BUYING ANTIQUES
REFERENCE BOOK
1971

For Collectors of English Antiques

BUYING ANTIQUES REFERENCE BOOK 1971

For Collectors of English Antiques

Museums and Collections
Books and Periodicals
Clubs and Societies
Auction Room Prices
Import and Export Regulations

by

A. W. COYSH and J. KING

PRAEGER PUBLISHERS
NEW YORK · WASHINGTON

BOOKS THAT MATTER

Published in the United States of America in 1971
by Praeger Publishers, Inc, 111 Fourth Avenue,
New York, N.Y. 10003

© 1971 in London, England, by A. W. Coysh and J. King

Library of Congress Catalog Card Number 73-115813

Printed in Great Britain

CONTENTS

LIST OF ILLUSTRATIONS

PREFACE

EXPERTS in the world of antiques acquire their knowledge and experience in three ways. They take every opportunity to see—and, if possible, to handle—fine specimens of the class of antiques they have chosen for study. They read extensively about their subject and build up their own store of reference books. And they talk with other specialists and discuss their problems. Nor is it necessary to be a full-time professional in order to be an expert: many an amateur collector working in a restricted field has become a specialist in his subject, a man whose advice is keenly sought. Even the ordinary buyer of antiques, who may have no strong urge to reach expert status, must nevertheless build up a background of knowledge or he will be misled by fake or forgery and waste his money.

This Reference Book sets out to smooth the path for those intent on acquiring this background. Part 1 indicates where and when fine collections of antiques may be seen in museum, gallery or historic house, dealing separately with each class of antique. Part 2 provides a very full bibliography for the specialist collector and for the general reader, some notes on museum publications, and information about books recently published. Part 3, for those who wish to make contact with other enthusiasts, gives detailed information about collectors' clubs and societies. Part 4 provides a comprehensive list of items sold at public auctions in the United Kingdom in 1969-70, together with prices for the previous twelve months, a list of salerooms and auctioneers, and gives some information about the Board of Trade regulations governing the export and import of antiques.

PREFACE

1
Looking at Antiques

ANTIQUE PERIODS AND
REIGNING MONARCHS

DYNASTY	ANTIQUE PERIODS
Tudor 1485-1603	*Tudor,* with antiques of the reign of Elizabeth I (1558-1603) referred to as *Elizabethan.*
Stuart 1603-1702	*Stuart,* with antiques of the reign of James I (1603-1625) and Charles I (1625-1649) referred to as *Jacobean.* This was followed by the *Cromwellian* or *Commonwealth* period (1649-1659) and then the *Restoration* (Charles II and James II). After this came the period of Dutch influence : *William and Mary* (1689-1702) and *Queen Anne* (1702-1714).
Hanoverian 1702-1901	The Georgian period embraces the reigns of George I (1714-1727), George II (1727-1760), George III (1760-1820) and George IV (1820-1830) but the period from 1800 to 1830 is often referred to as *Regency.* Few antiques are labelled William IV (1830-1837) : most post-Regency pieces are referred to as *Victorian.*

FURNITURE DESIGNERS

Furniture is more usually described by the style introduced by one of the great designers than by the period of the reigning monarch. Their influence dated roughly from the date of publication of their first design books and lasted, in most cases, for about twenty years, though 'reproduction furniture' in these styles is still made. The dates when their first design books were issued were :

William Kent	1744
Thomas Chippendale	1754
Robert and James Adam	1773
George Hepplewhite	1778
Thomas Sheraton	1791
Thomas Hope	1807
George Smith	1808

COLLECTIONS OF ANTIQUES
OPEN TO THE PUBLIC

ALL lovers of antiques enjoy seeing fine examples of early craftsmanship in art galleries, museums and historic houses, even though
it is not normally possible to handle them. Most large museums cover
many fields, while others specialise. Provincial museums usually pay
particular attention to local industries and crafts and exhibit material
with local associations. Some of the finest collections of early porcelain, pottery, silver and glass may be seen in the towns or cities where
these products were made—porcelain at Worcester and Derby, pottery at Stoke-on-Trent, silver at the assay cities and glass at London
and Newcastle. On the other hand, a collector who has bequeathed
his specimens to a local museum may provide specialist material far
from the manufacturing centre—the Willett Collection of Pottery
at Brighton, for example. If you are interested in particular branches
of antiques it is necessary to plan your visits. The first part of this
Reference Book aims to provide the signposts. It lists places in
Britain, and in the U.S.A., where various classes of antiques may be
properly studied, and mentions the nearest well-known town or city.
A list of museums, galleries and historic houses on pp. 80-102 gives
addresses and opening times.

THE ANTIQUE PERIODS

To understand an antique fully, it is necessary to know something
about the social history of the period—how the object was used, the
setting and the locality. A room in an eighteenth-century London
mansion would look very different from a room in an eighteenth-
century Yorkshire farmhouse. Yet the furniture they contained
may have been contemporary. Fortunately, many museums now
show furniture, porcelain, needlework and other household objects
in rooms or settings characteristic of a period, so giving the viewer a
clearer insight into the social life of the time than a study of individual items divorced from their surroundings can ever do.

PERIOD SETTINGS
In London
Fenton House. Eighteenth-century furnishings in a William and Mary house.
Geffrye Museum. Periods rooms showing middle-class furnishings from the
Jacobean period to the present. Children are obviously welcome.

Victoria and Albert Museum. Fine furniture from Elizabethan to *Art Nouveau* in period rooms.

Outside London

Barnsley: Cannon Hall Art Gallery and Museum. Eighteenth-century house with period rooms.

Birmingham: Aston Hall. One of the finest furnished Jacobean houses in Britain, with a panelled gallery and superb oak staircase.

Brighton: The Royal Pavilion. Furnished throughout in the Regency style.

Bristol: The Georgian House. Furniture of the late eighteenth and early nineteenth centuries arranged as it might have looked in a wealthy merchant's house of the period.

Bristol: The Red Lodge. Rooms furnished in styles of seventeenth and early eighteenth centuries.

Colchester: The Minories Art Gallery. Rooms in Georgian style.

Dumfries: Old Bridge House Museum. Seventeenth-century house with period rooms.

Hereford: The Old House. Jacobean period rooms.

Hull: Wilberforce House. Several period rooms. (See p. 79).

Huntingdon: The Cromwell Museum. Reflects life in the Commonwealth period. (See p. 74).

Kendal: Abbot Hall Art Gallery. Eighteenth-century period rooms.

Leeds: Abbey House Museum. Nineteenth-century houses, shops and workshops with working-class furnishings.

Lewes: Anne of Cleves House. Victorian room.

Northampton: Abington Museum. Period rooms, including Victorian.

Petersham: Ham House. Built before the Commonwealth and changed hands in Stuart times. The resurgence of craftsmanship in late seventeenth century is well evidenced.

Plymouth: Elizabethan House. Elizabethan furnishings.

Port Sunlight: Lady Lever Art Gallery. Tudor and Stuart, William and Mary, early eighteenth century, Adam, and Napoleon rooms.

Salford: Museum and Art Gallery. Reflects northern industrial life in a nineteenth-century 'street' with period rooms.

Salisbury: Salisbury and South Wiltshire Museum.

Scunthorpe: Borough Museum and Art Gallery. Period rooms.

Scunthorpe: Normanby Hall. Regency furnishings in a Regency mansion.

Southport: Botanic Gardens Museum. Victorian room.

Stockton: Preston Hall Museum. Period rooms.

Totnes: Elizabethan House. Elizabethan furniture.

Wakefield: City Museum. Period rooms and shops.

West Bromwich: Oak House Museum. Fifteenth-century building with period furniture.

Weymouth: No. 3 Trinity Street. Seventeenth-century house and furnishings.

Wolverhampton: Wightwick Manor. Furnished with William Morris wallpapers, glass, tiles, embroidery, etc., with Pre-Raphaelite paintings on the walls.

Worthing: Museum and Art Gallery. Period rooms.

York: Castle Museum. Period rooms and a cobbled street with period façades.

AMERICAN ANTIQUES IN BRITAIN

There is considerable trans-Atlantic traffic in antiques, though mainly from east to west. Nevertheless, there is considerable interest in American antiques in Britain. The American Museum at Claverton Manor, near Bath, has a series of twenty furnished rooms covering American domestic life from the late seventeenth century to the middle of the nineteenth century. See page 49.

Americana may also be seen at Capesthorne, near Macclesfield, which lies on the A34 between Wilmslow and Congleton. Ashburton Museum in Devon has some American Indian exhibits.

ARMS AND ARMOUR—see also *Edged Weapons* and *Firearms*
In London
H.M. Tower of London : The Armouries.
National Army Museum. (To open mid-summer, 1971.)
Victoria and Albert Museum.
Wellington Museum.

Outside London
Abingdon : Borough Museum Collections.
Arundel Castle.
Bournemouth : Rothesay Museum.
Bridgnorth : Acton Round Hall. European and Oriental arms and armour.
Calstock : Cotehele House.
Canterbury : The Westgate. Museum of Arms and Armour.
Edinburgh : National Museum of Antiquities. Highland weapons.
Edinburgh : Scottish United Services Museum.
Farleigh Hungerford : Castle Museum. Arms and armour of Civil War period.
Glasgow : Art Gallery and Museum. Scott and Whitelaw Collections.
Hatfield : Hatfield House. Armour.
Hungerford : Littlecote House. Cromwellian armoury : hide coats and seventeenth-century firearms on walls of the Great Hall.
Jersey : Gorey Castle Museum.
Kilmarnock : Dick Institute Museum. Walker Collection of basket-hilted swords.
Lincoln : City and County Museum.
Llandundno : Rapallo House.
Ludlow : The Museum.
Maidenhead : Cliveden. Suits of armour.
Newcastle-upon-Tyne : Keep and Black Gate Museum.
Nuneaton : Museum and Art Gallery.
Ormskirk : Rufford Old Hall.
Pontefract : The Castle Museum. Medieval arms and armour.
Poole : The Museum.
Stockton-on-Tees : Preston Hall Museum. Spence Collection.
Turton : Ashworth Museum.
Windsor Castle.

Many of the Services Museums have early weapons. For a complete list of these see *Museums and Galleries in Great Britain and Ireland*, an Index Publication, issued annually at 5s.

ART NOUVEAU
In London
Victoria and Albert Museum.
William Morris Gallery, Walthamstow.

Outside London
Accrington : Haworth Art Gallery. Good Tiffany glass.

BAROMETERS—see *Clocks and Watches*

BAYONETS—see *Edged Weapons*

BOW PORCELAIN
In London
Fenton House.
Victoria and Albert Museum.
Outside London
Bath: Holburne of Menstrie Museum.

BRASS WORK—see also *Horse Brasses*
Examples of brass work can be found in very many museums. There are particularly good exhibits at Berwick-on-Tweed Museum, Bridewell Museum, Norwich, and the Ashworth Museum, Turton.

BRISTOL PORCELAIN
In London
Fenton House. Includes Bristol 'Tebo' set of the Rustic Seasons.
Victoria and Albert Museum.
Outside London
William Cookworthy's Plymouth porcelain factory moved to Bristol in 1770. The two cities have examples from both centres.
Bath: Holburne of Menstrie Museum.
Bristol: City Museum and Art Gallery.
Plymouth: City Museum and Art Gallery.

BRONZES
Art Galleries often display bronze portrait-busts of famous people but relatively few have extensive collections of bronzes. The following are worth noting.
In London
British Museum.
Sir John Soane's Museum. Italian and Northern Renaissance bronzes.
Victoria and Albert Museum.
Wallace Collection.
Outside London
Bath: Holburne of Menstrie Museum. French and Italian bronzes.
Birmingham: Museum and Art Gallery.
Brighton: Art Gallery and Museum. Japanese bronzes.
Clacton: St Osyth's Priory.
Glasgow: Art Gallery and Museum.
Lewes: Glynde Place. Bronzes by Soldani.
Llandudno: Rapallo House Museum and Art Gallery.
Oxford: Ashmolean Museum. Italian, French, German and Chinese bronzes.
In the U.S.A.
Boston: Museum of Fine Arts.
Kansas City: William Rockhill Nelson Gallery of Art.
New York: Metropolitan Museum of Art.
Washington, D.C.: Freer Gallery of Art.

BYGONES—see *Folk Life*

CARD CASES
Preston: Harris Museum and Art Gallery. In the Mrs French Collection of Victoriana.

CARICATURES
In London
Wellington Museum. Many caricatures of the Duke of Wellington in the basement.

Outside London
Brighton: Royal Pavilion. Caricatures of the Prince Regent, with Gillray well represented.
Eastbourne: Towner Art Gallery.

CARPETS
In London
Victoria and Albert Museum. Superb display of carpets. A special study collection in Room 97 where you can examine both sides of a number of fine specimens.

Outside London
Many historic houses have fine carpets but it is not always possible to examine them closely.
Aylesbury: Waddesdon Manor. Savonnerie carpets.
Batley: Bagshaw Museum.
Burnley: Gawthorpe Hall.
Hungerford: Littlecote House. Aubusson carpets.
Pulborough: Parham.

CASTLEFORD EARTHENWARE
Castleford: Public Library and Museum.

CAUGHLEY and COALPORT PORCELAIN
Shrewsbury: Art Gallery and Museum.

CERAMICS
Most museums and country houses display pottery and porcelain. The following museums and houses have particularly good collections of British or European ceramics. (Specialized collections are listed under generic or factory names.)

In London
Bethnal Green Museum.
British Museum. Frank Lloyd Collection.
Fenton House. Lady Binnings Collection of Porcelain.
National Army Museum. Regimental china
Victoria and Albert Museum. Exhibits covering every period and every country. Schreiber and Herbert Allen Collections.
Wallace Collection. English and European porcelain.

Provinces
Bangor: Penrhyn Castle. Earthenware.
Barnard Castle: Bowes Museum. Includes European porcelain.
Bath: Holburne of Menstrie Museum. Mainly porcelain.
Bedford: Cecil Higgins Art Gallery. Mainly eighteenth-century English and Continental porcelain.
Belfast: Ulster Museum. British pottery.
Birmingham: Museum and Art Gallery. English and German porcelain. Wedgwood and other pottery.
Blackburn: Museum and Art Gallery.
Bolton: Museum and Art Gallery. Eighteenth-century English pottery.

B

Bournemouth: Rothesay Museum.
Bournemouth: Russell-Cotes Art Gallery and Museum.
Brighton: Art Gallery and Museum. Willett Collection of Pottery.
Bristol: City Art Gallery. Especially English delft.
Cambridge: Fitzwilliam Museum.
Carlisle: Museum and Art Gallery. Williamson Bequest of English porcelain.
Cheltenham: Art Gallery and Museum.
Chorley: Astley Hall. Leeds and other pottery.
Doncaster: Art Gallery and Museum.
Hastings: Public Museum and Art Gallery. German ceramics.
Hungerford: Littlecote House. English (especially Worcester) and German porcelain. Pottery (cow creamers, figures, pastille burners).
Leamington Spa: Art Gallery and Museum.
Leeds: City Art Gallery.
Leicester: The Museum.
Maidenhead. Henry Reitlinger Bequest.
Manchester: The Atheneum Annexe. A museum of ceramics.
Merthyr Tydfil: Art Gallery and Museum.
Northampton: Central Museum and Art Gallery.
Norwich: Castle Museum. Bulmer Collection of teapots.
Oxford: Ashmolean Museum. European ceramics.
Paisley: Museum and Art Gallery.
Perth: Scone Palace.
Port Sunlight: Lady Lever Art Gallery.
Preston: Harris Museum and Art Gallery.
Salisbury: Salisbury and South Wiltshire Museum.
Sheffield: City Museum.
Spalding: The Museum.
Stockport: Municipal Museum.
Stoke-on-Trent: City Museum and Art Gallery. Staffordshire wares.
Warrington: Municipal Museum and Art Gallery. Edelstein Collection.
Wisbech: Wisbech and Fenland Museum.
Worthing: The Museum.

In Canada
Montreal: The Museum of Art.

In the U.S.A.
Albany: Institute of History and Art.
Boston: Museum of Fine Arts. Early English and Continental porcelain.
Chicago: Art Institute. Steiglitz Collection of Worcester porcelain.
Detroit: Institute of Arts.
Kansas City: William Rockhill Nelson Gallery of Art. Burnap Collection of English Pottery.
Los Angeles: County Museum.
New York: Brooklyn Museum. American pottery.
          Metropolitan Museum of Art.
Newark: The Newark Museum.
Philadelphia: Museum of Art.
Williamsburg: Colonial Museum. Kauffman Collection of Chelsea porcelain and Kidd Collection of English pottery.
Winterthur: Henry Francis Dupont Museum. English pottery and porcelain.

CHATELAINES
Lewes: Anne of Cleves House.

CHELSEA PORCELAIN
In London
British Museum.
Fenton House. Includes Chelsea group of gold-anchor period of Winter and Spring.
Victoria and Albert Museum.

Outside London
Bath: Holburne of Menstrie Museum.
Bedford: Cecil Higgins Art Gallery.
Brighton: Art Gallery and Museum. Chelsea gold-anchor mark items.
Edgehill: Upton House. Chelsea figures.

CHINESE CERAMICS
In London
British Museum.
Fenton House. Blue porcelain room with examples of K'ang Hsi period (1662-1722) and a room with Sung ware (960-1279).
Percival David Foundation of Chinese Art. Examples of Sung, Yuan, Ming and Ch'ing dynasties.
Victoria and Albert Museum.

Outside London
Bath: Holburne of Menstrie Museum. Chinese porcelain.
Birmingham: Museum and Art Gallery. Chinese ceramic collection.
Bristol: City Art Gallery.
Burnley: Towneley Hall Art Gallery and Museum. Chinese pottery.
Cheltenham: Museum. Chinese porcelain room.
Durham: Gulbenkian Museum of Oriental Art and Archaeology. Malcolm MacDonald Collection of Chinese pottery and porcelain.
Hungerford: Littlecote House. Chinese collection including yellow Ming.
Leeds: Temple Newsam.
Northampton: Abington Museum.
Oxford: Ashmolean Museum. Collection from fourth to nineteenth century.
Port Sunlight: Lady Lever Art Gallery. Set out in chronological order in five separate rooms.
Sudbury: Melford Hall. Hyde Parker Collection of Chinese porcelain.
Wing: Ascott. Ming, K'ang Hsi and Chung porcelain.

CLAY TOBACCO PIPES
Tobacco pipes have a fascinating history. Smoking, or 'tobacco drinking' as it was called, was brought to Britain by Sir John Hawkins in 1565 and not, as is often supposed, by Sir Walter Raleigh, though he probably did much to make it fashionable.

In London
British Museum. Bragge Collection.
Guildhall Museum. Collection dates from 1570 when Raleigh was only 18 and spans the next 200 years, showing how pipe bowls increased in size as tobacco became cheaper.
London Museum.

Outside London
Cambridge: Museum of Archaeology and Anthropology.
Chester: Grosvenor Museum.
Guildford: Museum.
Ipswich: The Museum.

Jersey: Gorey Castle Museum.
Salisbury: Salisbury and South Wiltshire Museum.
Shrewsbury: Museum and Art Gallery. Thursfield Collection.
Taunton: Somerset County Museum.

CLOCKS, WATCHES AND BAROMETERS

Most of the finest makers of clocks and watches had their workshops in London. Many of the museum collections are also to be found there.

In London
British Museum. Ilbert Collection. A special room is available, by appointment, for students of horology.
Guildhall: Museum of the Clockmakers' Company.
Hampton Court. Barometers by Tompion.
London Museum.
National Maritime Museum.
Science Museum.
Victoria and Albert Museum.
Wallace Collection. French clocks.

Outside London
Basingstoke: Willis Museum.
Bath: Victoria Art Gallery. Horstmann Collection of watches.
Broadway: Snowshill Manor.
Bury St Edmunds: The Museum. Gershom-Parkington Memorial Collection of clocks and watches.
Cambridge: Fitzwilliam Museum.
Cardiff: National Museum of Wales.
Colchester: Minories Art Gallery. Locally-made clocks.
Dover: Corporation Museum. Locally-made clocks.
Dublin: National Museum of Ireland.
Edinburgh: Royal Scottish Museum.
Leicester: Newark Houses Museum. Locally-made clocks.
Lewes: Anne of Cleves House.
Lincoln: Usher Gallery. Usher Collection of watches.
Liverpool: City Museum.
Maidstone: Museum and Art Gallery. Kent clocks.
Norwich: Bridewell Museum. Locally-made clocks.
Oxford: Ashmolean Museum. Good collection, especially of watches.
Oxford: History of Science Museum.
Rochester: Public Museum. Kent clocks.
West Hoathley: The Priest House.
Windsor Castle.
York: Castle Museum. Clockmaker's shop.

In the U.S.A.
Boston: Museum of Fine Arts.
Bristol, Conn.: Bristol Clock Museum.
Colorado: Hagan's Clock Manor Museum at Manor Heights, Bergen Park, Evergreen.

COINS—see also *Medals*

Coins, tokens and medals are often grouped together in a single collection. Trade tokens are attracting considerable interest today. Small collections of tokens will often be found in the smaller museums: there is one at Reading, for example.

In London
British Museum. One of the finest collections of coins in Britain started with
  bequests made over 200 years ago.

Outside London
Basingstoke: The Willis Museum.
Bath: Victoria Art Gallery. Coins minted in Bath.
Bedford: The Museum.
Birmingham: Assay Office.
Blackburn: Museum and Art Gallery.
Brecon: Brecknock Museum.
Bristol: City Museum.
Cambridge: Fitzwilliam Museum.
Chelmsford: Chelmsford and Essex Museum.
Edinburgh: National Museum of Antiquities of Scotland. Scottish coins and
  medals.
Glasgow: The Hunterian Museum. Collection made by William Hunter and
  acquired in 1783.
Gloucester: City Museum and Art Gallery.
Jersey: Gorey Castle Museum.
King's Lynn: Museum and Art Gallery.
Leeds: Library of the Thoresby Society.
Luton: Museum and Art Gallery. Seventeenth-century trade tokens.
Lyme Regis: The Philpot Museum.
Merthyr Tydfil: Art Gallery and Museum.
Nuneaton: Museum and Art Gallery.
Oxford: Ashmolean Museum. Hebenden Coin Room with coins and medals
  from all over the world.
Peterhead: The Arbuthnot Museum.
Rochester: Public Museum.
Salisbury: Salisbury and South Wiltshire Museum. Trade tokens.
Sheffield: City Museum.
Shoreham: The Marlipins Museum.
Spalding: The Museum.
Swansea: Royal Institution of South Wales Museum.
Thetford: The Ancient House Museum.

COSTUME
Costume is of interest not only to the collectors but to the actor, painter,
producer, stage manager and writer. Fortunately, there are many places
where early costumes have been preserved.

In London
Bethnal Green Museum. Items in Spitalfields silk, a material made locally.
London Museum. Includes a collection of royal robes.
Victoria and Albert Museum. Costume Court (Room 40).

Outside London
Abergavenny: Abergavenny and District Museum.
Abingdon: Borough Museum. Stuart and Georgian costume.
Armagh: County Museum. Costume and uniforms.
Ashburton: Museum.
Aylesbury: Buckingham County Museum.
Basingstoke: The Willis Museum.
Bath: Museum of Costume. Probably the finest costume museum in Britain.
  Based on the collection of Mrs Doris Langley, it covers costume from

Elizabethan days to the present. Fashion plates may be seen by students.
Birmingham: Museum and Art Gallery. Costumes from the seventeenth century.
Brecon: Brecknock Museum.
Broadway: Snowshill Manor.
Burford: Tolsey Museum.
Chelmsford: Chelmsford and Essex Museum.
Christchurch: Red House Museum.
Colchester: Colchester and Essex Museum. Costume displayed in an eighteenth-century house 'The Holly Trees'.
Dunfermline: Pittencrief House Museum. Regency and Victorian costume.
Edinburgh: Canongate Tolbooth. Highland costume.
Edinburgh: Museum of Childhood. Children's dresses.
Edinburgh: National Museum Gallery. Eighteenth- and nineteenth-century costume.
Glasgow: Art Gallery. Oriental costumes.
Halifax: Bankfield Museum. Good costumes and some fabrics.
Hereford: City Museum and Art Gallery.
Hereford: Churchill Gardens Museum. Good costume collection.
Ipswich: Ipswich Museum.
King's Lynn: Museum and Art Gallery.
Leominster: Eye Manor.
Lewes: Anne of Cleves House.
Luton: Museum and Art Gallery. Nineteenth-century costume.
Manchester: The Gallery of English Costume.
Nottingham: City Museum and Art Gallery.
Preston: Museum and Art Gallery.
Rugeley: Blithfield Hall. Museum of Childhood and Costume.
Salisbury: Salisbury and South Wiltshire Museum.
Stoke-on-Trent: City Museum and Art Gallery.
Stratford-on-Avon: Royal Shakespeare Theatre Picture Gallery. Theatrical costumes.
Weybridge: Weybridge Museum.
Winslow: Claydon House. Seventeenth-century costumes.
Worthing: Museum and Art Gallery. Costumes displayed in period rooms.
Yeovil: Wyndham Museum. Bailward Collection.
York: Castle Howard. Costume galleries.

CUTLERY
In London
Guildhall Museum. Sixteenth-century knives with handles of wood, bone or iron.
Victoria and Albert Museum.
Outside London
Oxford: Ashmolean Museum.
Sheffield: City Museum. The best general collection of cutlery in Britain.

DELFTWARE
The Dutch town of Delft was the centre of a pottery industry in the seventeenth century. Similar ware was being made in London (Lambeth) and Bristol, and later in other places, notably Glasgow, Liverpool and Wincanton.
In London
Guildhall Museum. Mid-seventeenth-century Lambeth wares.
Victoria and Albert Museum.
The Pharmaceutical Society's Museum. Drug jars.

Outside London
Bath: Victoria Art Gallery. Bristol and West of England Delft Collection.
Birmingham: Art Gallery. Bristol and Liverpool tiles.
Brighton: Museum and Art Gallery. Seventeenth- and eighteenth-century delft in the Willett Collection.
Bristol: Museum and Art Gallery. A good range of wares, especially Bristol.
Lewes: Anne of Cleves House. Ointment and syrup jars.
Oxford: Ashmolean Museum. Robert Hall Warren Collection.
Reading: Museum and Art Gallery. Blatch Collection of English delft.

DERBY PORCELAIN
In London
Fenton House.
Victoria and Albert Museum.

Outside London
Derby: Museum and Art Gallery. Collection with over a thousand items of Derby porcelain ranging over the whole period of production.
Derby: Royal Crown Derby Works Museum. Derby porcelain of all periods from 1750.

DOLLS AND DOLLS' HOUSES
In London
Bethnal Green Museum. Good collection of dolls and dolls' houses.
London Museum. Queen Victoria's dolls.
Science Museum.
Victoria and Albert Museum.

Outside London
Bangor: Penrhyn Castle. Collection made by Miss Philippa Judge. Dolls from many parts of the world.
Bath: Museum of Costume.
Brighton: The Grange, Rottingdean. Now houses the National Toy Collection with many dolls.
Burford: Tolsey Museum. Dolls' house furnished in style of late eighteenth century.
Christchurch: Red House Museum.
Edinburgh: Museum of Childhood.
Farnham: The Willmer House Museum. Dolls and the Mainwaring dolls' house on the staircase dates from about 1788.
Glasgow: Tollcross Museum. A museum catering for children with a good collection of dolls.
Leeds: Abbey House Museum. Examples of musical automata including little eighteenth-century harpsichord dolls which dance.
Leominster: Eye Manor. Beck Collection of costume dolls.
Luton: Museum and Art Gallery.
Oxford: The Rotunda. Dolls' houses of eighteenth and nineteenth centuries.
Preston: The Harris Museum.
Salisbury: Salisbury and South Wiltshire Museum.
Stoke-on-Trent: City Museum and Art Gallery.
Taunton: Somerset County Museum.
Tunbridge Wells: The Royal Tunbridge Wells Museum.
Warwick: The Doll Museum. Joy Robinson Collection of period dolls.
Worthing: Museum and Art Gallery.
In the U.S.A.
New York: Museum of the City of New York.

Many of the dolls in this museum are described by John Noble, the Curator of the Toy Collection, in *Dolls* (1968).

In Europe
Dolls' house enthusiasts visiting Holland should see the delightful seventeenth- and eighteenth-century dolls' cabinets in the Rijksmuseum, Amsterdam.

EDGED WEAPONS
Many edged weapons—swords, bayonets, daggers, etc.—may be seen in military museums. These are listed in *Museums and Art Galleries in Great Britain and Ireland* (Index Publication) and in *A Guide to Military Museums* (Bellona Publication).

In London
H.M. Tower of London Armouries.
Hampton Court. Swords hung high on the walls.
National Maritime Museum.
Victoria and Albert Museum.
Wallace Collection.
Wellington Museum. Swords hung high on the walls.

Outside London
Edinburgh : Royal Scottish Museum.
Glasgow : Art Gallery and Museum.
Lincoln : City and County Museum.

In Canada
Toronto : Royal Ordnance Museum.

In the U.S.A.
Chicago, Ill : George F. Harding Museum.
Cleveland, Ohio : Museum of Art.
New York : Metropolitan Museum of Art.
New York : United States Military Academy (West Point).
Springfield, Mass : Armory Museum.
Washington, D.C : Smithsonian Institution.
Williamsburg, Virginia : The Powder Magazine.
Worcester, Mass : John Woodman Higgins Armoury.

ENAMELS
In London
Victoria and Albert Museum.

Outside London
Bath : Holburne of Menstrie Museum.
Norwich : Blickling Hall. Battersea enamel candlesticks.
Port Sunlight : Lady Lever Art Gallery. Bilston enamels.
Salisbury : Salisbury and South Wiltshire Museum.

EMBROIDERY—see *Needlework*

ENGRAVINGS—see *Prints*

FANS
Aylesbury : Waddesdon Manor.
Leominster : Eye Manor.
Worthing : Museum and Art Gallery.

FASHION PLATES
Fashion plates may often be seen in the print rooms of museums.

In London
Victoria and Albert Museum: The Costume Court.
Outside London
Bath: Museum of Costume.
Christchurch: Red House Museum.

FIGUREHEADS

Ship figureheads are occasionally seen in museums but there are notable collections at the following two places:
In London
Greenwich: The *Cutty Sark*. The 'Long John Silver' Collection.
Outside London
Portsmouth: The Victory Museum.

FIREARMS—see also *Arms and Armour, Weapons*

Firearms are to be seen in many military museums in addition to the following:
In London
National Army Museum. (To open mid-summer, 1971.)
H.M. Tower of London Armouries.
Victoria and Albert Museum.
The Wallace Collection.
The Artillery Museum, Woolwich Common. A large collection.
Outside London
Aylesbury: Waddesdon Manor. Collection of small arms open on Fridays from April to October.
Birmingham: City Museum Department of Science and Industry.
Canterbury: West Gate Museum.
Edinburgh: Art Gallery and Museum.
Glasgow: Art Gallery and Museum.
Lincoln: City Museum.
Shugborough: Staffordshire County Museum.
Warrington: Municipal Museum.
Yeovil: Wyndham Museum. Henry Stilby Collection.
In the U.S.A.
Boston, Mass: First Corps Cadets Armory.
Chicago, Ill: George F. Harding Museum.
Cleveland, Ohio: Museum of Art.
Fort Oglethorpe, Georgia: National Military Park.
Hartford, Conn: State Library and Wadsworth Atheneum.
Los Angeles, Cal: County Museum.
Newhaven, Conn: Winchester Museum.
New York: Metropolitan Museum of Art.
New York: United States Military Academy (West Point).
Springfield, Mass: Armory Museum.
Washington, D.C: Smithsonian Institution.
Williamsburg, Virginia: Powder Magazine.
Worcester, Mass: John Woodman Higgins Armory.

FIREBACKS—see *Ironwork*

FIRE MARKS

These are the small metal plates, now sought after by collectors, which were once placed on buildings by insurance policy holders in the days when fire-brigades were under the direction of private insurance companies. The head offices of many of today's insurance companies have collections.

In London
Chartered Insurance Institute. A fine collection.
Guildhall Museum.

Outside London
Grantham: Belvoir Castle.
Luton: Museum and Art Gallery.
Reading: Museum and Art Gallery.
York: The Castle Museum.

FOLK LIFE
Many antiques associated with domestic work, country crafts and agriculture, ranging from jelly moulds to sheep bells, from yokes to mangel-cutters, have often been grouped together as 'Bygones'. They are included in this Reference Book under Folk Life. Large collections of such objects, of course, merit the name of folk museums.

In London
Geffrye Museum. Houses a typical eighteenth-century kitchen with its domestic equipment and also a woodworker's shop.

Outside London
Abergavenny: Abergavenny and District Museum. Tools used in rural crafts.
Alton: Curtis Museum. Domestic and craft items.
Bacup: Natural History Society Museum. Domestic antiques.
Banbury: Sulgrave Manor. Fully equipped kitchen of the Tudor period.
Bangor: Museum of Welsh Antiquities. Farm and domestic equipment.
Belfast: Ulster Folk Museum. Every aspect of Ulster folk life.
Bradford: Bolling Hall. Three centuries of domestic antiques.
Bristol: Blaise Castle House Folk Museum. Reflects the life of the countryside over 500 years.
Cardiff: St Fagan's Castle. Welsh Folk Museum. Collection of Welsh love spoons.
Edinburgh: Huntly House. A Scottish eighteenth-century kitchen, reconstructed.
Evesham: Almonry Museum. Agricultural implements.
Gainsborough: The Old Hall. A folk museum.
Glamis: The Angus Folk Collection. Domestic and agricultural antiques.
Glasgow: Old Glasgow Museum. Domestic antiques.
Glenesk: Glenesk Folk Museum. Rooms furnished in country style.
Gloucester: Folk Museum. Old craft, farming and fishing equipment.
Great Yarmouth: Museum of Domestic Life.
Halifax: West Yorkshire Folk Museum. Rural craft antiques.
Hereford: City Museum. Agricultural implements.
Honiton: Honiton and All Hallows Public Museum. An old Devon kitchen with its domestic equipment.
Horsham: The Museum.
Isle of Man: Manx Village Folk Museum, Cregneash. Group of thatched buildings devoted to village crafts—the turner, blacksmith, weaver, etc.
Isle of Wight: Arreton Manor. Domestic and family items.
Keighley: Museum. Antique domestic and agricultural equipment.
Kilbarchan: Weaver's Cottage. A craftsman's home as it was in the eighteenth century.
Kingussie: Highland Folk Museum. Tools, craft-work and a furnished cottage.

Leeds: Abbey House Museum. Reflects three centuries of Yorkshire life.
Lewes: Anne of Cleves House. Domestic items.
Llandudno: Rapallo House Museum. An old Welsh kitchen.
Luton: Museum and Art Gallery. Domestic utensils and rural crafts.
Norwich: Bridewell Museum. Local industries and rural crafts. Strangers'
    Hall Museum of domestic antiques dating from the sixteenth century.
Plymouth: Buckland Abbey. A folk gallery.
Reading: English Rural Life Museum. Outstanding national collection
    reflecting every aspect of country life.
Salisbury: Salisbury and South Wiltshire Museum.
Shugborough: Staffordshire County Museum. Domestic and agricultural
    collection.
Stroud: The Museum. Craft and domestic equipment from the Cotswold
    countryside.
Tunbridge Wells: Royal Tunbridge Wells Museum. Farm and domestic
    antiques.
Wilmington: Wilmington Museum. Farm and domestic antiques.
York: Castle Museum. Folk museum of Yorkshire life.

FURNITURE

Fine individual items of furniture can be seen in many museums but some
of the finer collections are in historic houses where they can be seen in an
appropriate setting. Country-made furniture is often shown in folk museums
(see *Folk Life*).

In London
Buckingham Palace, The Queen's Gallery. Exhibitions from the Royal Col-
    lection.
Chiswick House. William Kent decoration.
Fenton House. Eighteenth-century furniture.
Forty Hall Museum. Stuart and Georgian furniture.
Geffrye Museum. Tudor to present day.
Ham House. Restoration period furniture.
Kenwood House. Fine examples of Robert Adam designs. The library is out-
    standing. Some contemporary furniture.
Osterley Park. Adam and French rococo furniture in a house mainly created
    and wholly decorated by Robert Adam.
Sir John Soane's Museum. Furniture of eighteenth and early nineteenth
    centuries used by Sir John Soane.
Victoria and Albert Museum. Furniture of all periods.
Wallace Collection. Fine Boulle furniture.

Outside London
Alnwick: Alnwick Castle. Victorian furniture.
Arundel: Arundel Castle. Furniture from Tudor times.
Aylesbury: Waddesdon Manor. Fine French furniture including many pieces
    by famous *ébénistes*.
Bakewell: Chatsworth House. Eighteenth-century furniture, including items
    by William Kent.
Bangor: Museum of Welsh Antiquities. Welsh furniture.
Barnard Castle: The Bowes Museum. French furniture.
Bath: Holburne of Menstrie Museum. Hepplewhite and Sheraton furniture.
Batley: Oakwell Hall. Period furniture in a sixteenth-century house; interest-
    ing English chairs.
Bedford: Cecil Higgins Art Gallery. English furniture.
Birmingham: Aston Hall. Jacobean house with period furniture.

Bolton: Smithills Hall. Stuart furniture.
Brighton: Art Gallery and Museum. Collection of fine late Georgian satinwood furniture, mainly 1780-1800. Also eighteenth-century French furniture—Louis XV and Louis XVI.
Brighton: Preston Manor. Furnished Georgian house.
Brighton: Royal Pavilion. Regency furniture.
Bristol: Georgian House. Furnished in Georgian style.
Bristol: Red Lodge. Furniture of several periods.
Bury St Edmunds: Ickworth. Eighteenth-century English and French furniture.
Cheltenham: Art Gallery and Museum. Eighteenth-century furniture.
Chesterfield: Hardwick Hall. Elizabethan house with period furniture.
Chippenham: Corsham Court. Georgian furniture.
Chorley: Astley Hall.
Colchester: Minories Art Gallery. Georgian furniture.
Derby: Kedleston Hall. Adam house with Adam furniture.
Dorking: Polesden Lacy. Louis XV and Louis XVI furniture.
Driffield: Sledmere House. Chippendale, Sheraton and French furniture.
Edinburgh: Lauriston Castle. Georgian and French furniture.
Exeter: Powderham Castle. Stuart and Regency furniture.
Fordingbridge: Breamore House. Tudor, Dutch marquetry and Chippendale.
Great Yarmouth: Museum of Domestic Life.
Guildford: Clandon Park.
Halifax: West Yorkshire Folk Museum. Stuart furniture.
Harrogate: Rudding Park. Regency furniture.
Hatfield: Hatfield House.
High Wycombe: Art Gallery and Museum. Windsor chairs.
High Wycombe: Hughenden Manor: Victorian furniture.
Hungerford: Littlecote House. All periods but mainly Tudor and Chinese Chippendale.
Isle of Wight: Arreton Manor. Stuart furniture.
Isle of Wight: Osborne House. Victorian furniture.
Knebworth: Knebworth House. Victorian furniture.
Leeds: Harewood House. Chippendale and Adam furniture.
Leeds: Temple Newsam. Stuart and Georgian furniture.
Leicester: Newarke Houses Museum. Victorian furniture.
Lewes: Anne of Cleves Museum. Tudor and country furniture.
Llanrwst: Gwydir Castle. Tudor furniture.
Maidenhead: Cliveden.
Manchester: Heaton Hall. Georgian furniture.
Manchester: Wythenshawe Hall. Stuart furniture.
Mere: Stourhead House. Chippendale furniture.
Norwich: Blickling Hall. Seventeenth- and eighteenth-century furniture.
Ormskirk: Rufford Old Hall. Tudor manor with period furniture.
Oxford: Ashmolean Museum.
Perth: Scone Palace. French furniture.
Port Sunlight: Lady Lever Art Gallery.
Preston: Samlesbury Old Hall. Collection of cabinets—English, European and Oriental.
Pulborough: Parham.
Saffron Walden: Audley End House. Chippendale, Hepplewhite and satinwood furniture.
Sandford Orcas: Manor House.
Sevenoaks: Knole. Stuart and Georgian furniture.

South Queensferry: Hopetoun House. Adam house with fine furniture, including Chippendale.
Steeple Ashton: Rousham House. Rooms decorated by William Kent. Good furniture.
Sutherland: Dunrobin Castle. Louis XV furniture.
Warminster: Longleat House. William and Mary, Louis XV and Empire furniture.
Warwick: Charlecote Park. Victorian furniture.
Whitchurch (Glamorgan): Castell Coch. Victorian furniture.
Winchcombe: Sudeley Castle. Walnut furniture of Queen Anne period.
Wilton: Wilton House. Chippendale and Kent furniture.
Wing: Ascott. French and Chippendale furniture.
Woburn: Woburn Abbey. French and English eighteenth-century furniture.
York: Castle Howard.

In the U.S.A.
Baltimore, Maryland: Museum of Art.
Boston: Museum of Fine Arts.
Chicago: Art Institute.
Delaware. Henry Francis du Pont Winterthur Museum. Pine kitchen of country-made furniture.
New York: Brooklyn Museum.
          Museum of the City of New York.
          Metropolitan Museum of Art. Many kinds of furniture, including country-made.
Lawrence, Mass: Art Museum. Davenport Collection.
Philadelphia: Museum of Art.

GLASS—see also *Paperweights*
In London
Bethnal Green Museum. Many countries, especially Venetian.
British Museum. Fine collection of glass.
Guildhall Museum. Old seventeenth- and early eighteenth-century wine bottles.
London Museum. Garton Collection.
Victoria and Albert Museum. Glass from many countries.
Wallace Collection.

Outside London
Aberdeen: Art Gallery and Industrial Museum. European glass.
Accrington: Haworth Art Gallery. Tiffany glass.
Alton: The Curtis Museum.
Barnard Castle: The Bowes Museum.
Bath: American Museum, Claverton Manor. American glass.
Bath: Holburne of Menstrie Museum.
Bath: Victoria Art Gallery. Carr Collection of English glass. Huth Collection of Bohemian glass.
Bedford: Cecil Higgins Art Gallery. Higgins Collection of English and European glass.
Belfast: The Ulster Museum. Irish glass.
Birmingham: City Museum and Art Gallery. Roman and Italian glass.
Blackburn: Museum and Art Gallery.
Bournemouth: Russell-Cotes Art Gallery and Museum.
Bradford: Bolling Hall Museum.
Brierley Hill, Staffordshire: Public Reference Library. The Glass Collection.
Bristol: Museum and Art Gallery. Bristol and Nailsea coloured glass.
Burnley: Towneley Hall Art Gallery and Museum. Eighteenth-century glass.

Bury St Edmund's: Moyse's Hall Museum. Eighteenth-century glass.
Buxton: The Museum.
Cambridge: Fitzwilliam Museum. Beves Collection.
Cardiff: National Museum of Wales. Eighteenth-century bottles. Silver-mounted crystal.
Castleford: Public Library and Museum. Local Victorian glass.
Chorley: Astley Hall Art Gallery and Museum.
Clevedon: Clevedon Court. Locally-made Nailsea glass.
Dublin: National Museum of Ireland. Early Irish glass from Cork, Dublin and Waterford.
Dudley: Branch Museum and Art Gallery. Mainly Brierley Hill glass.
Edinburgh: Royal Scottish Museum. English glass and items from many parts of the world.
Exeter: Royal Albert Memorial Museum. Henry Hamilton Clarke Collection of English glass.
Glasgow: Art Gallery and Museum. Mainly foreign glass.
Ipswich: Christchurch Mansion. Tibbenham Collection of English drinking glasses.
King's Lynn: Museum and Art Gallery. Drinking glasses.
Leamington Spa: Art Gallery and Museum. Georgian glass.
Lewes: Glynde Place. Jacobite glasses.
Liverpool: City Museum. European glass.
Maidenhead: Henry Reitlinger Bequest.
Manchester: City Art Gallery. South Lancashire glass.
Newcastle-upon-Tyne: Laing Art Gallery and Museum. Local glass made in the eighteenth and nineteenth centuries. There were over twenty glass-works in the area prior to 1750.
Norwich: Castle Museum. Early glass and some Absolon specimens.
Nottingham: City Museum and Art Gallery.
Oldham: Municipal Art Gallery and Museum. North of England glass from Francis Buckley Collection.
Oxford: Ashmolean Museum. Drinking glasses, white Bristol glass.
Preston: Harris Museum and Art Gallery. Nineteenth-century glass.
St Albans: City Museum. Roman and nineteenth-century glass.
Sheffield: City Museum. Yorkshire glass and German glass.
South Shields: Library and Museum. Local glass.
Swansea: Glynn Vivian Art Gallery.
Taunton: Castle Museum. Nailsea glass.
Truro: County Museum and Art Gallery. Small but good collection.
Wakefield: City Museum.
Warrington: Municipal Museum and Art Gallery. Local glass.

Those interested in techniques should visit the Pilkington Museum at St Helens where the development of glass-making is well shown with exhibits.

In the U.S.A.
Corning, N.Y: Corning Museum of Glass.
New York: Metropolitan Museum of Art.
Philadelphia: Museum of Art.
Toledo, Ohio: Museum of Art.

GOLF
Few people will connect golf with antiques, yet a form of the game was played over three hundred years ago. The history is reflected in the Spalding Golf Museum at Dundee.

HORSE BRASSES
The best collections of horse brasses are in provincial museums.
Hull: Transport Museum. Many brasses in this museum are illustrated in *Horse Brasses* by George Hartfield, 1965.
Luton: Museum and Art Gallery.
Oxford: Pitt Rivers Museum. Foreign brasses.
Taunton: Somerset County Museum. Brasses also in Mr Hartfield's book.
York: Castle Museum.

IRONWORK
Ironwork can be seen in many museums, especially folk museums, usually in the form of some antique implements and kitchen utensils But a few museums specialize in ironwork.

In London
Hampton Court. Fine firebacks.
Victoria and Albert Museum. Room 114 has a large collection of wrought ironwork, much of it Continental.

Outside London
Some of the earliest iron furnaces in England were in Sussex and many fine ironwork objects were made there: moulded firebacks are an example. It is not surprising, therefore, that Sussex museums figure largely in this list.
Battle: The Museum. Sussex ironwork relics.
Brighton: Art Gallery and Museum. Collection of iron firebacks.
Coalbrookdale: Museum of Ironfounding. Early engines and examples of iron casting.
Great Yarmouth: Old Merchant's House. Domestic ironwork from Stuart to Victorian times.
Hailsham: Michelham Priory. Sussex ironwork and a forge.
Horsham: The Museum. Sussex ironwork.
Lewes: Anne of Cleves House. Large collection of andirons, firebacks (with some rare fireback moulds), rush-holders and other ironwork.
Norwich: Bridewell Museum. The smithy.
Nottingham: City Museum and Art Gallery.
Petworth: Petworth House. The Mitford collection of firebacks.

JAPANESE PRINTS
This is a field for the expert since early coloured Japanese woodcuts have been reproduced freely. (See *Buying Antiques* 2nd Edition pp 128-31.) It is important, therefore, to see and study fine specimens. These can be seen at:
Blackburn: The Art Gallery.
Brighton: The Art Gallery and Museum.
Manchester: Whitworth Art Gallery.

IVORIES
A few ivory carvings are displayed in many museums.

In London
Courtauld Institute Galleries.
Victoria and Albert Museum.
Wallace Collection.

Outside London
Burnley: Towneley Hall Art Gallery.
Luton Hoo. Medieval ivories.
Oxford: Ashmolean Museum.
Perth: Scone Palace.

Sheffield : Graves Art Gallery. Chinese ivories.
Wolverhampton : Bantock House. Chinese ivories.

JADE
In London
Victoria and Albert Museum. Chinese jade carvings.
Outside London
Cardiff : National Museum of Wales.
Clacton : St Osyth's Priory. Collection of Chinese jade.
Durham : Gulbenkian Museum of Oriental Art and Archaeology. Sir Charles
Hardinge Collection of Chinese jade.

JEWELLERY
In London
British Museum.
H.M. Tower of London. The Crown Jewels.
Outside London
Barnard Castle : The Bowes Museum.
Brighton : Art Gallery and Museum.
Luton Hoo : Sixteenth- and seventeenth-century jewellery and Fabergé
jewels.
Oxford : Ashmolean Museum.
Rotherham : Museum and Art Gallery.
Worthing : Museum and Art Gallery.

LACE AND LACE BOBBINS
In London
Victoria and Albert Museum.
Outside London
Ashburton Museum.
Aylesbury : Buckingham County Museum. Lace bobbins.
Blair Atholl : Blair Castle.
High Wycombe : Art Gallery and Museum. Buckinghamshire lace.
Honiton : Honiton and All Hallows Public Museum. Honiton lace.
Luton : Museum and Art Gallery. Local pillow lace. Lace bobbins.
Nottingham : City Museum and Art Gallery. Nottingham lace.
   Collectors of lace will see much of interest in the many museums which
display costume (q.v.).

LACQUER
In London
Victoria and Albert Museum. Carved red lacquer throne of the Emperor
Chien Lung, made in the eighteenth century, together with fine red
lacquer vases.
Outside London
Edenbridge : Chiddingstone Castle. Japanese lacquer.

LEATHER ANTIQUES
In London
Guildhall Museum. Edmondson Collection of jacks or bombards, the leather
bottles used in England for centuries for holding ale. There are also
typically English mug-shaped leather drinking vessels—so typical that the
French in the seventeenth century used to say that the English drank out
of their boots ! The museum also has some seventeenth-century leather
gloves and gauntlets embroidered with silk, metal or ribbon.

Outside London
Kettering: Westfield Museum. Leather footwear.
Northampton: Central Museum and Art Gallery. Leather footwear.
Norwich: The Bridewell Museum. Leather room.

LEEDS EARTHENWARE
Alton: Curtis Museum. Bignall collection of early Leeds creamware—plain, painted and pierced, together with some later pieces produced in the 1870s from old moulds. Advisable to make an appointment.
Chorley: Astley Hall Art Gallery and Museum.
Leeds: City Art Gallery.

LINTHORPE EARTHENWARES
Middlesbrough: Dorman Memorial Museum.

LIVERPOOL PORCELAIN AND POTTERY—see also *Delftware*
Birkenhead: Williamson Art Gallery and Museum.
Bootle: Museum and Art Gallery. Bishop Collection of Liverpool pottery.
Liverpool: City Museum.

LONGTON HALL PORCELAIN
In London
Fenton House.
Victoria and Albert Museum.

LOWESTOFT PORCELAIN
Norwich: Castle Museum.

MAIOLICA
In London
Courtauld Institute Galleries. A few sixteenth-century pieces.
Victoria and Albert Museum. Sixteenth-century maiolica.
Wallace Collection.
Outside London
Bath: Holburne of Menstrie Museum of Art.
Birmingham: City Museum and Art Gallery.
Dorking: Polesden Lacy.
Oxford: Ashmolean Museum.

MARITIME ANTIQUES
Many people have a special interest in antiques connected with the sea—paintings, engravings, model ships, maps and charts, instruments, ships' furnishings, etc. Museums which exhibit these are often found in coastal towns and cities.
In London
National Maritime Museum. By far the most comprehensive maritime museum, with every kind of exhibit connected with the seafaring life, merchant and naval. The Annexe, the old Royal Observatory, has many early navigational instruments.
Outside London
Aberdeen: Art Gallery and Industrial Museum. A regional section includes maritime exhibits and models of sailing ships—the old Aberdeen clippers.
Barnstaple: Arlington Court. Maritime material, including model ships.
Barrow-in-Furness: The Museum. Vickers-Armstrong Collection of model ships.
Belfast: Transport Museum. Model ships.

C

Bournemouth: Rothesay Museum. Rooms devoted to maritime material.
Brixham: The Museum. Reflects commercial aspects of the seafaring life.
Buckler's Hard: Maritime Museum. Lies close to the old slipway on the Beaulieu River where ships of forest oak were built and launched in the eighteenth century. It has models of these ships, maps, charts, and paintings and prints of Beaulieu-built ships in action.
Dartmouth: Borough Museum. Maritime material.
Great Yarmouth: Maritime Museum for East Anglia.
Grimsby: The Doughty Museum. Exhibits concerned with fishing.
Hastings: Museum of Local History. Maritime items, including ship models.
Hull: Maritime Museum. Commercial aspects of shipping.
Littlehampton: The Museum. Maritime exhibits with sailing-ship material.
Middlesbrough: The Dorman Memorial Museum. Model ships.
Monmouth: Nelson Museum.
Norwich: The Bridewell Museum. River and sea room.
Plymouth. City Museum and Art Gallery. Model ships.
Plymouth: Buckland Abbey. Model ships.
Portsmouth: Victory Museum. Naval relics and pictures, including a panorama of the Battle of Trafalgar by W. L. Wyllie.
Rochester: Public Museum. Model ships.
Southampton: Maritime Museum. A relatively new museum with models, pictures, etc.
South Shields: Library and Museum. Model ships and early lifeboats.
Sunderland: Museum and Art Gallery. Model ships.
Whitby: Literary and Philosophical Society Museum. Maritime material and relics of Captain Cook.

MARTINWARE
The Martin brothers, who set up a small factory at Southall in Middlesex in 1877 to make a fine salt-glazed stoneware, produced a great variety of bowls, vases, jugs and grotesque figures of animals and birds. These are now much sought after by collectors. A few specimens may be seen in the Victoria and Albert Museum but enthusiasts should visit the Public Library at Southall to see the Martinware Pottery Collection.

MEDALS and MILITARIA
Medals are often exhibited with collections of coins (q.v.) and in Service museums with militaria.

MINIATURE PORTRAITS
In London
National Portrait Gallery.
Victoria and Albert Museum. Rooms 55 and 57.
The Wallace Collection.
Outside London
Bath: Holburne of Menstrie Museum.
Bournemouth: The Russell-Cotes Museum.
Brighton: Art Gallery and Museum. Falk Collection of English and French portrait miniatures.
Edinburgh: The National Gallery of Scotland.
Lincoln: Usher Gallery.
Manchester: City Art Gallery.
Oxford: Ashmolean Museum.
Port Sunlight: Lady Lever Art Gallery.

Steeple Ashton. Rousham House.
Windsor: The Royal Collection.

MUSICAL INSTRUMENTS
In London
British Piano Museum. Collection includes self-playing devices from cylinder and disc musical boxes to the piano, violin, reed organ and barrel piano.
Fenton House. Benton-Fletcher Collection of early musical instruments including seventeenth-century harpsichords and virginals.
Horniman Museum. Musical instruments from many parts of the world.
Royal College of Music. Donaldson Museum, with early musical instruments.

Outside London
Aylesbury: Waddesdon Manor.
Brighton: Art Gallery and Museum. Albert Spencer Collection of musical instruments.
Broadway: Snowshill Manor.
Hailsham: Michelham Priory.
Manchester: Heaton Hall. Music room with an organ built by Samuel Green.
Newport, I.O.W: Carisbrooke Castle Museum. Is said to have the oldest organ in the country.
Norwich: Blickling Hall. Pianoforte by Joseph Kirkman.
Oxford: Ashmolean Museum. Hill Music Room with Italian and English stringed and keyboard instruments.
Oxford: Pitt Rivers Museum.

In the U.S.A.
Newhaven, Conn.: Yale University Collection of musical instruments.

NEEDLEWORK—see also *Costume, Lace, Samplers* and *Tapestry*
Needlework is involved in every possible use of fabrics—clothing, shoes, and gloves; curtains and wall-hangings; bedcovers and upholstery; purses and cushions. There are samplers and needlework pictures; and there is lace. Many of the finest examples have been preserved in historic houses.

In London
Victoria and Albert Museum.

Outside London
Burnley: Gawthorpe Hall. Fine embroidery.
Calstock: Cotehele House. Needlework of seventeenth and eighteenth centuries.
Chesterfield: Hardwick Hall.
Edinburgh. Lauriston Castle. Wool mosaics.
Guildford: Museum and Muniment Room. Embroidery and stump work.
Hereford: City Museum.
Hockley Heath: Packwood House.
Hungerford: Littlecote House. Tudor needlework.
Leominster: Eye Manor. Many needlework silk pictures.
Lewes: Glynde Place. Victorian needlework pictures.
Pulborough: Parham.
Torpoint: Antony House.
West Hoathly: The Priest House. Embroidery.
Wolverhampton: Wightwick Manor. Needlework using William Morris designs.

NANTGARW AND SWANSEA PORCELAIN
Cardiff: National Museum of Wales.
Swansea: Glynn Vivian Art Gallery.
Swansea: Royal Institution of South Wales.

NEWHALL PORCELAIN
In London
Victoria and Albert Museum.
Outside London
Luton Museum.

PAINTINGS—see *Visiting Art Galleries* (pages 45 to 61)

PAISLEY SHAWLS
The history of Paisley shawls, which were made in the nineteenth century until about 1875, can be traced in Paisley Museum. There are also some fine Paisley shawls hung on the walls of the staircase at the Willmer House Museum, Farnham.

PAPERWEIGHTS
Collections of English and French paperweights are to be seen in Willmer House Museum, Farnham and at Littlecote House, near Hungerford. One of the most famous of all collections of paperweights is in the John Nelson Bergstrom Art Center and Museum in Neenah, Wisconsin, U.S.A.

PEWTER
Museums, historic houses and folk life collections often display some pewter articles, but there are no really comprehensive museum collections.
In London
Guildhall Museum. Pewter of sixteenth and seventeenth centuries.
London Museum.
Victoria and Albert Museum.
Outside London
Abingdon: Borough Museum.
Barnstaple: Arlington Court.
Cambridge: Fitzwilliam Museum.
Lewes: Anne of Cleves Museum.
Ormskirk: Rufford Old Hall.
Salisbury: Salisbury and South Wiltshire Museum.
South Molton: The Museum.
Taunton: Somerset County Museum.
In the U.S.A.
New York: Metropolitan Museum of Art. American pewter.

PIN CUSHIONS
Luton: Luton Museum and Art Gallery. The Doris Homan Collection of pincushions.

PINXTON PORCELAIN
Sheffield: City Museum. A collection of the period 1796-9.

PONTYPOOL WARE
The making of japanned wares began in Staffordshire in the late seventeenth century but the finest ware was made from about 1728 at Pontypool, when it became possible to use tin plate. Examples of the products of the Pontypool works, which was run by the Allgood family for nearly ninety

years, together with those of a second works established at Usk, can be seen in the Folk Life section of the Newport Museum and Art Gallery in Monmouthshire.

PLYMOUTH PORCELAIN—see *Bristol Porcelain*

PORCELAIN—see *Ceramics*

POTTERY—see *Ceramics*

PRATTWARE
Newcastle upon Tyne : Laing Art Gallery and Museum. Pot lids.
Oxford : Ashmolean Museum. Pot lids.

PRINTS, MAPS AND DRAWINGS—see also *Japanese Prints*
Early printed illustrations cover an enormous field—aquatints, engravings, etchings, lithographs, mezzotints, woodcuts and so on. There is scarcely a museum or historic house without one or two framed examples on show. It is only possible here to list places which have larger collections for study.
In London
British Museum. Prints, maps and drawings.
Museum of British Transport. Lithographs and engravings of transport subjects.
Victoria and Albert Museum. The collections may be seen in the Print Room (off Room 7). Rooms 70-73 are used for temporary displays from the collections.
Outside London
Aberdeen : Art Gallery and Industrial Museum. A print room.
Aberystwyth : National Library of Wales. Prints, maps and drawings.
Bangor : Museum of Welsh Antiquities. Prints, maps and drawings.
Bedford : Cecil Higgins Art Gallery. Original prints from sixteenth century.
Bradford : City Art Gallery and Museum. Print room for students.
Brighton : Art Gallery and Museum. Drawings and prints.
Cambridge : Fitzwilliam Museum. Prints.
Edinburgh : National Gallery of Scotland. Drawings and prints from fourteenth century.
Edinburgh : National Portrait Gallery. Reference collection of engraved portraits.
Liverpool : The Hornby Library. Prints and books illustrated with prints.
Manchester : Whitworth Art Gallery. Prints dating from Renaissance.
Oxford : Ashmolean Museum. Print Room.
Preston : Harris Museum and Art Gallery.
York : City Art Gallery.
In the U.S.A.
Boston, Mass : Boston Public Library.
Los Angeles, Cal : Los Angeles County Museum of Art.
New York, N.Y : The Brooklyn Museum, Metropolitan Museum of Art.
Philadelphia, Pa : Philadelphia Museum of Art.

ROCKINGHAM POTTERY AND PORCELAIN
Rotherham : Museum and Art Gallery.
Sheffield : City Museum.

SAMPLERS
In London
Victoria and Albert Museum.

Outside London
Bristol: The Georgian House.
Cardiff: National Museum of Wales.
Guildford: The Museum.
Stoke-on-Trent: City Museum and Art Gallery.

SCENT BOTTLES
Preston: Harris Museum and Art Gallery. In the Mrs French Collection.

SCIENTIFIC INSTRUMENTS—see also *Clocks, Watches and Barometers*
In London
British Museum.
Science Museum.
Outside London
Bury St Edmund's Museum. Instruments for measuring time.
Cambridge: Whipple Museum of the History of Science.
Edinburgh: Royal Scottish Museum.
Oxford: Museum of the History of Science.
In the U.S.A.
Chicago: Adler Planetarium.
Salem: Peabody Museum.
Washington D.C.: Smithsonian Institution.

SCULPTURE
In London
British Museum. Greek and Roman sculpture.
Foundling Hospital Art Treasures. Sculptures include the work of Roubillac and Rysbrack.
Sir John Soane's Museum. Works by J. Flaxman (all plaster).
Victoria and Albert Museum. Sculpture of all periods, especially Italian.
Outside London
Bakewell. Chatsworth House. A sculpture gallery.
Barnard Castle: The Bowes Museum.
Cambridge: Fitzwilliam Museum.
Durham: Gulbenkian Museum of Oriental Art and Archaeology. Indian sculpture.
Liverpool: Walker Art Gallery.
Llandudno: Rapallo House Museum and Art Gallery.
Manchester: City Art Gallery.
Oxford: Ashmolean Museum of Art and Archaeology.
Port Sunlight: Lady Lever Art Gallery. Sculpture halls which include works acquired from the collection of Thomas Hope.
Wilton: Wilton House.

SÈVRES PORCELAIN
Considerable quantities of fine porcelain from the Sèvres factory at Vincennes in France were imported into Britain in the eighteenth century by wealthy customers. Much of it is still to be seen in historic houses: the rest has been acquired by collectors or has found its way into museums.
In London
Victoria and Albert Museum. In the Jones Collection.
Wallace Collection. Finest Sèvres porcelain to be seen in Britain.
Outside London
Aylesbury: Waddesdon Manor.

Edgehill: Upton House.
Leeds: Harewood House.
Lewes: Firle Place.
Lewes: Glynde Place. Sèvres service decorated by Noel in 1764.
Windsor Castle.

SHEFFIELD PLATE
Some of the finest old Sheffield Plate can be seen in the cities where it was made in the eighteenth and early nineteenth centuries.
Birmingham: City Museum and Art Gallery.
Sheffield: City Museum.

SHELLS
Barnstaple: Arlington Court.

SHIP MODELS—see *Maritime Antiques*

SILHOUETTES
The Print Room at the Victoria and Albert Museum has the Desmond Coke Collection of Silhouettes and anyone interested may ask to see the work of particular artists. There are silhouettes by A. Edouart in the National Portrait Gallery.
Outside London
Wilton House.
Windsor Castle: Collection in the Royal Library.
Worthing Museum.

SILVER
In London
British Museum. Collection of early silver.
Goldsmith's Hall.
London Museum.
Victoria and Albert Museum. English, Irish and European silver—the finest collection in Britain.
The Wallace Collection.
Wellington Museum. Regency plate.
Outside London
Banbury: Chacombe Priory.
Barnsley: Cannon Hall Art Gallery and Museum.
Bath: Holburne of Menstrie Museum. Includes many early Apostle spoons.
Belfast: Ulster Museum. Irish silver.
Birmingham: Assay Office. By appointment.
Birmingham: Museum and Art Gallery.
Brighton: Art Gallery and Museum. Includes work by Paul de Lamerie and Paul Storr.
Bristol: City Art Gallery.
Burnley: Towneley Hall Art Gallery and Museum. Regimental silver.
Cambridge: Fitzwilliam Museum.
Cardiff: National Museum of Wales. Sir Charles Jackson Collection.
Edinburgh: National Museum of Antiquities of Scotland.
Edinburgh: Royal Scottish Museum. English and Scottish silver.
Glasgow: Art Gallery and Museum. Burrell Collection.
Hereford: City Museum and Art Gallery.
Leeds: Temple Newsam. Adam silver.
Leeds: Harewood House.

Manchester: Heaton Hall. **Assheton Bennett Collection.**
Merthyr Tydfil: Art Gallery and Museum.
Oxford: Ashmolean Museum. Many fine silversmiths represented, including Paul de Lamerie.
Plymouth: City Museum and Art Gallery.
Sheffield: City Museum.
Shugborough: Staffordshire County Museum.
Westport: Westport House. Irish silver.
Woburn: Woburn Abbey.

In the U.S.A.
Boston: Museum of Fine Arts.
Cambridge, Mass: Fogg Art Museum.
Los Angeles: County Museum of Art.
Minneapolis: Institute of Arts. Collection includes the famous Sutherland wine cistern by Paul de Lamerie.
New York: Metropolitan Museum of Art.
Philadelphia: Museum of Art.
San Marino, Cal: Huntingdon Library and Art Gallery.
Williamstown, Mass: Sterling and Francine Clark Art Institute.

SLIPWARE
In London
Guildhall Museum. Fourteenth-century slipware jugs and some seventeenth-century slipware from Wrotham found in the city, including porringers, posset pots and tygs.
Victoria and Albert Museum.
Outside London
Brighton: Museum and Art Gallery. Slipware from seventeenth century, including examples from Derbyshire and from Ilminster in Somerset.
Lewes: Anne of Cleves House. Sixteenth- and seventeenth-century slipware.
Oxford: Ashmolean Museum. Toft slipware.
Stoke-on-Trent: City Museum and Art Gallery.

SNUFF BOXES
In London
Wellington Museum, London. Collection of gold snuff boxes, some with inset miniature portraits.
Outside London
Oxford: Ashmolean Museum.

SPODE PORCELAIN AND POTTERY
Stoke-on-Trent: Spode-Copeland Museum and Art Gallery. Fine collection of Spode nineteenth-century porcelain and blue transfer-printed earthenware.

STAFFORDSHIRE FIGURES
In London
Fenton House.
Outside London
Bootle: Museum and Art Gallery.
Brighton: Museum and Art Gallery. Willett Collection has many Astbury and Whieldon figures: the Astbury figures representing 'Nebuchadnezzar's Band' (circa 1750) are remarkable. Also portrait figures by Ralph Wood and some vigorous and amusing groups by Obadiah Sherratt.

Melton Mowbray: Stapleford Park. Thomas Balston Collection of Victorian
   Staffordshire figures.
Salisbury: Salisbury and South Wiltshire Museum.
Stoke-on-Trent: City Museum and Art Gallery.

STEVENGRAPHS
These woven silk pictures, made in Coventry in the nineteenth century, are
much in demand, particularly since a Stevengraph Collectors' Association
was formed in America. They may be seen in the Herbert Art Gallery and
Museum in Coventry and there are a few specimens in the Rothesay Museum,
Bournemouth.

STONEWARE
In London
Victoria and Albert Museum. English (Room 137) and Continental (Rooms
   135-136).
Outside London
Brighton: Art Gallery and Museum. In Willett Collection.
Nottingham: City Museum. Local examples.
Southall: Public Library. See under *Martinware*, p. 34.

STRAW-WORK
In London
Victoria and Albert Museum
Outside London
Leominster: Eye Manor.
Luton Museum.
Peterborough Museum.

SUNDERLAND WARE
In London
Victoria and Albert Museum.
Outside London
Brighton: Art Gallery and Museum. In Willett Collection.
Newcastle-upon-Tyne: Laing Art Gallery and Museum.
Sunderland: Museum and Art Gallery.

SWANSEA PORCELAIN—see *Nantgarw*

TAPESTRY
In London
Hampton Court.
Victoria and Albert Museum. Gothic Tapestries Court (Room 38) with the
   Devonshire Hunting Tapestries (fifteenth-century Tournai), the Triumph
   Tapestries (early sixteenth-century Brussels) and others of the Tournai
   and Brussels Schools. The museum also has Beauvais and Gobelin tapes-
   tries.
Outside London
Aylesbury: Waddesdon Manor. French tapestries.
Barnard Castle: The Bowes Museum.
Calstock: Cotehele House.
Cambridge: Fitzwilliam Museum.
Chesterfield: Hardwick Hall.
Chorley: Astley Hall Art Gallery and Museum.
Dorking: Polesden Lacy. Brussels and Mortlake tapestries.

Edgehill: Upton House. Brussels tapestries.
Fordingbridge: Breamore House.
Grantham: Belvoir Castle. Brussels tapestries.
Harrogate: Rudding Park.
Hatfield: Hatfield House.
Hockley Heath: Packwood House.
Luton: Luton Hoo.
Maidenhead: Cliveden House.
Norwich: Blickling Hall. Flemish and Mortlake tapestries.
Oxford: Ashmolean Museum.
Port Sunlight: Lady Lever Art Gallery. Tapestry Room with Gobelin, Flemish and Mortlake examples.
Pulborough: Parham.
Shifnal: Weston Park. Gobelin and Aubusson tapestries.
Sutherland: Dunrobin Castle.
Winchcombe: Sudeley Castle. Elizabethan tapestries.
Woodstock: Blenheim Palace.
Yeovil: Montacute House.

THEATRE ART AND RELICS

Relics of the theatre are scattered widely in our museums: there are few true collections. The British Theatre Museum Association is anxious to see a National Theatre Museum established. Existing collections include:

In London
British Theatre Museum.
Victoria and Albert Museum. Theatre Art (Room 132).

Outside London
Bournemouth: Russell-Cotes Art Gallery and Museum. Room devoted to relics associated with Sir Henry Irving.
Richmond, Yorkshire: The Georgian Theatre.
Stratford-on-Avon: The Royal Shakespeare Picture Gallery. Costumes used by famous actors and actresses. Also portraits.

TOYS—see also *Dolls* and *Dolls' Houses*
Abingdon: Borough Museum.
Brighton: Grange Art Gallery and Museum, Rottingdean. National Toy Collection.
Broadway: Snowshill Manor.
Edinburgh: Museum of Childhood.
Hereford: City Museum.
Isle of Wight: Arreton Manor.
Luton: Museum and Art Gallery.
Rugeley: Blithfield Hall. Museum of Childhood and Costume.
Tunbridge Wells: Royal Tunbridge Wells Museum.

TRADE TOKENS—see *Coins*

TRANSPORT RELICS—see also *Horse Brasses*
Many museums have relics of the coaching age, sometimes including complete coaches or carriages. They include:
Halifax: West Yorkshire Folk Museum.
Horsham: The Museum. Section on horse transport, with comprehensive collection of driving and riding bits.
Hull: Transport Museum.
Maidstone: Museum of Carriages.

Nottingham: City Museum. Early vehicles.
Stoke Bruerne: Waterways Museum. Relics of canal life.
All interested in the early development of railway transport will find a great deal of valuable information in the *Railway Enthusiasts' Handbook* (David and Charles), which includes a list of railway museums in Britain.

TREEN
'Treen' is a generic term for the small wooden objects, often carved, which were mainly used in kitchens and on the table. The Victoria and Albert Museum has a collection next to Room 74 (West). In the Birmingham Museum and Art Gallery there is a good collection in the Pinto Gallery. Collections of treen are also to be seen in most folk museums (see pp. 26-7).

TRUNCHEONS
Birmingham: Museum and Art Gallery.
Cardiff: National Museum of Wales.
Liverpool: City Museums.
Nottingham: City Museum.
Oxford: Ashmolean Museum.
Salisbury: Salisbury and South Wiltshire Museum.
York: Castle Museum.
York: Railway Museum. Railway truncheons.

TUNBRIDGE WARE
Since the seventeenth century, Tunbridge has been known for boxes decorated with mosaic veneer—marquetry or parquetry, usually in geometrical designs. Games boxes, work boxes, dressing cases and many other small containers were made with this veneer. They can be seen in many museums, but particularly at the Royal Tunbridge Wells Museum and Art Gallery.

UNIFORMS
Most Service museums contain collections of uniforms.

WATCHES—see *Clocks, Watches* and *Barometers*

WATERCOLOUR DRAWINGS—see also *Visiting Art Galleries* (pp. 45-70).
In addition to Art Galleries, many watercolours may be seen in public libraries.
In London
British Museum. Print Room.
Courtauld Institute Galleries.
National Gallery.
Tate Gallery.
Victoria and Albert Museum.
Outside London
Bath: Victoria Art Gallery and Library.
Birkenhead: Public Library.
Birmingham: City Museum and Art Gallery.
Birmingham: Public Library.
Cambridge: Fitzwilliam Museum.
Glasgow: Art Gallery.
Glasgow: The University Library.
Leeds: City Art Gallery.
Manchester: Whitworth Art Gallery.
Newcastle upon Tyne: Laing Art Gallery.

Norwich: Castle Museum.
Oxford: Ashmolean Museum.
Whitby: Art Gallery.
Worthing: Museum and Art Gallery.
In the U.S.A.
Boston: Museum of Fine Arts.
Detroit: Institute of Arts.
Indiana: Rose Polytechnic Institute.
New York: Frick Art Reference Library.
New York: Grosvenor Library.
New York: Metropolitan Art Gallery.
Yale: University Library.

WEAPONS—see *Arms and Armour, Edged Weapons and Firearms*

WEDGWOOD WARE
In London
Victoria and Albert Museum.
Outside London
Birmingham: Museum and Art Gallery.
Nottingham: City Museum and Art Gallery.
Port Sunlight: Lady Lever Art Gallery. Wedgwood Room with ornamental wares, especially jasper. Flaxman's modelling tools.
Stoke-on-Trent: Wedgwood Museum.

WINE LABELS
Edinburgh: Royal Scottish Museum.

WORCESTER PORCELAIN
In London
Victoria and Albert Museum. Rooms 139 and 140.
Outside London
Brighton: Art Gallery and Museum. Stephens Collection.
Lewes: Glynde Place. Dr Wall tea-service decorated by Giles.
Oxford: Ashmolean Museum. Collection made by Rissik Marshall of coloured Worcester porcelain of the First Period (1751-83).
Wolverhampton: Bantock House.
Worcester: Dyson Perrins Museum. Unique collection.

WORK BOXES
Two exhibition cases of late eighteenth-century and early nineteenth-century fitted workboxes are to be seen in the Brighton Museum and Art Gallery, together with a showcase of needlework accessories. Guildford Museum has some nineteenth-century workboxes.

VISITING ART GALLERIES

MOST people buy pictures once or twice in a lifetime : for them it is the enjoyment of art that is of prime importance, not only in their own homes but wherever good pictures may be seen. Having acquired a taste for good painting it is possible to recognize work of quality even among relatively unknown artists and to buy pictures for the home that are not wildly expensive but which will wear well and appreciate in value. The study and understanding of pictures is almost an art in itself. For many of us, public art exhibitions are often so extensive as to be overwhelming. It is easy to wander round a gallery looking at picture after picture without really getting much from it. For this reason it is wise, especially for the amateur, to choose a few artists at a time and to try to get to know the range and style of their work well.

A list is given below of a selected number of eighteenth- and nineteenth-century painters of the British and American Schools, as well as some nineteenth-century French artists. In each case some places are mentioned where their work may be seen, together with the titles of a number of their better-known pictures. Reference is also made to relevant books about the artists and their work.

BRITISH AND AMERICAN PAINTERS

ALLSTON, WASHINGTON (1779-1843) was a visionary. He came from South Carolina but spent some time in Boston and was in London from 1801-1803.

In the U.S.A.
Boston : Museum of Fine Arts. *The Rising of the Thunderstorm at Sea; The Moonlit Landscape.*
Detroit : Institute of Fine Arts. *Belshazzar's Feast.*
New York. Metropolitan Museum of Art. *The Deluge.*
Pennsylvania : Philadelphia Academy of the Fine Arts. *The Dead Man Revived in the Tomb by Touching the Bones of the Prophet Elisha.*
See Richardson, E. P. *Washington Allston, A Study of the Romantic Artist in America.* Chicago, 1948.

ALMA-TADEMA, SIR LAWRENCE, R.A. (1836-1912) specialized in historical and classical subjects depicting life in Greece and Rome.

In London
Tate Gallery. *A Silent Greeting.*
Victoria and Albert Museum.

Outside London
Manchester City Art Gallery.

BLAKE, WILLIAM (1757-1827) was outside the main stream of British artists. His mystical philosophy produced unusual imaginative works.

In London
British Museum. Line engravings.
Tate Gallery. Many colour prints, watercolours and tempera on canvas.
In the U.S.A.
Boston : Museum of Fine Arts.
    See Blunt, Sir Anthony. *The Art of William Blake.* 1959
        Bronowski, J. *William Blake.* 1943
        Lister, R. *William Blake.* 1968
        Wilson, M. *The Life of William Blake.* 1927

BROWN, FORD MADOX (1821-1893) was born in Calais and studied in Belgium.

In London
National Portrait Gallery. *Portrait of D. G. Rossetti.*
Tate Gallery. *The Last of England; Lear and Cordelia; Christ Washing Peter's Feet; The Writing Lesson*—and others.
Outside London
Birmingham : City Art Gallery. *Portrait of Mrs Madox Brown.*
Glasgow : Art Gallery. *Wickliffe on his Trial,* and others.
Manchester : City Art Gallery. *Work.*
Oxford : Ashmolean Museum. *Pretty Baa-Lambs.*
Port Sunlight : Lady Lever Art Gallery. *Cordelia's Portion; Windermere.*
Wolverhampton : Wightwick Manor.
Canada
Ottawa : National Gallery of Canada. *Study of a Man's Head.*
    See Hueffer, F. M. *Ford Madox Brown.* 1896.

BURCHETT, RICHARD (1815-1875) was a student of art who became a teacher. He was a convert to Catholicism. At one time he did some farming but with little success. Noted for historical subjects but his landscapes are probably his best work.

In London
Victoria and Albert Museum. *Cornfield in the Isle of Wight; A Scene in the Isle of Wight.*

BURNE-JONES, SIR EDWARD COLEY (1833-1898), a great admirer of Rossetti, worked closely with William Morris over a wide field of craftsmanship, yet remained a painter.

In London
Tate Gallery. *King Cophetua and the Beggar Maid,* and others.
Victoria and Albert Museum. *The Mill,* and others.
    (Burne-Jones was responsible for the stained-glass windows of the Green Dining Room at the Victoria and Albert Museum.)
Outside London
Birmingham : City Museum and Art Gallery. *The Backgammon Players; The Feast of Peleus,* and many others.
Faringdon : Buscot Park.
Glasgow : City Art Gallery. *Danae: or The Tower of Brass.*
Port Sunlight : Lady Lever Art Gallery. *The Annunciation,* and others.
Wolverhampton : Wightwick Manor. *Love Among the Ruins.*

Canada
Ottawa: National Gallery of Canada. *Head of a Girl.*

In the U.S.A.
Cambridge, Mass: The Fogg Museum. *The Days of Creation.*
See Bell, M. *Sir Edward Burne-Jones.* 1902
See Burne-Jones, G. *Memorials of Edward Burne-Jones.* 1904

CANALETTO, GIOVANNI ANTONIO (1697-1768), A Venetian painter, although not of the British School, spent some ten years in England. Nevertheless, his finest paintings are of his beloved Venice. *A Regatta Scene on the Grand Canal* was sold in London in 1968 for £100,000, the highest price ever realized for one of his pictures.

In London
Dulwich College Picture Gallery. *The Bucintoro Returning to the Molo on Ascension Day; Old Walton Bridge.*
National Gallery. *A Regatta on the Grand Canal; Eton College; The Grand Canal—The Stonemason's Yard; Basin of S Marco on Ascension Day.*
Sir John Soane's Museum. *Venetian Scene.*

Outside London
Norwich: Blickling Hall. *A View of Chelsea.*
Oxford: Ashmolean Museum. *A View of Dolo on the River Brenta.*
Windsor: The Royal Collection. *The Thames seen from the Terrace of Somerset House; A Flight of Steps Leading up to a Loggia of a Palace.*
Woburn: Woburn Abbey. There are many Canaletto paintings in the private apartments (1s extra) but check that they are open before making a special visit.

Canada
Montreal: Museum of Fine Arts. *San Marco, the interior.*

In the U.S.A.
Boston, Mass: Museum of Fine Arts. *The Bacino di San Marco; The Molo; The Fonteghetto della Farina.*
See Constable, W. G. *Canaletto.* Oxford, 1962

COLLINS, CHARLES ALLSTON (1828-1873), a Pre-Raphaelite artist.
In London
Victoria and Albert Museum. *The Good Harvest of 1854.*

COLLINS, WILLIAM, R.A. (1788-1847), a painter of country scenes.
In London
Victoria and Albert Museum. *Seaford, Sussex.*

COLLINSON, JAMES (1825-1881), a painter of contemporary scenes.
Canada
Ottawa: National Gallery of Canada. *Childhood.*

CONSTABLE, JOHN, R.A. (1776-1837) a great landscape painter who was born in Suffolk, the scene of many of his pictures.

In London
Courtauld Institute Galleries. Constable watercolours.
National Gallery. *The Cornfield; Hay-Wain; Salisbury Cathedral; Weymouth Bay; Stoke-by-Nayland; View of Harwich.*
Tate Gallery.
Victoria and Albert Museum. The John Constable Collection.

Outside London
Cardiff: National Museum of Wales. *The Weir*.
Colchester: The Minories Art Gallery. Early works.
Ipswich: Christchurch Mansion (Wolsey Art Gallery).
Kilmarnock: Dick Institute Museum.
Port Sunlight: Lady Lever Art Gallery. *The Gamekeeper's Cottage*; *East Bergholt Church*.
In the U.S.A.
Chicago: Art Institute. *Stoke-by-Nayland*.
New York: Frick Collection. *The White Horse*.
New York: Metropolitan Museum of Art. *Salisbury Cathedral*.
Washington: National Gallery. *Wivenhow Park*.
See Basket, J. *Constable Oil Sketches*. 1966
See Leslie, C. R. *Memoirs of the Life of John Constable*. 1843, (Illustrated Edition 1937)

COPLEY, JOHN SINGLETON, R.A. (1738-1815) taught himself to paint in his home town of Boston in the 1750s, worked for many years as a portrait painter in America and finally settled in London.
In London
Tate Gallery. *The Death of the Earl of Chatham in the House of Lords*; *Death of Major Pierson*.
In the U.S.A.
Boston: Museum of Fine Arts. *Ann Tyng*; *Mary and Elizabeth Royall*; *Ezekiel Goldthwait*.
Detroit: Institute of Arts. *Col. William Montressor*; *Watson and the Shark*.
New York: Metropolitan Museum of Art. *Madam Sylvanus Bourne*.
Washington: National Gallery of Art. *Jane Browne*.
See Flexner, J. F. *John Singleton Copley*. Boston, 1948

COTMAN, JOHN SELL (1782-1842) one of the finest British watercolour artists.
In London
British Museum. *Greta Bridge, Yorkshire*; *Window of the Greyfriars Church, Norwich*.
Courtauld Institute Galleries. *Old Battersea Bridge* in Spooner Bequest of watercolours (1968).
Tate Gallery. *The Drop Gate*.
Outside London
Norwich: Castle Museum. The best of all collections of Cotman's paintings.
See Kitson, S.D. *The Life of John Sell Cotman*, 1937.

COX, DAVID (1783-1869) another watercolourist who also worked in oils.
In London
Courtauld Institute Galleries. In Spooner Bequest (1968).
Tate Gallery. Watercolour from Herbert Powell Collection acquired 1968.
Victoria and Albert Museum. *Rhyl Sands*.

CROME, JOHN (1768-1821) was born in East Anglia and became the first true British landscape painter, though he was greatly influenced by Dutch painting. He founded the Norwich Society of Artists in 1803.
In London
National Gallery. *Moonlight on the Yare*; *Poringland Oak*.
Tate Gallery. *Mousehold Heath, Norwich*.

Page 49: (above) The Greek Revival Room at the American Museum in Britain, Claverton Manor, Bath. The sofa and piano case are attributed to Duncan Phyfe of New York; (below) the Lee Room at the American Museum in Britain which came from New Hampshire and was used for both eating and sleeping. The chairs were made in Massachusetts, c 1710-30

Page 50: Humpen with Schwartzlot decoration probably made by Hermann Benckertt or Johann Keyl in Nuremberg, Germany, and dated 1691. This superb Humpen recently acquired by the Pilkington Glass Museum at St Helens has no known equal anywhere for quality with size

Outside London
Norwich Castle Museum. A good place to see the best of Crome's work and
that of other painters of the 'Norwich School'.
Port Sunlight: Lady Lever Art Gallery. *Marlingford Grove.*
See Clifford, D. and T. *John Crome.* 1968

DE WINT, PETER (1784-1849) was of Dutch-American descent. He trained
in London as a watercolourist. Many of his pictures are of the Lincoln-
shire countryside.
In London
British Museum.
Tate Gallery.
Victoria and Albert Museum.
Outside London
Cambridge: Fitzwilliam Museum. *Caernarvon Castle.*
Leeds: City Art Gallery.
Lincoln: Usher Gallery.
Worthing: Museum and Art Gallery.

EGG, AUGUSTUS (1816-1863).
In London
Tate Gallery. *Past and Present.*
Outside London
Leicester: Museum and Art Gallery. *Launce's Substitute for Proteus's Dog.*

ETTY, WILLIAM, R.A. (1787-1849) was born in York, studied at the
Royal Academy Schools in London and spent some time in Italy in his
thirties.
In London
Tate Gallery.
Victoria and Albert Museum.
Outside London
Bournemouth: Russell Cotes Art Gallery.
Hull: Ferens Art Gallery. *Titian's La Bella.*
York: City Art Gallery. *Venus and Cupid,* and others.
Canada
Montreal: Museum of Fine Arts. *A Bivouac of Cupid and his Company.*
See Farr, D. *William Etty.* 1958

FRITH, WILLIAM POWELL, R.A., (1819-1909)
In London
Tate Gallery. *Derby Day; Uncle Toby and the Widow Wadman.*
Victoria and Albert Museum. *The Bride of Lammermoor; Dolly Varden.*
Outside London
Birmingham: City Art Gallery. *Garden Flowers; Making a Posy.*
Bournemouth: Russell Cotes Art Gallery. *Ramsgate Sands.*
Derby: Museum and Art Gallery. *The Artist's Model.*
Harrogate: Art Gallery. *Many Happy Returns of the Day,* and others.
Leicester: Art Gallery. *The Railway Station.*
Liverpool: Walker Art Gallery. *The Marriage of Their Royal Highnesses
The Prince of Wales and the Princess Alexandra of Denmark; Claude
Duval.*
Manchester: City Art Gallery.
Oxford: Ashmolean Museum. *Before Dinner at Boswell's Lodgings, 1769.*

D

Sheffield: Graves Art Gallery. *The Love Token.*
Worthing: Museum and Art Gallery. *Blessing of the children at Boulogne.*
(Chalk on paper cartoon.)

Canada

Ottawa: National Gallery of Canada. *The Salon d'Or, Homburg.*
See Wallis, N. (Ed.) *A Victorian Canvas; The Memoirs of W. P. Frith, R.A.* 1957

GAINSBOROUGH, THOMAS, R.A. (1727-1788) was born in Suffolk where he developed a love of landscape painting, but when he moved to live in Bath and London social pressures forced him to specialize in portrait painting.

In London

Courtauld Institute Galleries. *Charles Tudway, M.P.* and Spooner Bequest watercolours.
Dulwich College Picture Gallery. *Mrs Moodey and her Children; The Linley Sisters;* and other portraits.
Foundling Hospital Art Treasures.
Kenwood House.
National Gallery. *The Painter's Daughter; White Dogs; John Plampin; The Morning Walk; Mr and Mrs Andrews; The Watering Place,* and others.
Tate Gallery.

Outside London

Abingdon: Guildhall Art Gallery.
Arundel: Arundel Castle.
Aylesbury: Waddesdon Manor.
Edinburgh: National Gallery of Scotland.
Grantham: Belvoir Castle.
Ipswich: Christchurch Mansion.
Lewes: Glynde Place.
Norwich: Blickling Hall.
Port Sunlight: Lady Lever Art Gallery.
Sheffield: Graves Art Gallery.
Sudbury: Gainsborough House (see p. 75).

In the U.S.A.

Boston: Museum of Fine Arts. *Portrait of Captain Thomas Mathew.*
New York: Frick Collection. *The Mall in St James's Park.*
New York: Metropolitan Museum of Art. *Portrait of Mrs Elliott.*
Washington: National Gallery. *Landscape with a Bridge.*
See Waterhouse, E. K. *Gainsborough.* 1958 (1966)
See Whitley, W. T. *Thomas Gainsborough.* 1915

HOGARTH, WILLIAM (1697-1764) has been described as the first really great British painter. He started as an engraver and he was over thirty years of age when he started painting what are now regarded as his masterpieces—moral and satiric histories such as *The Rake's Progress.*

In London

British Museum.
Foundling Hospital Art Treasures. *The March of the Guards to Finchley.*
National Gallery. *Marriage à la Mode; Shortly after the Marriage: Countess's Morning Levee; The Shrimp Girl.*
Sir John Soane's Museum. *The Rake's Progress; The Election.*
Tate Gallery.

Outside London
Wing: Ascott.
In the U.S.A.
New York: Frick Collection. *Portrait of Mrs Mary Edwards.*
Philadelphia: Museum of Art. *Portrait of Mrs Butler.*
See Antal, F. *Hogarth and his Place in European Art.* 1962
See Beckett, R. *Hogarth.* 1949

HUNT, WILLIAM HOLMAN, O.M. (1827-1910) shared a studio with
Rossetti and helped to form the 'Pre-Raphaelite Brotherhood.'
In London
National Portrait Gallery. *Portrait of Millais.*
Tate Gallery. *The Triumph of the Innocents; The Ship; Strayed Sheep,* and
others.
Victoria and Albert Museum. *Ponte Vecchio by Night.*
Outside London
Birmingham: City Art Gallery. *Valentine Rescuing Sylvia from Proteus,* and
others.
Manchester: City Art Gallery. *The Hireling Shepherd; The Shadow of the
Cross.*
Newcastle-upon-Tyne: Laing Art Gallery and Museum. *Isabella and the Pot
of Basil.*
Oxford: Ashmolean Museum. *Christians Escaping from the Druids.*
Port Sunlight: Lady Lever Art Gallery. *May Morning on Magdalen Tower.*
See Gissing, A. C. *William Holman Hunt.* 1936
LANDSEER, SIR EDWIN, R.A. (1803-1872) is best known for his animal
paintings, sentimental and humorous. He was immensely popular in his
lifetime, though violently criticised by Ruskin and the Pre-Raphaelites.
In London
Kenwood House. *Hawking in the Olden Times; The Hon E. S. Russell and
his Brother.*
National Portrait Gallery. *Portrait of Sir Walter Scott; Portrait of John
Landseer.*
Tate Gallery. *Dignity and Impudence; Shoeing the Mare,* and others.
Victoria and Albert Museum. *The Old Shepherd's Chief Mourner; The
Highland Drover's Departure,* and others.
Wallace Collection. *A Highland Scene; The Arab Tent,* and others.
Wellington Museum. *A Dialogue at Waterloo; The Illicit Still.*
Outside London
Bournemouth: Russell Cotes Art Gallery.
Macclesfield: West Park Museum and Art Gallery. Landseer sketches.
Sheffield: Graves Art Gallery.
See Manson, J. A. *Sir Edwin Landseer, R.A.* 1902

LAWRENCE, SIR THOMAS, P.R.A. (1765-1830) was famous as a portrait
painter.
In London
Tate Gallery.
Outside London
Brighton: Art Gallery and Museum.
Wilton House.
See Garlick, K. *Sir Thomas Lawrence.* 1954

LEIGHTON, FREDERICK, LORD, P.R.A. (1830-1896) travelled widely and learned his craft under distinguished artists.

In London

Tate Gallery. *The Bath of Psyche.*
Victoria and Albert Museum.

Outside London

Leeds: City Art Gallery. *The Return of Prosperine.*
Manchester: City Art Gallery. *Captive Andromache.*

LELY, SIR PETER (1618-1680) was invited to Britain from Holland in 1641 as a portrait painter of the nobility.

In London

Courtauld Institute Galleries. In the Lee Collection—*Sir Thomas Thynne; Lely and his Family; Figures in a Landscape.*
National Portrait Gallery.

Outside London

Abingdon: Guildhall Art Gallery.
Edinburgh: Scottish National Portrait Gallery. *Portrait of John, Duke of Lauderdale,* (acquired in 1968).
Manchester: City Art Gallery. *Sir John Cotton and his family.*
Sevenoaks: Knole.
Wilton: Wilton House. Many portraits.
See Baker, C. H. *Lely and the Stuart Portrait Painters.* 1912
See Beckett, R. B. *Lely.* 1951

LESLIE, CHARLES ROBERT, R.A. (1794-1859) was born of American parents and from 1800-1811 was educated in Philadelphia. He wrote a life of Constable (qv).

In London

Victoria and Albert Museum. *The Peasant Mistress of Don Quixote; Les Femmes Savantes; Le Bourgeois Gentilhomme; A Scene in the Artist's Garden.*
See Leslie, C. R. *Autobiographical Reflections.* 1860

MILLAIS, SIR JOHN EVERETT, P.R.A. (1829-1896) was influenced in his early days by the Pre-Raphaelites but broke away in the 1870s to produce work showing an outstanding technical skill.

In London

National Portrait Gallery. *Portrait of Sir Arthur Sullivan,* and others.
Tate Gallery. *The North West Passages; The Boyhood of Raleigh,* and others.
Victoria and Albert Museum. *Pizarro Seizing the Emperor of Persia.*

Outside London

Birmingham: City Art Gallery. *The Widow's Mite; The Blind Girl; The Ornithologist; The Forerunner.*
Glasgow: Art Gallery. *The Ruling Passion.*
Liverpool: Walker Art Gallery. *Lorenzo and Isabella.*
Manchester: City Art Gallery. *Autumn Leaves.*
Oxford: Ashmolean Museum. *The Return of the Dove to the Ark.*
Port Sunlight: Lady Lever Art Gallery. *Sir Isumbras at the Ford; Alfred, Lord Tennyson.*
Wolverhampton: Wightwick Manor. *Portrait of Effie Gray.*
See Baldry, A. *Sir John Everett Millais.* 1899

See Fish, A. *Sir John Everett Millais*. New York, 1923
See Millais, J. B. *The Life of Sir John Millais* (2 vols.) 1899

MORLAND, GEORGE (1763-1804) a painter who depicted life on the farm
and in the country.
In London
Tate Gallery.
Victoria and Albert Museum.

MULREADY, WILLIAM, R.A. (1786-1863) was born in Ireland. He
specialized in scenes of ordinary life.
In London
Tate Gallery. *The Last Inn.*
Victoria and Albert Museum. *Choosing the Wedding Gown; Open Your
Mouth and Shut Your Eyes; John Sheepshanks with his Maid; The Sonnet.*
Outside London
Dublin: National Gallery of Ireland. *The Bathers.*

OPIE, JOHN, R.A. (1761-1807) was a Cornish boy who made good as a
painter in London.
In London
Tate Gallery.
Outside London
Berwick-on-Tweed: Art Gallery.

PALMER, SAMUEL (1805-1881) started painting at an early age and by
the time he was fourteen had had three pictures accepted for the Royal
Academy Exhibition. His love of moonlight, seen in so many of his pictures,
dated from childhood. A portrait drawing by Samuel Palmer fetched
£1,300 at auction in 1968.
In London
Tate Gallery. *Rising Moon; Moonlight Landscape with Sheep; The Harvest
Moon*, and many others. A watercolour—*Rowe*—was acquired in 1968.
Victoria and Albert Museum. *Full Moon and Deer; Ruth Returning from
the Gleaning*, and others.
Outside London
Cambridge: Fitzwilliam Museum. *The Magic Apple Tree.*
Carlisle: Art Gallery. *The Harvest Moon.*
Manchester: City Art Gallery. *Bright Cloud and Ploughing; The Willow;
A Man with a Faggot.*
Oxford: Ashmolean Museum. *The Valley Thick with Corn; Shepherds
under a Full Moon*, and many others.
Canada
Ottawa: National Gallery of Canada. *Oak Trees in Lullingstone Park; Oak
Tree, Shoreham, Kent; The Young Angler.*
See Grigson, G. *Samuel Palmer: The Visionary Years.* 1947
Ashmolean Museum booklet: *Paintings and Drawings by Samuel
Palmer.*

PEALE, CHARLES WILLSON (1741-1827) was first and foremost a natural
craftsman and this is reflected in his painting. He spent two years in
London with Benjamin West (qv) learning portrait painting on the large
scale and also the painting of miniatures and engraving.

In the U.S.A.
Philadelphia: Museum of Art. *The Staircase Group.*
See Sellers, T. T. *Charles Willson Peale* (2 vols). Philadelphia, 1952

RAEBURN, SIR HENRY, R.A. (1756-1823) became pre-eminent as a portrait painter among Scottish artists and was knighted in 1822 by George IV.
In London
Courtauld Institute Galleries. *Mrs Malcolm.*
Tate Gallery.
Outside London
Aberdeen: Art Gallery and Regional Museum. *Robert Adam.*
Edinburgh: National Gallery of Scotland. *Mrs Campbell; Mrs. Colin Mackenzie of Portmore.*
Newcastle-upon-Tyne: Laing Art Gallery. *Robert Allan of Kirkliston, Midlothian.*

REDGRAVE, RICHARD, C. B., R.A. (1804-1888).
In London
Victoria and Albert Museum. *The Governess; An Old English Homestead.*
Outside London
Birmingham: City Art Gallery. *The Valleys also Stand Thick with Corn.*

REYNOLDS, SIR JOSHUA, P.R.A. (1723-1792) was greatly influenced by the work of Italian masters. He became the first president of the Royal Academy and had many opportunities of expressing his general views on the principles of art.
In London
Kenwood House.
National Gallery. *Lady Anne Lennox, Countess of Albermarle; Sir Watkin Williams-Wynn and his Mother; Colonel Tarleton.*
National Portrait Gallery. *Dr Johnson.*
Sir John Soane's Museum. *Love and Beauty.*
Wallace Collection.
Outside London
Aylesbury: Waddesdon Manor.
Faringdon: Buscot Park.
Grantham: Belvoir Castle.
Newcastle-upon-Tyne: Laing Art Gallery. *Mrs Elizabeth Riddell.*
Plymouth: City Museum and Art Gallery. *Portrait of Mrs Hamar.*
Port Sunlight: Lady Lever Art Gallery. *Mrs Paine with her Two Daughters; Elizabeth Gunning, Duchess of Hamilton and Argyll.*
Sevenoaks: Knole.
Shifnal: Weston Park.
Torpoint: Antony House.
Wilton: Wilton House.
Woburn: Woburn Abbey.
In the U.S.A.
Chicago: Art Institute. *Lady Sarah Bunbury.*
New York: Metropolitan Museum of Art. *Colonel Coussmaker.*
Washington: National Gallery. *Lady Elizabeth Delmé and her Children.*
See Waterhouse, E. K. *Reynolds.* 1941

ROMNEY, GEORGE (1734-1802) was a Lake District man who started as a cabinet maker and later set up in London as a portrait painter.

In London
Courtauld Institute Galleries. *Georgina, Lady Greville.*
Tate Gallery.
Outside London
Port Sunlight: Lady Lever Art Gallery. *Miss Rodbard; Mrs Oliver.*

ROSSETTI, DANTE GABRIEL (1756-1827) a Pre-Raphaelite painter who
was almost obsessed with the Middle Ages. He loved red hair and based
many of his female figures on Elizabeth Siddall whom he married, and
Jane Morris, wife of William Morris.
In London
National Portrait Gallery. *Self-Portrait; Madox Brown.*
Tate Gallery. *The Annunciation; Miss Siddall in a Chair; The Beloved,*
and many others.
Victoria and Albert Museum. *The Day Dream; Miss Siddall Standing at a*
Window (drawing).

Outside London
Bedford: Cecil Higgins Art Gallery. *Paolo and Francesca.*
Birmingham: City Art Gallery. *Sir Galahad at the Ruined Castle; Beata*
Beatrix (unfinished) and several studies.
Cambridge: Fitzwilliam Museum. *How They Met Themselves.*
Liverpool: Walker Art Gallery. *Dante's Dream.*
Oxford: Ashmolean Museum. *Dante Drawing an Angel.*
Port Sunlight: Lady Lever Art Gallery. *The Blessed Damozel; Sibylla*
Palmifera.
Southend-on-Sea: Beecroft Art Gallery. *Fanny Cornforth.*
Wolverhampton: Wightwick Manor. *Portrait of Rossetti and Madox*
Brown.
Canada
Ottawa: National Gallery of Canada. *The Roseleaf; Profile of a Woman;*
Salutatio Beatricis
See Angeli, H. *Dante Gabriel Rossetti.* 1949
See Doughty, O. *A Victorian Romantic: Daniel Gabriel Rossetti.* 1949
See Grylls, R. G. *Portrait of Rossetti.* 1964.

ROWLANDSON, THOMAS (1756-1827) mainly noted as a caricaturist
and illustrator.
In London
British Museum.
Courtauld Institute Galleries. In Spooner Bequest.
Tate Gallery.
Victoria and Albert Museum. *View of Vauxhall Gardens.*
Outside London
Northampton: Museum and Art Gallery.
Southend-on-Sea: Beecroft Art Gallery.
Worthing: Museum and Art Gallery.
See Oppé, A. P. *Thomas Rowlandson.* 1923.

SANDBY, PAUL (1725-1809) may be regarded as the first great English
watercolourist. He spent a good deal of time in Wales and loved its
scenery.
In London
British Museum.

Tate Gallery.
Victoria and Albert Museum.

Outside London
Belfast : Ulster Museum. *Caernarvon Castle by Moonlight.*
Cambridge: Fitzwilliam Museum. *Haymaking at Dolwyddelan below Moel Siabod.*
Plymouth : City Museum and Art Gallery. *Landscape.*

SARGENT, JOHN SINGER, R.A. (1856-1925) was born in Florence of American parents, brought up in Italy, studied in Paris and thereafter worked alternately in America and England, where he settled in 1887.

In London
Tate Gallery. *Miss Priestley; Ellen Terry as Lady Macbeth.*

Outside London
Aberdeen: Art Gallery. *Self Portrait.*
Cambridge: Fitzwilliam Museum. *Near the Mount of Olives, Jerusalem.*
Farnham : Willmer Museum. *A Portrait.*

In the U.S.A.
Boston: Museum of Fine Arts. *The Master and his Pupils.*
Chicago: Art Institute. *Venetian Glass Workers; Mrs Charles Gifford Dyer.*
Cincinnati: Taft Museum. *Robert Louis Stevenson; Two Girls Fishing.*
Los Angeles: County Museum. *Study of a Man Wearing Laurels.*
New York: Metropolitan Museum. *Study of Astronomy; Holy Land Mountains.*
Philadelphia: Museum of Art: *Duchess of Sutherland.*
See McKibben, David; *Sargent's Boston, with an Essay and Biographical Summary.* Boston, 1957. (This book contains a complete check list of Sargent's portraits.)
Mount, C. M. *John Singer Sargent,* 1957. (This book contains a complete list of Sargent's work in oil.

STUART, GILBERT (1755-1828), an American who showed early talent as a painter which attracted the attention of Cosmo Alexander, a Scot who took him to Edinburgh. For many years Stuart worked in London and in Ireland as a portrait painter before he returned to America.

In the U.S.A.
Boston: Museum of Fine Arts. *Washington at Dorchester Heights.*
New York: Metropolitan Museum of Art. *Portrait of George Washington.*
Washington: National Gallery. *Mrs Richard Yates.*
See Flexner, J. *Gilbert Stuart: A Great Life in Brief.* New York, 1955.

STUBBS, GEORGE (1724-1806) was well known as a painter of scenes with horses.

In London
Fenton House. A single picture.
Tate Gallery.

Outside London
Bath: Holburne of Menstrie Museum. *The Rev Carter Thelwell and his Wife and Daughter.*
Port Sunlight: Lady Lever Art Gallery. *Portrait of the Artist on Horseback; Hay Makers; Hay Carting.*
See Sparrow, W. S. *British Sporting Artists.* 1922 (1965). Chapter 5.

SULLY, THOMAS (1783-1872) was a great portrait painter who worked in Philadelphia. He has sometimes been called the Thomas Lawrence of America. For a time he joined Benjamin West in London.

In the U.S.A.
Boston: Museum of Fine Arts. *The Torn Hat; Washington at the Passage of the Delaware.*
Philadelphia: Museum of Art. *Queen Victoria.*
See Biddle, E. and Fielding, M. *The Life and Works of Thomas Sully, 1793-1872.* Philadelphia, 1921

TURNER, JOSEPH MALLORD WILLIAM, R.A. (1775-1851) had a meteoric career. He exhibited when fifteen, became a member of the Royal Academy at twenty-eight and a professor at thirty-three. He never married. A hard worker, he started as a watercolourist, then embarked on landscapes in oils and towards the end of his life his pictures depicted the forces of nature in all her moods.

In London
Courtauld Institute Galleries. Watercolours in Spooner Bequest (1968)
National Gallery. *Sunset at Petworth; Fire at Sea; Snow Storm at Sea; Rain, Steam and Speed; Calais Pier.*
Sir John Soane's Museum. *Refectory at Kirkstall Abbey* (watercolour).
Tate Gallery. A fine collection of Turner paintings including *Norham Castle; Sunrise; The Thames near Windsor; Calais Pier.*
Victoria and Albert Museum. *Salisbury Cathedral.*

Outside London
Lincoln: Usher Gallery. *Stamford, Lincs* (watercolour).
Luton Hoo: *Aberdulais Mill* (watercolour).
Oxford: Ashmolean Museum. Drawings and watercolours.
Petworth: Petworth House. Large collection.
Worthing: Museum and Art Gallery. Watercolours.

In the U.S.A.
Boston: Museum of Fine Arts: *The Slave Ship.*
Chicago: Art Institute. *Snow Storm in Val d'Aosta.*
New York: Metropolitan Museum of Art. *Grand Canal, Venice.*
Washington: National Gallery. *Mortlake Terrace.*
See Butlin, M. *Turner Watercolours.* 1962 (1967).
See Falk, B. *Turner the Painter: His Hidden Life.* 1938
See Finberg, A. J. *The Life of J. M. W. Turner, R.A.* 1939 (1961).

WATTS, GEORGE FREDERICK, O.M., R.A. (1817-1904) was a man who suffered from poor health and a retiring nature from childhood. Nevertheless, he was still working in his eighties and had a vast output.

In London
National Portrait Gallery. *Lord Tennyson; A. C. Swinburne; D. G. Rossetti; Cecil J. Rhodes; Dame Ellen Terry,* and many others.
St Paul's Cathedral. *Peace and Goodwill; Time, Death and Judgment.*
Tate Gallery. *Hope; Dray Horses; Life's Illusions,* and many others.
Victoria and Albert Museum.

Outside London
Aberdeen: Art Gallery and Museum. *Orpheus and Eurydice.*
Birmingham: City Art Gallery. *Burne-Jones.*
Compton, near Guildford: The Watts Gallery. A large collection. See p. 90.
Edinburgh: National Gallery of Scotland. *Mischief.*

Leeds: City Art Gallery. *Artemis.*
Leicester: City Art Gallery. *Fata Morgana.*
Liverpool: Walker Art Gallery.
Manchester: City Art Gallery. *The Good Samaritan,* and others.
Manchester: Whitworth Gallery. *Out of the Storm,* and others.
Oxford: Ashmolean Museum.
See Chapman, R. *The Laurel and the Thorn.* 1945

WEST, BENJAMIN (1738-1820) was the first American painter to gain a
reputation in Europe. He settled in London and eventually became
president of the Royal Academy. *The Death of General Wolfe* in the
National Gallery, Ottawa, has been used as an illustration in many school
history textbooks.

Outside London
Norwich: Blickling Hall. *Portrait of the Artist's Wife and Child.*
See Marceau, H. and Kemball, F. *Benjamin West 1738-1820.* Phila-
delphia, 1938.

WHISTLER, JAMES MCNEILL (1834-1903), son of an American army
officer, developed his skills in Russia and Paris before settling in England
in the 1860s.

In London
Tate Gallery. *Old Battersea Bridge; Valparaiso,* and others.

Outside London
Glasgow: City Art Gallery. *Portrait of Carlyle.*
Glasgow: The University has a large collection of oil paintings, etchings,
lithographs, pastel drawings and watercolours by Whistler.
Leicester: Art Gallery. *Thames, Nocturne in Blue and Gold.*
Oxford: Ashmolean Museum. *Portrait Drawing of Mrs L. Huth.*
Sheffield: Museum and Art Gallery.

In the U.S.A.
Boston: Museum of Fine Arts. *The Last of Old Westminster.*
Detroit: Institute of Arts. *Nocturne in Black and Gold—The Falling
Rocket.*
New York: Frick Collection. *The Pacific.*
Washington: Freer Gallery of Art. *The Music Room; Princesse du Pays de
la Porcelaine.*
See Holden, D. *Whistler Landscapes and Seascapes,* 1969.
See Laver, J. *James McNeill Whistler.* 1930 (revised edition, 1951)
See Pannel, E. R. *Life of James McNeill Whistler.* Philadelphia, 1919
See Sutton, D. *Nocturne: The Art of James McNeill Whistler.* 1963

WILKIE, SIR DAVID, R.A. (1785-1841) was a figure painter who delighted
in painting scenes of everyday life.

In London
Tate Gallery. *Peep o'day Boy's Cabin, West of Ireland.*
Victoria and Albert Museum.
Wellington Museum. *The Chelsea Pensioners reading the Gazette of the
Battle of Waterloo.*

Outside London
Birmingham: City Museum and Art Gallery. *Grace before Meat.*
Edinburgh: National Gallery of Scotland. *The Letter of Introduction.*

WILSON, RICHARD (1714-1782), a painter of many subjects, including figures and portraits, is known mainly for his landscapes. He worked for some time in Italy and painted many Italian scenes.

In London
National Gallery. *The Valley of the Dee; Holt Bridge: River Dee.*
Victoria and Albert Museum.

Outside London
Cardiff: National Museum of Wales.
Nottingham: City Museum and Art Gallery. *Snowdon.*
Port Sunlight: Lady Lever Art Gallery. *Castel Gondolfo: Lake Albano.*
Wilton: Wilton House. Many landscapes including two of Wilton.
See Constable, W. G. *Richard Wilson.* 1953

WRIGHT, JOSEPH (1734-1797), a portrait painter usually known as Wright of Derby. Much of his work is to be seen in Derby Museum and Art Gallery.
See Nicolson, B. *Joseph Wright of Derby, Painter of Light.* 2 vols 1968

ZOFFANY, JOHANN (1733-1810) was a master of the conversation piece and of scenes which illustrate the life of his time.

In London
The Royal Collection, Buckingham Palace. *Queen Charlotte and her Two Elder Sons; Life School at the Royal Academy; Cognoscenti in the Tribune of the Uffizi.*

NINETEENTH-CENTURY FRENCH PAINTERS

Many names have been used to describe French painting since the term 'Impressionist' was used by journalists after the Paris Exhibition of 1874 when a picture was shown entitled *Impression, Sunrise.* No attempt has been made to affix labels in the following list, which simply states some of the places where the work of French artists may be seen. English titles have been given where the particular gallery has translated the original title.

BAZILLE, JEAN-FRÉDÉRIC (1841-71) hired a studio in Paris in 1863 which he shared with Renoir. They had previously attended the same art school and were great admirers of Manet's work.

In France
Paris: The Louvre. *Vue de village; Mon atelier.*

BONNARD, PIERRE (1867-1947), who started as a poster artist, was greatly attracted by Japanese prints. His later pictures were intimate, many of them simply subjects or family groups in a home setting.

In London
Courtauld Institute Galleries. *The Blue Balcony.*

In the U.S.A.
Washington: Phillips Memorial Gallery. *La Palme.*

BOUDIN, EUGENE (1824-98) is noted for seascapes and harbour scenes and the striking way in which he painted skies.

In London
Courtauld Institute Galleries. *The Beach at Trouville.*
National Gallery. *Trouville.*

CÉZANNE, PAUL, (1839-1906), was born at Aix-en-Provence and went to Paris in 1861 to work as an artist. He is regarded by many as the greatest of French nineteenth-century painters.

In London
Courtauld Institute Galleries. Eight oil paintings including *The Card Players*; *Man Smoking a Pipe*; and *Trees at the Jas de Bouffau.*
National Gallery. *Les Grande Baigneuses*; *Dans le Parc du Chateau Noir*; *La Vielle au Chapelet.*
Tate Gallery. *Still Life with Water Jug*; *The Gardener*; *Mount Saint-Victoire.*

Outside London
Cardiff : National Museum of Wales.
Edinburgh : National Gallery of Scotland.
Glasgow : Art Gallery and Museum. Burrell Collection.

In the U.S.A.
Cambridge, Mass : Fogg Art Museum. *Petites Maisons à Auvers.*
Chicago : Art Institute. *Study of a Nude*; *View of Auvers.*
Cleveland, Ohio : Museum of Art. *The Pigeon Tower of Bellevue.*
Los Angeles : County Museum of Art.
Minneapolis : Institute of Arts.
New York : Brooklyn Museum. *View of Gardanne.*
New York : Museum of Modern Art. *Portrait of Uncle Dominique.*
Northampton, Mass : Smith College of Art Museum. *Turning Road at La Roche-Guyon.*
Philadelphia : Pennsylvania Museum of Art. *Mount Saint-Victoire seen from Les Louvres.*
St Louis : City Art Museum. *Portrait of the Artist's sister Marie.*
Washington, D.C. : National Gallery of Art. *Portrait of the Artist's son.*

In France
Paris : The Louvre. *Le Vase Bleu*; *La Table de Cuisine.*
See Hanson, L. *Mountain of Victory: A Biography of Paul Cézanne,* 1960.
See Perruchot, H. *Cézanne,* 1961.
See Rewald, J. *The Ordeal of Paul Cézanne,* 1950.

COROT, JEAN-BAPTISTE-CAMILLE (1796-1875), was born in Paris and became a painter, mainly of landscapes, working in France and Italy.

In London
National Gallery. *Roman Campagna with the Claudian Aqueduct*; *Dardagny View*; *The Cart.*
Wallace Collection. *Macbeth and the Witches.*

Outside London
Glasgow : Museum and Art Gallery. *View of Genoa.*
Oxford : Ashmolean Museum. *La Petit Chaville, near Ville d'Avray.*

In Canada
Ottawa : National Gallery of Canada. *The Bridge of Narni.*

In the U.S.A.
Boston: Museum of Fine Arts. *Old Man sitting on Corot's Trunk*; *The Forest of Fontainebleu.*
Chicago: Art Institute. *View of Genoa.*
New York: Brooklyn Museum. *The Young Girls of Sparta.*
Washington, D.C.: National Gallery of Art. *The Forest of Fontainebleu*; *A View near Volterra.*
In France
Paris: The Louvre. A large collection, including *Self Portrait at the age of 29*; *Florence from the Bobili Gardens*; *Portrait of Maurice Robert*; *La Dance de Bergères*; *The Belfry at Douai.*
See Roberts, K. *Corot*, 1965.

DEGAS, HILAIRE-GERMAIN EDGARD (1834-1917), started painting dancers, models, cabaret artists and working girls in the 1870s. He was also a sculptor.
In London
Courtauld Institute Galleries. *Two dancers on the stage*; *Woman drying herself*; *Woman at a window.*
National Gallery. *La La at the Cirque Fernando*; *Combing the Hair*; *Après le bain.*
Tate Gallery. *Femme à sa Toilette* (pastel) and sculptures.
Victoria and Albert Museum.
Outside London
Birmingham: City Museum and Art Gallery.
Edinburgh: National Gallery of Scotland. *Diego Martelli.*
Glasgow: Art Gallery. A fine selection in the Burrell Collection including *La Repetition de Danse*; *Portrait de Durauty.*
Liverpool: Walker Art Gallery. *Woman Ironing.*
In the U.S.A.
Boston: Museum of Fine Arts. *La Voiture au Courses: Le Père de Degas Écoutant Pagans.*
Chicago: Art Institute. *Chez la Modiste.*
New York: Metropolitan Museum of Art. *Répétition d'un Ballet sur la Scène*; *Bouderie*; *Danseuses a La Barre.*
Museum of Modern Art. *Après le Bain.*
Washington, D.C.: National Gallery of Art. *Avant la Course*; *En Attendant L'Entrée en Scène.*
In France
Paris: The Louvre. A large collection, including *Étude de Mains*; *Les Malheurs de la Ville d'Orléans*; *L'Orchestre de L'Opéra*; *L'Étoile*; *L'Absinthe*; *Femmes Devant un Café*; *Le Soir.*
See Bouret, J. *Degas*, 1965.

DELACROIX, EUGENE (1798-1863), was an admirer of English painting and rejected many prevailing classical trends. His influence on later painters such as Seurat was considerable.
In London
National Gallery.
Wallace Collection.
Outside London
Bristol: Art Gallery.

Dublin: Municipal Gallery of Modern Art.
Edinburgh: National Gallery of Scotland.
In the U.S.A.
Boston: Museum of Fine Arts.
Cambridge, Mass: Fogg Art Museum.
Chicago: Art Institute.
New York: Metropolitan Museum of Art.
Washington, D.C.: National Gallery.
In France.
Paris: The Louvre. *Femmes Algériennes* and many others.

GAUGUIN, PAUL (1848-1903), was born in Paris but spent some of his
early years in Peru. In his youth, he was for six years at sea. Then
followed a period of business life and it was not until 1883 that he started
to work as a full-time artist. He travelled a great deal, especially in the
Pacific Islands.

In London
Courtauld Institute Galleries. *Te Terioa*; *Nevermore*; *Madame Gauguin.*
National Gallery. *A Tahiti.*

Outside London
Bedford: Cecil Higgins Art Gallery. *Joiee de Bretagne* (lithograph).
Edinburgh: National Gallery of Scotland. *Vision après le sermon*; *Lutte de
Jacob avec l'ange.*

In the U.S.A.
Boston: Museum of Fine Arts. *D'où venons nous? Que sommes nous? Où
allons nous?*
Chicago: Art Institute. Tahitian pictures including *Te Burao*; *Mahana No
Atua*; *No Te Aha Oe Riri.*
Worcester, Mass: Museum. *Te Faatourama.*

In France
Paris: The Louvre. *Tahitiennes assises au bord de la mer*; *Le cheval blanc.*
See Alexandre, A. *Paul Gauguin.* Paris, 1930.
See Cogniat, R. *Gauguin.* 1947.
See Mittelstadt, K. *Paul Gauguin: Self Portraits.* 1969.

GOGH, VINCENT VAN (1853-90), was of Dutch extraction and was
employed for some years by his brother who worked for picture dealers.
He did not start to paint seriously until 1880. In 1886 he met a number
of well-known artists in Paris and in 1888 went to Arles, where he suffered
from mental trouble and eventually shot himself in 1890.

In London
Courtauld Institute Galleries. *Portrait of the artist with a bandaged ear*;
Peach trees in blossom.
National Gallery. *Sunflowers*; *Cornfield and Cypress Trees.*
Tate Gallery. *Sunflowers*; *La Chaise et la Pipe.*

Outside London
Glasgow: Art Gallery. Burrell Collection.

In the U.S.A.
Boston: Museum of Fine Arts.
Chicago: Art Institute. *Ma Chambre à coucher.*

New York: Metropolitan Museum of Art.
Toledo: Museum of Art. *Champ de blé.*
Washington: National Gallery.
In France
Paris: The Louvre. *Le Guinguette; Restaurant de la Sirène.*
See Coquiot, G. *Vincent Van Gogh. Paris,* 1923.
See Rewald, J. *Post-Impressionism from Gauguin to Van Gogh.* New
York, 1962.

MANET, EDOUARD (1832-83), rejected much of the teaching of his elders
and developed new techniques. For much of his life he was a rebel and
his work has only been fully recognized since his death.
In London
Courtauld Institute Galleries. *Bar au Folies-Bergère; Le Déjeuner sur
l'Herbe.*
National Gallery. *Musique aux Tuileries; Eva Gonzalès piegnant; La
Servante de Bocks.*
In the U.S.A.
Chicago: Art Institute. *Un philosophe; Courses à Longchamps.*
Washington: Phillips Memorial Gallery. *Le ballet espagnol.*
See Bex, M. *Manet.* 1948.
See Perruchot, H. *Manet.* 1962.

MATISSE, HENRI EMILE BENOIT (1869-1954), is included in this list
because, although primarily a twentieth-century painter, he trained and
was already exhibiting his work in the 1890s.
In London
Tate Gallery. *Nude Study in Blue; Standing Nude; Tree near Trivaux
Pond; Snail.*
Outside London
Glasgow: Art Gallery and Museum. *The Pink Tablecloth.*
In the U.S.A.
Baltimore: Museum of Art. *Girl in a Yellow Dress; Pink Nude; The Blue
Nude; The Invalid.*
Boston: Museum of Fine Arts. *Carmelina.*
Buffalo: Albright-Knox Art Gallery. *Music.*
Chicago: Art Institute. *Bathers in a River.*
Philadelphia: Museum of Art. *The Moorish Scene.*
Washington, D.C.: National Gallery of Art. *Odalisque with raised arms.*
See Brill, F. *Matisse.* 1967.

MILLET, JEAN FRANCOIS (1814-75) was the son of a French peasant.
He started to paint in Normandy, moving to Paris in 1837 and to
Barbizon in 1849. His country subjects, such as *The Angelus,* are full of
sentimentality.
In London
Victoria and Albert Museum
Outside London
Cardiff: National Museum of Wales.
Edinburgh: National Gallery of Scotland.
Glasgow: Art Gallery and Museum. Burrell Collection.

In the U.S.A.
Boston : Museum of Fine Arts.

MONET, CLAUDE-OSCAR (1840-1926), was born in Paris and became friendly with Boudin, Pissarro, Renoir, Cezanne and Manet.
In London
Courtauld Institute Galleries. *Vase of Flowers; Autumn at Argenteuil; Antibes.*
National Gallery. *Beach at Trouville; Bassin aux Nymphéas; Water Lilies.*
Tate Gallery. *Poplars on the Epte.*
In the U.S.A.
Boston : Museum of Fine Arts.
New York : Metropolitan Museum of Art. *La Terasse à Saint Adresse.*

MORISOT, BERTHE (1841-96), was the first woman to exhibit at the Impressionist exhibitions. She knew Manet well and in 1874 married his younger brother.
In London
Tate Gallery.
In the U.S.A.
Boston : Museum of Fine Arts.
Washington : National Gallery.

PISSARRO, CAMILLE (1830-1903), was born in the West Indies. He was desperately anxious to become an artist and by 1855 had made his way to Paris, where he started to work as a landscape painter. During the Franco-Prussian War and the Commune, he lived in London at Upper Norwood.
In London
British Museum. *Lucien Pissarro* (ink drawing).
Courtauld Institute Galleries. *Penge Station; The Quays at Rouen.*
National Gallery. *Lower Norwood; View of Louveciènnes; The Boulevard Montmartre at Night.*
In Paris
The Louvre. *Entrée de village.*

RENOIR, PIERRE AUGUSTE (1841-1919), started work as a decorator of porcelain. Later, he started to paint with Monet and in the 1880s travelled widely in Europe and Africa. His work was widely appreciated in America before it gained recognition in Europe. Many of his paintings are therefore to be found in American museums.
In London
Courtauld Institute Galleries. *Washerwomen; Woman tying her shoe; Portrait of Ambroise Vollard; The Theatre Box.*
National Gallery. *La Première Sortie; La Parapluies; Nu dans l'eau.*
In the U.S.A.
Boston : Museum of Fine Arts. *Venise, Gondola sur le Grand Canal; La danse à la campagne.*
Cambridge, Mass : Fogg Art Museum. *Portrait of Victor Chocquet; Chez la Modiste.*
Chicago : Art Institute. *Au cirque; Enfant en blanc; Dejeuner des canotiers.*
Minneapolis : Institute of Art. *Le parti de volant.*

Page 67 : Translucent red cameo vase acquired in 1970 by the Pilkington Glass Museum, St Helens. It was made by George Woodall, a master designer and glassworker at Thomas Webb & Sons, Stourbridge, and is inscribed on the base —*'Aquatic Life'*

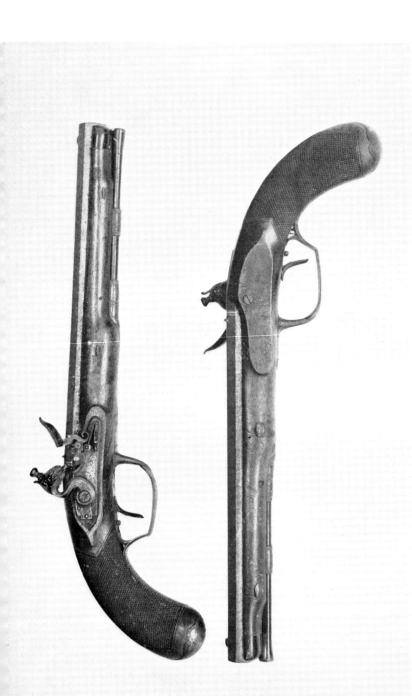

Page 68: A pair of early nineteenth-century ½ in-bore flintlock duelling pistols, 15¼ in overall, 10 in octagonal barrels, by Durs Egg, London. The maker's name is inlaid in gold on the barrels. Sold at Newbury, Berkshire, in January 1970 for £620

New York: Metropolitan Museum of Art: *Mme Charpentier et ses enfants*; *Au bord de la mere—femme assise.*

New York: Museum of Modern Art. *Brouillard à Guernesey.*

In France

Paris: The Louvre. *La liseuse*; *Le Moulin de la Galette*; *La Balancoire*; *La Dame à la violette*; *Chalands sur la Seine.*

See Renoir, J. *Renoir my Father.* 1958 (1962).

SEURAT, GEORGE (1859-91), evolved new techniques in painting which, in his short life, he was unable to develop fully.

In London

Courtauld Institute Galleries. A *young woman holding a powder puff*; *The Bridge at Courbevoie*; *Gravelines*; *Field of poppies.*

National Gallery. *Baignade.*

Tate Gallery. *Le Bec du Hoc, Granchamp*; *Bathers at Asnières.*

Outside London

Edinburgh: National Gallery of Scotland.

Glasgow: Museum and Art Gallery. Burrell Collection.

Liverpool: Walker Art Gallery.

In the U.S.A.

Chicago: Art Institute. *Un demanche d'été à la Grande Jatte.*

New York: Museum of Modern Art. *La brodeuse; Au Concert Europèen.*

In France

Paris: The Louvre. *Cirque.*

See Coquiot, G. *Seurat.* Paris, 1924.

SISLEY, ALFRED (1839-99), was a landscape painter of English descent.

In London

Courtauld Institute Galleries. *Snow at Louveciennes*; *Boats on the Seine.*

National Gallery. *L'Abreuvoir.*

Tate Gallery.

Outside London

Aberdeen: Art Gallery.

In the U.S.A.

Boston: Museum of Fine Arts.

Washington, D.C.: National Gallery of Art.

TOULOUSE-LAUTREC, HENRI-MARIE-RAYMOND DE (1864-1901), made his name as a poster artist.

In London

Courtauld Institute Galleries. *The tête-a-tête supper*; *Jane Avril in the entrance of the Moulin Rouge.*

Tate Gallery. *Les Deux Amies*; *Gabrielle*; *Femme assise au jardin.*

In the U.S.A.

Chicago: Art Institute. *Messaline a l'opera de Bordeaux*; *Au Moulin Rouge, La Table*; *Scène de ballet*; *Au Cirque Fernando*; *Bal au Moulin de la Gallette.*

New York: Brooklyn Museum of Fine Arts. *Femme à la cigarette*; *Paul Sescau.*

New York: Museum of Modern Art. *Mary Belfort en rose.*

E

In France
Albi: Musée Lautrec. A large collection in the birthplace museum.
Paris: Musée de l'Impressionisme.
  See Hanson, L. and E. *The Tragic Life of Toulouse-Lautrec, 1864-1901.*
    1956.
  See Perrochot, H. *Toulouse-Lautrec.* 1960.

ANTIQUES AND FAMOUS PEOPLE

THERE is a keen interest among collectors and historians in items which are linked in some way with well-known literary or historical figures. This is particularly so with books. If an author owned a book, wrote notes in a book, kept his original manuscripts or proof copies, or inscribed a book to present as a gift—all these are known as 'association copies'. The same is true of personal objects known to have been used by the famous—the snuff box, sewing box, desk, or walking stick. Furniture has a particular interest, as does the building in which it was housed. Fortunately the relics of many famous people have been preserved. In some cases they are still to be found in their original surroundings, a birthplace or a place where the person lived. In other cases they have found their way into museums or private collections. Napoleon's despatch case, for example, is to be seen in Wilton House, Wiltshire. The following list gives some of the better-known examples of association collections, listed alphabetically.

AUSTEN, JANE (1775-1817) was born at Steventon in Hampshire and lived for some time in Bath and Southampton. In the later years of her short life she lived with her sister and widowed mother at Chawton House, a mile south-west of Alton in Hampshire and this is when her novels started to appear—*Sense and Sensibility, Pride and Prejudice, Mansfield Park, Emma*. 'Jane Austen's House', as it is now called, has been preserved with some of its original furniture, manuscripts, needlework and other relics, including Jane's donkey cart. Chawton House is open daily from 11.00-16.30 hrs (except on Mondays and Tuesdays from November 1 to March 31 and on Christmas Day and Boxing Day.) Admission 2s; children (under 14) 1s.

BLAKE, ADMIRAL ROBERT (1599-1657) has been described as the greatest of English admirals next to Nelson. He was born and educated at Bridgwater in Somerset, probably in the actual house in Blake Street which is now the Admiral Blake Museum and which contains relics associated with him. Open daily 10.00-13.00 hrs and 14.00-17.00 hrs, except on Tuesdays when it closes at 13.00 hrs.

BOULTON, MATTHEW (1728-1809) was a shrewd and inventive engineer, manufacturer and businessman. He acquired some barren land in Soho, near Birmingham, and established a works there in 1762. Apart from making machinery, he produced a variety of small metal goods, especially in silver and Sheffield plate. He also succeeded in producing high-quality ormolu work which many people consider compared favourably with that of the French. He used many Adam designs. The Soho works was recognized as an authorized mint and many coins were struck there. After Boulton's death, the firm continued until 1898 as James Watt & Co. The Assay Office in Newhall Street, Birmingham, 3, contains not only examples of the work done in his Soho factory but also a vast volume of his correspondence. Visitors must make an appointment. Telephone: Birmingham CENtral 6951.

BRONTË, CHARLOTTE (1816-1855), the daughter of a clergyman, was brought up from the age of five in a small parsonage at Haworth on the Yorkshire moors, a few miles from Keighley. Her early home is now the Brontë Parsonage Museum and houses a number of relics, as well as the Bonnell Collection of manuscripts. It is open on weekdays 11.00-18.00 hrs and on Sundays 14.00-18.00 hrs. (In winter it closes an hour earlier.) Admission 2s; children 1s.

BRUNEL, SIR MARC ISAMBARD (1769-1849), the famous engineer, was born in France and did not settle in England until 1799. He worked on bridges, ships and railways, and the Great Western Railway Museum in Faringdon Road, Swindon, has a section devoted to items associated with him. Open weekdays 10.00-17.00 hrs and on Sundays 14.00-17.00 hrs. (Closed on Christmas Day, Boxing Day and Good Friday.) Admission 1s 6d; children 9d.

BUNYAN, JOHN (1628-1688), was born at Elstow, about one mile south of Bedford. Thirty-two years later he was committed to Bedford gaol where he did much of his writing. Elstow Moot Hall has material associated with Bunyan which can be seen from Tuesdays to Saturdays 11.00-17.00 hrs and Sundays 14.30-17.30 hrs.
In Bedford itself the Bunyan Meeting Library and Museum in Mill Street has the few personal relics which have survived. It is open from Tuesdays to Fridays 10.00-12.00 hrs and 14.30-16.30 hrs. Admission 1s. The Bunyan Collection in the Public Library in Harpur Street (open weekdays 10.00-18.00 hrs) includes many editions of Bunyan's works, among them the famous *Pilgrim's Progress*, which has been translated into more languages than any other book except the Bible.

BURNS, ROBERT (1759-1796) was born at Alloway near Ayr, in Scotland, in a small thatched cottage which is open on weekdays 09.00-19.00 hrs (in winter to dusk) and on Sundays in summer 14.00-19.00 hrs. Admission 1s. It is now a small museum with many relics associated with the poet. Some of his manuscripts are to be seen in the Burns' Monument and Museum, Kay Park, Kilmarnock. Open mid-April to mid-September 12.30-16.00 hrs and 17.00-20.30 hrs, and the rest of the year 10.00-12.00 hrs and 13.00-17.00 hrs. There is a Burns Collection in the Library of Broughton House, Kirkcudbright (open Mondays to Friday from April to September 11.00-13.00 and 14.00-16.00 hrs: Tuesdays and Thursdays only from October to March 14.00-16.00 hrs).
Souter Johnnie's House at Kirkoswald in Ayrshire (open daily from April to September, 14.30 hrs to 20.00 hrs. Admission 2s) was the home of John Davidson, the original Souter Johnnie of Burns' poem 'Tam o' Shanter.'

BYRON, GEORGE GORDON, 6th LORD (1788-1824), the poet, succeeded and inherited at an early age the estates of his great uncle, including Newstead Abbey, about nine miles north of Nottingham. After an education at Harrow and Cambridge he settled for some time in the family seat before travelling abroad. Newstead Abbey, which houses Byron relics and first editions of his works, is open daily from Good Friday until the end of September, 14.00-18.30 hrs. Admission 1s; children 6d. (Tea available.)

CARLYLE, THOMAS (1795-1881), the essayist and historian, was born at Ecclefechan, five miles from Lockerbie in Dumfries, and it is possible to visit the birthplace (The Arched House) to see personal relics and manuscripts. (Open from March to October 10.00-18.00 hrs. Admission 2s; children with adult free.) The Moat House at Annan in Dumfries is a museum with additional Carlyle material. (Open weekdays 09.00-17.00 hrs.)

In London, Carlyle's House at 24 Cheyne Row, Chelsea, S.W.3., contains a collection of his books with letters, manuscripts, prints and portraits. It is a National Trust property open weekdays (except Tuesdays) 10.00-13.00 hrs and 14.00-18.00 hrs (or dusk if earlier) and on Sundays 14.00-18.00 hrs (or dusk if earlier). Admission 3s; children and students 1s 6d. (Closed on Christmas Day, Boxing Day and Good Friday.)

CHATTERTON, THOMAS (1752-1770), the boy poet, was born and lived for the whole of his short life—a mere eighteen years—close to the famous church of St Mary Redcliffe in Bristol. His birthplace in Redcliffe Way can be seen on Wednesdays and Saturdays 15.00-17.00 hrs.

COBBETT, WILLIAM (1762-1835), writer on politics and the countryside, was born at Farnham. The Willmer House Museum at Farnham has busts and engravings.

COBDEN, RICHARD (1804-1865), the free-trader politician, was born at Heyshott near Midhurst in Sussex. The Richard Cobden Collection is at Dunford, three miles from Midhurst. It contains Cobden's library, diaries and papers connected with his campaign against the corn laws. It is maintained by the National Council of Y.M.C.As, and permission to view must be sought in advance from the Secretary. Telephone: Midhurst 2381.

COLERIDGE, SAMUEL TAYLOR (1772-1834) was born in Devon but it is the cottage at Nether Stowey in Somerset which has been preserved by the National Trust as a memorial. He lived there from 1797 to 1800, years in which he formed an intimate friendship with Wordsworth. Nether Stowey is on the Bridgwater to Minehead road and the Coleridge Cottage Museum is open from March to October every day except Friday and Saturday from 11.00-13.00 hrs and 14.00-17.00 hrs. Admission 1s; children 6d.

COOK, CAPTAIN JAMES (1728-1779), the navigator, was born in Yorkshire. He ran away to sea and was bound apprentice to Whitby shipowners. Relics are to be seen in Whitby Literary and Philosophical Society Museum in Panett Park. Open May to September on weekdays 09.00-13.00 hrs and 14.00-17.30 hrs. Sundays 14.00-17.00 hrs. Rest of year weekdays 10.30-13.00 hrs and also on Wednesdays, Saturdays and Sundays 14.00-16.00 hrs. Admission 1s; children 6d.

COWPER, WILLIAM (1731-1800), the poet, was never well. He suffered from fits of intense depression and, unable to face the rigours of a normal active life, went to Huntingdon at the age of thirty-four and boarded there with a retired clergyman and his wife—the Unwins. Two years later Mr Unwin died as the result of an accident and Cowper moved with his widow to Olney in Buckinghamshire. Here he formed a very close friendship with the curate, the Reverend John Newton. Together, they wrote the Olney hymns. In the Cowper Memorial Museum in the Market Place at Olney are some of their personal relics and manuscripts. Open weekdays 10.00-17.00 hrs. Admission 1s 6d.

CROMWELL, OLIVER (1599-1658) was born at Huntingdon and the Cromwell Museum in the Market Square has many exhibits associated with him and the Commonwealth period. Open weekdays (except Mondays) 11.00-13.00 hrs and 14.00-17.00 hrs, Sundays 14.00-16.00 hrs.

DARLING, GRACE (1815-1842), the daughter of a lighthouse keeper, is remembered for the help she gave her father in rescuing survivors from the wreck of the *Forfarshire*, which was sailing to Dundee in 1838. She was born at Bamburgh in Northumberland and the Grace Darling Museum, which is maintained there by the Royal National Lifeboat Institution, has relics of her life. Open from June to September on weekdays 11.00-12.30 hrs and 14.00-17.00 hrs, and on Sundays 15.00-17.00 hrs. Also on Sunday and Monday at Easter. Admission free but donation to R.N.L.I. funds appreciated.

DARWIN, CHARLES (1809-1882) after years of study and scientific work as naturalist to HMS *Beagle* in South American and Australian waters, married and later settled at Down House in Kent. Here he spent many years doing research and writing his great work *The Origin of the Species*. The house has been preserved as a Darwin Museum where it is possible to see the rooms in which he lived and worked, together with his relics and those of his family. Down House is in the village of Downe, about six miles south of Bromley, and is open daily (except Fridays) 10.00-17.00 hrs (11.00-17.00 hrs in winter). Admission 4s; children 1s.

DICKENS, CHARLES (1812-1870) was born in Commercial Road, Portsmouth and the house is now the Dickens' Birthplace Museum. It contains personal relics, many prints and first editions of his novels. Normally open weekdays 10.00-19.00 hrs (17.00 hrs in winter). At present closed.

Between 1837 and 1839, Dickens lived with his family in London, now Dickens House, 48 Doughty Street, W.C.1, where furnishings, manuscripts, letters and portraits are to be seen. Open weekdays 10.00-17.00 hrs, except Bank Holidays. Admission 2s 6d; students 1s 6d; children 6d.

In 1856 Dickens bought Gadshill Place, between Rochester and Gravesend, as a permanent home. There are more Dickens relics in Rochester Public Museum.

DISRAELI, BENJAMIN (1804-1881), who was Earl of Beaconsfield from 1847, was born in London. It was in 1847 that he bought Hughenden Manor, near High Wycombe in Buckinghamshire, now the Disraeli Museum (National Trust). It contains relics, manuscripts, books and pictures associated with him; his study remains as it was when he died. There is also a letter to him from Queen Victoria. The Manor is closed during January but is otherwise open daily (except Mondays) 14.00-18.00 hrs, and on Saturdays and Sundays also from 12.30-18.00 hrs. Open Bank Holiday Monday but closed the following day. Admission 4s.

DRAKE, SIR FRANCIS (1541-1596), who was born in Tavistock, is associated for most people with Plymouth. Buckland Abbey, which lies between them, was once the home of Sir Richard Grenville but was later acquired by Sir Francis. It now contains the Drake relics, including Drake's famous drum. Open from Easter to the end of September on weekdays, 11.00-18.00 hrs and on Sundays 14.00-18.00 hrs. In winter, it is open on Wednesdays, Saturdays and Sundays 15.00-17.00 hrs. Admission 2s; children 1s.

ELIOT, GEORGE (1819-1880), the novelist, whose real name was Mary Ann Evans, was born at Nuneaton in Warwickshire, where the Museum and Art Gallery (see p. 95) displays personal relics.

GAINSBOROUGH, THOMAS (1727-1788), one of the greatest of English portrait and landscape painters was born at Sudbury in Suffolk. His birthplace at 48 Gainsborough Street is open to the public as Gainsborough House and contains portraits and drawings by the artist. It is open on weekdays (except Mondays) and on Bank Holiday Mondays 10.30-12.30 hrs and 14.00-17.00 hrs. Sundays 14.00-17.00 hrs. Admission 2s; children 1s.

GEORGE IV—See *Prince Regent*

HANDEL, GEORGE FREDERICK (1685-1759) was born at Halle but became a naturalized British citizen in 1726 and then Court Composer. Handel relics are to be seen among the Foundling Hospital Art Treasures (see p. 81).

HARDY, THOMAS (1840-1928) was born in Dorset at Higher Bockhampton, three miles from Dorchester. The cottage (National Trust) can be visited only by written appointment with the tenant. Admission 2s; children 1s. The Dorset County Museum in Dorchester has a reproduction of Hardy's study and many relics, including the original handwritten manuscript of *The Mayor of Casterbridge* and a model ship—*The Triumph*—made by John Masefield and presented by him to Thomas Hardy. Open weekdays 10.00-13.00 hrs and 14.00-17.00 hrs. Admission 2s; children over ten, 6d.

HAZLITT, WILLIAM (1778-1830), essayist, painter and critic, was born at Maidstone where there are relics in the Museum and Art Gallery.

HOGARTH, WILLIAM (1697-1764) lived in the country at Chiswick during the latter part of his life in what is now called Hogarth's House, in Hogarth Lane, W.4., where there are relics and copies of his paintings and engravings. Open on weekdays 11.00-18.00 hrs (17.00 hrs in winter) and on Sundays 14.00 hrs-18.00 hrs (17.00 hrs in winter). Closed on Tuesdays in winter. Admission 1s; children 6d.

HUGO, VICTOR-MARIE (1802-1885), son of a French general, was an author of abounding vigour and mental activity, producing work unparalleled in the literature of his country. In 1852 he was exiled from France and settled in Guernsey, living for some years in Hauteville House, a tall storied building in Hauteville Street with a fine view across the harbour of St Peter Port. It remains very much as it was when Hugo lived there and is of interest since he concerned himself very much with the furnishings and layout of his home. There are rooms heavily furnished in oak with dark panelling. In one room are some fine Delft tiles and the attic room shows where the author worked, much of the time standing up. The house has a number of drawings and paintings, some by Hugo himself. Open weekdays 10.00-12.00 hrs and 14.00-16.30 hrs, but closed on Thursday afternoons. Admission 1s 6d; children 6d.

JEFFERIES, RICHARD (1848-1887), the naturalist, son of a Wiltshire farmer, was born in Swindon. At Coate, near Swindon, there is a Richard Jefferies Museum with manuscripts, personal relics and first editions of his works. Open Wednesday and Saturdays 14.00-17.00 hrs and in summer also on Sundays.

JOHNSON, SAMUEL (1709-1784) was born and educated in Lichfield. Dr Johnson's birthplace in Bread Market Street has material associated with his life and work. It is open daily 10.00-18.00 hrs in summer and 10.00-16.00 hrs in winter, but it closes on Monday afternoons.

KEATS, JOHN (1795-1821), the poet, was a Londoner who spent some years of his life in a Regency house in Wentworth Place, Hampstead, where he did much of his writing. It is now the Keats House and Museum, with personal relics and original manuscripts. Open weekdays 10.00-18.00 hrs. (Closed over Christmas and Easter, except on Easter Monday.)

KIPLING, RUDYARD (1865-1936) lived in Sussex when he returned from India. For some years he was at The Elms, Rottingdean. In the Grange Art Gallery and Museum at Rottingdean there is a Kipling Room with letters and copies of many editions of his works.
Bateman's, near Burwash, the seventeenth-century house where he spent the later years of his life and did much of his writing, is maintained by the National Trust. The author's study remains as it was when in use. The house may be seen by visitors from March to October. It is open Mondays to Thursdays 11.00-12.30 hrs and 14.00-18.00 hrs. Saturdays, Sundays and Good Friday 14.00-18.00. Admission 4s; children 2s. Refreshments.

KNOX, JOHN (1505-1572), the Protestant historian and reformer, spent the last twelve years of his life (with a few interruptions) in a minister's manse in the High Street of Edinburgh, now, No 45. This is John Knox's House, maintained by the Church of Scotland and with religious relics of the period. Open daily 10.00-17.00 hrs. Admission 1s; children 6d.

LIVINGSTONE, DAVID (1813-1873), the missionary and explorer, was born at Low Blantyre, Lanarkshire in a house which is now the Scottish National Memorial to David Livingstone. It contains a fine collection of personal relics and associated material. Open weekdays 10.00-22.00 hrs, Sundays 14.00-18.00 hrs. Admission 2s; children 9d. Tea available from April to September.

MARLBOROUGH, JOHN CHURCHILL, 1st DUKE OF (1650-1722). The National Army Museum has Marlborough's battle equipment and some commemorative flags.

MILLER, HUGH (1802-1856), noted Scottish geologist and author, was born at Cromarty in Ross-shire. Hugh Miller's cottage, his birthplace, is now a small geological museum with associated relics. It is open from April to October on weekdays 10.00-12.00 hrs and 13.00-17.00 hrs and on Sundays from June 14.00-17.00 hrs. Admission 2s. Children with adults free.

MILTON, JOHN (1608-1674), the poet, was born in Bread Street, London, but his personal relics are at Chalfont St Giles in Buckinghamshire in Milton's Cottage. There are portraits and busts of the poet and early editions of his works. Open weekdays (except Tuesdays) 10.00-13.00 hrs, and 14.15-18.00 hrs. Sundays 14.15-18.00 hrs. From November to January it opens only on Saturdays 10.00-13.00 hrs and 14.15 hrs to dusk and on Sundays 14.15 hrs to dusk. Admission 2s 6d; children 1s.

MORRIS, WILLIAM (1834-1896), artist, poet and socialist, was born at Walthamstow. The William Morris Gallery at Water House, Lloyd Park, Forest Road, is an eighteenth-century house which was at one time his home.

It has collections of the textiles, wallpapers, tiles and glass which helped so greatly to change English taste in design. There is also work by his contemporaries. The Gallery is open on weekdays 10.00-17.00 hrs (on Tuesdays and Thursdays in summer until 20.00 hrs). Also the first Sunday in each month, 10.00-12.00 hrs and 14.00-17.00 hrs. Closed on Bank Holidays.

NELSON, HORATIO, VISCOUNT NELSON (1758-1805) is best known as the admiral who fought the Battle of Trafalgar and who died in the hour of victory. HMS *Victory*, the flagship on which he died, can be seen in Portsmouth Dockyard. Quite near to the ship is the Victory Museum, which has many of Nelson's personal possessions and relics of those who served under him. They can be visited on weekdays 10.00-18.00 hrs (or sunset) and on Sundays 13.00-18.00 hrs (or sunset). Admission to the Museum, 1s; children 6d. There is no charge to visit HMS *Victory*. Nelson relics may also be seen in the Nelson Museum, Glendower Street, Monmouth—see p. 94.

NIGHTINGALE, FLORENCE (1820-1910) was named by her father— William Edward Nightingale of Embley Park, Hampshire—after the Italian city in which she was born. She was buried at her own request at East Wellow, near the family home. During her life she frequently visited her sister Parthe, who often demanded her presence at Claydon House, near Winslow in Buckinghamshire. Here are some of her personal possessions and many relics associated with the famous nurse. It is maintained by the National Trust and is open daily except Mondays from March to October 14.00-18.00 hrs, and in winter by appointment. Also open on Bank Holiday Monday but closes on the Tuesday following. Admission 3s. Children 1s 6d.

OWEN, ROBERT (1771-1858), the socialist reformer who spent much of his personal fortune in social experiments, was born at Newton in Montgomeryshire, where the Robert Owen Memorial Museum in Broad Street has many items associated with him, including books and manuscripts. Open daily 14.00-16.00 hrs.

PARK, MUNGO (1771-1806), traveller and explorer, was born near Selkirk. In the Selkirk Museum in Ettrick Terrace there is a collection of associated items. Open weekdays 09.00-18.00 hrs. (Closes at 16.00 hrs on Saturdays.)

PRINCE REGENT (1762-1830) who became George IV, had the Royal Pavilion built at Brighton by Henry Holland and John Nash when he was Prince of Wales. The State and Private Apartments are open daily 10.00-17.00 hrs (to 20.00 hrs July to September). Admission charges 3s to 4s according to season; children at reduced rates.

RHODES, CECIL (1853-1902), the South African statesman, was born at Bishop's Stortford in Hertfordshire, where the Rhodes Memorial Museum has been established with material showing the part he played in the history of South Africa. Open weekdays 10.00-16.00 hrs.

RUSKIN, JOHN (1819-1900), writer on art and sociology, was a Londoner. When his mother died in 1871, he went to live at Brantwood on Coniston Lake in Cumberland. The Ruskin Museum at Coniston has material associated with him. Open daily 10.00-18.00 hrs. Admission 6d.

Those who are particularly interested in Ruskin's paintings and writing should know of the Ruskin Gallery at Bembridge School in the Isle of Wight. Visitors must make an appointment. (Tel: Bembridge 2101.)

SCOTT, SIR WALTER (1771-1832), poet and novelist, was closely associated with the city of Edinburgh where he was born. Manuscripts and relics are in Lady Stair's House in Lady Stair's Close, Lawnmarket, Edinburgh, 1. Open weekdays 10.00-16.00 hrs (13.00 hrs on Saturday). Admission 1s; children 6d. In 1812 Scott built Abbotsford, a house near Melrose, which contains many of the original furnishings. It is open from the end of March to the end of October. Weekdays 10.00-17.00 hrs. Sundays 14.00-17.00 hrs. Admission 3s. Children 1s 6d. Tea available in summer.

SHAFTESBURY, ANTHONY ASHLEY COOPER, 7th EARL OF (1801-1885), reformer and philanthropist, had very close connections with Dorset, although he was born in London. He represented Dorset constituencies in Parliament and the family home—St Giles House at Wimborne St Giles, built by the 1st Earl of Shaftesbury in 1650, was his family home and it is there that his personal relics lie. Open daily (except Mondays) in August and on Wednesday and Sundays during the rest of the summer 14.00-18.00 hrs. Also on Bank Holidays 11.00-18.00 hrs. Admission 3s; children 1s 6d. Tea available.

SHAKESPEARE, WILLIAM (1564-1616) was born in a half-timbered house in Henley Street, Stratford-on-Avon. Shakespeare's birthplace houses a wealth of associated material. His wife's home, Anne Hathaway's Cottage at Shottery, and Mary Arden's House at Wilmcote, give the atmosphere of the period. All these Trust properties are open on weekdays in summer 09.00-18.00 hrs and on Sundays 14.00-18.00 hrs. In winter, they close on weekdays between 12.45 and 14.00 hrs, and at 16.00 hrs and on Sundays the Birthplace and Anne Hathaway's Cottage open 14.00-16.00 hrs. Admission to the Birthplace and Anne Hathaway's Cottage 2s 6d; children 1s; Mary Arden's House 2s; children 1s. (Inclusive ticket 7s.)

SOUTHEY, ROBERT (1774-1843), poet and biographer, settled in Keswick in 1803 and worked there steadily until his death. The Fitz Park Museum in Station Street has some of his orginal manuscripts. Open weekdays 10.00-20.00 hrs. Admission 6d; children 3d.

TENNYSON, ALFRED, 1st LORD (1809-1892), poet, was born at Somersby, Lincolnshire. Associated material is housed in the Usher Gallery in Lindum Road, Lincoln. Open weekdays 10.00-17.30 hrs, Sundays 14.30-17.00 hrs.

VICTORIA, QUEEN, who reigned from 1838 to 1901, regarded Osborne House at East Cowes in the Isle of Wight as her informal home. Here she spent many happy summers with Prince Albert. The State Apartments and Private Rooms are on view to the public: they have a fine range of Victoriana. Open between Easter and Spring Bank Holiday on Mondays, Wednesdays and Fridays 11.00-17.00 hrs and thereafter until September on Mondays to Fridays at the same time. Admission 2s 6d; children 1s 3d.

WALTON, IZAAK (1593-1683), who wrote *The Compleat Angler*, was born at Stafford. For many years he was a hosier in London and made enough money to retire at the age of fifty and spend the rest of his life—some forty years—in the country, where he enjoyed his favourite sport of angling. His country home at Shallowford, near Stafford, is now the Izaak Walton Cottage and Museum with interesting relics associated with the author. Open daily (except Tuesdays) 10.00-13.00 hrs, and 14.30-16.30 hrs. Admission 1s; children 6d.

WATT, JAMES (1736-1819), the engineer who entered into partnership with Matthew Boulton, was born at Greenock and there are items in the McLean Museum, Greenock (15 Kelly Street, West End) associated with him. Open Tuesdays to Saturdays 10.00-17.00 hrs.

WELLINGTON, ARTHUR WELLESLEY, 1st DUKE OF (1769-1852) lived at Apsley House, Hyde Park Corner, W.1. This is now the Wellington Museum with a collection of personal relics and trophies, and some of the chinaware and paintings he owned. Some of the most interesting associative material is in the basement—a series of caricatures in the form of hand-coloured etchings by William Heath and John Doyle published 1828-9, and a collection of commemorative items in a glazed alcove collected by a commercial firm because they used his portrait in their trade mark. They include medallions, snuff boxes, printed jugs and statuettes. There are also relics at Walmer Castle in Kent, the residence of the Lord Warden of the Cinque Ports. Open daily 09.30-19.00 hrs, but closes early in winter and does not open on Sunday mornings in winter. It is closed when the Lord Warden is in residence.

WESLEY, JOHN (1703-1791), the founder of Methodism, when not travelling as a preacher, lived in London at 47 City Road, EC1, and it was here that he died. This is now Wesley's House and Museum, with a good collection of personal relics. Open weekdays 10.00-13.00 hrs and 14.00-16.00 hrs. Admission 2s, (closed on Bank Holidays). Wesley's childhood home at the Old Rectory, Epworth, Lincolnshire, is open on weekdays 10.00-12.00 hrs and 14.00-16.00 hrs. Sundays 14.00-16.00 hrs.

WHITE, GILBERT (1720-1793), the famous naturalist who wrote *The Natural History and Antiquities of Selborne*, published in 1789, was born in this Hampshire village and lived there for much of his life. The house, known as 'The Wakes', is now the Oates Memorial Library and Museum (with relics of the Antarctic explorer). Visitors can see the room where White worked, his garden and a fine collection of the many editions of his books. Open weekdays (except Fridays) 14.30-17.30 hrs. April to October also 11.00-13.00 hrs. Sundays 14.30-17.30 hrs. Admission 2s; children 6d.

WILBERFORCE, WILLIAM (1759-1833), the philanthropist who worked for the abolition of slavery, was born in Hull. His birthplace at 25 High Street is a Tudor building now known as Wilberforce House. Open weekdays 10.00-17.00 hrs, and Sundays 14.30-16.30 hrs.

WOLFE, GENERAL JAMES (1727-1759), the conqueror of Quebec, was born at Westerham in Kent, where he spent his childhood. Personal relics are now kept in Quebec House which is maintained by the National Trust. Open from March to October on Sundays, Tuesdays and Wednesdays 14.00-18.00 hrs, and on Bank Holiday Mondays 10.00-13.00 and 14.00-18.00 hrs. Admission 1s 6d; children 9d.

WORDSWORTH, WILLIAM (1770-1850), the Lake District poet, was born at Cockermouth. The house, in the main street, is open from Easter to September on Mondays, Wednesdays and Saturdays 10.00-12.00 and 14.00-17.00 hrs. Admission 1s 6d; children 9d.

Wordsworth was educated at Penrith and Hawkshead. After years at Cambridge, in France and at Alfoxden in Somerset, he returned to the Lakes and settled with his sister Dorothy at Dove Cottage, Grasmere, where they lived from 1799 to 1808. The cottage is open to visitors and a Wordsworth Museum at Grasmere houses some of his manuscripts. Cottage and museum are open on weekdays between Easter and October 10.00-18.00 hrs. In winter 10.00-16.30 hrs except from mid-January to March 1. Admission 2s each, or 3s to visit both. Some Wordsworth manuscripts are preserved in the Fitz Park Museum and Art Gallery in Station Street, Keswick. Open weekdays 10.00-20.00 hrs. Admission 6d; children 3d.

ART GALLERIES, MUSEUMS AND HISTORIC HOUSES
Addresses and Opening Times

UNLESS otherwise stated, admission is free and the collections are closed to the public on Christmas Day, Boxing Day and Good Friday. Many of the buildings, particularly the historic houses, have fine floors and the wearing of stiletto heels is discouraged. Dogs are not normally admitted. Care has been taken to ensure that all opening times and admission fees are correct at the time of going to press, but the Publishers cannot guarantee that there may not have been subsequent changes. National Trust properties are marked (N.T.). Members of the Trust may visit these free of charge.

IN BRITAIN

IN AND AROUND LONDON

Artillery Museum, The Rotunda, Woolwich Common. Weekdays, 10.00-12.45 hrs 14.00-17.00 hrs. Saturdays, 10.00-12.00 hrs. Sundays, 14.00-17.00 hrs. (Closes at 16.00 hrs in winter.)

Bethnal Green Museum, Cambridge Heath Road, London, E.2. Weekdays, 10.00-18.00 hrs. Sundays, 14.30-18.00 hrs.

British Museum, Great Russell Street, London, W.C.1. Weekdays, 10.00-17.00 hrs. Sundays, 14.30-18.00 hrs. Refreshments available.

British Piano Museum, 368 High Street, Brentford, Middlesex. April to September on Saturdays and Sundays, 14.30-18.00 hrs. Admission by donation of 3s 6d.

British Theatre Museum, Leighton House, 12 Holland Park Road, Kensington, London, W.14. Tuesdays, Thursdays and Saturdays, 11.00-17.00 hrs. Closed Bank Holidays.

Museum of British Transport, Clapham High Street, London, S.W.4. Weekdays 10.00-17.30 hrs. Admission 2s 6d; children 1s 6d.

Buckingham Palace, The Queen's Gallery, Buckingham Palace Road, London, S.W.1. Tuesday to Saturday, 11.00-17.00 hrs. Sundays, 14.00-17.00 hrs. Bank Holiday Mondays, 11.00-17.00 hrs. Admission 2s 6d.

Chartered Insurance Institute Museum, 20 Aldermanbury, London, E.C.2. Monday to Friday during normal office hours.

Courtauld Institute Galleries, Woburn Square, London, W.C.1. Weekdays, 10.00-17.00 hrs. Sundays, 14.00-17.00 hrs.

Cutty Sark, Cutty Sark Gardens, Greenwich Pier, London, S.E. 10. Weekdays, 11.00-18.00 hrs. Sundays, 14.30-18.00 hrs. Closes an hour earlier in winter. Admission 2s; children (with adults) 1s.

Dulwich College Picture Gallery, College Road, London, S.E.21. Tuesdays to Saturdays, 10.00-16.00 hrs (open to 18.00 hrs in summer). Sundays from April to September 14.00-17.00 hrs (18.00 hrs in summer).

Fenton House (N.T.), Hampstead Grove, Hampstead, London, N.W.3. Weekdays (except Tuesdays) 11.00-17.00 hrs. Sundays 14.00-17.00 hrs (or dusk if earlier). Admission 4s. Children 2s.

Forty Hall Museum, Forty Hall, Enfield, Middlesex. Daily from Easter to September (except Mondays) 10.00-20.00 hrs. 18.00 at weekends). Rest of year 10.00-17.00 hrs (or dusk if earlier).

Foundling Hospital Art Treasures, 40 Brunswick Square, London, W.C.1. Mondays and Fridays 10.00-12.00 hrs and 14.00-16.00 hrs. Closed Bank Holidays. Admission 1s.

Geffrye Museum, Kingsland Road, Shoreditch, London, E.2. Tuesday to Saturday, 10.00-17.00 hrs. Sundays, 14.00-17.00 hrs. Open Bank Holiday Mondays.

Goldsmiths' Hall, Foster Lane, Cheapside, London, E.C.2. By appointment.

Guildhall Museum, Gillett House, 55 Basinghall Street, London, E.C.2. Weekdays, 10.00-17.00 hrs.

Ham House (N.T.), Petersham, Richmond. Daily, except Mondays, from March to October, 14.00-18.00 hrs. Rest of year 12.00-16.00 hrs. Admission 2s; children 1s. Tea available in summer.

Hampton Court Palace, Hampton Court. From May to September, weekdays 09.30-1800 hrs. Sundays 11.00-1800 hrs. November to February weekdays 10.00-16.30 hrs. Sundays 10.00-16.30 hrs. March, April and October weekdays 09.30-17.00 hrs. Sundays 14.00-17.00 hrs. Admission 4s; children 1s. In winter 2s; children 1s.

Horniman Museum, London Road, Forest Hill, London, S.E.23. Weekdays, 10.30-18.00 hrs. Sundays, 14.00-18.00 hrs. Open Good Fridays. Tea available in summer and always on Saturdays.

Kenwood House (Iveagh Bequest), Hampstead, London, N.W.3. Weekdays, 10.00-19.00 hrs. Sundays, 14.00-19.00 hrs. Closes at 1700 hrs in winter on Saturdays and Mondays only. Tea available. Admission 3s; children 1s.

Leighton House Art Gallery and Museum, 12 Holland Park Road, Kensington, London, W.14. Weekdays, 11.00-17.00 hrs. Closed Bank Holidays. Children must be with adult.

London Museum, Kensington Palace, The Broad Walk, Kensington Gardens, London, W.8. Weekdays, 10.00-17.00 hrs. Sundays, 14.00-17.00 hrs. Open until 18.00 hrs from March to September.

Martinware Pottery Collection, Public Library, Osterley Park Road, Southall, Middlesex. Monday to Friday, 09.00-20.00 hrs. Saturdays, 09.00-17.00 hrs.

National Army Museum, Royal Hospital Road, London, S.W.3 To open mid-summer, 1971. Telephone 01-730-3477.

National Gallery, Trafalgar Square, London, W.C.2. Weekdays, 10.00-18.00 hrs. Sundays and Boxing Day, 14.00-18.00 hrs. Closed Christmas Eve. Restaurant.

National Maritime Museum, Romney Road, Greenwich, London, S.E.10. Weekdays, 10.00-18.00 hrs. Sundays, 14.30-18.00 hrs. Closed Christmas Eve. Restaurant in summer (licensed).

National Portrait Gallery, St Martin's Place, Trafalgar Square, London, W.C.2. Weekdays, 10.00-17.00 hrs, (18.00 on Saturdays). Sundays, 14.00-18.00 hrs. Closed Christmas Eve.

Osterley Park House, Isleworth. Daily (except Mondays) from March to October, 14.00-18.00 hrs. November to February, 12.00-16.00 hrs. Open Bank Holidays 12.00-16.00 hrs. Admission 2s; children 1s. Car park 1s.

Percival David Foundation of Chinese Art, 53 Gordon Square, London, W.C.1. Mondays, 14.00-17.00 hrs. Tuesday to Friday, 10.30-17.00 hrs. Saturdays, 10.30-13.00 hrs. Closed first fortnight of August and on Bank Holidays.

Pharmaceutical Society Museum, 17 Bloomsbury Square, London, W.C.1. By appointment. Telephone 01-405 8967.

Royal College of Music (Donaldson Museum), Prince Consort Road, South Kensington, London, S.W.7. During term time from Monday to Friday, by appointment. Telephone 01-589 3643.

Old Royal Observatory, National Maritime Museum, Greenwich Park, Weekdays, 10.00-18.00 hrs. Sundays, 14.30-18.00 hrs. Closed Christmas Eve.

Science Museum, Exhibition Road, South Kensington, London. Weekdays, 10.00-18.00 hrs. Sundays, 14.30-18.00 hrs.

Sir John Soane's Museum, 13 Lincoln's Inn Fields, London, W.C.2. Tuesday to Saturday, 10.00-17.00 hrs. Closed on Bank Holidays and during August.

Tate Gallery, Millbank, London, S.W.1. Weekdays, 10.00-18.00 hrs. Sundays and Boxing Day, 14.00-18.00 hrs. Closed Christmas Eve. Restaurant.

Tower of London, Tower Hill, London, E.C.3. Weekdays in summer, 10.00-17.30 hrs. Sundays in summer, 14.00-17.00 hrs. Closes 1 hour or more earlier in winter. Admission 2s; children 6d. Restaurant.

Victoria and Albert Museum, Cromwell Road, South Kensington, London, S.W.7. Daily, 10.00-18.00 hrs. (Some galleries closed on Sunday.) Restaurant.

Wallace Collection, Hertford House, Manchester Square, London, W.1. Weekdays, 10.00-17.00 hrs. Sundays, 14.00-17.00 hrs. Closed Christmas Eve.

Wellington Museum, Apsley House, Hyde Park Corner, London, W.1. Weekdays, 10.00-18.00 hrs. Sundays, 14.30-18.00 hrs. Admission 1s; children 6d.

William Morris Gallery, Water House, Lloyd Park, Forest Road, Walthamstow, London, E.17. Weekdays 10.00-17.00 hrs (later on Tuesdays and Thursdays in summer).

OUTSIDE LONDON

Aberdeen: Art Gallery and Regional Museum, School Hill. Weekdays, 10.00-17.00 hrs. Sundays, 14.00-17.00 hrs.

Abergavenny and District Museum. Tuesday, Thursday, Saturday, Sunday, April to May, 14.30-17.00 hrs. Daily, June to September, 14.30-17.00 hrs. Admission 6d; children 3d.

Aberystwyth: National Library of Wales. Weekdays 09.30-18.00 hrs.

Abingdon: Borough Museum Collection, The County Hall. Daily, 14.00-17.00 hrs.

Abingdon: Guildhall Art Gallery. Daily when not in use.

Accrington: The Haworth Art Gallery, Haworth Park. April to October, weekdays, 14.00-17.00 hrs and Sundays, 14.00-17.00 hrs and 18.00-20.00 hrs.

Acton Round Hall: see Bridgnorth.

Alcester: Ragley Hall (2 miles out on A435). Daily, except Mondays and Fridays, from May to end of September, 14.00-18.00 hrs. Open same time Bank Holiday Monday. Admission 5s; children 1s. Tea available.

Alnwick: Alnwick Castle. Daily (except Fridays and Saturdays) from May to late September, 13.00-16.30 hrs. Admission 3s; children 1s 6d.

Alton: The Curtis Museum, High Street. Weekdays (except Wednesdays) 14.00-17.00 hrs. Also open Saturdays 10.00-13.00 hrs.

Antony House: see Torpoint.

Arlington Court: see Barnstaple.

Armagh: County Museum, The Mall. Weekdays, 10.00-13.00 hrs and 14.00-17.00 hrs. Closed Bank Holidays.

Arreton Manor: see Isle of Wight.

Arundel Castle, Sussex. Monday to Thursday, from Easter Monday to mid-June, 13.00-16.30 hrs. Then Monday to Friday to end of September, 12.00-16.30 hrs. Admission 4s; children 2s. Refreshments available.

Ascott: see Wing.

Ashburton Museum (Devon), 1 West Street. Tuesdays, Thursdays and Saturdays, June to August, and Saturdays only from September to May, 14.30-17.00 hrs.

Aylesbury: Buckingham County Museum. Monday to Friday, 09.30-17.00 hrs. Saturdays, 09.30-12.30 hrs and 13.30-1700 hrs.

Aylesbury: Waddesdon Manor (N.T.) (6 miles from Aylesbury at Waddesdon Village). Wednesday to Sunday, April to the end of October, 14.00-18.00 hrs. Bank Holidays, 11.00-18.00 hrs. Admission 6s. Fridays 10s. (Children under 12 not admitted to house.) Tea available.

Bacup: Natural History Society Museum, 24 Yorkshire Street. Saturdays, 14.00-17.00 hrs.

Bakewell: Chatsworth House (4 miles from Bakewell on the A623). End of March to beginning of October, Wednesdays, Thursdays and Fridays, 11.30-16.00 hrs. Saturdays and Sundays, 14.00-17.30 hrs. Open Bank Holiday Monday and Tuesday and Good Friday, 11.30-17.30 hrs. Admission 5s; children 2s. Car park 2s.

Banbury: Chacombe Priory. Sundays and Bank Holidays, April to September and also Saturdays from June to August and Fridays in August. 14.30-18.30 hrs. Admission 4s 6d; children 3s. Car park 1s. Tea available.

Bangor: Museum of Welsh Antiquities, University College of North Wales, College Road. Weekdays, April to October, 10.00-16.00 hrs. Monday to Friday, November to March, 13.00-16.00 hrs.

Bangor: Penrhyn Castle (N.T.) (the Castle is about 1 mile from the centre of the town). Weekdays, June to September, 11.00-18.00 hrs, and on Sundays in July and August, 14.00-18.00 hrs. In April, May and October, open Mondays, Wednesdays and Thursdays, 14.00-17.30 hrs. Admission 5s; children 2s 6d. Tea available in summer.

Barnard Castle: The Bowes Museum. Weekdays, May to October, 10.00-17.30 hrs. (Closed up to an hour and a half earlier in winter.) Sundays, 14.00-17.00 hrs, closing an hour earlier in winter. Admission 1s; children 6d. Refreshments available in summer.

Barnsley: Cannon Hall Art Gallery and Museum. Weekdays, 10.30-17.00 hrs. Sundays, 14.30-17.00 hrs. (Closing at dusk in winter.)

Barnsley: Cooper Art Gallery, Church Street. Weekdays, 11.30-17.00 hrs.

Barnstaple: Arlington Court (N.T.) (7 miles from Barnstaple on A39). Daily, April to September (except Saturdays, 11.00-13.00 hrs and 14.00-18.00 hrs. Admission 6s; children 3s. Refreshments available until 18.00 hrs.

Barrow-in-Furness Museum, Ramsden Square. Weekdays, 10.00-19.00 hrs. Closed Bank Holidays.

Basingstoke: The Willis Museum, New Street. Monday to Friday, 14.00-17.30 hrs. Saturdays, 10.00-12.30 hrs and 14.00-17.00 hrs. Closed Bank Holidays.

Bath: American Museum, Claverton Manor (about 2½ miles from Bath railway station). Daily, from April to mid-October (except Mondays), 14.00-17.00 hrs. Admission 3s 6d; children 2s 3d. Tea available.

Bath: Dyrham Park, Gloucestershire (N.T.) (8 miles from Bath and 10 miles from Bristol). Daily, except Monday and Tuesday, from Easter to September, 14.00-18.00 hrs. Bank Holidays 12.00-18.00 hrs. Wednesdays, Saturdays, and Sundays only in October, November and March 14.00-18.00 hrs or dusk if earlier. Admission 5s; children 2s 6d. Refreshments available from April to September.

Bath: Holburne of Menstrie Museum of Art, Great Pulteney Street. Weekdays (except Wednesdays), 11.30-13.00 hrs and 14.00-16.00 hrs. Open until 17.00 hrs in summer and also on Sundays, 14.00-17.00 hrs. Admission 2s 6d; children and students 1s.

Bath: Museum of Costume, The Assembly Rooms. Weekdays, 10.00-17.00 hrs. Sundays, 14.00-17.00 hrs. (Open at 09.30 hrs and until 18.00 hrs in summer.) Admission 3s; children 1s 6d.

Bath: Victoria Art Gallery, Bridge Street. Weekdays (except Mondays), 10.00-13.00 hrs and 14.30-18.00 hrs.

Batley: Bagshaw Museum, Wilton Park. Weekdays (except Monday mornings) 11.00-18.00 hrs. Sundays 14.00-19.00 hrs. Closes at 16.30 hrs in winter.

Batley: Oakwell Hall, Birstall. Daily, (except Fridays), 14.00-17.00 hrs in summer and 12.00-17.00 hrs in winter.

Battle Museum, Old Church House. Weekdays, 10.00-13.00 hrs and 14.00-17.00 hrs. Sundays, 14.30-17.30 hrs. Admission 1s; children 6d.

Beaulieu: see Buckler's Hard, Maritime Museum.

Bedford: Cecil Higgins Art Gallery, Castle Close. Weekdays, 11.00-18.00 hrs. Sundays, 14.30-17.00 hrs.

Belfast: Ulster Museum, Stranmillis. Weekdays, 10.00-18.00 hrs. Wednesdays, open until 21.00 hrs.

Belfast: Transport Museum, Witham Street, Newtownards Road. Weekdays, 10.00-18.00 hrs. Wednesday open until 21.00 hrs. Admission 1s; children 6d.

Belfast: Ulster Folk Museum (Cultra Manor, Craigavad, 8 miles from the city). Daily (except Mondays), from May to September, 14.00-21.00 hrs. October to April, 14.00-17.00 hrs. Admission 2s; children 6d.

Belvoir Castle: see Grantham.

Berwick-on-Tweed Museum and Art Gallery, Marygate. Weekdays, 10.00-19.00 hrs, except Thursdays and Saturdays when closing time is 17.00 hrs.

Beverley Art Gallery, Champney Road. Weekdays, 10.00-18.00 hrs, except Wednesdays, when 10.00-13.00 hrs.

Bibury: Arlington Mill. Daily, 11.30-13.00 hrs and 14.00-19.00 hrs (dusk if earlier). Admission 3s; children 6d.

Birkenhead: Williamson Art Gallery and Museum, Slatey Road. Weekdays, 10.00-18.30 hrs. Sundays, 14.00-17.00 hrs. Closes at 17.00 hrs weekdays in winter.

Birmingham: City Museum and Art Gallery, Department of Art, Congreve Street. Weekdays, 10.00-18.00 hrs. Sundays, 14.00-17.30 hrs.

Birmingham: City Museum and Art Gallery, Department of Science and Industry, Newhall Street. Weekdays, except Mondays, 10.00-17.00 hrs. (17.30 hrs on Saturdays.) Sundays, 14.00-17.30 hrs.

Birmingham: Assay Office, Newhall Street. By appointment only. Telephone CENtral 6951.

Birmingham: Aston Hall, Trinity Road, Aston (about 3 miles from the city). Weekdays, 10.00-17.00 hrs. Closes at dusk in winter. Sundays (in summer only), 14.00-17.00 hrs. Admission 1s; children 6d. Family tickets 2s 6d.. Tea available.

Birmingham: Blakesley Hall, Blakesley Road, Yardley. Weekdays, 09.30-18.00 hrs (20.00 hrs on Wednesdays). Sundays, 14.00-17.00 hrs. Closed Good Friday.

Blackburn: Museum and Art Gallery, Library Street. Weekdays, 09.30-20.00 hrs. (18.00 hrs. on Saturdays.)

Blackpool: Grundy Art Gallery, Queen Street. Weekdays, 10.00-17.00 hrs, and on Sundays in summer, 14.00-17.00 hrs.

Blair Atholl: Castle and Atholl Museum (8 miles from Pitlochry on A9). Weekdays, 10.00-18.00 hrs. Sundays, 14.00-18.00 hrs, from early May to early October, and on Sundays and Mondays in April. Admission 4s 6d; children 2s. Refreshments available. Free car park.

Blickling Hall: see Norwich.

Blithfield Hall: see Rugeley.

Bolton: Museum and Art Gallery, Civic Centre. Mondays to Fridays, 10.00-18.00 hrs. Saturdays, 10.00-17.30 hrs.

Bolton: Smithills Hall, Smithills Dean Road. Weekdays (except Thursdays), 10.00-18.00 hrs. (17.00 hrs in winter). Sundays, from April to September only, 14.00-18.00 hrs. Closed Good Friday.

Bootle: Museum and Art Gallery, Oriel Road. Mondays to Fridays, 09.00-19.00 hrs. Saturdays, 09.00-13.00 hrs.

Bournemouth: Rothesay Museum, 11 Bath Road. Weekdays, 10.00-18.00 hrs in summer. 10.00-17.00 hrs in winter. Sundays, 14.30-17.00 hrs.

Bournemouth: Russell-Cotes Art Gallery and Museum, East Cliff (close to Rothesay Museum). Weekdays, 10.00-18.00 hrs in summer; 10.00-17.00 hrs in winter. Sundays, 14.30-17.00 hrs. Admission on Thursdays 2s.

Bradford: City Art Gallery and Museum, Cartwright Hall. Daily, 10.00-17.00 hrs. Open at least two hours later from April to September.

Bradford: Bolling Hall, Bowling Hall Road. Daily 10.00-17.00 hrs. Open at least two hours later from April to September.

Breamore House: see Fordingbridge.

Brecon: Brecknock Museum, Glamorgan Street. Weekdays, 10.00-12.00 hrs, and 13.00-16.00 hrs. Closed Monday afternoons.

Bridgnorth: Acton Round Hall (6 miles from the town). Thursdays, mid-May to mid-September, 14.30-18.00 hrs. Admission 3s 6d; children 2s.

Brighton: Art Gallery and Museum, Church Street. Monday to Friday, 10.00-19.00 hrs. Saturdays, 10.00-17.00 hrs. Sundays, 14.00-17.00 hrs. (18.00 hrs in summer.)

Brighton: The Grange Art Gallery and Museum, Rottingdean. Monday to Friday, 10.00-19.00 hrs. Saturdays, 10.00-17.00 hrs. Sundays, 14.00-17.00 hrs. (18.00 hrs in summer.)

Brighton: Thomas-Stanford Museum, Preston Manor. Weekdays, 10.00-13.00 hrs and 14.00-17.00 hrs. Sundays, 14.30-17.00 hrs. Admission 2s; children 6d.

Brighton: The Royal Pavilion. Weekdays, 10.00-17.00 hrs. (20.00 hrs in

F

July, August and September.) Admission up to 4s according to season; children at reduced prices.

Bristol: City Museum and Art Gallery, Queen's Road. Weekdays, 10.00-17.30 hrs.

Bristol: Georgian House, 7 Great George Street. Weekdays, 11.00-17.00 hrs.

Bristol: The Red Lodge, Park Row. Weekdays, 13.00-17.00 hrs.

Bristol: Blaise Castle Folk Museum, Henbury. Weekdays, 14.00-17.30 hrs. Sundays, 15.00-17.00 hrs. (In winter closing time is 16.30 hrs.) Closed on Sundays in December, January and February. Tea available.

Brixham Museum. Weekdays, from June to September, 10.00-13.00 hrs 14.30-17.30 hrs and 19.15-21.00 hrs. Sundays, 14.30-17.30 hrs. In October and from March to May, Wednesdays and Sundays only, 14.30-17.00 hrs. Admission 1s; children 3d.

Broadway: Snowshill Manor (N.T.) Wednesdays, Thursdays, Saturdays and Sundays, from May to September, 11.00-13.00 hrs and 14.00-18.00 hrs (or dusk if earlier). Saturdays and Sundays only in April and October, same opening times. Open on Bank Holiday Mondays. Admission 5s; children 2s 6d.

Buckler's Hard: Maritime Museum near Beaulieu, Hampshire. April to October, daily 10.00-21.00 hrs. November to March, Saturdays and Sundays, 10.00-17.00 hrs. Admission 2s 6d.; children 1s.

Burford: Tolsey Museum, High Street. Daily, from April to September, 14.30-17.30 hrs. Admission 1s; children 6d.

Burnley: Towneley Hall Art Gallery and Museum. Weekdays, 10.00-17.30 hrs. Sundays, 14.00-17.00 hrs. Refreshments available.

Bury: Art Gallery and Museum, Moss Street. Weekdays, 10.30-19.45 hrs. Closes at 17.00 hrs in winter and on Saturdays.

Bury St Edmunds: The Gershom-Partington Collection of Clocks and Watches, 8 Angel Hill. Weekdays, 10.00-13.00 hrs and 14.00-17.00 hrs.

Bury St Edmunds: Ickworth (N.T.) (a country house 3 miles from the town). Wednesdays, Thursdays, Saturdays, Sundays and Bank Holiday Mondays Easter to first Sunday in October, 14.00-18.00 hrs. Admission 5s; children with adult 2s 6d.

Buscot Park: see Faringdon.

Buxton Museum, Terrace Road. Mondays to Fridays, 10.00-19.00 hrs. Saturdays, 10.00-17.00 hrs.

Calstock: Cotehele House (N.T.) Cornwall (2 miles from village; 8 miles from Tavistock, Devon). Daily (except Mondays), from April to September, 11.00-18.00 hrs (or dusk if earlier). Open Bank Holidays. Admission 5s; children 2s 6d. Refreshments available.

Cambridge and County Folk Museum, 2-3 Castle Street. Tuesday to Saturday, 11.00-13.00 hrs and 14.30-16.30 hrs. Sundays, 14.30-16.30 hrs. Open Bank Holidays. Admission 6d; children 3d.

Cambridge: Fitzwilliam Museum, Trumpington Street. Weekdays, 10.00-16.00 hrs (17.00 hrs May to August). Sundays, (Picture Gallery), 14.00-16.00 hrs. (17.00 hrs May to August). Closed first Wednesday in month.

Cambridge: Whipple Museum of the History of Science, Free School Lane. Mondays to Fridays, 10.00-13.00 hrs. and 14.00-16.00 hrs.

Canterbury: The Westgate. Weekdays in summer, 10.00-13.00 hrs and 14.00-18.00 hrs. In winter, afternoons only, 14.00-16.00 hrs. Admission 6d; children 3d.

Cardiff: National Museum of Wales, Cathays Park. Weekdays, 10.00-17.00 hrs (18.00 hrs in summer). Sundays, 14.30-17.00 hrs.

Cardiff: St Fagan's Castle: Welsh Folk Museum (4 miles from Cardiff). Weekdays. 10.00-19.00 hrs. (Closes 17.00 hrs in winter.) Sundays, 14.30-19.00 hrs. (17.00 hrs in winter.) Admission 1s; children 6d. Refreshments available.

Carisbrooke: see Isle of Wight.

Carlisle: Museum and Art Gallery, Tullie House, Castle Street. Weekdays, 09.00-20.00 hrs. (Closing 17.00 hrs in winter.) Open on Sundays, in June, July and August, 14.30-17.00 hrs.

Castleford: Castleford Public Library and Museum, Carlton Street. Weekdays, 09.30-18.00 hrs. Closes on Thursdays at 12.00 hrs and on Saturdays, 17.30 hrs.

Castle Howard: see York.

Chacombe Priory: see Banbury.

Chatsworth House: see Bakewell.

Chelmsford and Essex Museum, Oaklands Park, Chelmsford. Weekdays, 10.00-17.00 hrs. Sundays, 14.00-17.00 hrs.

Cheltenham: Art Gallery and Museum, Clarence Street. Weekdays, 10.00-18.00 hrs. Museum closed 13.00-14.15 hrs.

Chester: Grosvenor Museum. Weekdays, 10.00-17.00 hrs. Sundays, 14.00-17.00 hrs.

Chesterfield: Hardwick Hall (N.T.) (on A617, 2 miles south of town). Wednesdays, Thursdays, Saturdays and Sundays, from Easter Saturday to end of October: also Bank Holiday Mondays, 14.00-18.00 hrs (or dusk if earlier). Admission 6s; children 3s. Tea available from 15.00 hrs. Free car park.

Chiddingstone Castle: see Edenbridge.

Chippenham: Corsham Court (in village of Corsham 4 miles from town). Open 11.00-12.30 hrs and 14.00-18.00 hrs daily (except Mondays and Fridays) from mid-July to mid-September. From April to October Sundays, Wednesdays and Thursdays only. Rest of year Sundays only, closing at 16.30 hrs in winter. Admission 3s 6d; children 1s 6d.

Chorley: Astley Hall Art Gallery and Museum, Astley Park. Daily from April to September 14.00-18.00 hrs. Open to 20.00 hrs from May to August. Weekdays only in winter 14.00-16.00 hrs. Admission 6d; children 3d. (Free on Tuesdays and Thursdays.) Tea available in summer.

Clacton: St Osyth's Priory, Gatehouse (4 miles from town on B1027). Open August only, daily, 14.30-16.30 hrs. Admission 4s; children 2s.

Clandon Park: see Guildford.

Claverton Manor: see Bath.

Claydon House: see Winslow.

Clevedon Court, near Clevedon, Somerset (N.T.). From April to September on Wednesdays, Thursdays, Sundays and Bank Holiday Mondays 14.30-17.30 hrs. Admission 4s; children 2s. Tea available.

Cliveden: see Maidenhead.

Coalbrookdale: Museum of Ironfounding. Summer only from Monday to Friday, 10.00-12.00 hrs and 14.00-16.00 hrs. Saturdays, 14.00-16.00 hrs.

Colchester and Essex Museum, The Holly Trees. Weekdays, 10.00-17.00 hrs.

Colchester: Minories Art Gallery, High Street. Weekdays, 10.00-13.00 hrs and 14.00-17.00 hrs. Admission 1s; children 6d. Free on Saturdays.

Corsham Court: see Chippenham.

Cotehele House: see Calstock.

Cregneash: see Isle of Man.

Dartmouth: Borough Museum, The Butterwalk. Weekdays, in summer, 11.00-17.00 hrs: in winter, 14.00-16.00 hrs. Admission 6d; children 3d.

Derby: Museum and Art Gallery, The Strand. Weekdays, 10.00-18.00 hrs (17.00 hrs on Saturdays.) Sundays, 14.30-16.30 hrs.

Derby: Royal Crown Derby Works Museum, Osmaston Road, Derby, DE3 8J2. Telephone 47051/3 and 40196/7. Museum open to public only by appointment.

Derby: Kedleston Hall (5 miles from town). Sundays, from May to September, 14.00-18.00 hrs. (Also Bank Holiday Mondays.) Admission 4s (House and gardens); Children 1s 6d. Museum extra. Tea available.

Derby: Melbourne Hall (8 miles from town on A514). Daily, except Mondays and Fridays, from first Saturday in July to last Sunday in September, 14.00-18.00 hrs. Open at Easter (except Good Friday) and thereafter on Sundays only until July. Open at 11.00 hrs on Bank Holidays. Admission 4s; children under fourteen, 1s 6d. Refreshments available.

Doncaster Museum and Art Gallery, Chequer Road. Weekdays, 10.00-17.30 hrs. Sundays, 14.00-17.00 hrs.

Dorking: Polesden Lacey (N.T.) (3 miles from town). March to mid-December, on Saturdays and Sundays, 11.00-12.45 hrs and 14.00-18.00 hrs (or dusk if earlier) and Wednesdays 14.00-18.00 hrs (or dusk if earlier). Open Tuesdays from May to August and on Bank Holiday Monday. Admission 6s; children (with adult) 3s. Tea available April to October.

Dover: Corporation Museum, Ladywell. Weekdays, 10.00-17.00 hrs (except Wednesdays.)

Driffield: Sledmere House (8 miles from the town). Daily, except Mondays and Fridays, from mid-May to late September, 13.30-17.30 hrs including Bank Holiday Mondays. Admission 4s; children 2s. Restaurant and cafeteria.

Dublin: National Museum of Ireland, Kildare Street. Tuesday to Saturday, 10.00-17.00 hrs. Sundays, 14.00-17.00 hrs.

Dudley: Branch Museum and Art Gallery, Moor Street, Brierley Hill. Weekdays, 10.00-19.00 hrs. Closes at 13.00 hrs on Wednesdays and 17.00 hrs on Saturdays.

Dumfries: Old Bridge House Museum, Old Bridge Street. Weekdays, 10.00-13.00 hrs and 14.00-18.00 hrs. (17.00 hrs in winter). Sundays, April to September only, 14.00-17.00 hrs.

Dundee: City Museum and Art Galleries, Albert Square. Weekdays, 10.00-17.30 hrs.

Dunfermline: Pittencrief House Museum. Weekdays, 11.00-13.00 hrs: 14.00 hrs to dusk. Sundays, 14.00 hrs to dusk.

Durham: Gulbenkian Museum of Oriental Art and Archaeology, Elvet Hill. Monday to Friday, 09.30-13.00 hrs and 14.15-17.00 hrs. Saturdays, 9.30-12.00 hrs and 14.15-17.00 hrs. Sundays, 14.15-17.00 hrs. Closed on Bank Holidays. Admission 1s; children 6d.

Eastbourne: The Towner Art Gallery, Manor House, 9 Borough Lane. Weekdays, 10.00-18.00 hrs (17.00 hrs in winter.) Sundays, 14.00-18.00 hrs (17.00 hrs in winter.)

Edenbridge: Chiddingstone Castle (in Chiddingstone village, 5 miles from Edenbridge: 27 miles from London via A21). Daily (except Mondays), from Easter Saturday to end of October, 14.00-17.30 hrs. Saturdays, Sundays and Bank Holiday Mondays, 11.30-17.30 hrs and in winter on Sundays only, 14.00-16.00 hrs. Closed December, January and February. Admission 3s 6d; children 2s. Bank Holidays 5s; children 2s 6d.

Edgehill: Upton House (N.T.) (in Warwickshire, 1 mile south of town on

A422). Wednesdays and Saturdays, 14.00-18.00 hrs from July to September. Wednesdays only, rest of year, 14.00-18.00 hrs, or dusk if earlier. Admission 4s.

Edinburgh: National Gallery of Scotland, The Mound. Weekdays, 10.00-17.00 hrs. Sundays, 14.00-17.00 hrs.

Edinburgh: Scottish National Portrait Gallery, Queen Street. Weekdays, 10.00-18.00 hrs. Sundays, 14.00-18.00 hrs. In winter, weekdays 11.00-18.00; Sundays 14.00-17.00 hrs or dusk if earlier.

Edinburgh: National Museum of Antiquities of Scotland, Queen Street. Weekdays, 10.00-17.00 hrs. Sundays, 14.00-17.00 hrs.

Edinburgh: The Museum Gallery, 18 Shandwick Place. Weekdays, 10.00-17.00 hrs. Closed on Sundays.

Edinburgh: Royal Scottish Museum. Chambers Street. Weekdays, 10.00-17.00 hrs. Sundays, 14.00-17.00 hrs. Tea available.

Edinburgh: Scottish United Services Museum, Crown Square, Edinburgh Castle. Weekdays, 09.30-18.00 hrs. (16.30 hrs in winter.) Sundays, (June to September only), 11.00-18.00 hrs. Admission 2s; children 1s.

Edinburgh: Canongate Tolbooth, Canongate. Weekdays, 10.00-17.00 hrs. Admission 1s; children 6d.

Edinburgh: Huntly House, Canongate. Weekdays, 10.00-17.00 hrs. Also open on Wednesday evenings in summer 18.00-21.00 hrs. Admission 1s; children 6d.

Edinburgh: Lady Stair's House, Lady Stair's Close, Lawnmarket. Weekdays, 10.00-16.00 hrs, except Saturdays when it closes at 13.00 hrs. Admission 1s; children 6d.

Edinburgh: Lauriston Castle, Cramond Road South. Daily, from April to October, except Fridays, 11.00-13.00 hrs and 14.00-17.00 hrs. In winter, Saturdays and Sundays only, 14.00-16.00 hrs. Admission 2s; children 1s.

Edinburgh: Museum of Childhood, Hyndford's Close, 34 High Street. Weekdays, 10.00-17.00 hrs. Admission 1s; children 6d.

Evesham: Almonry Museum, Vine Street. Daily from March to September, except Mondays and Wednesdays, 14.30-18.30 hrs. Admission 1s; children 3d.

Exeter: Powderham Castle, Kenton (8 miles from the City on Dawlish road —A379). Daily, except Saturdays, from third Sunday in May to third Sunday in September, 14.00-18.00 hrs. Admission 4s; children 2s 6d. Tea available.

Eye Manor: see Leominster.

Faringdon: Buscot Park (N.T.) (3 miles from town on A417). Wednesdays, 14.00-18.00 hrs from April to September and on the first Saturday and Sunday in each of these months, 14.00-18.00 hrs. Admission 4s; children 2s.

Farleigh Hungerford: Castle Museum. Weekdays, 09.30-19.00 hrs. Sundays, 14.00-19.00 hrs. Closes earlier from October to April. Admission 1s; children 6d.

Farnham: Willmer House Museum, 38 West Street. Tuesday to Saturday, 11.00-17.00 hrs. Sundays and Bank Holiday Mondays, 14.30-17.00 hrs.

Firle Place: see Lewes.

Fordingbridge: Breamore House (3 miles north of town near A338). Daily, April to September, except Mondays and Fridays, 14.00-17.30 hrs. Open also Bank Holidays. Admission 4s; children 2s. Tea available from June.

Gateshead: Saltwell Park Museum, Saltwell Park. Weekdays, 10.00-18.00 hrs. Sundays, 15.00-17.00 hrs. Closed Sundays and Friday afternoons in winter.

Glamis: Angus Folk Collection, Kirkwynd. Easter weekend and daily from June to September, 13.00-18.00 hrs. Admission 2s; children 1s.

Glasgow: Art Gallery and Museum, Kelvingrove. Weekdays, 10.00-17.00 hrs. Sundays, 14.00-17.00 hrs. Tea available.

Glasgow: Old Glasgow Museum, People's Palace. Weekdays, 10.00-17.00 hrs. Sundays, 14.00-17.00 hrs.

Glasgow: Tollcross Museum, Tollcross Park. Weekdays, 11.00-17.00 hrs. Sundays, 14.00-17.00 hrs. Closes at dusk in winter.

Glasgow: Hunterian Museum, The University. Weekdays, 10.00-17.00 hrs. Saturdays, 10.00-12.00 hrs.

Glenesk: Folk Museum. Open daily in summer, 14.00-18.00 hrs. Admission 1s; children 6d. Tea available.

Gloucester: City Museum and Art Gallery, Brunswick Road. Weekdays, 10.00-17.30 hrs.

Gloucester: Folk Museum and Regimental Museum, 99-103 Westgate Street. Weekdays, 10.00-17.30 hrs.

Glynde Place: see Lewes.

Grantham: Belvoir Castle (7 miles from the town off the A607). Wednesdays, Thursdays and Saturdays, from April to September, 12.00-18.00 hrs. Sundays, 14.00-19.00 hrs and Sundays in October, 14.00-18.00 hrs. Admission 4s 6d; children 2s. Refreshments available.

Great Yarmouth: Maritime Museum for East Anglia, Marine Parade. Daily in summer, 10.00-13.00 hrs and 14.00-20.00 hrs. Admission 1s; children 6d.

Great Yarmouth: Museum of Domestic Life (N.T.), 4 South Quay. Daily in summer, except Saturdays, 10.00-13.00 hrs and 14.00-17.30 hrs. Admission 1s; children 6d.

Grimsby: Doughty Museum, Town Hall Square. Weekdays, except Mondays, 10.00-12.30 hrs and 14.00-17.30 hrs. Open until 20.00 hrs on Wednesdays and Thursdays.

Guernsey: Lukis and Island Museum, St Barnabas, Cornet Street, St Peter Port. Weekdays, except Wednesdays and Bank Holidays. Admission 1s 6d; children with adult 6d. Free on Thursdays and Saturdays.

Guildford: Museum and Muniment Room, Castle Arch. Weekdays, 11.00-17.00 hrs.

Guildford: Clandon Park (N.T.) (3 miles from town near A246). Mondays, Wednesdays, Saturdays and Sundays, June to September, 14.00-18.00 hrs. Bank Holiday Monday, 11.00-18.00 hrs. Admission 6s; children 3s.

Guildford, Compton: The Watts Gallery. Daily except Thursdays, 14.00-18.00 hrs (16.00 hrs in winter), also Wednesdays and Saturdays, 11.00-13.00 hrs.

Gwydir Castle: see Llanrwst.

Hailsham: Michelham Priory (7 miles from Eastbourne). Daily, from June to September, 11.00-17.30 hrs. From April to May and in early October, 14.00-17.30 hrs. Admission 4s; children 2s. Tea available.

Halifax: Bankfield Museum and Art Gallery, Akroyd Park. Weekdays, 11.00-17.00 hrs. (19.00 hrs in spring and summer.) Sundays, 14.30-17.00 hrs.

Halifax: West Yorkshire Folk Museum, Shibden Hall, Shibden Park. Weekdays, except Fridays, April to September, 11.00-19.00 hrs. Sundays, 14.00-17.00 hrs. October, November, December and March, Wednesdays, Thursdays, and Saturdays, 14.00-17.00 hrs. Admission 1s; children 3d.

Hardwick Hall: see Chesterfield.

Harewood House: see Leeds.

Harrogate: Rudding Park (3 miles from town off A661). Daily (except

Fridays), Easter Saturday to September, 14.00-18.00 hrs. Bank Holidays, 11.00-19.00 hrs. Admission 3s 6d; children 2s. Tea available.

Hartlepool: Gray Art Gallery and Museum, Clarence Road. Weekdays, 10.00-17.30 hrs. Closes at 13.00 hrs Thursdays. Sundays, 15.00-17.00 hrs.

Haslemere: Educational Museum, High Street. Weekdays. 10.00-17.00 hrs. (16.00 hrs in winter.) Sundays, in spring and summer only, 14.00-17.00 hrs. Admission 1s; children 3d.

Hastings: Public Museum and Art Gallery, John's Place, Cambridge Road. Weekdays, 10.00-13.00 hrs: 14.00-17.00 hrs. Sundays, 15.00-17.00 hrs.

Hastings: Museum of Local History. Weekdays, in spring and summer, 09.00-12.30 hrs: 14.00-17.30 hrs. Closed Thursday afternoons.

Hatfield: Hatfield House. May to September. Weekdays (except Mondays), 12.00-17.00 hrs. Sundays, 14.30-17.30 hrs. Admission 5s; children 2s 6d. Tea available.

Hereford: City Museum and Art Gallery, Broad Street. Weekdays, 10.00-18.30 hrs. (Closes 17.00 hrs Thursdays and Saturdays.) Sundays, 14.00-17.30 hrs.

Hereford: Churchill Gardens Museum, Venn's Lane. Daily, 14.00-17.00 hrs.

Hereford: The Old House, High Town. Weekdays, 10.00-13.00 hrs: 14.00-17.30 hrs. Sundays, 14.00-17.30 hrs. In winter closes on Saturdays at 13.00 hrs and all day Sunday. Admission 1s; children 3d (free with adults).

High Wycombe: Art Gallery and Museum, Castle Hill. Weekdays (except Wednesdays), 10.00-18.00 hrs. Closes at 17.30 hrs in winter.

Hinwick House: see Wellingborough.

Hockley Heath: Packwood House (N.T.) Warwickshire. (11 miles from Birmingham.) From April to September on Tuesdays, Wednesdays, Thursdays, Saturdays and Bank Holiday Mondays, 14.00-19.00 hrs. Sundays, 14.30-19.00 hrs. Rest of Year, Wednesdays, Saturdays, 14.00-17.00 hrs. Sundays, 14.30-17.00 hrs. Admission 3s (House only); children 1s 6d (House only).

Honiton and All Hallows Public Museum, High Street. Weekdays, from April to November, 10.00-17.00 hrs. Admission 6d.

Hopetoun House: see South Queensferry.

Horsham: Museum, Causeway House. Wednesdays, Thursdays and Saturdays, 14.30-16.30 hrs.

Hughenden Manor: see High Wycombe.

Hull: Maritime Museum, Pickering Park. Weekdays, 10.00-17.00 hrs. Sundays, 14.30-16.30 hrs.

Hull: Transport Museum, 36 High Street. Weekdays, 10.00-17.00 hrs. Sundays, 14.30-16.30 hrs.

Hull: Wilberforce House, 25 High Street. Weekdays, 10.00-17.00 hrs. Sundays, 14.30-16.30 hrs.

Hungerford: Littlecote House (3 miles from Hungerford off A4). April to mid-October, Mondays, Tuesdays, Wednesdays, and Saturdays, 14.00-17.00 hrs. Also Sundays, 14.00-18.00 hrs. Admission 5s; children 2s 6d. Tea available.

Ickworth: see Bury St Edmunds.

Ipswich: Christchurch Mansion, Christchurch Park. Weekdays, 10.00-17.00 hrs. Sundays, 15.00-17.00 hrs. Closes at dusk in winter.

Isle of Man: Manx Village Folk Museum, Cregneash, nr. Port St Mary. Summer weekdays, 10.00-13.00 hrs: 14.00-17.00 hrs. Admission 6d.

Isle of Wight: Arreton Manor (3 miles from Newport). Weekdays, April to

November, 10.00-18.00 hrs. Sundays, 14.30-18.30 hrs. Admission 3s; children 1s 6d. Refreshments available.

Isle of Wight: Carisbrooke Castle Museum, Newport. Weekdays, 9.30-19.00 hrs in summer, closing earlier in winter. Sundays, 14.00-17.00 hrs in spring and summer only. Admission 2s 6d; children 1s 3d. Tea available in summer.

Jersey: Gorey Castle Museum. Daily, 10.00-17.00 hrs. Closed in winter. Admission 2s; children 6d.

Kedleston Hall: see Derby.

Keighley: Art Gallery and Museum, Cliffe Castle. Weekdays, 10.30-17.30 hrs; Sundays, 14.00-17.00 hrs. Closes at dusk in winter; sometimes open until 20.00 hrs in summer.

Kendal: Abbot Hall Art Gallery. Weekdays (except Thursdays), 10.30-17.30 hrs. Sundays, 14.00-17.00 hrs. Closed second half of December.

Kettering: Westfield Museum, West Street. Weekdays, 10.00-17.00 hrs (20.00 hrs Wednesdays and Fridays in summer.) Sundays, 14.00-18.00 hrs.

Kilbarchan: Weaver's Cottage, The Cross. Tuesdays, Thursdays and Saturdays, 14.00-17.00 hrs, and Sundays in summer, 14.00-17.00 hrs. Admission 2s; children (with adult) free.

Kilmarnock: Dick Institute Museum, Elmbank Avenue. May to September, 10.00-20.00 hrs. Closes 17.00 hrs Wednesdays and Saturdays. October to April, 10.00-17.00 hrs.

King's Lynn: Museum and Art Gallery, Market Street. Weekdays, 10.00-17.00 hrs.

Kingussie: The Highland Folk Museum. Weekdays, in summer, 10.00-16.00 hrs.

Kirkcaldy: Museum and Art Gallery, War Memorial Grounds. Weekdays, 11.00-17.00 hrs. Sundays, 14.00-17.00 hrs.

Knebworth: Knebworth House (28 miles north of London). Saturdays and Sundays from May to September and Spring and Summer Bank Holidays, 14.30-17.30 hrs. Admission 3s 6d; children 2s. Tea available.

Knole: see Sevenoaks.

Lancaster Museum, Old Town Hall, Market Square. Weekdays, 10.00-17.30 hrs.

Lauriston Castle: see Edinburgh.

Leamington Spa: Art Gallery and Museum, Avenue Road. Weekdays, 10.45-12.45 hrs: 14.30-17.00 hrs. Thursdays, also 18.00-20.00 hrs. Sundays, 14.30-17.00 hrs. Closed on Wednesday afternoons.

Leeds: Art Gallery. Weekdays, 10.30-18.30 hrs. Sundays, 14.30-17.00 hrs.

Leeds: Abbey House Museum, Kirkstall. April to September, weekdays, 10.00-18.00 hrs. October to March closes 1 hr earlier. Sundays, April to September, 14.30-18.00 hrs. October to March, 14.00-17.00 hrs.

Leeds: Harewood House (8 miles from the city on A61). Daily from Good Friday to end of September, and on Sundays in October, 11.00-18.00 hrs. Admission 4s; children 2s. Refreshments available.

Leeds: Temple Newsam (5 miles from the city). Daily, 10.30-18.15 hrs (or dusk if earlier). Wednesday, from May to September, to 20.30 hrs. Admission 2s; children with adult 1s.

Leeds: Library of the Thoresby Society, 16 Queen Square. Tuesdays and Thursdays, 11.00-15.00 hrs.

Leicester: Museum and Art Gallery, New Walk. Monday to Friday, 10.00-17.00 hrs (later in summer). Saturdays, 10.00-19.00 hrs. Sundays, 14.00-17.00 hrs.

Leicester: Newarke Houses Museum, The Newarke. Weekdays, 10.00-17.00 hrs (open later in summer). Sundays, 14.00-17.00 hrs.

Leominster: Eye Manor (4 miles from the town). Sundays, Wednesdays, Thursdays and Saturdays, from Easter Sunday to last Sunday in September, 14.30-17.30 hrs. Admission 3s; children 1s 6d.

Lewes: Anne of Cleves House, High Street, Southover. Weekdays, 10.00-18.00 hrs or dusk if earlier. Admission 2s; children 1s.

Lewes: Firle Place (4 miles from the town on A27). Wednesdays and Thursdays, from July to September, 14.15-17.30 hrs. Sundays, 15.00-18.00 hrs. Also Sundays in June and Sundays and Mondays of Bank Holiday weekends, 15.00-18.00 hrs. Admission 3s 6d; children 2s. Tea available.

Lewes: Glynde Place (4 miles from the town on A27). Thursdays, Saturdays and Sundays, from May to September, 14.15-17.30 hrs and on Bank Holiday Mondays. Admission 3s; children 1s 6d. Tea available.

Lincoln: City and County Museum, Broadgate. Weekdays, 10.00-17.30 hrs. Sundays, 14.30-17.00 hrs.

Lincoln: Usher Gallery, Lindum Road. Weekdays, 10.00-17.30 hrs. Sundays, 14.30-17.00 hrs.

Littlecote House: see Hungerford.

Littlehampton: Museum, 12a River Road. Monday, Wednesday, and Saturday, 10.30-13.00 hrs and 14.15-16.30 hrs. Also open on Fridays in summer.

Liverpool: City Museums, William Brown Street. Weekdays, 10.00-17.00 hrs. Sundays, 14.00-17.00 hrs.

Liverpool: Walker Art Gallery, William Brown Street. Weekdays, 10.00-17.00 hrs. Sundays, 14.00-17.00 hrs.

Liverpool: Sudley Art Gallery and Museum, Mossley Hill Road. Weekdays, 10.00-17.00 hrs. Sundays, 14.00-17.00 hrs.

Llandundno: Rapallo House Museum and Art Gallery. Weekdays, (except Tuesdays), 10.00-13.00 hrs: 14.00-17.00 hrs. Closes one hour earlier from September to April.

Llanrwst: Gwydir Castle. Open daily 09.30 hrs-dusk. Admission 3s.

Longleat House: see Warminster.

Ludlow: Museum, Butter Cross. Weekdays in summer (except Thursdays), 10.30-12.30 hrs: 14.00-17.00 hrs. In winter afternoons only (except Thursdays). Saturdays in winter, 10.30-12.30 hrs and 14.00-17.00 hrs.

Luton: Museum and Art Gallery, Wardown Park. Weekdays, 10.00-18.00 hrs (earlier closing time in winter). Sundays, (except December and January) 14.00-18.00 hrs (earlier closing time in winter).

Luton: Luton Hoo (30 miles from London via M1 to the Luton A6 turning). Daily, from April 25 to last Sunday in September, (except Tuesdays and Fridays). Open Good Fridays. Weekdays 11.00-18.00 hrs. Sundays, 14.00-18.00 hrs. Admission 4s; children 1s 6d. Refreshments available.

Lyme Regis: The Philpot Museum, Bridge Street. Daily, in summer, 10.00-13.00 hrs: 14.30-17.30 hrs. In winter, on Tuesdays, Saturdays and Sundays, 10.30-12.30 hrs: 14.30-16.30 hrs and on Thursday afternoons.

Macclesfield: Capesthorne (on A34 road between Wilmslow and Congleton). April to September, on Sundays, 14.00-17.30 hrs (and Wednesdays from mid-May). Open Good Friday and Bank Holiday Mondays. Admission 4s; children 1s 6d. Refreshments available.

Maidenhead: Henry Reitlinger Bequest, Oldfield, Riverside. Tuesdays and Thursdays, 10.00-12.30 hrs: 14.15-16.30 hrs.

Maidenhead: Cliveden (N.T.) (3 miles from town). Wednesdays, Saturdays, and Sundays, from April to October, 14.30-17.30 hrs. Admission to gardens 4s; house 1s. Children half-price.

Maidstone: Museum and Art Gallery, St Faith's Street. Weekdays, 10.00-18.00 hrs. Closing 17.00 hrs in winter. Closed on Bank Holidays.

Manchester: City Art Gallery, Mosley Street. Weekdays, 10.00-18.00 hrs. Sundays, 14.30-17.00 hrs.

Manchester: Athenaeum Annexe, Princes Street. Weekdays, 10.00-18.00 hrs. Sundays, 14.30-17.00 hrs.

Manchester: Whitworth Gallery, Oxford Road. Weekdays, 10.00-17.00 hrs. (Thursdays until 21.00 hrs.)

Manchester: Fletcher Moss Museum, The Old Parsonage, Wilmslow Road, Didsbury. May to August, weekdays, 10.00-20.00 hrs. Sundays, 14.00-20.00 hrs. Closes at 18.00 hrs in spring and autumn and at 16.00 hrs in winter.

Manchester: Heaton Hall, Heaton Park, Prestwich (6 miles from city centre). May to August, weekdays, 10.00-20.00 hrs. Sundays, 14.00-20.00 hrs. Closes at 18.00 hrs in spring and autumn and at 16.00 hrs in winter. Tea available.

Manchester: The Gallery of English Costume, Platt Hall, Rusholme (2 miles from city centre). May to August, weekdays, 10.00-20.00 hrs. Sundays, 14.00-20.00 hrs. Closes at 18.00 hrs in spring and autumn and at 16.00 hrs in winter.

Manchester: Queen's Park Art Gallery, Harpurhey. May to August, weekdays, 10.00-20.00 hrs. Sundays, 14.00-20.00 hrs. Closes at 18.00 hrs in spring and autumn and at 16.00 hrs in winter.

Manchester: Wythenshawe Hall, Wythenshawe Park, Northenden. May to August, weekdays, 10.00-20.00 hrs. Sundays, 14.00-20.00 hrs. Closes at 18.00 hrs in spring and autumn and at 16.00 hrs in winter. Tea available.

Melford Hall: see Sudbury.

Melton Mowbray: Stapleford Park. May to September, Wednesdays, Thursdays and Sundays, 14.30-18.30 hrs. Open Bank Holidays. Admission 4s; children 2s. Admission to Thomas Balston Collection of Staffordshire Figures, 1s. N.T. members free. Tea available.

Mere: Stourhead (N.T.). (3 miles from Mere in Wiltshire village of Stourton). Wednesdays, Saturdays and Sundays from March to November: also Thursdays and Bank Holidays from Easter to September: 14.00-18.00 hrs. (or dusk if earlier). Admission to house, 5s; children 2s 6d.

Merthyr Tydfil: Art Gallery and Museum, Cyfarthfa Castle. Weekdays, 10.00-13.00 hrs: 14.00-18.30 hrs (closing 17.00 hrs in winter). Sundays, 14.00-17.00 hrs. Admission 6d on Sundays and Bank Holidays.

Michelham Priory: see Hailsham.

Middlesbrough: Dorman Museum, Linthorpe Road. Weekdays, 10.00-20.00 hrs (18.00 hrs in winter). Sundays April to September, 14.00-20.00 hrs.

Monmouth: Nelson Museum, Glendower Street. Weekdays, 10.00-13.00 hrs and 14.00-17.00 hrs. July to September open an hour later and also on Sundays 14.00-17.00 hrs. Admission 1s; children 6d.

Montacute House: see Yeovil.

Newcastle-under-Lyme: Borough Museum and Art Gallery, Brampton Park. Weekdays, 10.00-13.00 hrs: 14.00-18.00 hrs and Sundays, in summer only, 14.00-17.30 hrs.

Newcastle upon Tyne: Laing Art Gallery and Museum, Higham Place. Weekdays, 10.00-18.00 hrs (until 20.00 hrs on Tuesdays and Thursdays). Sundays, 14.30-17.30 hrs.

Newcastle upon Tyne: Higham Place Gallery. Weekdays, 10.00-13.00 hrs: 14.30-18.00 hrs.

Newport (Mon.): Museum and Art Gallery, John Frost Square. Weekdays, 10.00-17.30 hrs. Closed on Bank Holidays.

Northampton: Central Museum and Art Gallery, Guildhall Road. Weekdays, 10.00-18.00 hrs. (Thursdays and Saturdays to 20.00 hrs.)

Northampton: Abington Museum, Abington Park. Weekdays, 10.30-12.30 hrs: 14.00-18.00 hrs. (Closes earlier in winter.) Sundays, April to September, 14.30-17.00 hrs.

Norwich: Blickling Hall (N.T.) (15 miles from Norwich on west side of A140). Wednesdays, Thursdays, Saturdays and Sundays from Easter to end of September, 14.00-18.00 hrs. Admission 5s; children with adult 2s 6d. Tea available.

Norwich: Bridewell Museum of Local Industries and Crafts, Bridewell Alley, St Andrew Street. Weekdays, 10.00-17.00 hrs.

Norwich: Castle Museum. Weekdays, 10.00-17.00 hrs. Sundays, 14.30-17.00 hrs. Admission 2s 6d in summer; 6d in winter; children free.

Norwich: Strangers' Hall Museum of Domestic Life, Charing Cross. Weekdays, 10.00-17.00 hrs. Admission 1s in summer; free in winter.

Nottingham: City Museum and Art Gallery, The Castle. Weekdays, 10.00-18.45 hrs. (17.45 hrs, on Fridays and at dusk in winter.) Sundays, 14.00-16.45 hrs. Admission usually free but 6d on Sundays and Bank Holidays.

Nuneaton: Museum and Art Gallery, Riversley Park. Monday to Friday, 12.00-19.00 hrs. Saturdays and Sundays, 10.00-19.00 hrs. Closes 17.00 hrs in December, January and February.

Oldham: Municipal Art Gallery and Museum, Union Street. Monday to Friday, 10.00-19.00 hrs. Saturdays, 10.00-17.00 hrs.

Ormskirk: Rufford Old Hall (N.T.) (east of A59, five miles north of town). Weekdays, except Mondays, 12.00-20.00 hrs (or dusk if earlier). Sundays, 13.00-20.00 hrs (or dusk if earlier). Closed on Wednesdays from October to March. Admission 3s; children with adult 2s. Tea available.

Oxford: The Ashmolean Museum of Art and Archaeology, Beaumont Street. Weekdays, 10.00-16.00 hrs. Sundays, 14.00-16.00 hrs. Closes during St Giles Fair in early September.

Oxford: Museum of the History of Science, Broad Street. Weekdays, 10.30-13.00 hrs: 14.30-16.00 hrs.

Oxford: Pitt Rivers Museum, Parks Road. Weekdays, 14.00-16.00 hrs.

Oxford: The Rotunda, Grove House, 44 Iffley Turn. May to mid-September on Sundays, 14.15-17.15 hrs. Admission 2s; no children under 16.

Packwood House: see Hockley Heath.

Paisley: Museum and Art Galleries, High Street. Weekdays, 10.00-17.00 hrs (to 20.00 hrs on Tuesdays and 18.00 hrs on Saturdays).

Parham House: see Pulborough.

Penrhyn Castle: see Bangor.

Perth: Scone Palace (2 miles from Perth on A93). Daily (except Fridays) from end of April to mid-October. Weekdays, 11.00-17.00 hrs. Sundays, 14.00-17.00 hrs. Admission 4s; children 2s. Refreshments available.

Peterborough: Museum and Art Gallery. Weekdays, 10.00-13.00 hrs, 14.00-17.00 hrs. Closed on Monday mornings. Admission 6d.

Peterhead: Arbuthnot Museum, St Peter Street. Weekdays, (except Tuesdays), 14.00-17.00 hrs.

Petworth House (N.T.) (5½ miles east of Midhurst). Wednesdays, Thursdays, Saturdays and Bank Holidays, from April to October, 14.00-18.00 hrs. Admission 5s; children 2s 6d. (Connoisseur's days on 1st and 3rd Tuesday of each month. Admission 7s.)

Plymouth: City Museum and Art Gallery, Tavistock Road. Weekdays, 10.00-18.00 hrs (20.00 hrs on Fridays). Sundays, 15.00-17.00 hrs.

Plymouth: Elizabethan House, 32 New Street. Weekdays, 10.00-13.00 hrs: 14.15-18.00 hrs (or dusk if earlier). Sundays in summer, 15.00-17.00 hrs.

Plymouth: Buckland Abbey (N.T.) (11 miles from city). Daily, from Good Friday to September 30. Weekdays, 11.00-18.00 hrs. Sundays, 14.00-18.00 hrs. Rest of year on Wednesdays, Saturdays and Sundays, 15.00-17.00 hrs. Admission 2s; children 1s. Car park 1s. Refreshments available.

Plymouth: Saltram House (N.T.) Daily, from April to mid-October (except Tuesdays), 14.00-18.00 hrs. Admission 6s; children 3s. (Connoisseur's Day on Friday. 10s.) Teas available.

Polesden Lacy: see Dorking.

Pontefract Castle Museum: Weekdays, 09.00 hrs to dusk. Sundays, 10.00 hrs to dusk. Admission 2d.

Poole Museum, South Road. Weekdays, 10.00-17.00 hrs.

Poole: Old Town House, Scaplen's Court, High Street. Daily, mid-May to September, 10.00-19.00 hrs. Admission 1s; children 6d.

Portsmouth: The Victory Museum, H.M. Dockyard. Weekdays, 10.00-18.00 hrs (or dusk if earlier). Sundays, 13.00-18.00 hrs (or dusk if earlier). Admission 1s; children 6d.

Port Sunlight: Lady Lever Art Gallery. Weekdays, 10.00-17.00 hrs. Sundays 14.00-17.00 hrs.

Powderham Castle: see Exeter.

Preston: Harris Museum and Art Gallery, Market Square. Weekdays, 10.00-17.00 hrs.

Pulborough: Parham House (4 miles from Pulborough on A283). Sundays, Wednesdays, Thursdays and Bank Holidays from Easter Sunday to first Sunday in October, 14.00-17.30 hrs. Admission until May 31 4s. Rest of season 5s; children 2s 6d. On last Sunday in each month 7s 6d.; children 4s.

Ragley Hall; see Alcester.

Reading: Museum and Art Gallery, Blagrave Street. Weekdays, 10.00-17.30 hrs.

Reading: English Rural Life Museum, Whitenights Park. Tuesday to Saturday, 10.00-13.00 hrs: 14.00-16.30 hrs.

Rochester: Public Museum, Eastgate House. Daily (except Fridays), 14.00-17.30 hrs.

Rotherham: Museum and Art Gallery. Weekdays (except Fridays), 10.00-18.00 hrs. (17.00 hrs in winter.) Sundays, 14.30-17.00 hrs. (16.30 in winter).

Rottingdean: see Brighton.

Rousham House: see Steeple Ashton.

Rudding Park: see Harrogate.

Rufford Old Hall: see Ormskirk.

Rugeley: Museum of Childhood and Costume, Blithfield Hall (4 miles from Rugeley). Wednesdays, Thursdays, Saturdays and Sundays, from Good Friday to first Sunday in October, 14.30-18.00 hrs and Bank Holiday Mondays, 12.00-19.00 hrs and Tuesdays, 14.30-18.00 hrs. Admission 4s; children 2s. Cars 2s. Refreshments available.

St Albans: City Museum, Hatfield Road. Weekdays, 10.00-17.30 hrs (17.00 hrs in winter).

Saffron Walden: Audley End House (one mile west of town on A11). Daily, except Mondays, from April to early October, 11.30-17.30 hrs. Admission 3s; children and O.A.Ps 1s. Tea available from 2 p.m.

St Fagans Welsh Folk Museum: see Cardiff.

St Helens: Pilkington Glass Museum, Prescot Road. Monday to Friday, 10.00-17.00 hrs. Saturdays and Sundays, 14.00-16.30 hrs.

St Osyth's Priory: see Clacton.

Salford: Museum and Art Gallery, The Crescent, Peel Park. Weekdays, 10.00-18.00 hrs. (17.00 hrs in winter.) Sundays, 14.00-17.00 hrs.

Salisbury and South Wiltshire Museum, St Ann Street. Weekdays (except Mondays), 10.00-13.00 hrs: 14.00-17.00 hrs. (Closing 16.00 hrs in winter.) Sundays (summer only), 15.00-17.00 hrs. Admission 2s 6d. Children with adult free.

Saltram House: see Plymouth.

Sawston Hall: see Cambridge.

Scone Palace: see Perth.

Sevenoaks: Knole (N.T.). Wednesdays, Thursdays, Fridays, Saturdays and Bank Holidays, from March to December, 10.00-12.00 hrs: 14.00-17.00 hrs. (15.30 hrs in winter.) Admission 6s; children 3s. (Or 7s 6d for all on Fridays, Connoisseurs' Day—except Good Friday.)

Sheffield: City Museum, Weston Park. Weekdays, 10.00-17.00 hrs. (Open to 20.30 hrs in summer.) Sundays, 13.00-16.00 hrs.

Sheffield: Graves Art Gallery, Surrey Street. Weekdays, 10.00-20.00 hrs. Sundays, 14.00-17.00 hrs.

Sheffield: Mappin Art Gallery, Weston Park. Weekdays, 10.00-17.00 hrs. (20.30 hrs in summer). Sundays, 13.00-16.00 hrs.

Sherborne: The Manor House (at Sandford Orcas, 3 miles from the town). Daily from mid-March to October, 11.00-17.00 hrs. Rest of year Fridays, Saturdays and Sundays only, 11.00-16.00 hrs. Admission 3s; children (under 10) 1s.

Shifnal: Weston Park (5 miles from Shifnal in Shropshire, off the A5). Wednesdays, Thursdays, Saturdays and Sundays, from May to early September, 14.00-19.00 hrs. Also Bank Holiday Mondays and Tuesdays and Sundays in April. Admission 5s; children 3s. Tea available.

Shoreham: The Marlipins Museum, High Street. Daily, from May to October, 10.00-12.30 hrs: 14.00-17.00 hrs.

Shrewsbury: Museum and Art Gallery, Castle Gates. Daily 10.00-18.00 hrs.

Shugborough, near Stafford: Staffordshire County Museum. Weekdays in summer (except Mondays), 11.00-17.30 hrs. Sundays and Bank Holidays in summer, 14.00-17.30 hrs.

Sledmere House: see Driffield.

Snowshill Manor: see Broadway.

South Molton Museum, Town Hall. Summer: Wednesdays in summer, 14.30-16.30 hrs. Thursdays, 11.00-12.00 hrs and 14.30-16.30 hrs. Winter. Thursdays, 11.00-12.30 hrs and 14.30-16.00 hrs. All year: Saturdays, 11.00-12.30 hrs.

South Queensferry: Hopetoun House (12 miles from Edinburgh on A9). Daily, May to September (except Thursdays and Fridays), 13.30-17.30 hrs. Admission 4s; children 2s. Tea available.

South Shields: Library and Museum, Ocean Road. Weekdays, 10.00-19.00 hrs. Saturdays, 10.00-17.00 hrs.

Southampton: Tudor House, St Michael's Square. Weekdays, 10.00-17.00 hrs. Sundays, 14.30-16.30 hrs.

Southampton: Wool House Maritime Museum, Bugle Street. Weekdays, 10.00-17.00 hrs. Sundays, 14.30-16.30 hrs.

Southend-on-Sea: Beecroft Art Gallery, Station Road, Westcliff-on-sea. Weekdays. 10.30-17.30 hrs. Sundays, 14.00-17.30 hrs.

Southport: Botanic Gardens Museum, Churchtown. Weekdays, 10.00-18.00 hrs. Sundays, 14.00-17.00 hrs. Closes at dusk in winter.

Spalding: Museum, Broad Street. By appointment only.

Steeple Ashton: Rousham Hall (12 miles from Oxford). Wednesdays and Bank Holidays, from June to August, 14.00-18.00 hrs. Admission 3s.

Steyning: St Mary's (in village of Bramber, 1 mile from the town on A283). Weekdays from Good Friday to mid-October (except Mondays) 11.00-18.00 hrs. Sundays, 14.00-18.00 hrs. Admission 3s; children 2s.

Stockport: Municipal Museum, Vernon Park, Turncroft Lane. Weekdays, 10.00-18.00 hrs (17.00 hrs in winter). Sundays, 14.00-17.00 hrs. Closed from November to February.

Stockton-on-Tees: Preston Park Museum of Social History, Preston Park, Eaglescliffe. Weekdays, 10.00-20.00 hrs. Sundays, 14.00-17.00 hrs.

Stoke Bruerne, near Towcester: Waterways Museum. Daily, 10.00-12.30 hrs, 14.00-17.00 hrs, 18.00-20.00 hrs. Closes on Mondays and at 5 p.m. in winter. Admission 2s; children 6d.

Stoke-on-Trent: City Museum and Art Gallery, Broad Street, Hanley. Weekdays, 10.00-18.00 hrs. Sundays, 14.30-17.00 hrs.

Stoke-on-Trent: Spode-Copeland Museum and Art Gallery, Church Street. Monday to Friday, 10.00-16.00 hrs.

Stoke-on-Trent: Wedgwood Museum, J. Wedgwood & Sons Ltd, Barlaston. By appointment. Tel. Barlaston 2141.

Stourhead: see Mere.

Stratford-upon-Avon: Royal Shakespeare Theatre Picture Gallery. Daily from April to November, 10.00-13.00 hrs: 14.00-18.00 hrs. Sundays, 14.00-18.00 hrs. In winter, Saturdays, 10.00-13.00 hrs and 14.00-16.00 hrs. Sundays, 14.00-16.00 hrs. Admission 3s.; students 2s; children 1s.

Stroud: Museum, Lansdown. Weekdays, 10.30-13.00 hrs: 14.00-17.00 hrs.

Sudbury: Melford Hall (N.T.) (3 miles from the town in village of Long Melford). Wednesdays, Thursdays, Sundays from Easter to the end of September, and Bank Holidays, 14.30-18.00 hrs. Admission 4s; children (with adult) 2s.

Sunderland: Museum and Art Gallery, Borough Road. Weekdays, 09.30-18.00 hrs. (17.00 hrs on Saturdays.) Sundays, 15.00-17.00 hrs.

Sutherland: Dunrobin Castle, Golspie. Weekdays end of July to early September, 11.00-18.00 hrs. Admission 3s; children 1s 6d. Tea available.

Swansea: Glynn Vivian Art Gallery, Alexandra Road. Weekdays, 10.30-17.30 hrs.

Swansea: Royal Institution of South Wales Museum, Victoria Road. Weekdays, 10.00-17.00 hrs. Admission 1s; children 6d.

Taunton: Somerset County Museum, Taunton Castle. Weekdays, 09.30-13.00 hrs: 14.15-17.30 hrs. Admission 1s; children 6d.

Teeside: see Middlesbrough and Stockton.

Temple Newsam: see Leeds.

Thetford: The Ancient House Museum, White Hart Street. Weekdays in summer, 14.00-17.00 hrs. Tuesday, Thursday and Saturday in winter, 14.00-16.00 hrs. Open on Saturday mornings from 10.00 hrs.

Torpoint: Antony House (N.T.) (5 miles from Plymouth). Tuesdays, Wednesdays and Thursdays, from April to September, also Bank Holiday Mondays, 14.00-18.00 hrs. Admission 5s; children 2s 6d.

Totnes: The Elizabethan House. Weekdays, April to September, 10.30-13.00 hrs: 14.00-17.30 hrs. Admission 6d; children 3d.

Truro: County Museum and Art Gallery, River Street. 10.00-17.00 hrs (16.00 hrs in winter). Closed on Bank Holidays.

Tullynally Castle, West Meath, Eire : see Castlepollard.

Tunbridge Wells: Royal Tunbridge Wells Museum and Art Gallery, Civic Centre. Weekdays, 10.00-17.30 hrs.

Turton: The Ashworth Museum, Turton Tower, Chapletown Road. Wednesdays and Saturdays, 14.00 hrs to dusk. Admission 1s; children 3d.

Upton House: see Edgehill.

Waddesdon Manor: see Aylesbury.

Wakefield: City Art Gallery, Wentworth Terrace. Weekdays, 11.00-17.00 hrs. Sundays, 14.30-17.00 hrs.

Wakefield: City Museum, Wood Street. Weekdays, 11.00-18.00 hrs. Sundays, 14.30-17.30 hrs.

Warminster: Longleat House (4 miles from the town). Daily, 10.00-18.00 hrs (16.00 hrs in winter). Admission 5s; children 2s. Refreshments available.

Warrington: Municipal Museum and Art Gallery, Bold Street. Weekdays, 10.00-19.00 hrs (17.00 hrs on Saturdays). Closed on Bank Holidays.

Warwick: Charlcote Park (N.T.) Daily except Mondays from April to September, 11.15-17.45 hrs. Admission 4s; children 2s.

Warwick: Doll Museum, Oken's House, Castle Street. Weekdays, 10.00-18.00 hrs. Sundays, 14.30-17.00 hrs. Admission 2s; children 1s.

Wellingborough: Hinwick House (6 miles from the town). Thursdays and Bank Holidays from Easter to September and on Easter Monday, 14.00-17.00 hrs. Admission 2s 6d; children 1s 6d.

West Bromwich: Oak House Museum, Oak Road. Weekdays, 11.00-17.00 hrs (16.00 hrs in winter) and Sundays in summer only 14.30-17.00 hrs. Closed on Thursday afternoons.

West Hoathly: The Priest House, Sussex. Weekdays, from April to September (except Fridays), 11.00-17.30 hrs. Sundays, 14.00-17.30 hrs. Admission 2s; children 1s.

Weston Park: see Shifnal.

Westport: Westport House, County Mayo, Eire. From April to mid-October daily 14.00-18.00 hrs and in August 10.30-18.30 hrs. Admission 5s; children 2s. Refreshments available.

Weybridge: Museum, Church Street. Monday to Friday, 14.00-17.00 hrs. Saturdays, 10.00-17.00 hrs.

Weymouth: No 3 Trinity Street. Easter Saturday to late September. Wednesdays, Saturdays and Bank Holiday Mondays, 14.30-17.00 hrs. Admission 2s; children 6d.

Whitby: Art Gallery, Panett Park. May to September, weekdays, 09.00-13.00 hrs: 14.00-17.30 hrs. Sundays, 14.00-17.00 hrs. In winter, weekdays, 10.30-13.00 hrs and on Wednesdays and Saturdays, 14.00-16.00 hrs.

Whitby: Literary and Philosophical Society Museum, Pannett Park. May to September, weekdays, 09.00-13.00 hrs: 14.00-17.30 hrs. Sundays, 14.00-17.00 hrs. In winter, weekdays, 10.30-13.00 hrs, and on Wednesdays, Saturdays and Sundays, 14.00-16.00 hrs. Admission 1s; children 6d.

Whitchurch: (Glamorgan): Castell Cock. Weekdays, 09.30-19.00 hrs, Sundays, 14.00-19.00 hrs. Closes earlier in winter. Admission 1s 6d; children 9d.

Wightwick Manor: see Wolverhampton.

Wilmington: Museum, Wilmington Priory, Sussex. Weekdays (except Fridays), from May to September, 10.00-18.00 hrs. Sundays, 14.00-17.00 hrs. Admission 2s; children 1s.

Wilton House, near Salisbury (in Wilton, off the A30). Weekdays (except Mondays), from April to September, 11.00-17.30 hrs (open Bank Holiday

Mondays). Also on Sundays, 14.00-17.30 hrs. Admission 4s; children 2s. Teas available.

Winchcombe: Sudeley Castle. Daily (except Mondays and Fridays) from April to September, 13.30-17.30 hrs. Admission 4s 6d; children 3s. Tea available.

Windsor Castle: State Apartments. Weekdays (subject to needs of Court), June to September, 11.00-17.00 hrs. (Closes rest of year earlier—15.00 hrs in winter.) Sundays from May to October, open from 13.30 hrs. Admission 2s; children 6d.

Wing: Ascott (N.T.) (2 miles from Leighton Buzzard). Wednesdays, Saturdays and Bank Holiday Mondays, from April to September, 14.00-18.00 hrs. Also open some Sundays in July and August. Admission 5s; children 2s 6d.

Winslow: Claydon House (N.T.) Buckinghamshire. Daily (except Mondays), March to October, 14.00-18.00 hrs. Open Bank Holiday Mondays but closes the next day instead—i.e. Tuesdays. Admission 5s; children 2s 6d.

Wisbech: Wisbech and Fenland Museum, Museum Square. Weekdays (except Mondays), 10.00-13.00 hrs: 14.00-17.00 hrs. (16.00 hrs in winter.)

Woburn Abbey (43 miles from London via M1). Daily, April to October, 11.30-17.00 hrs. Daily, in winter, 13.30-16.00 hrs. Admission 6s; children 3s. Refreshments available.

Wolverhampton: Municipal Art Gallery and Museum, Lichfield Street. Weekdays, 10.00-18.00 hrs.

Wolverhampton: Bantock House, Bantock Park. Weekdays, 10.00-19.00 hrs. Sundays, 14.00-17.00 hrs.

Wolverhampton: Wightwick Manor (N.T.) (3 miles from Wolverhampton). Thursdays, 14.30-17.30 hrs. Saturdays, 10.30-12.30 hrs and 14.30-17.30 hrs. Wednesdays, in summer, 14.00-18.00 hrs. (Last party of visitors 16.30 hrs.) All Bank Holiday Mondays, 14.30-17.30 hrs. Admission 3s. (Saturday afternoons 5s.)

Woodstock: Blenheim Palace (8 miles north of Oxford). Mondays, Tuesdays, Wednesdays and Thursdays, from April to October, also Saturdays and Sundays in summer holiday season, Easter weekend (except Good Friday), 13.00-18.00 hrs. Closed over Spring Bank Holiday weekend. Admission 5s; children 2s 6d. Tea available in summer.

Woodstock: Oxford City and County Museum. Weekdays, from May to September, 10.00-17.00 hrs. Sundays, 14.00-18.00 hrs. From October to April, weekdays only, 10.00-17.00 hrs.

Worcester: City Museum and Art Gallery, Foregate Street. Weekdays, 10.00-13.00 hrs and 14.00-18.00 hrs.

Worcester: Dyson Perrins Museum of Porcelain, The Royal Porcelain Works, Severn Street. Weekdays, 10.00-13.00 hrs; 14.00-17.00 hrs. Closes at 13.00 hrs on Saturdays from April to October.

Worthing: Museum and Art Gallery, Chapel Road. Weekdays, 10.00-19.00 hrs. (17.00 hrs in winter.)

Yeovil: Borough Museum, Hendford Manor Hall. Weekdays (except Thursdays), 10.30-13.00 hrs: 14.15-17.00 hrs.

Yeovil: Montacute House (N.T.) (in village of Montacute, 4 miles from the town). Daily (except Mondays and Tuesdays), from Easter to September, 12.30-18.00 hrs. From March to Easter and in October and November, open only on Sundays, Wednesdays and Saturdays, 14.00-18.00 hrs (or dusk if earlier). Connoisseur's Day on Fridays, 10s. Admission 5s on other days; children 2s 6d. Refreshments available in summer.

York: City Art Gallery, Exhibition Square. Weekdays, 10.00-17.00 hrs. Sundays, 14.30-17.00 hrs.

York: Castle Museum, Tower Street. Weekdays, 09.30-19.30 hrs. Sundays, 14.00-19.30 hrs. (Closes 16.30 hrs in winter.) Admission 3s; children 1s 6d.

York: Railway Museum, Queen Street. Weekdays, 10.00-17.00 hrs. Admission 1s 6d; children 9d.

York: The Yorkshire Museum, Museum Street. Weekdays, 10.00-17.00 hrs.

York: Castle Howard (14 miles from York off the A64). Daily (except Mondays and Fridays), from Easter Sunday to the first Sunday in October, 13.30-17.00 hrs. Also Bank Holiday Mondays from 11.30 hrs. Admission to House, Grounds and Costume Galleries, 7s; children 3s 6d. House and Grounds only 5s; children 2s 6d. Refreshments available.

IN CANADA AND THE U.S.A.

Many of the following museums and galleries are closed on Christmas Day, New Year's Day, Thanksgiving Day and July 4.

Albany: Institute of History and Art, 125 Washington Avenue. Tuesdays to Saturdays, 10.00-16.45 hrs. Sundays, 13.00-18.00 hrs. Open until 21.00 hrs on Tuesdays from October to May.

Boston: Museum of Fine Arts. Tuesdays to Saturdays, 10.00-17.00 hrs. Sundays, 13.30-17.30 hrs. Open on Tuesdays until 22.00 hrs from October to May.

Cambridge, Mass.: Fogg Art Museum, Quincy Street at Broadway (38). Mondays to Saturdays, 09.00-17.00 hrs. Sundays, 14.00-17.00 hrs. Closed on Sundays from mid-June to October.

Chicago: Adler Planetarium, 900E, Achsah Bond Drive, 60605. Daily, 09.30-17.00 hrs. Open until 21.30 hrs on Tuesdays and Fridays from October to May. Admission 50 cents; children 25 cents.

Chicago: Art Institute, Michigan Avenue at Adams Street (3). Weekdays, 10.00-17.00 hrs. Sundays, 12.00-17.00 hrs. Open until 21.30 hrs on Wednesday evenings.

Cincinatti: Taft Museum, 316, Pike Street (2). Weekdays, 10.00-17.00 hrs. Sundays and holidays, 14.00-17.00 hrs.

Cleveland, Ohio: Museum of Art, 11150 East Boulevard, 44106. Tuesdays to Fridays, 10.00-18.00 hrs. Saturdays, 09.00-17.00 hrs. Sundays and holidays, 13.00-18.00 hrs. Open 09.00-22.00 hrs on Wednesdays.

Corning, N.Y.: Museum of Glass, Corning Glass Center, Houghton Park, 14832. Daily, 09.30-17.00 hrs from June to August and from Tuesdays to Saturdays, 09.30-17.00 hrs from September to May.

Dearborn, Michigan: Henry Ford Museum. Daily 09.00-17.00 hrs. Admission $1.40.

Detroit: Institute of Arts, 5200 Woodward Avenue, 48202. Tuesdays to Fridays, 09.00-21.00 hrs. Saturdays and Sundays, 09.00-18.00 hrs from September to June. Closes 18.00 hrs in July and August.

Fort Oglethorpe, Georgia: Chickamanga and Chattanooga National Military Museum. Daily, 08.00-17.00 hrs.

Los Angeles: County Museum of Art, 5905 Wilshire Boulevard, 90036. Tuesday to Saturday, 10.00-17.00 hrs.

Minneapolis: Institute of Arts, 201E 34th Street, 55404. Tuesdays, 10.00-22.00 hrs. Wednesdays and Saturdays, 10.00-17.00 hrs. Sundays and holidays, 13.00-17.00 hrs.

Montreal: Museum of Fine Arts, 1379 Sherbrooke Street West (25). Week-days, 10.00-17.00 hrs (20.00 hrs on Wednesdays). Sundays, 14.00-17.00 hrs. Closed on Mondays in July and August.

New York: The Frick Collection, 1 West 70th Street, 10021. Tuesday to Saturday, 10.00-17.00 hrs. Sundays, 13.00-17.00 hrs. Children under ten not admitted.

New York: Metropolitan Museum of Art, Fifth Avenue at 82nd Street, 100 28. Monday to Saturday, 10.00-17.00 hrs. Sundays and holidays, 13.00-17.00 hrs.

New York: Museum of the City of New York, 1220 Fifth Avenue (29). Tuesdays to Saturdays, 10.00-17.00 hrs. Sundays and holidays, 13.00-17.00 hrs.

New York: U.S. Military Academy, West Point. Daily, 10.30-16.30 hrs.

Newark, N.J.: Newark Museum, 43-49 Washington Street. Mondays to Saturdays, 12.00-17.30 hrs. Sundays, 14.00-18.00 hrs. Open on Wednes-days and Thursday evenings 19.00-21.30 hrs from September to June.

Newhaven, Conn.: Winchester Museum, 275 Winchester Avenue. Mondays to Saturdays, 09.00-16.00 hrs.

Ottawa: National Gallery of Canada, Elgin and Albert Streets (4). Weekdays, 10.00-18.00 hrs. (22.00 hrs on Tuesdays and Thursdays). Sundays, 14.00-18.00 hrs.

Philadelphia, Pa.: Museum of Art, Benjamin Franklin Parkway at 26th Street (1). Daily, 09.00-17.00 hrs. Admission free on Mondays. Other days 50 cents. Children with adults, 25 cents.

Salem: Peabody Museum, 161 Essex Street. Weekdays, 09.00-17.00 hrs. Sundays, 14.00-17.00 hrs. Closes one hour earlier from November to March.

San Marino, Cal.: Henry E. Huntington Library and Art Gallery, 1151 Oxford Road. Tuesday to Sunday, 13.00-16.30 hrs. Closed in October.

Springfield, Mass.: Springfield Armory and Benton Small Arms Museum, Federal Building, Federal Street (1). Tuesdays to Saturdays, 13.00-16.00 hrs.

Toledo, Ohio: Museum of Art, Monroe Street and Scottwood Avenue. Wednesdays, Fridays and Saturdays, 09.00-17.00 hrs. Tuesdays and Thurs-days, 09.00-21.00 hrs. Sundays, Mondays and holidays, 13.00-17.00 hrs.

Washington, D.C.: National Gallery, Constitution Avenue at Sixth Street (25). Weekdays, 10.00-17.00 hrs. Sundays, 14.00-20.00 hrs.

Washington, D.C.: Smithsonian Institution, Freer Gallery of Art, Jefferson Drive at Twelfth Street, S.W. on the Mall, 20560. Daily 09.00-16.30 hrs.

Williamstown, Mass.: Sterling and Rancine Clark Art Institute, South Street. Tuesdays to Sundays, 14.00-17.00 hrs. Closed in February.

Winterthur, Delaware: Henry Francis du Pont Winterthur Museum. Tues-days to Saturdays, 09.30-16.30 hrs. Sixteen period rooms open April, May and June. Admission to sixteen museum rooms $1.00, and to South Wing, adults 50 cents. No children under sixteen admitted.

Worcester, Mass.: John Woodman Higgins Armory, 100 Barber Avenue (6). Mondays to Fridays, 08.30-16.30 hrs. Saturdays, 08.30-12.00 hrs.

2

Reading about Antiques

BOOKS FOR READING AND REFERENCE

THE lover of antiques is always searching for clues which will help him to solve his problems. They may turn up almost anywhere—in an article, an auction sale catalogue, a question-and-answer column, or in a book. Some books embody the results of many years of original research; others, usually for the general reader, derive much of their material from earlier publications though they often contain some discoveries made by the author. Few books, therefore, are to be despised as possible sources of information. The following list contains most of the books in English that are readily available from booksellers or public libraries, together with many that are now hard to find, though most reference libraries are helpful in trying to obtain books for those who make a serious study of any subject. It must be realised, however, that some scholarly books published many years ago have already become rare and valuable. Many of them are difficult to obtain and cost a good deal of money.

The dates given are usually those of first publication but in some cases the date of a later reprint or new edition is indicated in brackets. Unless otherwise stated, it may be assumed that the books were published in London.

It is often difficult to understand and appreciate antiques without some knowledge of the social history of the periods when they were used. For this reason, this bibliography starts with a short list of general books on the antique periods and on collecting; thereafter, the various classes of antiques are listed alphabetically.

ANTIQUE PERIODS

Bentley, N. *The Victorian Scene, 1837-1907*. 1968
Burton, E. *The Elizabethans at Home*. 1958; *The Jacobeans at Home*. 1962; *The Georgians at Home*. 1967
Clark, K. *The Gothic Revival*. 1950
Dutton, R. *The Victorian Home*. 1954
Edwards, R. and Ramsey, L. G. G. *The Connoisseur Period Guides; Tudor Period, 1500-1603; Stuart Period, 1603-1714; Early Georgian Period, 1714-1760; Late Georgian Period, 1760-1810; Regency Period, 1810-1830; Victorian Period, 1830-1860*. 1956-8. These are also combined in one volume—*The Connoisseur's Complete Period Guide*. 1968
Gloag, J. *Georgian Grace*. 1956 (1967); *Victorian Comfort*. 1961
Gordon, H. *Antiques in their Periods*. 1952 (1964)
Hayward, H. *Thomas Johnson and English Rococo*. 1964
Honour, H. *Chinoiserie*. 1961

Reade, B. *Regency Antiques.* 1953
Roe, F. G. *The Georgian Child.* 1961; *The Victorian Child.* 1959; *Victorian Corners.* 1968.
Richardson, A. E. *Georgian England, 1700-1820.* 1931.
Wells, G. *The English Life Series,* 6 vols. 1967; *c. 1550-1610 Elizabeth I and James I*; *c. 1610-1700 Charles I to William and Mary*; *c. 1700-1760 Anne to George II*; *c. 1760-1820 George III*; *c. 1820-1855 George IV to Victoria; c. 1855-1900 Victoria: Later Years.*

ANTIQUE COLLECTING: GENERAL
Many of the books in this list cover a number of classes of antiques, often unusual pieces which are not dealt with in any single volume.
Bagnall, D. *Collecting Cigarette Cards.* 1965
Bedford, J. *The Collecting Man.* 1968
Boger, L. A. and H. B. *The Dictionary of Antiques and the Decorative Arts.* 1957 (1969)
Du Cann, C. G. L. *Antiques for Amateurs.* 1962; *Adventures in Antiques.* 1965
Comstock, H. *The Concise Encyclopaedia of American Antiques.* 2 vols. London, New York and Toronto, 1958
Cooper, D. and Clark, K. *Great Private Collections.* 1963
Cowie, D. and Henshaw, K. *Antique Collectors' Dictionary.* 1962
Coysh, A. W. and King, J. *Buying Antiques General Guide.* 1967 (1970); *The Buying Antiques Reference Book.* Newton Abbot, 1968 (1971)
Eccles, Lord. *On Collecting.* 1968
Gohm, D. C. *Small Antiques for the Collector.* 1969
Goodwin, M. *A Pocket Dictionary of Collectors' Terms.* 1967
Gordon, H. *The Lure of Antiques.* 1961
Hughes, G. B. *Collecting Antiques.* 1950 (1961); *More About Collecting Antiques.* 1952; *The Country Life Collector's Pocket Book.* 1963
Hughes, T. *Cottage Antiques.* 1967; *Small Antiques for the Collector.* 1964 (1965); *Small Decorative Antiques.* 1959; *More Small Decorative Antiques.* 1962
Johnson, S. *Collector's Luck.* 1968
Mebane, J. *New Horizons in Collecting.* 1967
McClinton, K. M. *A Handbook of Popular Antiques.* New York, 1945
Mitchell, P. *An Introduction to Picture Collecting.* 1968
Ramsay, L. G. G. (Ed.) *Concise Encyclopaedia of Antiques.* 5 vols. London and New York, 1955-60
Savage, G. *The Antique Collector's Handbook.* 1959
Scott, A. and C. *Collecting.* 1968
Speck, G. E. and Sutherland, E. *English Antiques.* 1969
Toller, J. *Living with Antiques.* 1969
Wills, G. *Antiques.* 1961
Wenham, A. *Antiques A-Z.* 1954 (1968)
Woodhouse, C. P. *Investment in Antiques and Art.* 1969

ARMS AND ARMOUR: GENERAL—see also *Edged Weapons and Firearms*
The armour enthusiast will find a great deal to interest him in early monumental brasses which very often depict the armour of a period with almost photographic accuracy. Books on the subject are listed under *Monumental Brasses.*
Anderson, L. J. *Japanese Armour.* 1969

Aylward, J. D. *The English Master of Arms.* 1956; *European Armour.* 1958

Blair, C. *European Armour 1066-1700.* 1958; *European and American Arms.* 1962 (1964)

Blackmore, H. L. *Arms and Armour.* New York, 1965

Buehn, W. *Warrior's Weapons.* New York, 1962

Egerton, Lord, of Tatton. *Indian and Oriental Armour.* New Edition, 1968.

Ellacott, S. E. *Collecting Arms and Armour.* 1964

Ffoulkes, C. J. *Arms and Armament.* 1945

Fryer, D. J. *Antique Weapons A to Z.* 1969

Hayward, J. F. *Armour.* 1951

Holmes, M. *Arms and Armour in Tudor and Stuart London.* 1957

Mann, J. *Outline of Arms and Armour in England.* 1960; *Wallace Collection Catalogue of European Arms and Armour.* 1962

Martin, P. *Armour and Weapons.* 1968

Norman, V. *Arms and Armour.* 1964

Oakeshott, R. E. *The Archaeology of Weapons.* 1960; *A Knight and his Armour.* 1961; *A Knight and his Weapons.* 1964; *The Sword in the Age of Chivalry.* 1965

Peterson, H. L. *Arms and Armour in Colonial America.* Harrisburg, 1956

Robinson, B. W. *Arms and Armour of Old Japan.* 1951

Stone, G. C. *A Glossary of the Construction, Decoration and Use of Arms and Armour in All Countries at All Times.* Portland, Maine, 1934

Wilkinson, H. *Engines of War.* 1841

ART—see *Visiting Art Galleries* pp. 45-70

ART DECO
Battersby, H. *The Decorative Twenties.* 1969

Hillier, B. *Art Deco of the 20s and 30s.* 1968

ART NOUVEAU
Amaya, M. *Art Nouveau.* 1966; *Tiffany Glass.* 1968

Barilli, R. *Art Nouveau.* 1969

Battersby, M. *The World of Art Nouveau.* 1968

Burdett, D. *The Beardsley Period.* 1925

Howard, T. *Charles Rennie Mackintosh and the Modern Movement.* 1952

Koch, R. *Tiffany Coloured Glass.* 1964 (1966)

Madsen, S. T. *Art Nouveau.* 1967

Rheims, M. *The Age of Art Nouveau.* 1966

Schmutzler, R. *Art Nouveau.* New York, 1962

Taylor, J. R. *The Art Nouveau Book in Britain.* 1966

Walker, R. A. (Introduction by) *The Best of Beardsley.* 1948 (1967)

AUTOGRAPHS
Benjamin, M. A. *Autographs: A Key to Collecting.* New York, 1946

Broadley, A. M. *Chats on Autographs.* 1910

Munby, A. N. L. *The Cult of the Autograph Letter in England.* 1962

BADGES
Chichester, H. M. and Short, G. B. *Records and Badges of the British Army.* 1900

Cole, H. N. *Badges on Battledress.* Aldershot, 1953

Edwards, T. J. *Regimental Badges.* Aldershot, 1951 (1966)

Farmer, J. S. *Regimental Records.* 1901
Parkyn, M. *Shoulder Belt Plates and Buttons.* 1956
Perry, O. L. *Rank and Badges.* 1887

BAROMETERS
Bell, G. H. and E. F. *Old English Barometers.* Winchester, 1951 (1970)
Goodison, N. *English Barometers.* 1969
Middleton, W. E. K. *The History of the Barometer.* Baltimore, 1964

BAYONETS—see *Edged Weapons*

BELLS
Ingram, T. *Bells in England.* 1954
Morris, E. *Bells of All Nations.* 1957; *Tintinabula.* 1959

BOOKS AND BOOK COLLECTING—see also *Prints*
Bland, D. *A History of Book Illustration.* 1958 (1969)
Boughot, H. F. *The Printed Book, Its History.* 1887
Carter, J. *Taste and Technique in Book Collecting.* 1948; *Books and Book Collectors.* 1956; *A B C for Book Collectors.* 1952 (1966)
Collison, R. L. *Book Collecting.* 1957
Crane, W. *Of the Decorative Illustration of Books Old and New.* 1896
Deringer, D. *The Illuminated Book.* 1958
Doyle, B. *The Who's Who of Children's Literature.* 1968
Duff, E. G. *Early English Printing.* 1896
Ede, C. *The Art of the Book.* 1951
Ellis, R. W. *Book Illustration.* Kingsport, 1952
Franklin, C. *The Private Presses.* 1969
Garvey, E. M. and Hofer, P. *The Artist and the Book, 1860-1960.* Boston, 1961
Glaister, G. A. *Glossary of the Book.* 1960
Goldschmidt, E. P. *The Printed Book of the Renaissance.* Cambridge, 1950
Hamilton, S. *Early American Book Illustration.* Princeton, 1958
James, P. *English Book Illustration, 1800-1900.* 1947
Jennett, S. *The Making of Books.* 1951
McLean, R. *Victorian Book Design and Colour Printing.* 1963
Macmurtrie, D. C. *The Book: The Story of Printing and Bookmaking.* New York, 1937; London, 1938
Muir, P. H. *English Children's Books, 1600-1900.* 1954; *Book Collecting as a Hobby.* 1944
Pitz, H. A. *Treasury of American Book Illustration.* New York, 1947
Pollard, A. W. *Fine Books.* 1912
Prideaux, S. T. *Aquatint Engraving.* 1909 (1968)
Ramsden, C. *London Bookbinders, 1780-1840.* 1956
Reid, F. *Illustrators of the Sixties.* 1928
Sadleir, M. *The Evolution of Publishers' Binding Styles.* 1930
Simon, H. *Five Hundred Years of Art in Illustration.* New York, 1942
Slater, J. H. *How to Collect Books.* 1905
Smith, J. A. *Illustrated Children's Books.* 1948
Steinberg, S. H. *Five Hundred Years of Printing.* 1955
Storm, C. and Peckham, H. *Invitation to Book Collecting.* New York, 1947
Thomas, A. G. *Fine Books.* 1967
Thorpe, P. *English Book Illustration: The Nineties.* 1935
Tooley, R. V. *English Books with Coloured Plates, 1790-1860.* 1954
White, G. *English Book Illustration: The Sixties (1855-1870).* 1897

BOOK PLATES
Fincham, H. W. *The Artists and Engravers of British and American Bookplates*. 1897

BOTTLES—see *Glass*

BOXES—see also *Snuff Boxes*
Bedford, J. *All Kinds of Small Boxes*. 1964
Berry-Hill, H. and S. *Antique Gold Boxes*. London, New York and Toronto, 1960
Delieb, E. *Silver Boxes*. 1968
Snowman, A. K. *Eighteenth-Century Gold Boxes of Europe*. 1965 (1968)

BRASSWORK—see also *Horse Brasses and Monumental Brasses*
Burgess, F. W. *Chats on Old Copper and Brass*. 1954
Franklyn, J. *Brasses*. 1964
Grove, J. R. *Antique English Brass Candlesticks, 1450-1750*. 1968
Hamilton, H. *The English Brass and Copper Industries to 1800*. 1926
Lindsay, J. S. *Iron and Brass Instruments of the English House*. 1964
Wills, G. *Collecting Copper and Brass*. 1962; *Copper and Brass*. 1969

BRONZES
Dent, H. C. *Old English Bronze Wool-Weights*. 1927
Koop, A. J. *Early Chinese Bronzes*. 1924
Lamb, W. *Greek and Roman Bronzes*. 1928
Lanfer, B. *Archaic Chinese Bronzes*. New York, 1922
Montague, J. *Bronzes*. 1963
Pope-Hennessy, J. *Italian Bronze Statuettes*. 1961
Radcliffe, A. *European Bronze Statuettes*. 1966
Savage, G. *A Concise History of Bronzes*. 1968
Underwood, L. *Bronzes of West Africa*. 1967

BUTTONS—see also *Badges*
Albert, L. S. and Kent, K. *The Complete Button Book*. 1949 (1952)
Epstein, D. *Buttons*. 1969
Parkyn, M. *Shoulder Belt Plates and Buttons*. 1956

BYGONES—see also *Treen*
Monson-Fitzjohn, C. J. *Drinking Vessels of Bygone Days*. 1927
Robins, F. W. *The Story of the Lamp and the Candle*. 1939
Scott, A. and C. *Collecting Bygones*. 1964
Wright, P. *Old Farm Implements*.

CANDLESTICKS—see *Brass*

CARE OF ANTIQUES—see *Restoration*

CARPETS AND RUGS
Campana, M. *Oriental Carpets*. 1969
Dilley, A. U. *Oriental Rugs and Carpets*. New York, 1931 (1960)
Edwards, A. C. *The Persian Carpet*. 1953
Erdmann, K. *Seven Hundred Years of Oriental Carpets*. 1961 (1970)
Hawley, W. A. *Oriental Rugs, Antique and Modern*. New York, 1913
Hopf, A. *Oriental Carpets and Rugs*. 1962 (1969)
Jacoby, H. *How to Know Oriental Carpets and Rugs*. 1963

Kendrick, A. F. and Tattersall, C. E. C. *Handwoven Carpets, Oriental and European.* 2 vols. 1922

Liebham, P. *Oriental Rugs in Colour.* New York, 1963

Martin, F. R. *A History of Oriental Carpets before 1800.* 1908

May, C. D. *How to Identify Persian and other Oriental Rugs.* 1952 (1968)

Mumford, J. K. *Oriental Rugs.* 1901; *The Yerkes Collection of Oriental Carpets.* 1910

Sarre, F. and Trenkwald, H. (trans. by A. F. Kendrick) *Old Oriental Carpets.* 2 vols. Leipzig, 1926

Schurmann, U. *Caucasian Rugs.* 1965

Tattersall, C. E. C. *Handwoven Carpets, Oriental and European.* 2 vols. 1922; *The Carpets of Persia.* 1931

Tattersall, C. E. C. and Reed, S. *A History of British Carpets.* Leigh-on-Sea, 1934 (1966)

Thatcher, A. B. *Turkoman Rugs.* 1940

Von Bode, W. and Köhnel, E. (trans. by C. G. Ellis) *Antique Rugs from the Near East.* Braunschweig, 1958

CARRIAGES AND WAGGONS

Arnold, J. *The Farm Waggons of England and Wales.* 1969

Damase, J. *Carriages.* 1968

Tubbs, D. B. *Horseless Carriages.* 1969

CHESSMEN

Copley, F. S. *Improved Geometrical and Universal Chessmen.* Staten Island, 1864

Graham, F. L. *Chess Sets.* 1969

Hammond, A. *A Book of Chessmen.* 1950

Harbeson, J. F. *Nine Centuries of Chessmen.* Philadelphia, 1964

Liddell, D. M. and others. *Chessmen.* New York, 1937

Mackett-Beeson, A. E. J. *Chessmen.* 1968

Murray, H. J. R. *A History of Chess.* 1913

Wichmann, H. and S. *Chess and Chessmen.* 1964

CHRISTMAS AND GREETINGS CARDS

Buday, G. *The History of the Christmas Card.* 1954 (1965)

Chase, E. D. *The Romance of Greeting Cards.* Cambridge, Mass., 1926

Laver, J. *Victoriana* (pp. 97-106). 1966

CLOCKS AND WATCHES

Baillie, G. H. *Watchmakers and Clockmakers of the World.* 1947 (1966); *Clocks and Watches: an historical bibliography.* 1951

Bentley, W. J. *The Plain Man's Guide to Antique Clocks.* 1963

Britten, F. J. *Old Clocks and Watches and Their Makers.* 1899. (The seventh edition of this classic, with new illustrations, was issued in 1956 with the material largely rewritten by G. H. Baillie, C. Clutton and C. A. Ilbert and was reprinted with corrections in 1969); *The Watch and Clockmaker's Handbook, Dictionary and Guide.* 1955

Bréguet, C. A. L. *Bréguet—Horologer.* 1964

Bruton, E. *The True Book about Clocks.* 1957; *Clocks and watches, 1400-1900.* 1967

Chamberlain, P. *It's About Time.* 1941 (1964). (A book about watches and watchmaking.)

Clutton, C. and Daniels, D. *Watches of Europe and America.* 1965

Cumhaill, P. W. *Investing in Clocks and Watches.* 1967

Dawson, P. G. *The Design of English Domestic Clocks.* 1956
De Carle, D. *Watch and Clock Encyclopaedia.* 1959; *Clocks and their Values.* 1968.
Drepperd, C. W. *American Clocks and Clockmakers.* Boston, 1958
Edey, W. *French Clocks.* 1968
Edwards, E. L. *The Grandfather Clock.* 1952 (1956)
Fleet, S. *Clocks.* 1961
Goaman, M. *English Clocks.* 1967
Gordon, G. F. C. *Clockmaking, Past and Present.* 1949
Hayden, A. *Chats on Old Clocks.* 1918
Hill, R. R. *Early British Clocks.* 1949
Jordan, B. and von Bertele, H. *The Book of Old Clocks and Watches.* 1964
Joy, E. T. *The 'Country Life' Book of Clocks.* 1967
Lee, R. A. *The Knibb Family—Clockmakers.* 1964
Lloyd, H. A. *Some Outstanding Clocks over Seven Hundred Years, 1250-1950.* 1958; *The Collector's Dictionary of Clocks.* 1964; *Old Clocks.* 1965
Morpurgo, E. *Precious Watches.* 1966
Palmer, B. *The Book of American Clocks.* New York, 1950; *A Treasury of American Clocks.* New York, 1968
Peate, I. C. *Clock and Watch Makers in Wales.* Cardiff, 1960.
Robertson, J. D. *The Evolution of Clockwork.* 1931
Smith, J. *Old Scottish Clockmakers.* 1921
Symonds, R. W. *A History of English Clocks.* 1947; *The Life and Work of Thomas Tompion.* 1951 (1969)
Tait, H. *Clocks in the British Museum.* 1968
Tyler, E. J. *European Clocks.* 1969
Ullyett, K. *British Clocks and Clockmakers.* 1947; *In Quest of Clocks.* 1950 (1962); *Watch Collecting for Amateurs.* 1969
Wenham, E. *Old Clocks.* 1951 (1965)
Willard, J. W. *Simon Willard and his Clocks.* 1969

COINS AND TRADE TOKENS: GENERAL
Beyne, W. *Trade Tokens issued in the Seventeenth Century.* 2 vols. 1891
Brown, L. *Coin Collecting.* 1962
Carson, R. A. G. *Coins.* 1962
Chamberlain, C. C. *Guide to Numismatics.* 1960
Craig, W. D. *Coins of the World, 1750-1850.* Wisconsin, 1966
Davis, W. J. *Nineteenth-Century Token Coinage.* 1906
Einzig, P. *Primitive Money.* 1957
Johnson, R. F. *Coin Collecting.* 1969
Linecar, H. W. A. *Beginner's Guide to Coin Collecting.* 1966; *Coins.* 1967
Narbeth, C. *The Coin Collector's Encyclopaedia.* 1968
Linecar, H. W. A. *Beginners Guide to Coin Collecting.* 1967
Porteous, J. *Coins.* 1964
Rayner, P. A. *Coin Collecting for Amateurs.* 1967

COINS AND TRADE TOKENS: SPECIAL AREAS
Andrews, A. *Australasian Tokens and Coins.* Sydney, 1921
Askew, G. *The Coinage of the Roman Empire.* 1951
Brooke, G. C. *English Coins.* 1932 (1955)
Charlton, J. E. *Catalogue of Canadian Coins, Tokens and Paper Money.* Toronto, 1960
Craig, J. *The Mint.* Cambridge, 1953
Grant, M. *Roman History from Coins.* Cambridge, 1958

Grueber, H. A. *Handbook of the Coins of Great Britain and Ireland in the British Museum.* 1899

Linecar, H. W. A. *Crown Pieces of Great Britain and the Commonwealth.* 1962

Mack, R. P. *The Coinage of Ancient Britain.* 1953

Mathias, P. *English Trade Tokens.* 1962

North, J. J. *English Hammered Coinage.* 1960

Oman, C. *The Coinage of England.* Oxford, 1931

Rowe, C. M. *Salisbury's Local Coinage.* 1966 (1968)

Schlumberger, H. *Gold Coins of Europe since 1800.* 1900

Seaby, H. A. (Ed.) *Notes on English Silver Coins (1066-1648).* 1948

Seaby, H. A. *Standard Catalogue of the Coins of Great Britain and Ireland.* Published annually.

Seaby, H. A. and Kozolubski, J. *Greek Coins and their Values.* 1959

Seaby, H. A. and Rayner, P. *The English Silver Coinage from 1649.* 1968

Seaby, P. J. *The Story of the English Coinage.* 1952

Stewart, I. H. *The Scottish Coinage.* 1955

Sutherland, A. *Numismatic History of New Zealand.* Wellington, 1941

Wang, Yu-Ch'uian. *Early Chinese Coinage.* American Numismatic Society, New York, 1951

Waters, A. W. *Notes on Eighteenth-Century Tokens.* 1954; *Notes on Nineteenth-Century Tokens.* 1957

COPPERWORK

Burgess, F. W. *Chats on Old Copper and Brass.* 1954

Hamilton, H. *The English Brass and Copper Industries to 1800.* 1926

Wills, G. *Collecting Copper and Brass.* 1962; *The Book of Copper and Brass.* 1968

COSTUME—see also *Fashion Plates* and *Monumental Brasses*

Boucher, F. *A History of Costume in the West.* 1966

Bradfield, N. *Women's Dress, 1730-1930.* 1968; *Costume in Detail.* 1969

Bradshaw, A. *World Costumes.* 1962

Brooke, I. *English Children's Costume Since 1775.* 1930; *A History of English Costume.* 1937 (1968)

Bruhn, W. and Tilke, M. *A Pictorial History of Costume.* 1955

Buck, A. *Victorian Costume and Costume Accessories.* 1961

Calthrop, D. C. *English Costume.* London, 1907. (Also published in four parts—Early English, Middle Ages, Tudor and Stuart, Georgian.)

Contine, M. *Fashion.* 1965 (1967)

Cunnington, C. W. *English Women's Clothing in the Nineteenth Century.* 1937; *The Art of English Costume.* 1948; *Handbook of English Medieval Costume.* 1952; *Handbook of English Costume in the Sixteenth Century.* 1954; *Handbook of English Costume in the Seventeenth Century.* 1955; *Handbook of English Costume in the Eighteenth Century.* 1957; *Handbook of English Costume in the Nineteenth Century.* 1959; *A Picture History of English Costume.* 1960

Cunnington, C. W. and P. *The History of Underclothing.* 1951; *Handbook of English Medieval Costume.* 1969

Cunnington, P. and Lucas, C. *Occupational Costume in England.* 1968

Cunnington, P. and Mansfield, A. *English Costume for Sports and Indoor Recreation.* 1969

Fairholt, F. W. *Costume in England.* 1846

Gibbs-Smith, C. H. *The Fashionable Lady in the Nineteenth Century.* 1960

Hartley, D. *Medieval Costume and Life.* 1931
Hill, M. H. and Bucknell, P. A. *The Evolution of Fashion: Pattern and Cut, 1066-1930.* 1967
Holmes, M. R. *Stage Costumes and Accessories in the London Museum.* 1968
Houston, M. G. *Medieval Costume in England and France.* 1939
Laver, J. *Taste and Fashion from the French Revolution until today.* 1937; *Costume Through the Ages.* 1963
Lister, M. *Costume, An Illustrated Survey from Ancient Times to the Present Day.* 1967
Martin, P. *European Military Uniforms.* 1963 (1968)
Maxwell, S. and Hutchinson, R. *Scottish Costume.* 1958
McQuoid, P. *Four Hundred Years of Children's Costume from the Great Masters, 1400-1800.* 1923
Moses, F. *Modern Costume.* 1823
Planché, J. R. *A Cyclopaedia of Costume.* 1876-79
Rhead, C. W. *Chats on Costume.* 1906
Waugh, N. *The Cut of Women's Clothes, 1600-1930.* 1968
Yarwood, D. *English Costume from the Second Century B.C. to 1960.* 1952 (1967)

DAGGERS—see *Edged Weapons*

DOLLS—see also *Toys*
Early, A. K. *English Dolls, Effigies and Puppets.* 1955
Fraser, A. *Dolls.* 1963
Hillier, M. *Dolls and Dollmakers.* 1968
Johnson, A. *Dressing Dolls.* 1969
Low, F. H. *Queen Victoria's Dolls.* 1894
Noble, J. *Dolls.* 1968
St George, E. *Dolls of Three Centuries.* 1951
Singleton, E. *Dolls.* 1927
Von Boehn, M. *Dolls and Puppets.* 1965
White, G. *Dolls of the World.* 1962; *European and American Dolls.* 1966

DOLLS' HOUSES
Benson, A. C. and Weaver, Sir Laurence. *The Book of Queen Mary's Dolls' House and the Book of Queen Mary's Dolls' House Library.* 1924
Grant, J. *The Doll's House.* 1934
Greene, V. *English Dolls' Houses.* 1967
Jacobs, F. G. *A History of Dolls' Houses.* 1954
Latham, J. *Dolls' Houses.* 1969

DRUG JARS
Howard, G. E. *Early English Drug Jars.* 1931

DUMMY BOARD FIGURES
Scott, A. and C. *Dummy Board Figures.* 1966

EDGED WEAPONS (Bayonets, Daggers and Swords)
Altmayer, J. P. *American Presentation Swords.* Alabama, 1958
Atwood, J. *The Dagger and Edged Weapons of Hitler's Germany.* Berlin, 1965
Aylward, J. D. *The Small Sword in England.* 1960
Bosanquet, H. T. *The Naval Officer's Sword.* 1955

Burton, R. F. *Book of the Sword.* 1884
Carrington-Pierce, P. *A Handbook of Court and Hunting Swords, 1660-1820.* 1937
Dean, B. *Catalogue of European Court and Hunting Swords.* New York, 1929; *Catalogue of European Daggers.* New York, 1929
Ellacott, S. E. *Armour and Blade.* 1962
Ellis-Davidson, H. R. *The Sword in Anglo-Saxon England.* Oxford, 1962
Ffoulkes, C. T. *Sword, Lance and Bayonet.* 1967
German, M. C. *A Guide to Oriental Daggers and Swords.* 1967
Hawley, W. M. *Japanese Sword Smiths.* California, 1966
Hayward, J. F. *Swords and Daggers.* 1951
Henderson, J. *Sword Collecting for Amateurs.* 1969
Hutton, A. *Fixed Bayonets.* 1890; *The Sword and the Centuries.* 1901
Joby, H. L. *Japanese Sword Mounts.* 1910
Knutsen, R. M. *Japanese Polearms.* 1963
Latham, R. J. W. *British Military Swords.* 1966; *British Military Bayonets.* 1967
Norman, A. V. *Small Swords and Military Swords.* 1967
Oakeshott, R. E. *Archaeology of Weapons.* 1960; *The Sword in the Age of Chivalry.* 1964
Peterson, H. L. *American Knives.* New York, 1958; *American Indian Tomohawks.* New York, 1965; *Daggers and Fighting Knives of the Western World.* 1968
Rawson, P. S. *The Indian Sword.* Copenhagen, 1969
Robinson, B. W. *Primer of Japanese Sword Blades.* 1955; *The Art of the Japanese Sword.* 1961
Stephens, S. J. *Bayonets.* 1968
Valentine, E. *Rapiers.* 1968
Wagern, E. *Cut and Thrust Weapons.* 1967
Wayne, B. *Exercise of Broadsword.* Washington, 1850
Webster, D. B. *American Socket Bayonets, 1717-1873.* Ottawa, 1964
Wilkinson, F. *Swords and Daggers.* 1967
Wilkinson Latham, R. J. *British Military Swords from 1800 to the Present Day.* 1966; *British Military Bayonets.* 1967
Yumoto, J. M. *The Samurai Sword.* Tokyo, 1958

EMBROIDERY
Campbell, C. *Linen Embroideries.* 1935
Church, E. R. *Artistic Embroidery.* New York, 1880
Dolby, A. *Church Embroidery.* 1867
Higgin, L. *Handbook of Embroidery.* 1880
Johnstone, P. *Byzantine Tradition in Church Embroidery.* 1967; *Greek Island Embroidery.* 1961
Jourdain, M. A. *English Secular Embroidery.* 1910
Kendrick, A. F. *English Embroidery.* 1905
Morris, B. *History of English Embroidery.* 1954; *Victorian Embroidery.* 1962
Wheeler, C. *The Development of Embroidery in America.* New York and London, 1921

ENAMELS—ENGLISH
Brown, W. N. *The Art of Enamelling on Metal.* 1900
Cunynghame, H. *The Art of Enamelling on Metals.* 1906
Hughes, T. and B. *English Painted Enamels.* 1951
Ilford, Lord. *Staffordshire Coloured Enamels.* 1965

Mew, E. *Battersea Enamels.* 1926
Turner, W. *Transfer Printing on Enamels, Porcelain and Pottery.* 1907

ENAMELS—EUROPEAN
Gauthier and Marcheaux, M. *Limoges Enamels.* 1962

ENAMELS—ORIENTAL
Bowes, J. L. *Japanese Enamels.* 1884
Garner, H. M. *Chinese and Japanese Cloisonné Enamels.* 1962

FAKES AND FORGERIES, AND THEIR DETECTION
Arnau, F. *Three Thousand Years of Deceptions in Art and Antiques.* Dusseldorf, 1959; London, 1961
Cescinsky, H. *The Gentle Art of Faking Furniture.* 1931 (American reprint, 1968)
Kurz, O. *Fakes: A Handbook for Collectors and Students.* 1948 (Revised edition, 1969)
Savage, G. *Forgeries, Fakes and Reproductions: A Handbook for Collectors.* 1963
Schüller, S. *Forgers, Dealers and Experts.* 1960
Tilley, F. *Ultra-Violet Fluorescence and Micro-Analysis of English Porcelain.* 1957

FANS
Cust, L. *Fans and Fan-Leaves.* 1893
MacIver, P. *The Fan Book.* 1920
Rhead, G. W. *The History of the Fan.* 1910
Salwey, C. M. *The Fans of Japan.* 1894
Schreiber, Lady Charlotte. *Fans and Fan-Leaves: English.* 1888; *Fans and Fan-Leaves: Foreign.* 1890
Uzanne, O. *The Fan.* 1884

FASHION PLATES
Holland, V. *Hand Coloured Fashion Plates, 1770-1899.* 1955
Laver, J. *Fashion and Fashion Plates, 1800-1900.* 1943; *Costume Illustration, The Nineteenth Century.* 1947

FIREARMS
Akehurst, R. *Sporting Guns.* 1968; *Game Guns and Rifles.* 1969
Atkinson, J. A. *Duelling Pistols.* 1964
Baker, E. *Remarks on Rifle Guns.* 1825
Baxter, D. R. *Superimposed Load Firearms, 1360-1860.* Hong-Kong, 1966
Blackmore, H. L. *British Military Firearms, 1650-1850.* 1961 (1967); *Firearms.* 1964; *Guns and Rifles of the World.* 1965
Blair, C. *European and American Arms, c 1100-1850.* 1962; *Pistols of the World.* 1968
Blanch, H. J. *A Century of Guns.* 1909
Boothroyd, G. *Gun Collecting.* 1961
Bowman, H. *Antique Guns.* New York, 1953
Busk, H. *The Rifleman's Manual.* 1858
Carey, A. M. *English, Irish and Scottish Firearms Makers.* 1967
Carman, W. Y. *History of Firearms.* 1955
Chapel, C. E. *U.S. Martial and Semi-Martial Single-shot Pistols.* New York, 1962

Dowell, W. C. *The Webley Story.* Leeds, 1962
Dunlap, J. *American, British and Continental Pepperbox Firearms.* California, 1964
Edwards, W. B. *The Story of Colt's Revolver.* Harrisburg, 1953
Ellacott, S. E. *Guns.* 1955
Ffoulkes. *The Gunfounders of England.* Cambridge, 1937
Folkard, H. C. *The Wild Fowler.* 1864
Forsyth, J. *The Sporting Rifle.* 1867
Freemantle, T. F. *The Book of the Rifle.* 1901
George, J. N. *English Pistols and Revolvers.* Onslow County, North Carolina, 1938; London, 1963; *English Guns and Rifles.* Pennsylvania, 1947
Glendenning, I. *British Pistols and Guns, 1640-1840.* 1951 (1969)
Gyngell, D. S. H. *Armourers' Marks.* 1959 (1960)
Hastings, M. *English Sporting Guns.* 1969
Hayward, J. F. *European Firearms.* 1955; *The Art of the Gunmaker.* Vol. I 1500-1660: Vol II 1660-1830. 1962-3
Held, R. *The Age of Firearms.* New York, 1957; London, 1959
Jackson, H. J. *European Hand Firearms of the Sixteenth to Eighteenth Centuries.* 1959
Kauffman, H. J. *The Pennsylvania-Kentucky Rifle.* Harrisburg, 1960
Lavin, J. *A History of Spanish Firearms.* 1965
Lenk, T. *The Flintlock, Its Origin and Development.* Stockholm, 1939; London, 1965
Lister, R. *Antique Firearms: Their Care, Repair and Restoration.* 1963
Logan, H. C. *Underhammer Guns.* Harrisburg, Pennsylvania, 1960
Neal, W. K. *Spanish Guns and Pistols.* 1955
Neal, W. K. and Back, D. H. L. *The Mantons: Gunmakers.* 1967; *Forsyth & Co., Patent Gunmakers.* 1969
Partington, J. R. *A History of Greek Fire and Gunpowder.* Cambridge, 1960
Peterson, H. L. (Ed.) *Encyclopaedia of Firearms.* 1964 (1967); *The Book of the Gun.* 1963 (1967)
Pollard, H. B. C. *History of Firearms.* 1926
Pope, D. *Guns.* 1965
Reynolds, E. G. B. *The Lee Enfield Rifle.* 1960
Ricketts, H. *Firearms.* 1962
Riling, R. *Guns and Shooting: A Bibliography.* New York, 1951; *The Powder Flask Book.* New Hope, Pennsylvania, 1953
Roads, C. H. *The British Soldiers' Firearms, 1850-1864.* 1964
Serven, J. E. *Colt Firearms.* California, 1954 (1959)
Smith, W. H. B. *Gas, Air and Spring Guns of the World.* Pennsylvania, 1957
Taylerson, A. W. F. *The Revolver, 1865-1888.* 1966; *Revolving Arms.* 1967
Taylerson, A. W. F., Andrews, R. A. N. and Frith, J. *The Revolver, 1818-1865.* 1968
Walsh, J. H. *The Modern Sportsman's Gun and Rifle.* 1882
Wilkinson, F. *Small Arms.* 1965 (1966); *Flintlock Pistols.* 1969
Winant, L. *Early Percussion Firearms.* New York, 1959; London. 1961; *Fire arms Curiosa.* New York, 1955 (1961); *Pepperbox Firearms.* New York, 1952

FIRE MARKS

Fothergill, G. A. *Fire Marks from 1680.* 1911
Williams, B. *Fire Marks and Insurance Office Fire Brigades.* 1927; *Specimens of British Fire Marks.* 1934

FIREPLACES

Kelly, A. *The Book of English Fireplaces.* 1969
William, T. *Designs of Monuments and Chimney Pieces.* 1843

FURNITURE—GENERAL

Aronson, J. *The Encyclopaedia of Furniture.* Third edtn., 1966
Binstead, H. E. *English Chairs.* 1923
Blake, J. P. and Hopkins, A. E. R. *Old English Furniture.* 1930
Boger, L. A. *The Complete Guide to Furniture Styles.* 1961
Boynton, L. *English Furniture.* 1969
Davies, L. T. and Lloyd-Johnes, N. J. *Welsh Furniture.* 1950
Dean, M. *English Antique Furniture.* 1968
Edwards, R. *A History of the English Chair.* 1951 (1965); *The Shorter Dictionary of English Furniture.* 1964
Fastnedge, R. *English Furniture Styles from 1500 to 1830.* 1955 (1962)
Foley, E. *Book of Decorative Furniture:* 2 vols. 1910-11
Gloag, J. A. *Short Dictionary of Furniture.* 1952 (Revised and enlarged edition, 1969); *The Englishman's Chair.* 1964
Gordon, H. *Old English Furniture.* 1948
Hayden, A. *Chats on Cottage and Farmhouse Furniture.* 1912 (1950)
Hayward, H. (Ed.) *World Furniture.* 1965
Heal. A. *The London Furniture Makers, 1660-1840.* 1953
Henderson, J. *Furniture.* 1967
Honour, H. *Cabinet Makers and Furniture Designers.* 1969
Hughes, B. *The Pocket Book of Furniture.* 1968
Hughes, T. *Old English Furniture.* 1949
Joy, E. T. *English Furniture.* 1962; '*Country Life*' *Book of Furniture.* 1964 (1969)
Litchfield, F. *Illustrated History of Furniture.* 1922
Macquoid, P. *A History of English Furniture:* 4 vols. 1904
Macquoid, P. and Edwards, R. *The Dictionary of English Furniture from the Middle Ages to the late Georgian Period:* 3 vols. 1924-27 (1954)
Menzies, W. G. *Period Furniture for Everyman.* 1939 (1950)
Mercer, E. *Furniture, 700-1700.* 1969
Negus, A. *Going for a Song: English Furniture.* 1969
Penderel-Brodhurst, J. G. J. and Layton, E. J. *Glossary of English Furniture.* 1925 (1954)
Ramsey, L. G. G. (Ed.) *Antique English Furniture.* 1961
Ramsey, L. G. G. and Comstock, H. (Eds.) *The Connoisseur Guide to Antique Furniture.* 1957 (1969)
Symonds, R. W. *The Present State of Old English Furniture.* 1927; *English Furniture from Charles II to George II.* New York, 1929; *Old Furniture.* 1939 (1964)
Wanscher, O. *The Art of Furniture: 5,000 years of Furniture and Interiors.* Copenhagen, 1966; English Translation, London, 1968
Wenham, E. *The Collector's Guide to Furniture Design.* 1928; *Old Furniture.* 1964
Wheeler, G. O. *Old English Furniture.* 1909

FURNITURE—AMERICAN

Andrews, E. D. and F. *Shaker Furniture.* New Haven, 1950
Bjerkoe, E. H. *The Cabinetmakers of America.* Garden City, New York, 1957
Burton, E. M. *Charleston Furniture, 1700-1825.* Charleston, 1955

H

Carpenter, R. E. Jr. *The Arts and Crafts of Newport, Rhode Island, 1640-1820.* Newport, 1954

Comstock, H. *American Furniture: Seventeenth, Eighteenth and Nineteenth Century Styles.* New York, 1962

Downs, J. *American Furniture of the Queen Anne and Chippendale Styles.* New York, 1952

Hinkley, F. L. *A Directory of Antique Furniture.* New York, 1953

Hipkiss, E. J. *The M. and M. Karolik Collection of Eighteenth Century American Arts.* Boston, 1941

Horner, W. M. Jr. *Blue Book, Philadelphia Furniture.* Philadelphia, 1935

Iverson, M. D. *The American Chair, 1630-1890* New York, 1957

Kettell, R. H. *The Pine Furniture of Early New England.* New York, 1929 (1956)

McClelland, N. *Duncan Phyfe and the English Regency, 1795-1830.* New York, 1939

Miller, E. G. *American Antique Furniture.* 2 vols. 1967

Montgomery, C. F. *American Furniture. The Federal Period, 1788-1825.* New York, 1966; London, 1967

Nagel, C. *American Furniture, 1650-1850.* 1949

Ormsbee, T. H. *Early American Furniture Makers.* New York, 1930; *The Windsor Chair.* New York, 1962

Otto, C. J. *American Furniture of the Nineteenth Century.* New York, 1965

Sack, A. *Fine Points of Furniture: Early American.* New York, 1950 (1963)

Williams, H. *Country Furniture of Early America.* 1964

FURNITURE: EARLY ENGLISH DESIGN BOOKS

Chippendale, T. *Gentleman and Cabinet Maker's Director.* 1754; Re-issued in London and New York, 1957

Hepplewhite, A. & Co. *Cabinet Maker and Upholsterer's Guide.* 1788

Hope, T. *Household Furniture and Interior Decoration.* 1807

Ince, W. and Mayhew, T. *Universal System of Household Furniture.* 1762-3; Reprinted 1960

Manwaring, R. *Cabinet and Chairmaker's Real Friend and Companion.* 1765; Reprinted 1954

Sheraton, T. *Cabinet-Maker and Upholsterer's Drawing Book.* 1791-4; *The Cabinet Directory.* 1803

Smith, G. *Cabinet-Maker and Upholsterer's Guide.* 1826; *Designs for Household Furniture and Interior Decoration.* 1808

FURNITURE—ENGLISH BEFORE 1800

Brackett, O. *Thomas Chippendale.* 1924

Cescinsky, H. *English Furniture of the Eighteenth Century.* 3 vols. 1911-12

Coleridge. A. *Chippendale Furniture: The Work of Thomas Chippendale and his Contemporaries in the Rococo Taste: c. 1745-1765.* 1968

Edwards, R. *Sheraton Furniture Designs.* 1949; *Hepplewhite Furniture Design.* 1955

Edwards, R. and Jourdain, M. *Georgian Cabinet Makers.* 1944; Revised Edition London and New York, 1963

Ellwood, G. M. *English Furniture and Decoration, 1680-1800.* 1933

Fastnedge, R. *Hepplewhite Furniture Design.* 1954; *Sheraton Furniture.* 1961

Harris, E. *The Furniture of Robert Adam.* 1963

Hayward, C. H. *English Period Furniture, 1580-1800.* 1936; *Period Furniture Designs.* 1968

Jourdain, M. *English Decoration and Furniture of the Early Renaissance, 1500-1650.* 1924; *The Work of William Kent.* 1948
Lenyon, F. *Furniture in England from 1660-1760.* 1914 (1925)
Musgrave, C. *Adam and Hepplewhite Furniture.* 1965
Nickerson, D. *English Eighteenth-Century Furniture.* 1963
Rogers, J. C. *English Furniture.* 1923 (1968)
Strange, T. A. *Eighteenth-Century Furniture, Woodwork and Decoration.* 1958
Symonds, R. W. *Old English Walnut and Lacquer Furniture.* 1923; *English Furniture from Charles II to George II.* 1929; *The Ornamental Designs of Chippendale.* 1949; *Chippendale Furniture Design.* 1954; *Furniture Making in the Seventeenth and Eighteenth Century in England.* 1955; *Veneered Walnut Furniture.* 1952
Tipping, H. A. *Old English Furniture of the Cabriole Period.* 1922
Ward-Jackson, P. J. *English Furniture Designs of the Eighteenth Century.* 1959
Watkin, D. *Thomas Hope and the Neo-Classical Idea.* 1968
Wolsey, S. W. and Luff, R. W. P. *Furniture in England: The Age of the Joiner.* 1968

FURNITURE—ENGLISH REGENCY
Aslin, E. *Nineteenth-Century English Furniture.* 1962
Harris, J. *Regency Furniture Designs from Contemporary Sources Books, 1803-26.* 1961
Jourdain M. and Fastnedge, R. *Regency Furniture.* 1965 (Revision of earlier publication.)
Musgrave, C. *Regency Furniture* (1800-1830). 1961
Reade, B. *Regency Antiques* (Contains a useful appendix giving the names and addresses of London furniture makers in 1817.) 1953

FURNITURE—ENGLISH VICTORIAN
Aslin, E. *Nineteenth-Century English Furniture.* 1962
Bird, A. *Early Victorian Furniture.* 1964
Braund, J. *Illustrations of Furniture from the Great Exhibition.* 1858
Jervis, S. *Victorian Furniture.* 1968
Joel. D. *The Adventures of British Furniture, 1851-1951.* 1953
Lawford, H. *The Cabinet of Practical, Useful and Decorative Furniture Designs.* 1859
Roe, F. *Victorian Furniture.* 1952
Symonds, R. B. and Whineray, B. B. *Victorian Furniture.* 1962

FURNITURE—FRENCH
Packer, C. *Paris Furniture, 1710-1810.* New York. 1956
Souchal, G. *French Eighteenth-Century Furniture.* 1961
Strange, T. A. *French Interiors, Furniture, Woodwork and Decoration.* 1958
Verlet, P. *French Royal Furniture.* 1963; *French Furniture and Interior Decoration of the Eighteenth Century.* 1967
Watson, F. J. B. *Louis XVI Furniture.* 1960; *French Furniture in the Wallace Collection.* 1956

FURNITURE—ITALIAN
Hunter, G. L. *Italian Furniture and Interiors.* 2 vols. 1920
Morazzoni, G. *Italian Furniture of the Neo-Classic Period (1760-1820).* 1955

GAMES—see also *Toys*
Whitehouse, F. R. B. *Table Games of Georgian and Victorian Days.* 1951

GLASS—AMERICAN

Belknap, E. McC. *Milk Glass*. New York, 1949
Chipman, F. W. *The Romance of Old Sandwich Glass*. New York, 1952
Koch, R. *Tiffany Coloured Glass*. 1964 (1966)
Lee, Ruth W. *Early American Pressed Glass*. New York, 1946
McKearin, G. S. and H. *American Glass*. New York, 1941; *Two Hundred Years of American Blown Glass*. New York, 1949
Revi, A. C. *American Pressed Glass*. New York, 1964
Watkins, L. W. *American Glass and Glass Making*. New York, 1950

GLASS—ENGLISH, IRISH AND SCOTTISH—see also *Paperweights*

Angus-Butterworth, L. M. *British Table and Ornamental Glass*. 1956
Ash, D. *How to Identify English Drinking Glasses and Decanters (1680-1830)*. 1961
Barrington-Haynes, E. *Glass Through the Ages*. 1948
Bate, P. *English Table Glass*. 1905 (1913)
Bedford, J. *English Crystal Glass*. 1966
Bles, J. *Rare English Glasses of the Seventeenth and Eighteenth Centuries*. 1920; *European Glass*. 1926
Buckley, F. *The Glass Trade in England in the Seventeenth Century*. 1914; *History of Old English Glass*. 1925
Crompton, S. (Ed.) *English Glass*. 1967
Davis, D. *The 'Country Life' Book of Glass*. 1967; *English and Irish Antique Glass*. 1965
Dillon, E. *History of Glass*. 1907
Elville, E. M. *The Collector's Dictionary of Glass*. 1961 (1967); *English Table Glass*. 1951; *English and Irish Cut Glass (1750-1960)*. 1953
Fleming, J. A. *Scottish and Jacobite Glass*. Glasgow, 1938
Francis, G. R. *Old English Drinking Glasses*. 1926
Godden, G. A. *Antique China and Glass under £5*. 1966
Guttey, D. R. *From Broad Glass to Cut Crystal*. 1956
Hartshorne, A. *Old English Glasses*. London and New York, 1897
Haynes, E. B. *Glass Through the Ages*. 1948 (1959)
Honey, W. B. *English Glass*. 1946
Hughes, G. B. *Table Glass in England, Scotland and Ireland from the Sixteenth Century to 1820*. 1956; *English Glass for the Collector*. 1958 (1967)
Kampfer, F. and Beyer, K. G. *Glass: A World History*. 1967
Lewis, J. S. *Old Glass and How to Collect It*. 1948
Lloyd, W. *Investing in Georgian Glass*. 1969
Marson, P. *Glass*. 1918
Pellatt, A. *Glass Manufactures*. 1821; *Curiosities of Glass-making*. 1849 (Reprint 1969)
Robertson, R. A. *Chats on Old Glass*. 1954
Ruggles-Brise, S. *Sealed Bottles*. London and New York, 1949
Savage, G. *Glass*. 1965
Stanmus, G. *Old Irish Glass*. 1920
Thorpe, W. A. *A History of English and Irish Glass*. 2 vols. 1929 (1969); *English Glass*. 1935 (1968)
Wakefield, Hugh. *Nineteenth-Century British Glass*. 1961
Warren, P. *Irish Glass*. 1970
Westropp, M. S. D. *Irish Glass*. 1920
Whistler, L. *Engraved Glass*. 1958
Wilkinson, O. N. *Old Glass: Manufacture, Style, Uses*. 1968
Wilkinson, R. *The Hallmarks of Antique Glass*. 1969

Wills, Geoffrey. *The 'Country Life' Pocket Book of Glass.* 1966
Winbolt, S. E. *Wealden Glass.* 1933
Yoxall, J. H. *Collecting Old Glass.* 1966

GLASS—COLOURED AND OPAQUE
Amic, Y. *French Opaline Glasses of the Nineteenth Century.* 1952
Beard, G. A. *Nineteenth-Century Cameo Glass.* Newport, 1955
Bedford, J. *Bristol and other Coloured Glass.* 1964
Belknap, E. McC. *Milk Glass.* New York, 1949
Charleston, R. J. *English Opaque—White Glass.* 1962
Davis, D. C., and Middlemas, K. *Coloured Glass.* 1968

GLASS PICTURES
Clarke, H. G. *The History of Old English Glass Pictures from 1690-1810.* 1928

HORSE BRASSES
Hartfield, G. *Horse Brasses.* London, New York, and Toronto, 1965
Hughes, G. B. *Horse Brasses.* 1956 (1962)

ICONS
Irimie, C. *Roumanian Icons on Glass.* 1969
Kondokov, N. P. *The Russian Icon.* 1927
Onasch, K., revised by T. Rice. *Icons.* 1964
Papageorgiou, A. *Icons in Cyprus.* 1969
Rice, T. *Russian Icons.* 1947 (1963)
Skrobuche, H. *Icons.* 1964
Weitzmann, K. *Icons from South-Eastern Europe and Sinai.* 1968

IRONWORK
Eras, V. M. *Locks and Keys throughout the Ages.* 1957
Gardner, J. S. *English Ironwork of the Seventeenth and Eighteenth Centuries.* 1911
Harris, J. *English Decorative Ironwork from Contemporary Source Books, 1693-1836.* 1960
Lindsay, J. S. *An Anatomy of English Wrought Iron, 1000-1800.* 1964; *Iron and Brass Implements of the English House.* 1964
Lister, R. *Decorative Wrought Ironwork in Great Britain.* 1956 (1960)
Shuffney, L. A. *The English Fireplace.* 1920
Taylor, S. *Opercula: London Coal Plates.* 1966
Young, W. A. *Old English Pattern Books of the Metal Trades.* 1913

IVORY
Beibeder, O. *Ivory.* 1965
Longhurst, M. H. *History of English Ivories.* 1926
Maskall, A. *Ivories.* 1905
Natanson, J. *Early Christian Ivories.* 1953
Williamson, G. C. *The Book of Ivory.* 1938
Wills, G. *Ivory.* 1968

JADE
Bedford, J. *Jade and other Hardstone Carvings.* 1969
Hansford, S. H. *Chinese Carved Jades.* 1968
Jenyns, S. *Chinese Archaic Jades in the British Museum.* 1951
Lawfer, B. *Jade.* Chicago, 1912
Luzzato-Bilitz, D. *Antique Jade.* 1969

Nott, S. C. *Chinese Jade through the Ages.* 1936 (1962); *Chinese Jade, Its Characteristics, Decoration, Folklore and Symbolism.* 1963
Palmer, J. P. *Jade.* 1967
Pope-Hennessy, U. *Early Chinese Jades.* 1923; *A Jade Miscellany.* 1946
Savage, G. *Chinese Jade.* 1964
Wills, G. *Jade.* 1964
Zara, L. *Jade.* 1969

JAPANESE PRINTS

Binyon, L. *Catalogue of Japanese and Chinese Woodcuts in the British Museum.* 1916
Binyon, L. *Painting in the Far East.* 1934
Binyon, L. and Sexton, J. J. *Japanese Colour Prints.* 1923; Revised 1960
Blunt, W. *Japanese Colour Prints from Harunobu to Utamaro.* 1952
Boller, W. *Masterpieces of the Japanese Woodcut.* 1958
Ficke, A. C. *Chats on Japanese Prints.* 1915
Hillier, J. *Japanese Drawings, 17th-19th Century.* 1966; *Japanese Masters of the Colour Print.* 1954; *Japanese Prints, Drawings and Paintings (Kegan Paul Catalogue)* 1967
Modansha. *Library of Japanese Art.* Rutland, Vermont and Tokyo. First English edtn. 1955
Lane, R. *Masters of the Japanese Print.* New York, 1962
Michener, J. *Japanese Prints from the Early Masters to the Present Day.* Rutland, Vermont, 1963
Munsterberg, H. *The Landscape Painting of China and Japan.* Tokyo, 1955

JAPANNED WARES

John, W. D. *English Decorated Trays (1550-1850).* 1964; *Pontypool and Usk Japanned Wares.* 1965
Stalker, J. *A Treatise on Japanning and Varnishing.* 1688 (1962)

JEWELLERY—see also *Enamel*

Bainbridge, H. C. *Fabergé, Goldsmith and Jeweller to the Russian Imperial Court.* 1949 (1967)
Bedford, J. *Jewellery.* 1964
Benda, K. *Ornament and Jewellery.* 1967
Bradford, E. *English Victorian Jewellery.* 1959 (1967); *Four Centuries of European Jewellery.* 1953 (1967)
Burgess, F. W. *Antique Jewellery and Trinkets.* 1919
Castellani, A. *Antique Jewellery and its Revival.* 1862
Curran, M. *Collecting Jewellery.* 1963; *Jewels and Gems.* 1961
Emanuel, H. *Diamonds and Precious Stones.* 1865
Evans, J. *A History of Jewellery 1100-1870.* 1953 (1970)
Eyles, W. C. *The Book of Opals,* 1964
Falkiner, R. *Investing in Antique Jewellery.* 1968
Flower, M. *Victorian Jewellery.* 1951; (Revised 1967); *Jewellery, 1837-1901.* 1968
Fregnac, C. *Jewellery.* 1965
Jones, W. *Finger Ring Lore.* 1898
Hinks, P. *Jewellery.* 1969
Hughes, T. and B. *English Painted Enamels.* 1951
King, C. W. *Antique Gems and Rings.* 1872
Kunz, G. F. *The Book of the Pearl.* 1908
Leechman, F. *The Opal Book.* 1961

Lewis, M. D. S. *Antique Paste Jewellery.* 1969
Oved, S. *The Book of Necklaces.* 1953
Prosser, W. *Birmingham Inventions.* 1881
Rogers, F. and Beard, A. *Five Thousand Years of Gems and Jewellery.* 1947
Ryley, A. B. *Old Paste.* 1913
Snowman, K. *The Art of Carl Fabergé.* 1954
Steingraber, E. *Antique Jewellery: Its History in Europe from 800 to 1900.* 1957
Vilimkova, M. and Darbois, D. *Egyptian Jewellery.* 1969
Wigley, T. B. *The Art of the Goldsmith and Jeweller.* 1898
Wright, J. S. *The Jewellery and Gilt Toy Trades.* 1866

KEYS—see *Locks and Keys*

LACE
Caplin, J. *The Lace Book.* 1932
Head, R. E. *The Lace and Embroidery Collector: A Guide to Collectors of Old Lace, Samplers, etc.* 1921
Hoare, K. *The Art of Tatting.* 1910
Jackson, F. N. *A History of Hand-made Lace.* 1928
Jourdain, M. *Old Lace.* 1908
Moore, N. H. *The Lace Book.* 1908
Palliser, B. *History of Lace.* 1875
Pollen, J. H. *Seven Centuries of Old Lace.* 1928
Ricci, E. *Old Italian Lace:* 2 vols. 1913
Wardle, P. *Victorian Lace.* 1968

LACQUER
Bedford, J. *Chinese and Japanese Lacquer.* 1969
Boyer, M. *Japanese Export Lacquers (1600-1800).* 1959
Herberts, K. *Oriental Lacquer.* 1962
Koizumi, G. *Lacquer Work.* 1923
Strange, E. F. *Catalogue of Chinese Lacquer in the Victoria and Albert Museum.* 1925; *Chinese Lacquer.* 1926

LEADWORK
Weaver, L. *English Leadwork.* 1909

LEATHERWORK
Waterer, J. W. *Leather Craftsmanship.* 1968

LOCKS AND KEYS
Eras, V. M. *Locks and Keys Throughout the Ages.* 1957

MAPS AND GLOBES
Bagrow, L. *History of Cartography.* English Edition, 1964
Baynton-Williams, R. *Investing in Old Maps.* 1969
Crone, G. R. *Maps and Their Makers.* Second edtn. 1962
Darlington, I. and Howgego, G. *Printed Maps of London, c. 1553-1830.* 1964
Fite, D. E. and Freeman, E. *The Book of Old Maps.* New York, 1965
Fordham, H. G. *The Road Books and Itineraries of Great Britain, 1570-1850.* 1924; *John Cary: Engraver, Map, Chart and Print-Seller, and Globe Maker, 1754-1835.* 1925
Lee, R. J. *English County Maps.* 1953

Lister, R. *How to Identify Old Maps and Globes.* 1965; *Antique Maps and their Cartographers.* 1970
Lynham, E. *British Maps and Map-Makers.* 1944; *Ornamental Writing and Symbols on Maps, 1250-1800.* 1945
Quixley, R. C. E. *Antique Maps of Cornwall and the Isles of Scilly.* 1966
Radford, P. J. *Antique Maps.* Portsmouth, England, 1965
Robinson, A. H. W. *Marine Cartography in Britain.* 1962
Skelton, R. A. *Decorative Printed Maps of the Fifteenth to Eighteenth Centuries.* (Based on a book compiled in 1922 by A. L. Humphreys and rewritten by R. A. Skelton in 1952. It is well documented with a useful bibliography to each chapter.) Reprinted 1967
Stevenson, E. L. *Terrestrial and Celestial Globes.* 2 vols. Yale, 1921
Taylor, E. G. R. *Tudor Geography, 1485-1583.* 1935; *Late Tudor and Early Stuart Geography, 1583-1650.* 1934
Tooley, R. V. *Maps and Mapmakers.* 1962

MARITIME ANTIQUES
Dow, G. F. *Whale Ships and Whaling During Three Centuries.* Salem, Mass., 1935
Frere-Cook, G. *The Decorative Arts of the Mariner.* 1966

MATCHBOX LABELS
Rendall, J. *Matchbox Labels.* Newton Abbot, 1968

MEDALS
Cole, H. H. *Coronation and Commemorative Medals.* Aldershot, 1953
Dorling, H. T. *Ribbons and Medals.* 1946
Gordon, L. L. *British Battles and Medals.* Aldershot, 1962
Hieronymussen, P. *Orders, Medals and Decorations of Britain and Europe.* First English edtn. London, 1967
Irwin, D. H. *War Medals and Decorations, 1588-1898.* 1899
Kerr, J. N. *Notes on War Medals, 1794-1840.* 1948
Laffin, J. *British Campaign Medals.* London, New York, Toronto, 1964
Purves, A. A. *Collecting Medals and Decorations.* 1968

MILITARIA—see also *Medals*
Johnson, A. C. *Chats on Military Curios.* 1915
Wilkinson, F. *Militaria.* 1969

MINIATURES
Bolton, T. *Early American Portrait Painters in Miniature.* New York, 1921
Bradley, J. W. *A Dictionary of Miniaturists, Illuminators, Calligraphers and Copyists.* 3 vols. 1958
Bussagli, M. *Indian Miniatures.* 1969
Delaissé, L. M. J. *Medieval Miniatures.* 1965
Foskett, D. *British Portrait Miniatures.* 1963 (1968); *John Smart: The Man and his Miniatures.* 1964
Foster, J. J. *Miniature Painters.* 2 vols. 1903
Hand, S. *Signed Miniatures.* 1925
Heath, D. *Miniatures.* 1905
Lister, R. *The British Miniature.* 1951
Long, B. S. *British Miniaturists 1520-1860.* 1929 (1967)
O'Brien, D. *Miniatures of the Eighteenth and Nineteenth Centuries.* 1952
Porcher, J. *French Miniatures.* 1960
Propert, J. L. *A History of Miniature Art.* 1887

Reilly, D. R. *Portrait Waxes*. 1953
Reynolds, G. *English Portrait Miniatures*. 1953
Schidlof, L. *The Miniature in Europe*. 4 vols. (Edition of 750 copies.) 1965
Williamson, G. C. *The Miniature Collector*. 1921

MIRRORS
Roche, S. *Mirrors*. English translation 1957
Wills, G. *English Looking-Glasses*. 1965

MODEL SOLDIERS—see also *Toys*
Featherstone, D. F. *War Games*. 1962; *Tackle Model Soldiers This Way*.
   1963; *Battles with Model Soldiers*. Newton Abbot, 1970
Garratt, J. G. *Model Soldiers*. 1962
Harris, E. *Model Soldiers*. 1962
Nicollier, J. *Collecting Toy Soldiers*. Rutland, Vermont, 1967
Wells, H. G. *Floor Games*. 1911; *Little Wars*. 1913
Young, P. and Lawford, J. P. *Charge*. 1967

MONUMENTAL BRASSES
Busby, R. J. *The Beginner's Guide to Brass Rubbing*. 1969
Davis, C. T. *The Monumental Brasses of Gloucestershire*. 1889 (1969)
Druitt, H. *Manual of Costume as illustrated by Monumental Brasses*. 1906
Kite, E. *The Monumental Brasses of Wiltshire*. 1860 (1969)
Macklin, H. W. *Monumental Brasses*. 1905 (1953)
Trivick, H. *The Craft and Design of Monumental Brasses*

MUSICAL AUTOMATA
Chapius, A. and Droz, E. *Automata*. 1960

MUSICAL BOXES
Clarke, J. E. T. *Musical Boxes: A History and Appreciation*. (Contains a
   valuable appendix with a list of makers of musical boxes, mechanical
   singing birds and automata.) 1948 (1961)
Hoke, H. and J. *Music Boxes: Their Lure and Lore*. New York, 1957
Ord-Hume, A. W. J. G. *Collecting Musical Boxes and How to Repair Them*.
   1967
Webb, G. *The Cylinder Musical Box Handbook*. 1968

MUSICAL INSTRUMENTS—see also *Violins*
Anderson, O. *The Bowed Harp: A Study of the History of Early Musical
   Instruments*. 1930
Armstrong, R. B. *English and Irish Instruments*. 1908
Baines, A. *European and American Musical Instruments*. 1966
Blades, J. *Percussion Instruments and Their History*. 1969
Boalch, D. *Makers of the Harpsichord and Clavichord (1440-1840)*. 1955
Boyden, D. D. *Catalogue of the Hill Collection of Musical Instruments in
   the Ashmolean Museum, Oxford*. 1969
Bragard, R. *Musical Instruments in Art and History*. 1969
Buchner, A. *Mechanical Musical Instruments*. 1961; *Musical Instruments
   through the Ages*. 1957
Carse, A. *Musical Wind Instruments*. New York, 1939 (1965)
Clemencic, R. *Old Musical Instruments*. 1968
Donington, R. *The Instruments of Music*. Third edtn. 1953
Galpin, F. W. *Old English Instruments of Music*. 1932 (1964); *A Textbook
   of European Instruments*. 1937

126   THE BUYING ANTIQUES REFERENCE BOOK

Geiringer, K. *Musical Instruments.* 1943 (1965)
Harding, R. *The Pianoforte, its History to 1851.* 1933
James, P. *Early Keyboard Instruments: Their History from the Stone Age to the Present Day.* 1961
Marcuse, S. *Musical Instruments: A Comprehensive Dictionary.* 1966
Rendall, G. *The Clarinet.* 1954
Russell, R. *The Harpsichord and Clavichord.* 1959
Sharpe, A. P. *The Story of the Spanish Guitar.* 1954

NEEDLEWORK—see also *Embroidery*
Alford, Lady M. *Needlework as an Art.* 1886
Armes, A. *Early Smocks.* Leicester, 1950
Day, L. F. *Art in Needlework.* 1900
Finley, R. E. *Old Patchwork Quilts.* New York, 1929
Glaister, E. *Needlework.* 1880
Groves, S. *The History of Needlework Tools and Accessories.* 1967
Hall, M. R. *English Church Needlework.* 1901
Harbeson, G. B. *American Needlework.* New York, 1938
Hughes, T. *English Domestic Needlework (1660-1860).* 1961
Kendrick, A. F. *English Needlework.* 1933 (1967). (Latest edition revised by Patricia Wardle.)
Morris, J. A. *The Art of Ayrshire White Needlework.* Glasgow, 1916
Morris, M. *Decorative Needlework.* 1893
Symonds, M. and Preece, L. *Needlework through the Ages.* 1928

NETSUKE
Brockhaus, A. *Netsuke.* Leipzig, 1905
Jonas, F. M. *Netsuke.* 1928 (1969)
Newman, A. R. *Japanese Art.* 1965
O'Brien, M. L. *Netsuke: A Guide for Collectors.* Rutland, Vermont, U.S.A., and Tokyo, Japan, 1965
Reitichi, U. *The Netsuke Handbook.* (English translation from the Japanese.) 1964
Ryerson, E. *The Netsuke of Japan.* 1968

PAINTING
This list includes only a number of general books on American, English and French painting. Biographical books on some individual artists are given under their names on pp. 45-70. The most useful book of reference is Bénézit's *Dictionary of the Painters, Sculptors and Engravers of every country and of every age to the year 1966* in 8 volumes, though, unfortunately for English-speaking readers, the text is in French.
Baker, C. N. and Constable, W. C. *English Paintings of the Sixteenth and Seventeenth Centuries.* 1930
Barker, A. *American Painting: History and Interpretation.* New York, 1950
Baur, J. I. H. *American Painting in the Nineteenth Century.* New York, 1953
Boase, T. S. R. *English Art (1800-1870).* 1959
Combrech, E. H. *The Story of Art.* London and New York, 1950
Croft-Murray, E. *Decorative Painting in England.* 1963
Daniel, H. *Adventures in Art: A Guide to Gallery-going.* London, New York and Toronto, 1960
Dickes, W. F. *The Norwich School of Painting.* 1905
Etheridge, K. *Collecting Drawings.* 1970
Flexner, J. H. *A Short History of American Paintings.* Boston, 1950

Freedman, W. B. *Pre-Raphaelitism: a Bibliocritical Study.* Harvard, 1965
Gaunt, W. *The Observer's Book of Painting and Graphic Art.* 1958; *A Concise History of English Painting.* 1964; *The Pre-Raphaelite Tragedy.* 1942
Graves, A. *A Dictionary of Artists.* Third Edition 1907. Reprinted 1969
Hardie, M. *Water Colour Painting in Britain.* Vol I. The Eighteenth Century. 1966 (1967); Vol. II. The Romantic Period. 1967
Hauser, A. *The Social History of Art.* New York, 1951
Hughes, C. E. *Early English Water Colour.* 1913; Revised by J. Mayne, 1960
Ironside, R. and Gere, J. A. *Pre-Raphaelite Painters.* 1948
Larkin, O. W. *Life and Art in America.* New York, 1949
Maas, J. *Victorian Painters.* 1969
Newton, E. *British Painting.* 1945; *European Painting and Sculpture.* London and New York, 1950
Proctor, I. *Masters of British Nineteenth-Century Art.* 1961
Redgrave, S. and R. *A Century of Painters of the English School.* 1866; Revised edtn., 1947
Reynolds, G. *Painters of the Victorian Scene.* 1953; *Victorian Painting.* 1966
Richardson, E. P. *Painting in America.* 1956. (With a very good bibliography.)
Sparrow, W. S. *British Sporting Artists.* 1922 (1965)
Taylor, B. *Animal Painting in England.* 1955
Waterhouse, E. *Painting in Britain (1530-1790).* 1953
Wilenski, R. H. *English Painting.* 1933; *Modern French Painters.* 1911 (1947)
Williams, I. *Early English Water Colours.* 1952

PAPERWEIGHTS
Bedford, J. *Paperweights.* 1968
Bergstrom, E. H. *Old Glass Paperweights.* 1947 (1968)
Cloak, E. C. *Glass Paperweights.* 1970
Elville, E. M. *Paperweights and other Glass Curiosities.* 1954
Imbert and Amic, Y. *French Crystal Paperweights.* 1948
Jokelson, P. *Antique French Glass Paperweights.* New York, 1955; *Glass Paperweights and Cameo Heads.* New York, 1968
Manheim, F. J. *A Garland of Weights.* Limited Edition, 1968

PAPIER MÂCHÉ
Dickinson, G. *English Papier Mâché.* 1925
Toller, J. *Antique Papier Mâché in Great Britain and America.* 1962

PEWTER
Bedford, J. *Pewter.* 1965
Bell, M. *Old Pewter.* New York, 1905; Revised Edtn. London, 1913
Cotterell, H. H. *Old Pewter and How to Collect It.* 1913; *Bristol and West-Country Pewterers.* 1918; *Old Pewter: Its Makers and Marks in England, Scotland and Ireland.* 1929 (1965); *Pewter Down the Ages.* Plymouth, 1932
Cotterell, H. H. and Westropp, M. *Irish Pewterers.* 1917
de Navarro, A. *Causeries on English Pewter.* 1911 (1924)
Englefield, E. *A Treatise on Pewter and its Manufacture.* 1933
Gale, E. J. *Pewter and the Amateur Collector.* 1910
Ingleby Wood, L. *Scottish Pewterware and Pewterers.* Edinburgh, 1907
Markham, C. H. *Pewter Marks and Old Pewter Ware.* 1928 (1948)

Massé, H. J. *Pewter Plate*. 1904 (1911); *The Pewter Collector: A Guide to English Pewter*. 1921; *Chats on Old Pewter*. 1911; Revised by R. F. Michaelis, 1949

Michaelis, R. F., *Antique Pewter of the British Isles*. 1955; *British Pewter*. 1969

Price, F. G. H. *Old Base Metal Spoons*. 1908

Verster, A. J. G. *Old European Pewter*. 1959

Ullyett, K. *Pewter Collecting for Amateurs*. 1967

Welch, C. *History of the Worshipful Company of Pewterers*. 2 vols. 1902

PICTURE POSTCARDS

Alderson, F. *The Comic Postcard in English Life*. Newton Abbot, 1970

Carline, R. *Pictures in the Post*. 1959

Staff, F. *The Penny Post, 1680-1918*. 1964; *The Picture Postcard and its Origins*. 1966

PIPES, TOBACCO

Sources listed in *The Concise Encyclopaedia of Antiques*. Vol. 4, p. 208. 1959

Scott, C. and A. *Tobacco and the Collector*. 1966

PLAYING CARDS

Benham, W. G. *Playing Cards*. 1931

Hargrave, C. P. *A History of Playing Cards*. Boston, 1930

Mann, S. *Collecting Playing Cards*. Reprint, 1967

Morley, H. I. *Old and Curious Playing Cards*. 1931

Taylor, E. S. *The History of Playing Cards*. 1865

Tilley, R. *Playing Cards*. 1967

PONTYPOOL AND USK WARES—see also *Japanned Wares*

John, W. D. *Pontypool and Usk Japanned Wares*. 1965

PORCELAIN AND POTTERY MARKS

Chaffers, W. *Marks and Monograms on Pottery and Porcelain*, Fifteenth Edition, 2 vols. 1965; *Collector's Handbook of Marks and Monograms on Pottery and Porcelain*. Fourth Edition, 1968.

Cushion, J. P. *Pocket Book of English Ceramic Marks*. 1959 (1965); *Pocket Book of German Ceramic Marks*. 1961; *Pocket Book of French and Italian Ceramic Marks*. 1965

Cushion, J. P. and Honey, W. B. *Handbook of Pottery and Porcelain Marks*. 1956

Godden, G. A. *Encyclopaedia of British Pottery and Porcelain Marks*. 1964; *Illustrated Encyclopaedia of British Pottery and Porcelain*. 1966; *Handbook of British Pottery and Porcelain Marks*. 1968

Kovel, R. M. and T. H. *A Dictionary of Marks*. 1953

Macdonald-Taylor, M. *A Dictionary of Marks*. 1962

Rhead, G. W. *British Pottery Marks*. 1910

PORCELAIN AND POTTERY—GENERAL

Barber, E. A. *Pottery and Porcelains of the United States*. 1901

Bedford, J. *Talking About Teapots*. 1964

Bemrose, G. *Nineteenth-Century English Pottery and Porcelain*. 1952 (1968)

Binns, W. M. *The First Century of English Porcelain*. 1906

Blacker, J. F. *The A.B.C. of Nineteenth Century English Ceramics.* 1911 (1920)

Burton, W. *History and Descriptions of English Porcelain.* 1902; *History and Description of English Earthenware and Stoneware.* 1904; *Porcelain, Its Nature, Art and Manufacture.* 1906; *General History of Porcelain.* 2 vols. 1921

Charleston, R. J. (Ed.) *English Porcelain, 1745-1850.* 1965; *World Ceramics.* 1968

Church, A. *English Earthenware.* 1914

Cox, W. E. *The Book of Pottery and Porcelain.* New York, 1945

Cushion, J. P. *English China Collecting for Amateurs.* 1967

Dixon, J. L. *English Porcelain of the Eighteenth Century.* 1952

Fisher, S. W. *English Blue and White Porcelain of the Eighteenth Century.* 1947; *China Collector's Guide.* 1957; *British Pottery and Porcelain.* 1962; *English Ceramics.* 1966

Fleming, J. A. *Scottish Pottery.* Glasgow, 1923

Godden, G. A. *British Pottery and Porcelain, 1780-1850.* 1963; *Victorian Porcelain.* 1961

Hagger, R. G. *English Country Pottery.* 1950

Hayden, A. *Chats on English China.* 1904; *Chats on English Earthenware.* 1909.

Hillier, B. *Pottery and Porcelain, 1700-1914.* 1968

Hobson, R. *British Museum Catalogue of English Pottery.* 1903; *British Museum Catalogue of English Porcelains.* 1905

Hodgson, W. *How to Identify Old China.* 1903; *Old English China.* 1913

Hodkin, J. E. and E. *Examples of Early English Pottery.* 1896

Honey, W. B. *Old English Porcelain.* 1928 (1948); *English Pottery and Porcelain.* 1947 (Revised by R. J. Charleston, 1968)

Hughes, G. B. *Victorian Pottery and Porcelain.* 1959 (1968); *English and Scottish Earthenware, 1660-1860.* 1961; *English Pottery and Porcelain Figures.* 1964

Hughes, G. B. and T. *English Porcelain and Bone China, 1743-1850.* 1955 (1968)

Jewitt, W. *The Ceramic Art of Great Britain.* 2 vols. 1878-1883

King, W. *Porcelain Figures of the Eighteenth Century.* 1925

Lane, A. *English Porcelain Figures of the Eighteenth Century.* 1961

Lewis, G. *A Picture History of English Pottery.* 1956; *A Collector's History of English Pottery.* 1969

Litchfield, F. *Pottery and Porcelain: A Guide for Collectors.* 1900; Rewritten by Frank Tilley, 1963

Mankowitz, W. and Haggar, R. G. *The Concise Encyclopaedia of English Pottery and Porcelain.* London and New York, 1957

Morley-Fletcher, H. *Investing in Pottery and Porcelain.* 1968

Nightingale, J. E. *Contributions towards the History of Early English Porcelain.* 1881

Rackham, B. *Catalogue of the Schreiber Collection in the Victoria and Albert Museum.* Vol 1 *Porcelain* (1915); Vol. 2 *Earthenware* (1929); *Medieval English Pottery.* 1947; *Early Staffordshire Pottery.* 1951

Rackham, B. and Read, H. *English Pottery.* 1924

Rhead, G. W. *Staffordshire Pots and Potters.* 1906; *The Earthenware Collector.* 1920

Roscoe, W. *English Porcelain Figures, 1744-1848.* 1947

Rosenfeld, B. *Eighteenth-Century Porcelain Figures.* 1950

Savage, G. *Eighteenth-Century English Porcelain.* 1952; *Porcelain through the Ages.* 1954 (1961); *Pottery through the Ages.* 1959; *English Pottery and Porcelain.* 1961

Scott, G. R. *Antique Porcelain Digest.* 1962

Shaw, S. *A History of the Staffordshire Potteries.* 1829; Reprinted, Newport, Mon., 1968

Solon, M. L. *Pâte-sur-Pâte.* 1894; *History of Old English Porcelain.* 1903

Tilley, F. *Teapots, Pottery and Porcelain.* 1957

Turner, W. *Transfer Printing on Enamels, Porcelain and Pottery.* 1907

Wakefield, H. *Victorian Pottery.* 1962

Watney, B. *English Blue and White Porcelain of the Eighteenth Century.* 1963

Wedgwood, J. C. *Staffordshire Pottery and Its History.* 1914

Wedgwood, J. and Ormsbee, T. H. *Staffordshire Pottery.* New York, 1947

Wills, G. *'Country Life' Book of English China.* 1964

PORCELAIN—DECORATION

Ballantyne, A. R. *Robert Hancock and his Work.* 1885

Cook, C. *Robert Hancock, His Life and Work.* 1948; *Supplement to the Life and Work of Robert Hancock.* 1955

Fisher, S. W. *Decoration of English Porcelain.* 1954

John, W. D. with Simcox, A. and J. *William Billingsley, 1758-1828.* 1968

Tapp, W. H. *The Brothers Brewer, 1764-1820.* 1932; *Jefferys Hamett O'Neale.* 1938

Turner, W. *Transfer Printing on Enamels, Porcelain and Pottery.* 1907

PORCELAIN—ENGLISH FACTORIES

Bow

Bemrose, W. *Bow, Chelsea and Derby Porcelain.* 1898

Egan, M. *Old Bow Porcelain.* 1909

Hurlbutt, F. *Bow Porcelain.* 1926

Lewer, H. W. *Bow Porcelain Early Figures.* 1919

Stoner, F. *Chelsea, Bow and Derby Porcelain Figures.* 1955

Tait, H. *Bow Porcelain 1744-1776.* 1959

Tiffin, W. F. *Chronograph of the Bow, Chelsea and Derby Manufacturers* 1847

Bristol and Plymouth

Barrett, F. *Worcester Porcelain and Lund's Bristol.* 1966

Hurlbutt, F. *History of British Porcelain.* 1928

Mackenna, F. S. *Champion's Bristol Porcelain.* 1947; *Cookworthy's Plymouth and Bristol Porcelain.* 1946

Owen, H. *Two Centuries of Ceramic Art in Bristol.* 1873

Trapnell, A. *Dispersal Catalogue of the Trapnell Collection of Bristol and Plymouth Porcelain.* 1912

Caughley and Coalport

Barrett, F. A. *Caughley and Coalport Porcelain.* Leigh-on-Sea, 1951

Godden, G. A. *Caughley and Worcester Porcelain, 1775-1800.* 1969

Chelsea

Blunt, R. *The Cheyne Book of Chelsea China.* 1924

Bryant, G. E. *Chelsea Porcelain Toys, 1745-84.* 1925

Hackenbroch, Y. *Chelsea and other English Porcelain; In the Irwin Intermyer Collection.* 1956

Hurlbutt, F. *Chelsea China*. 1922 (1937)
King, W. *Chelsea Porcelain*. New York, 1922
Mackenna, F. S. *Chelsea Porcelain: Gold Anchor Wares*. 1952; *Chelsea Porcelain: Red Anchor Wares*. 1951 (1967); *Chelsea Porcelain: Triangle and Raised Anchor Wares*. 1948 (Limited Edition, 1969)
Stoner, F. *Chelsea, Bow and Derby Porcelain Figures*. 1955
Tiffin, W. F. *Chronograph of the Bow, Chelsea and Derby Manufacturies*. 1847

Derby
Bemrose, W. and Wallis, A. *The Pottery and Porcelain of Derbyshire*. 1870
Gilhespy, F. B. *Derby Porcelain*. 1961 (1965); *Crown Derby Porcelain*. Leighon-Sea, 1951
Gilhespy, F. B. with Budd, D. M. *Royal Crown Derby China*. 1964
Haslem, J. *The Old Derby China Factory*. 1876
Hurlbutt, F. *Old Derby Porcelain and its Artist Workmen*. 1925
Hyam, E. E. *The Early Period of Derby Porcelain*. 1926
Stoner, F. *Chelsea, Bow and Derby Porcelain Figures*. 1955
Tapp, W. H. *The Brothers Brewer, 1764-1820*. 1932
Williamson, F. *The Derby Pot-Manufactory known as Cockpit Hill, Derby*. 1931

Liverpool
Boney, K. *Liverpool Porcelain of the Eighteenth Century and its Makers*. 1957

Longton Hall
Bemrose, W. *Longton Hall Porcelain*. 1906
Watney, B. *Longton Hall Porcelain*. 1957

Lowestoft
Casley, H. C. *The Lowestoft China Factory*. 1903
Crisp, F. A. *The Lowestoft China Factory and the Moulds Found There*. 1907; *Catalogue of Lowestoft China*. 1907
Fairbairn, G. *Oriental Lowestoft: The Book of Crests of the Families of Great Britain and Ireland*. 2 vols. 1892-1905
Godden, G. A. *The Illustrated Guide to Lowestoft Porcelain*. 1969
Hyde, J. A. L. *Oriental Lowestoft*. Newport, Mon. 1936 (Revised 1964)
Kiddel, A. J. B. *Lowestoft Porcelain: Collection of Mrs Russell Colman*. 1937
Spelman, W. W. R. *Lowestoft China*. London and Norwich, 1905

Minton
Godden, G. A. *Minton Pottery and Porcelain of the First Period, 1793-1850*. 1968

Nantgarw and Swansea
Charles, R. L. *A Picture Book of Welsh Porcelain*. 1951
Dennis, C. R. *The Nantgarw Pottery and Porcelain Site*. 1948
John, W. D. *Nantgarw Porcelain*. 1948; *Nantgarw Porcelain*: Supplement No. 1 1956; Supplement No. 2. *The 'Mackintosh' Nantgarw Porcelain Bird Services*. 1965; *Swansea Porcelain*. 1957
Meager, K. S. *The Swansea and Nantgarw Potteries*. 1950
Morton-Nance, E. *The Pottery and Porcelain of Swansea and Nantgarw*. 1942

Turner, W. *The Ceramics of Swansea and Nantgarw*. 1897
Williams, I. J. *Catalogue of Welsh Porcelain in the National Museum of Wales. Cardiff*, 1931; *The Nantgarw Pottery and its Products: An examination of the Site*. 1932

New Hall
Charleston, R. J. *New Hall Porcelain*. 1965
Stringer, G. E. *New Hall Porcelain*. 1949

Pinxton
Barrett, F., Exley, C. L. and Thorpe, A. L. *The Pinxton China Factory.* Derby, 1963

Plymouth—see *Bristol*

Rockingham
Eaglestone, A. A. and Lockett, T. A. *The Rockingham Pottery, Its Fine Porcelain and Earlier Earthenware*. Rotherham, 1964 (1967)
Llewellyn, G. R. *Rockingham Pottery and Porcelain* (See *Connoisseur Year Book*, 1962.).
Rice, D. G. *Rockingham Ornamental Porcelain*. 1965

Spode
Bedford, J. *Old Spode China*. 1969
Cannon, T. G. *Old Spode*. 1927
Hayden, A. *Spode and his Successors*. 1925

Swansea—see *Nantgarw and Swansea*

Worcester
Barrett, F. A. *Worcester Porcelain*. 1953
Bedford, J. *Old Worcester China*. 1966
Binns, R. W. *A Century of Potting in the City of Worcester, 1751-1851.* London and Worcester, 1865; *Worcester China, 1852-1892*. 1897
Fisher, S. *Worcester Porcelain*. 1968
Godden, G. A. *Caughley and Worcester Porcelains, 1775-1800*. 1969
Hobson, R. L. *Worcester Porcelain*. 1910
Mackenna, F. S. *Worcester Porcelain*. 1950
Marshall, H. R. *Armorial Worcester, First Period*. 1964; *Coloured Worcester Porcelain, First Period*. 1954
Sandon, H. *Worcester Porcelain*. 1970

POTTERY—WARES, POTTERIES AND MAKERS
Adams
Adams, P. W. L. *History of the Adams Family*. 1914
Nicholls, R. *The Adams Family*. 1928
Peel, D. *A Pride of Potters*. 1957
Turner, W. *William Adams, an old English Potter*. 1904

Black Basaltes
Grant, M. H. *The Makers of Black Basaltes*. 1910 (1966)

Bristol Potteries
Pountney, W. J. *Old Bristol Potteries*. Bristol, 1920

Creamware—see also—*Leeds* and *Wedgwood*
Towner, D. *English Cream Coloured Earthenwares.* 1957

Delftware
Bedford, J. *Delftware.* 1966
Berendsen, A. *Tiles: A General History.* 1967
Downman, E. A. *Blue Dash Chargers and other Early English Tin Enamel Circular Dishes.* 1919
Garner, F. H. *English Delftware.* 1948 (1965)
Hodgkin, J. E. and E. *Examples of Early English Pottery.* 1891
Howard, G. E. *Early English Drug Jars.* 1931
Imber, D. *Collecting Delft.* 1968
Justice, J. *Dictionary of Marks and Monograms on old Dutch Delft Pottery.* 1930
Lane, A. *The Collection of Pottery Tiles in the Victoria and Albert Museum.* 1939 (1961); *French Faience.* 1948
Mundy, R. G. *English Delft Pottery.* 1928
Neurdenbury, E. and Rackham, B. *Old Dutch Pottery and Tiles.* 1923
Pountney, W. J. *The Old Bristol Potteries.* London and Bristol, 1920
Ray, A. *English Delft Pottery in the Robert Hall Warren Collection, Ashmolean Museum, Oxford.* 1968

Doulton
Eyles, D. *Doulton Pottery, 1815-1965.* 1965

Leeds Pottery
Grabham, O. *Yorkshire Potteries, Pots and Potters.* 1916
Kidson, J. R. and F. *Historical Notices of the Leeds Old Pottery.* 18?2
Rackham, B. *Leeds Pottery.* 1938
Towner, D. C. *English Cream Coloured Earthenware.* 1957; *Leeds Pottery.* 1963

Liverpool Potteries
Entwhistle, P. *Catalogue of Liverpool Pottery and Porcelain.* Liverpool, 1907
Gatty, C. F. *The Liverpool Potteries.* Liverpool, 1882
Lancaster, H. B. *Liverpool and her Potters.* Liverpool, 1936
Mayer, J. *History of the Art of Pottery in Liverpool.* Liverpool, 1873 (1885)

Lustreware—see also *Sunderland Potteries*
Bedford, J. *Old English Lustre Ware.* 1965
Bosanko, W. *Collecting Old Lustre Ware.* 1916
Evans, Lady. *Lustre Pottery.* 1920
Hodgdon, J. R. *Collecting Old English Lustre.* Portland, Maine, 1937
Hughes, G. B. *English Lustrewares.* (See 'Country Life' Annual.) 1955
John, W. D. and Baker, W. *Old English Lustre Pottery.* Newport, Mon., 1951 (1962)
John, W. D. and Simcox, J. *Early Wedgwood Lustre Wares.* 1963
Thorne, A. *Pink Lustre Pottery.* 1926

Martinware
Beard, C. R. *Catalogue of the Collection of Martinware formed by F. J. Nettleford with a short history of R. W. Martin and Bros., Southall, Middlesex.* 1936

Mason
Haggar, R. G. *The Masons of Lane Delph.* 1952

I

Minton
Godden, G. A. *Minton Pottery and Porcelain of the First Period, 1793-1850.* 1968

Prattware
Clarke, H. G. *Colour Pictures on Pot Lids.* 1924 (1927); *The Pot Lid Book.* 1931; *The Centenary Pot Lid Book.* 1949; *Underglaze Colour Picture Prints on Staffordshire Pottery.* 1950; *Pictorial Pot Lid Book.* 1955 (1960); *The New Pot Lid Book.* 1969

Rockingham Pottery
Eaglestone, A. A. and Lockett, T. A. *The Rockingham Pottery.* Rotherham, 1964 (1967)

Salt Glaze Ware
Blacker, J. F. *The ABC of English Saltglaze Stoneware.* 1922
Burton, W. *English Earthenware and Stoneware.* 1904
Luxmoore, C. F. C. *Early Salt Glaze Ware.* (Limited edition of 100.) 1924

Slipware
Cooper, R. G. *English Slipware Dishes (1600-1850).* 1965 (1968); *Pottery of Thomas Toft.* Leeds, 1952
Lomax, C. J. *Quaint Old English Pottery.* Manchester, 1909

Spode
Bedford, J. *Old Spode China.* 1969
Hayden, A. *Spode and his Successors.* 1925
Williams, S. B. *Antique Blue and White Spode.* 1943 (Third edition, enlarged, 1949)

Staffordshire Blue
Larsen, E. B. *American Historical Views on Staffordshire China.* New York, 1939
Little, W. L. *Staffordshire Blue.* 1969
Williams, S. B. *Antique Blue and White Spode.* 1943 (Third edition, enlarged, 1949)

Staffordshire Busts and Figures
Andrade, C. *Astbury Figures.* 1924
Balston, T. *Staffordshire Portrait Figures of the Victorian Age.* 1958
Bedford, J. *Staffordshire Pottery Figures.* 1964; *Toby Jugs.* 1968
Bristowe, W. S. *Victorian China Fairings.* 1965
Cummings, A. D. *Portraits of John Wesley in Pottery.* 1962
Cushion, J. P. *Animals in Pottery and Porcelain.* 1962
Eyles, D. *Good Sir Toby: The Story of Toby Jugs through the Ages.* 1955
Haggar, R. G. *English Pottery Figures, 1660-1860.* 1947; *Staffordshire Chimney Ornaments.* 1955
Hughes, G. B. *English Ceramic Figures.* 1963 (1964)
Latham, B. *Victorian Staffordshire Portrait Figures.* 1953
Lee, A. *Portraits in Pottery.* Boston, Mass., 1931
Mackintosh, Lord. *Early English Figure Pottery.* 1938
Price, R. K. *Astbury, Whieldon and Ralph Wood Figures and Toby Jugs.* 1922
Rackham, B. and Jeremy, P. *Animals in Staffordshire.* 1953
Read, H. *Staffordshire Pottery Figures.* 1929
Stanley, L. T. *Collecting Staffordshire Pottery Figures.* 1962

Sunderland Potteries
Crawley, J. *The Sunderland Potteries.* 1961
Shaw, J. T. *The Potteries of Sunderland and District.* Sunderland, 1961

Turner
Grant, H. M. *The Makers of Black Basaltes.* 1910 (1967)
Hillier, B. *The Turners of Lane End.* 1965

Wedgwood
Barnard, H. *Chats on Wedgwood Ware.* 1924
Bedford, J. *Wedgwood Jasper Wares.* 1964
Burton, W. *Josiah Wedgwood and his Pottery.* 1922
Buten, H. M. *The Wedgwood A.B.C.* 1964
Chellis, E. *The Wedgwood Bibliography.* 1966
Church, A. H. *Josiah Wedgwood, Master Potter.* 1903
Farrer, K. E. (ed.) *Wedgwood's Letters to Bentley.* 1903
Finer, A. and Savage, G. *The Selected Letters of Josiah Wedgwood.* 1965
Grant, H. M. *The Makers of Black Basaltes.* 1910 (1967)
Haynes, D. E. L. *The Portland Vase.* 1964
Heilpern, G. *Josiah Wedgwood, Eighteenth Century English Potter: A Bibliography.* 1968
Hobson, R. L. *Wedgwood Pottery in the Lady Lever Gallery.* 1924
Honey, W. B. *Wedgwood Ware.* 1948
Jewitt, L. *The Wedgwoods—being a life of Josiah Wedgwood.* 1865
John, W. D. and Simcox, J. *Early Wedgwood Lustre Wares.* 1962
Kelly, A. *Decorative Wedgwood.* 1965; *The Story of Wedgwood.* 1962
Litchfield, R. B. *Tom Wedgwood (1771-1805).* 1903
Mankowitz, W. *The Portland Vase and the Wedgwood Copies.* 1952; *Wedgwood* 1953 (1967)
Meteyard, E. *The Life of Josiah Wedgwood.* 2 vols. 1865; *The Younger Wedgwoods (1795-1815).* 1871; *Wedgwood and his Works.* 1873; *Memorials of Wedgwood.* 1874; *Handbook of Wedgwood Ware.* 1875. Reprinted 1964; *Wedgwood's Catalogue of 1787.* 1877; *Choice Examples of Wedgwood.* 1879
Moore, M. H. *Wedgwood and his Imitators.* 1912
Rathbone, F. *Old Wedgwood.* 1893; *The Sanderson Collection of Old Wedgwood.* 1902; *The Wedgwood Museum at Etruria.* 1909
Savage, G. and Finer, A. *Selected Letters of Josiah Wedgwood I.* 1965
Smiles, S. *Josiah Wedgwood.* 1894
Warrillow, E. J. D. *History of Etruria.* 1953
Williamson, G. C. *The Wedgwood Imperial Russian Dinner Service.* 1909
Woods of Burslem
Falkner, F. *The Wood Family of Burslem.* 1912

AMERICAN PORCELAIN AND POTTERY
Barber, E. A. *The Pottery and Porcelain of the United States.* New York, 1901
Ramsey, J. *American Potters and Pottery.* New York, 1939
Watkins, L. W. *Early New England Potters and Their Wares.* Cambridge, Mass., 1950

CONTINENTAL PORCELAIN AND POTTERY
GENERAL
Bacci, M. *European Porcelain.* 1969
Charles, R. L. *Continental Porcelain of the Eighteenth Century.* 1963

Cushion, J. *Continental China Collecting for Amateurs.* 1970

Hagger, R. *The Concise Encyclopaedia of Continental Pottery and Porcelain.* London and New York, 1960

Honey, W. B. *A Dictionary of European Ceramic Art:* Vol. 1. Illustrated Historical Survey. 1949; Vol. 2. Dictionary of Factories. 1952

DUTCH POTTERY
Neurenburg, E. *Old Dutch Pottery and Tiles.* 1923

Rackham, B. *Early Netherland Maiolica.* 1926

FRENCH PORCELAIN AND POTTERY
Auscher, E. S. *French Porcelain.* 1905

Cushion, J. P. *A Pocket Book of French and Italian Ceramic Marks.* 1965

Dauterman, C. C. *Sèvres.* 1969

Erikson, S. *Sèvres Porcelain: The James A. de Rothschild Collection at Waddesdon Manor.* 1969

Garnier, E. *The Soft Paste Porcelain of Sèvres.* 1892

Giacomotti, J. *French Faience.* 1963

Honey, W. B. *French Porcelain of the Eighteenth Century.* 1960

Laking, G. F. *Sèvres Porcelain of Buckingham Palace and Windsor Castle.* 1907

Landais, H. *French Porcelain.* 1961

Lane, A. *French Faience.* 1948 (1969)

Savage, G. *Seventeenth and Eighteenth Century French Porcelain.* 1958 (1967)

Solon, M. L. E. *A History and Description of old French Faience.* 1903

GERMAN PORCELAIN AND POTTERY
Cushion, J. P. *A Pocket Book of German Ceramic Marks.* 1961

Ducret, S. *German Porcelain and Faience.* 1962

Hayward, J. F. *Vienna Porcelain of the du Pacquier Period.* 1952

Honey, W. B. *Dresden China.* 1934 (1954); *German Porcelain.* 1947

Hughes, G. M. *Meissen Porcelain Figures in the Collection of the Hon Mrs Ionides.* 1950

Savage, G. *Eighteenth-Century German Porcelain.* 1958

GREEK POTTERY
Lane, A. *Greek Pottery.* 1948 (1970)

ITALIAN PORCELAIN
Cushion, J. P. *A Pocket Book of French and Italian Ceramic Marks.* 1965

Lane, A. *Italian Porcelain.* 1954

Rackham, B. *Italian Maiolica.* 1952 (1964); *Islamic Pottery and Italian Maiolica.* 1959

Romano, E. *Capo-di-Monte Porcelain.* 1960

Solon, M. L. E. *A History and Description of Italian Maiolica.* 1901

Stazzi, F. *Italian Porcelain.* 1963 (1967)

ORIENTAL POTTERY AND PORCELAIN
Blacker, J. F. *Chats on Oriental China.* 1908

Bluett, E. E. *Ming and Ching Porcelains.* 1933

Brankston, A. *Early Ming Wares of Ching-te-Chen.* 1938

Donnelly, P. J. *Blanc de Chine.* 1969

du Boulay, A. *Chinese Porcelain.* 1963

Garner, H. *Oriental Blue and White.* 1964 (1970)

Gompertz, St G. M. *Chinese Celadon Wares*. 1958; *Korean Celadon and other Wares of the Koryŏ Period*. 1963; *Korean Pottery and Porcelain of the Yi Period*. 1969; *Celadon Wares*. 1969
Gray, B. *Early Chinese Pottery and Porcelain*. 1953
Gulland, W. G. *History of Chinese Porcelain*. 2 vols. 1918
Hetherington, A. L. *Chinese Ceramic Glazes*. 1937 (1948); *The Early Ceramic Wares of China*. 1922
Hobson, R. L. *Chinese Pottery and Porcelain*. 2 vols. 1915; *Wares of the Ming Dynasty*. 1923; *The Later Ceramic Wares of China*. 1925; *The Leonard Gow Collection of Chinese Porcelain*. 1931; *The Sir Percival David Collection of Chinese Pottery and Porcelain*. 1934
Hobson, R. L. and Hetherington, H. L. *The Art of the Chinese Potter*. 1923
Hodgson, W. *How to Identify Old Chinese Porcelain*. 1912
Honey, W. B. *The Ceramic Art of China and other Countries of the Far East*. 1945 (1954); *Corean Pottery*. 1947
Jenyns, S. *Later Chinese Porcelain*. 1952 (1966); *Ming Pottery and Porcelain*. 1953; *Japanese Porcelain*. 1965; *Japanese Pottery*. 1969
Jourdain, M. and Jenyns, S. *Chinese Export Art in the Eighteenth Century*. 1963 (1968)
Kem, C. and Gompertz, G. St G. M. *The Ceramic Art of Korea*. 1961
Lloyd-Hyde, J. A. *Chinese Porcelain for the European Market*. 1946 (1957)
Metcalf, C. J. B. *Introduction to Chinese Pottery and Porcelain*. 1955
Miller, R. A. *Japanese Ceramics*. Tokyo, 1960
Monkhouse, C. *A History and Description of Chinese Porcelain*. 1902
Mudge, J. M. *Chinese Export Porcelain for the American Trade, 1735-1835*. New York, 1962
Phillips, J. G. *China-Trade Porcelain*. 1956
Prodan, M. *The Art of the T'ang Potter*. 1960
Sayer, G. R. *The Potteries of China*. 1949
Spinks, C. N. *The Ceramic Wares of Siam*. Bangkok, 1965
Sullivan, M. *Chinese Ceramics, Bronzes and Jades in the Collection of Sir Alan and Lady Barlow*. 1963
Willetts, W. *Foundations of Chinese Art*. 1965
Williamson, G. C. *The Book of Famille Rose*. 1927

POSTERS
Abdy, J. *The French Poster from Chéret to Capiello*. 1969

PRINTS—see also *Japanese Prints*
Adheman, J. *Graphic Art of the Eighteenth Century*. New York, 1964
Bedford, J. *Victorian Prints*. 1969
Cardus, N. and Arlott, J. *The Noblest Game*. 1969
Clark, H. G. *Baxter Colour Prints: Their History and Production*. 1919; *The Centenary Baxter Book*. 1936
Cliffe, H. *Lithography*. New York, 1965
Crookshank, C. de W. *Prints of British Military Operations, 1066-1868*. 1921
Falk, B. *Thomas Rowlandson: His Life and Art*. 1949
George, M. D. *Hogarth to Cruikshank: Social Change in Graphic Satire*. 1967 (1968)
Gray, B. *The English Print*. 1937
Hayden, A. *Chats on Old Prints*. 1900 (1928)
Hayter, S. *About Prints*. 1962
Hill, D. *McGillray, the Caricaturist*. 1965
Keble Chatterton, E. *Old Ship Prints*. 1927 (1967)

Lewis, C. T. *George Baxter: His Life and Work*. 1908; *The Le Blond Book*. 1920; *The Picture Printer of the Nineteenth Century—George Baxter*. 1924; *The Story of Picture Printing in England*. 1928
Linssen, F. F. *The Appreciation of Old Engravings and Etchings*. 1957
Linton, W. J. *The Masters of Wood Engraving*. 1889
Lister, R. *Samuel Palmer and His Etchings*. 1969
Mayor, A. H. *Guide to the Print Collection, Metropolitan Museum of Art*. New York, 1964
McLean, R. *George Cruickshank*. 1948
Neville, R. *British Military Prints*. 1909
Prideaux, S. T. *Aquatint Engraving*. 1909 (1968)
Sarzano, F. *Sir John Tenniel*. 1948
Stone, R. *Wood Engravings of Thomas Bewick*. 1953
Thomber, H. *James Gillray*. 1891
Tromp, E. *Gustave Doré*. 1932
Weber, W. *The History of Lithography*. 1966
Wechsler, H. J. *Great Prints and Printmakers*. 1967
Wedmore, F. *Fine Prints* (Contains a good bibliography of earlier books on prints.) 1897
Weekley, M. *Thomas Bewick*. 1953
Wilder, F. L. *How to Identify Old Prints*. 1969
Wolf, E. C. J. *Rowlandson and his Illustrations of Eighteenth-Century English Literature*. 1945
Wright, J. B. *Engraving and Etching*. 1952
Zigrosser, C. and Gaehde, C. M. *A Guide to the Collecting and Care of Original Prints*. New York, 1965. London, 1966

PRISONERS-OF-WAR WORK
Toller, J. *Prisoners-of-War Work, 1756-1815*. (Includes work in straw, wood, paper, horn, thread-lace, hair, etc.) 1965

THE REPAIR OF AND RESTORATION OF ANTIQUES
Doerner, M. *The Materials of the Artist*. London and New York, 1949
Gunn, M. J. *Print Restoration and Picture Cleaning*. 1911
Johnson, A. *How to Repair and Dress Old Dolls*. 1967
Laurie, A. P. *Pigments and Mediums of the Old Masters*. 1914
Lister, J. *Antique Firearms: Their Care, Repair and Restoration*. 1963
Lucas, A. *Antiques, Their Restoration and Preservation*. 1932
Mills, J. F. *The Care of Antiques*. London and New York, 1964
Parsons, C. S. M. and Curl, F. H. *China Mending and Restoration*. 1963
Plenderleith, H. J. *The Conservation of Prints and Drawings*. 1937; *The Conservation of Antiquities and Works of Art*. 1956; *The Preservation of Leather Bookbindings*. 1946 (1957)
Rosimer, J. J. *Ultra-Violet Rays and their Use in the Examination of Works of Art*. New York, 1931
Ruhemann, H. *The Cleaning of Paintings*. 1968
Savage, G. *The Art and Antique Restorers' Handbook*. 1954

RUGS—see *Carpets*

SAMPLERS
Ashton, L. *Samplers*. 1926
Christie, A. *Samplers and Stitches*. 1920

Colby, A. *Samplers.* 1964
Huish, M. B. *Samplers and Tapestry Embroideries.* 1900
Jones, M. E. *British Samplers.* Oxford, 1948
King, D. *Samplers.* 1960
Oddy, R. *Samplers in Guildford Museum.* 1951
Payne, F. G. *Guide to the Collection of Samplers and Embroideries of the National Museum of Wales,* 1939
Trendall, P. G. *Catalogue of Samplers in the Victoria and Albert Museum.* 1922

SCENT BOTTLES
Foster, K. *Scent Bottles.* 1965

SCIENTIFIC INSTRUMENTS
Michel, H. *Scientific Instruments in Art and History.* 1966; English translation 1967. This survey (see review on p. 114) contains a bibliography and references to sources of information.

SCULPTURE
Ashton, L. *An Introduction to the Study of Chinese Sculpture.* 1924
Basche, H. and Lohse, B. (Eds.) *Gothic Sculpture.* 1963
Chancellor, E. B. *The Lives of the British Sculptors.* 1911
Cheney, S. *Sculpture of the World: A History.* 1968
Esdaile, K. A. *English Monumental Sculpture since the Renaissance.* 1927
Gunnis, L. *Dictionary of British Sculptors, 1660-1857.* 1953
Pope-Hennessy, J. *Essays on Italian Sculpture.* 1968
Wingert, P. A. *Sculpture in Negro Africa.* New York, 1950

SHEFFIELD PLATE
Bradbury, F. *Old Sheffield Plate Makers' Marks, 1740-1860.* 1932; *History of Old Sheffield Plate.* Sheffield, 1912 (1968)
Hayden, A. *Chats on Old Sheffield Plate.* 1908
Robertson, R. A. *Old Sheffield Plate.* 1957
Veitch, H. M. *Sheffield Plate, its history, etc.* 1908
Watson, B. *Old Silver Platers and their Marks.* 1908
Wenham, E. *Old Sheffield Plate.* 1955
Wyler, S. B. *The Book of Sheffield Plate. New York,* 1949
Wylie, B. *History of Sheffield Plate.* 1913

SHELLS
Dance, S. P. *Rare Shells.* 1969

SILHOUETTES
Bolton, E. S. *Wax Portraits and Silhouettes.* 1914
Coke, D. *The Art of Silhouette.* 1913 (1928)
Edouart, A. *A Treatise on Silhouette Likenesses.* 1835
Hickman, P. *Silhouettes.* 1968
Jackson, E. Nevill. *Ancestors in Silhouette cut by August Edouart.* 1921; *The History of Silhouettes.* 1911; *Silhouette: Notes and Dictionary.* 1938
Lister, R. *The British Miniature.* 1951
Mayne, A. *British Profile Miniaturists.* 1970
Morgan, L. M. *A Master of Silhouette.* 1938
Woodiwiss, J. *British Silhouettes.* 1966

SILK PICTURES

Baker, W. S. Le Van. *The Silk Pictures of Thomas Stevens*. New York, 1957
Sprake, A. and Darby, M. *Stevengraphs*. Guernsey, 1968

SILVER—AMERICAN AND CANADIAN

Avery, C. L. *Early American Silver*. New York, 1930
Bigelow, F. H. *Historic Silver of the Colonies*. 1950
Buhler, K. C. *American Silver*. Cleveland, Ohio, 1950
Jones, E. A. *Old Silver of Europe and America*. 1928
Langdon, J. E. *Canadian Silversmiths, 1700-1900*. Lunenburg, Vermont, 1967; *Guide to the Marks on Early Canadian Silver*. 1969
Phillips, J. M. *American Silver*. London, New York and Toronto. 1949

SILVER—BRITISH

Ash, D. *How to Identify English Silver Drinking Vessels, 600-1830*. 1963; *Dutch Silver*. 1965
Banister, J. *An Introduction to Old English Silver*. 1965; *English Silver*. 1969
Bligh, J. *Discovering Hallmarks on British Silver*. 1968
Bradbury, F. *Guide to Marks of Origin on British and Irish Silver Plate*. Sheffield, 1860; Latest edtn. 1968
Brunner, H. *Old Table Silver for Collectors and Amateurs*. 1967
Came, R. *Silver*. 1961
Chaffers, W. *Handbook to Hallmarks on Gold and Silver Plate*. Ninth Edition, 1966
Cripps, W. J. *Old English Plate*. 1879; Reprinted 1967
Curran, M. *Collecting English Silver*. 1963
Delieb, E. *Bibliography of Hallmarking*. 1965; *Investing in Silver*. 1967; *Silver Boxes,* 1968
Dixon, S. C. *Antique English Silver Trays and Tazze*. 1964
Ellenbogen, E. *English Vinaigrettes*. Cambridge, 1956
Finlay, I. *Scottish Gold and Silver Work*. 1956
Gask, N. *The Old Silver Spoons of England*. 1926
Hayward, J. F. *Huguenot Silver in England, 1688-1727*. 1959 (1964)
Heal, A. *The London Goldsmiths (1200-1800)*. 1935
Henderson, J. *Silver Collecting for Amateurs*. 1965
How, G. E. P. and J. P. *English and Scottish Silver Spoons*. 3 vols. 1952-7
Hughes, G. B. *Small Antique Silverware*. 1957
Hughes, G. B. and T. *Three Centuries of English Domestic Silver, 1500-1820*. 1952
Jackson, C. J. *English Goldsmiths and their Marks*. 1905 (1967); *An Illustrated History of English Plate*. 2 vols. 1911 (1968)
Miles, E. B. *Antique English Pocket Silver Nutmeg Graters*. 1967
Oman, C. C. *English Domestic Silver*. (Now in seventh edition.) 1968; *English Silversmiths Work*. 1965
Penzer, N. M. *Paul Storr, The Last of the Goldsmiths (1771-1844)*. 1954
Phillips, P. A. S. *Paul de Lamerie, Silversmith of London, 1688-1757*. 1935 (1968)
Prideaux, W. S. *Memorials of the Goldsmiths' Company, 1335-1815*. 2 vols. 1896-7
Ramsey, L. G. G. (ed.) *Antique English Silver and Plate*. 1962
Ridgway, M. H. *Chester Goldsmiths from Early Times to 1726*. 1969
Rowe, R. *Adam Silver*. 1965
Rupert, C. G. *Apostle Spoons*. 1929

Shure, D. S. *Hester Bateman*. 1959
Stone, J. *English Silver of the Eighteenth Century*. 1965
Taylor, G. *Silver: An Illustrated Introduction*. 1956 (1965)
Wardle, P. *Victorian Silver and Silver Plate*. 1963
Watts, W. W. *Old English Silver*. 1924
Wenham, E. *Domestic Silver of Great Britain and Ireland*. 1931; *Old Silver*. 1964
Wyler, S. B. *The Book of Old Silver*. New York, 1949

SILVER—EUROPEAN
Andron, E. *Introduction to Swedish Silver*. 1968
Davis, F. *French Silver, 1450-1825*. 1969
Fredericks, J. W. *Antique Dutch Silver*. 4 vols. 1965
Jones, E. A. *Old Silver of Europe and America*. 1928
Kieland, T. *Norwegian Goldwork: Middle Ages*. 1926
Oman, C. C. *The Golden Age of Hispanic Silver, 1400-1665*. 1969

SILVER—ORIENTAL
Coombes, K. *Paktong*. 1969
(Chinese silver-like alloy used about 1730-60)
Roth, L. *Oriental Silverwork, Chinese and Malay*. 1968

SNUFF BOTTLES AND BOXES
Curtis, M. M. *The Book of Snuff and Snuff Boxes*. 1935
Le Corbeiller, C. *European and American Snuff Boxes, 1730-1830*. 1966
MacCausland, H. *Snuff and Snuff Boxes*. 1951
Norton, R. and M. *A History of Gold Snuff Boxes*. 1935
Perry, L. S. *Chinese Snuff Bottles*. 1954 (1960)

SPURS
James, J. *The Book of Spurs*. 1858
Lacy, C. *The History of the Spur*. 1911

STEVENGRAPHS—see *Silk Pictures*

SWORDS—see *Edged Weapons*

TABLEWARE
Bailey, C. T. P. *Knives and Forks*. 1927
Price, H. *Old Base Metal Spoons*. 1908

TAPESTRY
Thomson, W. G. *A History of Tapestry*. 1930
Wace, A. *The Marlborough Tapestries at Blenheim Palace*. 1968
Weigert, R. *French Tapestry*. 1956

TEXTILES
Volbach, W. F. *Early Decorative Textiles*. 1969

TOYS—see also *Model Soldiers*
Daikin, L. *Children's Toys Throughout the Ages*. 1953 (1963)
Frazer, A. *A History of Toys*. 1966
Gordon, L. *Peepshow into Paradise, A History of Children's Toys*. 1953
Gröber, K. *Children's Toys of Bygone Days*. 1928

Holme, G. *Children's Toys of Yesterday.* 1932
Jackson, N. *Toys of Other Days.* 1908
Speaight, G. *A History of the English Toy Theatre.* 1946 (1969)

TRADESMEN'S CARDS
Heal, A. *London Tradesmen's Cards of the Eighteenth Century.* 1925

TREEN
Gould, M. E. *Early American Wooden Ware.* Springfield, Mass., 1942; *Household Life in America, 1620-1850.* Rutland, Vermont, 1965
Pinto, E. H. *Treen, or Small Woodware through the Ages.* 1949; *Encyclopaedia and Social History of Treen and other Wooden Bygones.* 1969
Thomas, O. E. *Domestic Utensils of Wood.* 1932

TRUNCHEONS
Clark, E. F. *Truncheons, Their Romance and Reality.* 1935
Dicken, E. R. H. *Truncheons, Their History.* North Devon, 1952

UNIFORMS—see also *Costume*
Barnes, R. M. *History of Regiments and Uniforms of the British Army.* 1957; *Military Uniforms of Britain and the Empire.* 1960
Blakeslee, F. *Uniforms of the World.* New York, 1929
Carman, W. Y. *British Military Uniforms from Contemporary Pictures.* 1957 (1968); *Indian Army Uniforms.* 1961 (1968)
Coggins, J. *Arms and Equipment of the Civil War.* New York, 1962
Hyatt, S. *Uniforms and Insignia of the Third Reich.* U.S.A., 1962
Islam, D. *Ranks and Uniforms of the German Army, Navy and Air Force.* 1939
Lawson, C. P. *History of Uniforms of the British Army.* 5 vols. 1940-67
Luard, J. *History of the Dress of the British Soldier.* 1852
Macdonald, R. J. *History of the Dress of the Royal Regiment of Artillery, 1625-1897.* 1899
Martin, P. *European Military Uniforms.* 1963 (1968)
Molls, J. *Uniforms of the Royal Navy during the Napoleonic Wars.* 1965
Smitherman, P. H. *Cavalry Uniforms of the British Army.* 1962; *Uniforms of the Scottish Regiments.* 1962; *Infantry Uniforms of the British Army.* 1965; *Uniforms of the Yeomanry Regiments.* 1967
Thorburn, W. A. *French Army Regiments and Uniforms.* 1969

VALENTINES
Lee, R. W. *A History of Valentines.* 1953
Staff, S. *The Valentine and its Origins.* 1969

VICTORIANA
Laver, J. *Victoriana.* 1966
Peter, M. *Collecting Victoriana.* 1965
Spellman, D. and S. *Victorian Music Covers.* 1969
Toller, J. *Regency and Victorian Crafts.* 1969
Vres, L.de. *Victorian Advertisements.* 1968
Wood, V. *Victoriana: A Collector's Guide.* 1960 (1968)
Woodhouse, C. P. *Victoriana Collectors Handbook.* 1970
The Official Catalogue of the Great Exhibition. 1851 (1970)

VIOLINS
Hamma, F. *German Violin Makers*. 1961
Haweis, H. R. *Old Violins and Violin Lore*. 1898
Jalovec, K. *Italian Violin Makers*. 1957 (1964); *Beautiful Italian Violins*. 1962; *German and Austrian Violin Makers*. 1967; *Encyclopaedia of Violin Makers*. 1968
Mason-Clarke, A. *The Violin and Old Violin Makers*. n.d.
Morris, W. M. *British Violin Makers*. 1920
Sandys, W. and Forster, S. A. *The History of the Violin*. 1864
Stainer, C. *A Dictionary of Violin Makers*. 1896

WAX PRINT PORTRAITS
Bolton, E. S. *Wax Portraits and Silhouettes*. 1914

WEAPONS—see *Arms and Armour, Edged Weapons, Firearms*

WINE LABELS
Cropper, P. J. *Bottle Labels*. 1924
Penzer, N. M. *Book of the Wine Label*. 1947
Whitworth, E. W. *Wine Labels*. 1966

———

MUSEUM BOOKS AND PAMPHLETS

Museum catalogues, books and pamphlets, particularly those that are illustrated, can be of great help to collectors. A selection is listed below. Normally they can be obtained from museum curators whose addresses are given on pp 80-102. Victoria and Albert Museum (V & A) pamphlets, which are published by Her Majesty's Stationery Office, can be bought from Government bookshops where a complete list (Section List No 55) can be obtained. Prices in brackets include postage.

ARMS AND ARMOUR
Arms and Armour in Tudor and Stuart London. London Museum Catalogue. 7s 6d (8s) (approx.)
Hayward, J. *European Armour*. Illustrated. V & A. 7s 6d (8s); *Swords and Daggers*. V & A. 5s (5s 4d)
Robinson, B. W. *Arms and Armour of Old Japan*. Illustrated. V & A. **3s 6d** (3s 10d)
European Armour in the Tower of London. 70s (74s 6d)

CLOCKS AND WATCHES
Hayward, J. F. *English Watches*. V & A. 12s 6d
Peate, I. C. *Clock and Watchmakers in Wales*. National Museum of Wales, Cardiff. 6s (7s 6d)

COSTUME
A Brief Guide to the Costume Court. V. & A. 6d (10d)
Synopsis of Nineteenth-Century Women's Costume. A card showing 21 draw-
ings. V. & A. 6d (10d)
Payne, F. G. *Welsh Peasant Costume.* National Museum of Wales, Cardiff.
2s (2s 6d)

DOLLS AND TOYS
Dolls. V & A small picture book. 3s (3s 4d)
Dolls in the Worthing Museum Collection. Illustrated. Introduction by Mary
Hillier. 3s 6d (4s)
Dolls Houses. V & A small picture book. 2s 6d (2s 10d)
Toys. V & A small picture book. 2s 6d (2s 10d)

DRAWINGS
English Drawings in the Ashmolean Museum, Oxford. Illustrated. 2s 6d
(2s 11d)

EMBROIDERY
*Illustrated Catalogue of English Samplers and Embroideries at the Georgian
House.* City Art Gallery, Bristol. 6d (11d)
Flowers in English Embroidery. V & A small picture book. 4s (4s 6d)
King, D. *Samplers.* V & A large picture book. 12s 6d (13s 4d)
Wade, N. W. *Basic Stitches in Embroidery.* V & A. 2s 6d (2s 10d)

FIREARMS
Russell, G. *An Introduction to the History of Firearms.* Rothesay Museum,
Bournemouth. 2s 6d (2s 11d)

FOLK LIFE
Welsh Folk Museum. St Fagan's Castle, Cardiff. 1s (1s 6d)

FURNITURE
A Short History of English Furniture. V & A large picture book. Bound 25s
(27s 6d). Paper 17s 6d (18s 6d)
Chests of Drawers and Commodes. V & A. Illustrated. 3s (3s 6d)
Victorian Furniture. V & A small picture book. 4s (4s 6d)
Edwards, R. *English Chairs.* V & A large picture book. (Reprinting)
Hayward, J. F. *English Cabinets. Illustrated.* V & A. 5s (5s 6d)
Hayward, J. F. *English Desks and Bureaux.* V & A large picture book.
12s 6d (13s 2d)
Hayward, J. F. *Tables.* Illustrated. V & A. 5s 6d (6s 1d)

GLASS
English Glass. V & A large picture book. 10s 6d (11s 2d)
Glass Tableware. V & A small picture book. 2s 6d (2s 10d)
Bohemian Glass. V & A large picture book. 7s 6d (8s)

HATS
Luton and the Hat Industry. Luton Museum. 3s 6d (4s)

LACE
Pillow Lace in the East Midlands. Luton Museum. 4s 6d (5s)

MINIATURES
Portrait Miniatures. V & A small picture book. 2s 6d (2s 11d)

MUSICAL INSTRUMENTS
Catalogue of Musical Instruments. V & A. Vol 1, *Keyboard Instruments.*
40s (41s 6d). Vol 2, *Non-keyboard Instruments.* 50s (54s 6d)
Early Keyboard Instruments. V & A small picture book. 3s (3s 4d)

PEWTER
Blair, C. V & A small picture book. 2s 6d (2s 10d)

PORCELAIN
Chinese Porcelain of the Ch'ing Dynasty. V & A small picture book. 3s
(3s 5d)
Porcelain Figures. V & A small picture book. 5s (5s 6d)
One Hundred and Eleven Coffee Cups with 16 plates to illustrate 96
examples. Harris Museum and Art Gallery, Preston. 1s 6d, post free
The R. H. Smith Collection of English Porcelain. Illustrated. Harris Museum
and Art Gallery, Preston. 1s 6d post free

POTTERY
American Studio Pottery. V. & A. 8s 6d (9s 2d)
Cream Coloured Earthenware. V & A small picture book. 2s 6d (2s 11d)
Le Vine, J. R. A. *Linthorpe Pottery.* Tees-side Museums and Art Galleries
Service, Dorman Museum, Middlesbrough. 5s (5s 6d)
Guide to the Collection of English Lustre Ware. Stoke-on-Trent Museum and
Art Gallery. 1s (1s 4d)
The N. Teulon-Porter Collection of Mocha Ware. Stoke-on-Trent Museum
and Art Gallery. 1s (1s 4d)
The Potteries of Sunderland and District. Sunderland Museum and Art Gal-
lery. 5s (5s 6d)
Rhymes and Mottoes on Sunderland Pottery. Sunderland Museum and Art
Gallery. 2s (2s 6d)
Wedgwood. V & A small picture book. 4s 6d (5s)

PRINTS
Handbook to the Department of Prints, Drawings and Paintings. V & A. 3s
6d (4s)

SILVER AND SHEFFIELD PLATE
There are many V & A small picture books on silver and Sheffield plate.
They are listed here with their numbers.

Sheffield Plate	No 39	3s	(3s 4d)
English Medieval Silver	No 27	2s	(2s 4d)
Early Stuart Silver	No 24	2s	(2s 4d)
Charles II Domestic Silver	No 17	3s	(3s 4d)
Queen Anne Domestic Silver	No 25	2s	(2s 4d)
Mid-Georgian Domestic Silver	No 28	4s	(4s 6d)
Adam Silver	No 35	2s 6d	(2s 10d)
Regency Domestic Silver	No 33	2s	(2s 4d)
Irish Silver	No 46	2s 6d	(2s 10d)
Scandinavian Silver	No 47	2s 6d	(2s 10d)
Golden Age of Dutch Silver	No 29	2s	(2s 4d)
French Domestic Silver	No 52	2s 6d	(2s 10d)
German and Swiss Domestic Silver of the Gothic *Period.* By C. C. Oman	No 55	2s 6d	(2s 10d)

German Domestic Silver of the Eighteenth Century No 58   3s 6d (4s)
German Domestic Silver (1618-1700)   No 64   3s 6d (3s 10d)
Norwich Castle Museum issues a booklet on *Norwich Silver, 1565-1706*. 5s (5s 6d)

TUNBRIDGE WARE
A duplicated sheet describing how Tunbridge Ware was made and giving a list of makers may be obtained by sending a stamped and addressed envelope to The Curator, Tunbridge Wells Museum, Civic Centre, Tunbridge Wells.

SOME RECENT BOOKS

The most attractive books on antiques, whether for the amateur or for the specialist collector, are those which contain a relatively large number of new and good illustrations, preferably from private collections rather than well-known museums. This poses a real problem for any publisher. Inevitably illustrations put up the price, especially if an attempt is made to place them adjacent to the relevant text. A valuable reference book can carry a high price which specialist dealers and collectors will pay, but a general book on antiques must attract the amateur in both presentation and price. The problem has been solved in *English Antiques*, compiled and edited by G. E. Speck and E. Sutherland (Ward Lock, 1969, 50s), which contains over 280 clear illustrations of ceramics, silver, glass, firearms, furniture, clocks, pewter, jewellery, maps and so on. This struck me as a fantastic achievement for the price, until I realised that the book is really a digest of material already published in Ward Lock's 'Creative Leisure' series and 'Collectors Monographs', both text and illustrations. Nevertheless, unless one has previously acquired these books, *English Antiques* is wonderful value for money.

BOOK COLLECTING
A History of Book Illustration: David Bland, Faber & Faber, 1969. £10
This scholarly work, first published in 1958, deals with the whole history of book illustration from the earliest illustrated manuscripts to illustrations of the 1950s. This new edition consists of a revision of the earlier text with additional material at the end of the book dealing with the work of such artists as Rex Whistler, Anthony Gros, Lovat Fraser, Eric Ravilious and many American and European illustrators. The coverage is international and the illustrations copious and well produced. Great care has obviously been taken to ensure quality reproduction. The illustrations, of which there are

over 400, are presented in three ways; some appear within the text, others are grouped on art paper, and there are twenty-three in colour, printed on special sheets which are inserted in the relevant chapters. It is a fine book which no collector can afford to be without.

Nevertheless, there are many of modest means who will wish that the need to be comprehensive had not involved the exclusion of artists whose work is now creating interest, or the rather scanty reference to such illustrators as Arthur Rackham (who gets a six-line mention) and Beatrix Potter, whose work was also reproduced by the three-colour process. These are surely the most sought after of twentieth-century illustrators? The prolific photo-process work of Hugh Thomson is mentioned briefly and so are the wood engravings of Eric Gill and Robert Gittings. But many of the illustrators of the 1890s and later are not referred to at all—the Brocks, Chris Hammond, George Morrow, Charles and Heath Robinson and Ernest Sheperd, whose *Everybody's Boswell* (1930), though in the Hugh Thomson tradition, surely compares favourably with the work of W. A. Dwiggins, the American, who illustrated *Tartarin of Tarascon* in the same year. Do not, however, be deterred by these remarks from securing this admirable work which will greatly reward all who take the trouble to read it and will always remain a valuable book of reference.

BYGONES

The Farm Waggons of England and Wales by James Arnold, published in 1969 in a limited edition of 1,800 copies by John Baker, reminds us that the days of the working farm horse are virtually gone. Today the old waggons, triumphs of country craftsmanship involving the skills of wheelwright, carpenter and blacksmith, lie decaying in yard and barn. A few have been retrieved and restored and have taken their place with other bygones in the folk museums. This book, which deals with twenty-four representative types—for they differed in construction from county to county—is the result of twenty-five years of study. There is a substantial introduction which describes their construction, followed by beautifully drawn coloured plates. Unfortunately, the descriptive text does not face them: in each case it follows on the succeeding page so that there must be a continual turning to and fro as one studies the book. One can only assume that this is intended, to ensure that when the book becomes a 'breaker' the relevant text will not be separated from its plate. There can surely be no other explanation for so inept a layout. One hopes the plates will not end up in frames because this is a beautiful book which will become a classic in its field.

CERAMICS

A Collector's History of English Pottery: Griselda Lewes, Studio Vista, 1969. 84s

This is another 'comprehensive' book in the sense that it sets out to cover the history of English pottery from the Stone Age to the 1960s. However, by the time you reach page 27 you are already well into the eighteenth century and you do not leave the nineteenth century until you turn page 191. So the bulk of the book is certainly of interest to the collector of antique earthenware. It has 372 clear illustrations, a few in colour, many of them taken from pieces in private collections or provincial museums. There is no impression, when turning the pages, that you have seen the illustrations before, except perhaps for the grinning face on the jug by Wallace Martin which leers from the page to tell you that once again his portrait has been chosen from the V and A. The choice of Victorian portrait figures is particularly good and shows a wide range. There are a few minor errors here and there. The captions to plates 273 and 274 on page 146 have unfortunately been reversed and surely Dillwyn & Co of Swansea were not operating in 1820? The pottery was then being run by Bevington & Co. Plate 309 shows a 'relish or mustard pot' in pale blue earthenware with a two-colour transfer decoration. This could well be true but it is interesting to note that examples of this type of pot (the design was registered by F. and R. Pratt & Co) are occasionally found complete with the lid on which is clearly printed 'POTTED MEAT'. There is one in the Bignall Collection at the Hampshire County Museum Service Headquarters at Chilcomb House, Winchester.

Continental China: John Cushion, Frederick Muller, 1970. 25s
This book in the 'Collecting for Amateurs' series meets a real need. It is divided into three parts. The first part deals briefly with materials and techniques—the first use of hard-paste porcelain, the way in which groups and figures were moulded, the techniques which produced maiolica in Italy, faience in France and Delftware in Holland.
The second part covers the production of pottery in all the major centres in Europe, while part three deals with the main porcelain factories. Particularly valuable are the ceramic marks by which the wares of the various centres can be recognized. There are twenty-four illustrations and a useful index makes it possible to find information about factories, makers, modellers and decorators with ease. An excellent book which provides useful signposts for the beginner who does not want to start building up a battery of specialist reference books before he has found his way around.

Old Spode China: John Bedford, Cassell, 1969. 12s 6d
For every fifteen books that have been written about Josiah Wedgwood and his wares, only one has been written about Josiah Spode. There are at least eight Wedgwood clubs and societies in America: I have still to hear of a Spode society. Yet the introduction of bone china by Josiah Spode II at the end of the eighteenth century was a turning-point in the ceramics industry and in the years that followed the factory made not only fine porcelains but excellent earthenwares: the wares printed in underglaze blue have never been surpassed.
In 1925 Arthur Hayden's book on *Spode and his Successors* was published and in 1943 a book by S. B. Williams on *Antique Blue and White Spode*, which deals almost exclusively with earthenwares. A new book on Spode to celebrate the bi-centenary is now due. Meanwhile, Mr Bedford's little book, one of the 'Collectors Pieces' series, is very welcome. It is perhaps a pity that so much of the book should be devoted to ceramic history and to the life of Josiah Spode I before he started on his own as a potter, and so little space to a description of the actual wares illustrated, most of them V and A pieces. There are, however, some useful items of information in some of the captions. It is interesting to know, for example, that the 'Lucano' pattern was taken from an aquatint of 1798, though surely more detail could have been provided? The accepted names of some of the other patterns illustrated such as the 'Filigree' pattern on p 24 and the 'Bird and Grasshopper' pattern on p 29 might also have been given.

An Illustrated Guide to Worcester Porcelain: Henry Sandon, Herbert Jenkins, 1969. 84s
This comes near to being the definitive work on the subject. It is written

Page 149 : Louis Quinze-style serpentine-front kingwood vitrine, richly mounted in ormolu, the *bombé* lower section with Vernes-Martin panels; the doors with lovers in a landscape, and landscapes to the sides. Sold at Retford, Nottinghamshire, in January 1970 for £250

Page 150: (left) Silver asparagus servers by George Smith, London, c 1780-90, 10¼ in, recently given by the 'Friends of the National Museum of Wales' to the Museum; (right) eighteenth-century silver race ticket of oval form issued for the Doncaster Course, the ground engraved with symbols of sport. Sold at Retford, Nottinghamshire, in December 1969 for £410

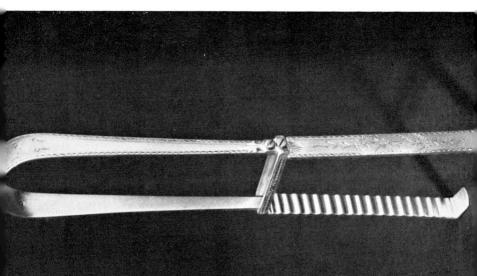

by the Curator of the Dyson Perrin's Museum at the Worcester Works and has a new range of 150 illustrations. Its value is based on the fact that Mr Sandon, helped by a number of enthusiasts, excavated part of the site of the original Worcester factory and discovered thousands of discarded factory 'wasters' which have made it possible to revise the attributions of many pieces of porcelain formerly thought to have been produced at the Caughley factory or elsewhere. Scientific evidence has replaced 'aesthetic reasoning', as the work of earlier so-called experts has been delicately described. Perhaps the fact that it is now known that the well known 'Fisherman' pattern, always attributed to Caughley, was also used by the Worcester Factory will cause people to beware of attributions based solely on printed decoration. Having studied this excellent and valuable book, it was a great disappointment to read Mr Sandon's other book *British Pottery and Porcelain for Pleasure and Investment:* John Gifford Ltd, 1969. 21s. This is well illustrated with ninety-nine plates in black and white and another sixteen in colour, but gives the impression that it was written in a hurry, lacked final revision and also careful proof-reading. How else could some of the sentences and errors have escaped notice? 'The impressed word "Salopian" is also rarely found impressed', starts one sentence which has to be read several times before the real meaning emerges. And on another page we are told that 'Willaim Ball' of Liverpool, produced 'polycrome prints'. Nevertheless, if you can bear such irritations, the book is good value for money.

DOMESTIC CRAFTS
Regency and Victorian Crafts: Jane Toller, Ward Lock, 1969. 30s

The sub-title of this book gives it a period atmosphere which the real title lacks. In a sense 'The Genteel Female—Her Arts and Pursuits' is more descriptive. It makes one think of embroidery and beadwork, of pictures made of shells or sand or seaweed, of cut paper flowers, feather tippets and felt-work pictures, of woolwork and wax flowers. I know of no other book which brings together so much useful information about these dusty productions of our great-great-grandmothers. Perhaps that is why so many people react against them : they have been in the attic or shed so long that they are damp and soiled. Perhaps they are worth bringing out and cleaning up, for those that have been preserved in pristine condition by houseproud ladies or have found their way before dissolution into museum galleries have a certain period charm. Occasionally, especially in the field of embroidery, the work displays real artistry. The author of this book tells us that instructions on shell-work, paper-work, and feather-work are finding their way into today's women's magazines. One can understand that these crafts have an antiquarian interest but has the reaction against mass production gone so far? Though, come to think of it, the competitions held by Women's Institutes today on 'what to do with a detergent bottle' or 'landscape gardening on a plate' hardly measure up to Victorian standards and the entries are (we hope) even more ephemeral.

FIREARMS AND EDGED WEAPONS

Two books on firearms come from G. Bell & Sons—*Game Guns and Rifles:* Richard Akehurst, 1969, 50s, and *Antique Weapons A-Z:* Douglas J. Fryer, 1969, 50s.

Mr Akehurst's book, which has the sub-title 'From Percussion to Hammerless Ejector in Britain', and covers the period from about 1830 to 1900, is a serious study of the subject for those who have a specialist interest either as

K

collectors or shooters. There is much technical information, especially on firing mechanisms, with some valuable diagrams to show how they operate. There are over fifty black and white illustrations, including some charming old wood engravings showing barrel welding and the proofing of barrels in the 1850s. The eighty-nine plates, well produced on art paper, show guns by such famous makers as John Manton, James Purdey, Charles Lancaster, W. & J. Rigby, John Dickson, J. Woodward and Westley Richards, including examples in labelled cases. Collectors will particularly value this book for the last chapter on 'Gunmakers of the Period' which contains historical notes, dates and addresses and other information not readily available elsewhere.

Antique Weapons A-Z covers a wider field. There are five main sections —Firearms and Accessories, European Swords and Daggers, Sundry Weapons (Polearms, Maces, Crossbows and Flails), Eastern and Native Weapons, and Japanese Weapons. Each section consists of a glossary of terms followed by a series of photographs. In all there are 425 illustrations. The book ends with a good bibliography.

Antique Weapons: Richard Akehurst, John Gifford. 21s
   This covers much of the same ground as *Antique Weapons A-Z*, with pictures not only of weapons but also reproductions of old prints showing the weapons in use. These include elephant hunting in the days of the muzzle-loader; a horseman, using a heavy-calibre revolver, riding down a buffalo; and Miss Annie Oakley of Buffalo Bill's Wild West Show, the peerless lady wing-shot, with her Winchester repeating rifle. This is a colourful and readable book which clothes much valuable factual information in a mantle of history.

FURNITURE
Cabinet Makers and Furniture Designers: Hugh Honour, Weidenfeld & Nicholson, 1969. £5 5s
   This book deals with fifty of the most notable and influential cabinet-makers and designers of the last four hundred years, covering the whole of Europe and America. The author starts in the sixteenth century with Jacques Andromet de Cerceau and ends in the twentieth century with the American, Charles Eames. It is not surprising to find that most of the names are from the eighteenth century and early nineteenth century. Four to eight pages are devoted to each 'name' and these include illustrations, sometimes in colour. The treatment is well balanced. In each case the work of the designer or craftsman is placed in historical perspective so that one can understand the influences that played upon him. Then follows a brief biography which begins with his birth and early training, expands upon his developing skills and indicates the influence that he, in turn, has had on those who trained under him. This treatment gives the book a real sense of continuity despite the fact that it consists of fifty self-contained essays. The Parisian *ébénistes* of the eighteenth century emerge as a family network rather than as isolated individuals. Early in the nineteenth century the noted New York cabinet maker, Duncan Phyfe, is seen to climb the social and professional ladder, much as a doctor might move to Harley Street, starting in the main cabinet-making centre of Broad Street and moving on to develop the elegant showrooms and workshops of a fashionable designer in Partition Street. We learn how, late in the nineteenth century, the Belgian painter and art nouveau designer, Henry Van de Velde, was influenced by the people

he met when he moved from Antwerp to Paris—Monet, Whistler, Pissaro, Debussy and Verlaine. This is a book not only for the lover of old furniture but for all who have a sense of history and who visit museums and historic houses to see the work of early craftsmen.

LACQUER
Chinese and Japanese Lacquer: John Bedford, Cassell, 1969. 12s 6d
This most useful little book on a highly specialized subject explains what lacquer is, the techniques involved, and the methods of decoration—carving, painting, inlay with gold, shell or silver foil, and so on. It describes the kind of articles which are usually made with lacquer, paying particular attention to inro which were used in Japan for carrying medicines and personal trivia. A brief concluding section deals with the 'Lacquer Masters,' some of whom became as famous as carvers of netsuke. A page is devoted to artists' signatures on Japanese lacquer.

MILITARIA
Militaria: Frederick Wilkinson, Ward Lock, 1969. 35s
An increasing number of people are interesting themselves in military history and collecting militaria—a word used not only for the objects used by the soldier but for anything connected with the armed services. This book deals with prints, medals, books, and miniatures. It also deals with uniforms together with the helmets, headdresses, belts, badges and buttons that go with them. There is a chapter on military weapons, though this is such a wide and specialized field that it can only touch briefly on the subject. As in the other books in this series for collectors, the emphasis is on good illustrations and there is a most valuable final section on reference books and collections of militaria.

PEWTER
British Pewter: Ronald F. Michaelis, Ward Lock, 1969. 25s
This is one of the 'Collectors Monograph' series written by one of the greatest of all experts on pewter who has been Honorary Librarian of the Pewter Society of Great Britain for some twenty years and a collector of pewter for nearly twice that period. It is well illustrated with examples, which include Scottish, Irish and Channel Island wares, chosen mainly from private collections. The text is crisp, concise and informative. It is exactly the kind of book a collector needs. The early history is dealt with briefly; much more space is devoted to practical details—touch marks, decoration, standards of quality, the care of old pewterware and the detection of fakes. The book has a very useful appendix on Britannia Metal.

PRINTS
How to Identify Old Prints: F. L. Wilder, Bell, 1969. £4
Mr Wilder started at Sotheby's in 1911 and the dust-wrapper blurb does not exaggerate when it states that 'the author's lifelong interest in the subject has enabled him to bring to this book an authority and experience unequalled in the art markets of the world'. For anyone who wants to understand prints and the processes of production, this book is what educationists would call 'required reading'. The various types of print—woodcut, line-engraving, etching, mezzotint, stipple and aquatint are all described in detail, including the work of well-known artists who used the various methods. There is much advice for the collector about paper and watermarks, platemarks, borderlines,

margins, inscriptions and reprints. Over a hundred plates and a number of line drawings illustrate this excellent work.

Victorian Prints: John Bedford, Cassell, 1969. 12s 6d

This little book deals with the kind of print which can still be found (with luck) in an old portfolio at an auction sale, a pile of prints in an antique shop or bookshop, or in an old book, fit only for 'breaking', bought at a jumble sale. On the other hand cleaned, mounted and framed, they some-times sell for considerable sums in shops where the dealer understands these things. It will also be of interest to those who like to collect books illustrated with old prints. The field is immense and the author has wisely been selec-tive. He deals in eight short chapters with landscape prints, often engraved after artists such as J. M. W. Turner, John Constable or Clarkson Stanfield; fashion prints by such artists as Anaïs Toudouze, the prints of birds and flowers which illustrated so many Victorian books on natural history and gardening: transport prints with scenes of road, rail or sea; music covers; and the painter-etchers and lithographers. The technical aspects have only been touched on. This book will certainly stimulate the interest of the amateur who will need to study the subject in depth before he can decide with certainty how a particular print was produced.

Maps and Prints for Pleasure and Investment: D. C. Gohm, John Gifford, 1969. 21s

This is a useful book for the new collector. It is mainly about prints and starts by dealing briefly with the various styles and methods of engraving and then gives many useful hints on paper, states, mounting, restoration, and on how one may identify fakes and reproductions. More than half the book consists of lists of engravers and map-makers. These bring together much information about the men and their work and include a catalogue of George Baxter's prints, though Abraham Le Blond, the most famous of his licensees, is omitted. However, a comprehensive list of engravers would fill a large volume in itself so the amateur need not be too discouraged if the engraver of his favourite print does not appear in Mr Gohm's book; let it encourage him to search larger dictionaries of artists and engravers.

POSTCARDS

The Comic Postcard in English Life: Frederick Alderson, David & Charles, 1970. 50s

The first postcard was posted in England in 1870 so 1970 was an appropri-ate year in which to publish a book on the more amusing picture-postcards, especially those of Edwardian days. These early colourful ephemera are now approaching the time when they will become 'antiques' in the strict trade sense of the word. It was the advent of the statutory Bank Holiday and the expansion of seaside resorts which provided the opportunity to open up a lucrative trade in comic postcards and many of them have a seaside or holiday theme. This book illustrates over 300 examples, some in colour, and its main interest lies in the way the selection illustrates the social history of the twentieth century. Indeed, one can almost date a postcard within a year or so by studying the costume, setting, style of humour, 'blueness' of joke, and the social attitude it reflects. This historical aspect has obviously been one of the main interests of the author, rather than the skill of the commercial artists who designed them. It is a pity that more space was not devoted to a discussion of the work of Donald McGill, Arnold Taylor and

Douglas Tempest, who had the advantage of colour when their *Punch* contemporaries had to work mainly in black and white. Incredibly, Louis Wain, some of whose comic drawings of dogs and cats were certainly on postcards, is not mentioned at all, though his name became a household word. Most of the examples shown in the book are of cards published by Bamforth & Company of Holmfirth, Yorkshire.

SILVER
Silver for Pleasure and Investment: Geoffrey Wills, John Gifford. 21s
This is another in the 'For Pleasure and Investment' series. What a pity it was not given its proper title: 'A Dictionary of Silver Articles', for this occupies more than three-quarters of the book. It is a useful book for reference but like the 'Directory of Huntingdonshire Cabmen' will need to be read in short bursts—Apple Corers to Coffee Pots, Dog Collars to Porringers, Quaiches to Stirrup Cups, and Sugar Tongs to Wine Labels. Anyway, that gives some idea of the scope of the book. The illustrations are first-rate and are chosen from pieces that have passed through the salerooms and could therefore have been acquired by anyone with a deep enough pocket.

A. W. COYSH

PERIODICALS

THE following may normally be obtained through booksellers or newsagents.

Antique Collector
Illustrated articles of interest to collectors. Published six times a year at 7s 6d. Annual subscription £2 5s. ($7·50 in Canada and the U.S.A.)
Offices: 16 Strutton Ground, Victoria Street, London, S.W.1.

Antique Dealer and Collector's Guide
Articles of special interest to collectors. Published monthly at 6s. Annual subscription £4 8s ($15.00 in Canada and the U.S.A.)
Subscription Dept., Berrow's House, Hylton Road, Worcester, England.

Antique Finder
Articles and many trade advertisements. Published monthly, exclusive to antique dealers, art dealers, auctioneers and allied and associated trades. Annual subscription £4 post free ($12·50 for Canada and the U.S.A.).
Offices: Antique Finder Ltd., 34-40 Ludgate Hill, London, E.C.4.

Apollo
An international magazine on the fine arts with informative articles, often including the results of recent research. Published monthly at 12s 6d. Annual subscription £7 10s. ($24·00 in Canada and the U.S.A.) Apollo Magazine Ltd., Bracken House, Cannon Street, London, E.C.4.

Art and Antiques Weekly
A newspaper with articles, auction reports, and a section on exhibitions and coming events. Published weekly at 2s. Annual subscription, including postage, £5 5s ($18.00 in the U.S.A. and Canada)
Offices: Morland Publications Ltd., 2 Arundel Street, London, W.C.2.

Art in America
Articles on all classes of antiques. Published six times a year. Annual subscription £6 5s. ($18·00 in the U.S.A.)
Art in America, 635 Madison Avenue, New York, 22.

Arts Review and Gallery Guide
Articles on painting, book reviews and a detailed gallery guide. The Review contains a guide to prices of pictures in two London salesrooms. Published fortnightly by Richard Gainsborough Periodicals at 2s 6d. Annual subscription £3 17s 6d. ($12·00 by surface mail to Canada and the U.S.A., $35·00 by air mail.)
Offices: 8 Wyndham Place, Bryanston Square, London, WIH 2A7.

Book Collector, The
Articles on the collection and study of printed books and manuscripts. Published quarterly at 10s
Offices: 'The Book Collector', 58 Frith Street, London, W.1

Burlington Magazine
Articles which make a new contribution to knowledge in all spheres of art. Published monthly at 10s. Annual subscription £6 15s (or $20·00).
Offices: 258 Gray's Inn Road, London, W.C.1.

The Clique
The antiquarian booksellers' medium. Published weekly. Annual subscription £3. (First class post U.K. £3 10s). Canada and the U.S.A. $9·00.
Offices: 170 Finchley Road, London, N.W.3.

Coin Monthly
Published at 3s. Annual subscription £2 5s ($5.40 in the U.S.A. and Canada)
Offices: Numismatic Publishing Co., Sovereign House, High Street, Brentwood, Essex.

Coins Weekly
An international weekly newspaper in colour. Annual subscription £4 ($16.00 in the U.S.A. and Canada)
Offices: Morland Publications, 2 Arundel Street, London, W.C.2.

Coins and Medals
A monthly magazine published at 2s 6d. Annual subscription £1 17s. Write to Subscription Department, Link House, Dingwall Avenue, Croydon, CR9 2TA.

The Connoisseur
A magazine with authoritative articles on the fine arts and antiques. Published monthly at 12s 6d. Annual subscription £7 10s. Letters to the Publicity Department, 22 Armoury Way, London, S.W.18.

Gun Review
An international magazine devoted to all aspects of guns and shooting with articles on antique firearms. Annual subscription £2 8s. ($6·50 in Canada and the U.S.A.). Published by Ravenhill Publishing Co, Standard House, Bonhill Street, London, E.C.2.

Tradition
A magazine for collectors of militaria published six times a year by Belmont-Maitland Publishers Ltd., 188 Piccadilly, London, W.1. Annual subscription £5 ($12·50 in the U.S.A.) which includes membership of the International Society of Military Collectors (see p. 169).

YEAR BOOKS AND ANNUALS

Antiques in Britain
A directory of over 2,000 shops with maps showing where to find them. £1 8s post free from 13 High Street, Wendover, Bucks.

Buying Antiques Reference Book
A book full of information about collections, books, collecting clubs, prices, etc. published at 50s by David & Charles, South Devon House, Newton Abbot, Devon.

The British Antiques Year Book
A comprehensive guide to the British art and antique trade published annually in the spring at 25s (or 27s 6d by post) by Apollo Magazine Publications Ltd., 22 Davies Street, London, W.1.

Guide Emer
A directory of 60,000 names and addresses of antique dealers, picture galleries, markets, fairs, etc., classified in 24 European countries, published at £3 (two volumes), postage extra, by G. and F. Gillingham, 4 Crediton Hill, Hampstead, London, N.W.6.

The International Antiques Year Book
A guide to the leading art and antique dealers in Europe and the U.S.A. with a selective guide to the British trade. Published annually in the autumn at 25s (27s 6d by post) by Apollo Magazine Publications Ltd, 22 Davies Street, London, W.1.

Historic Houses, Castles and Gardens in Great Britain and Ireland.
Published annually in January at 5s (6s 6d post free) by Index Publishers, 30 Finsbury Square, London, E.C.2.

Guide to Irish Antiques and Antique Dealers
Published at 10s by the Mercier Press, 4 Bridge Street, Cork.

A Guide to Military Museums
Published annually at 5s, or by post 5s 6d, by Bellona Publications Ltd., Hawthorn Hill, Bracknell, Berkshire.

Museums and Galleries in Great Britain and Ireland
Published annually in July at 5s (6s 6d post free) by Index Publishers, 30 Finsbury Square, London, E.C.2.

On View
An annual guide to museum and gallery acquisitions at 8s 6d ($1·50) or 9s 6d to cover postage and packing. Published by Plaistow Publications, 3 New Plaistow Road, Stratford, London, E.15.

PRICE GUIDES AND BULLETINS

ART SALES
The Connoisseur Art Sales Index
A record of current art prices and an analytical guide to future sales. The service provides a series of publications to its subscribers in loose-leaf form for filing in a special binder. Subscription rates, £25 ($60) a year (for ten issues between October and July).

The Connoisseur Art Sales Annual
This lists over 17,000 oil paintings, pastel and gouache sold for £100 ($240) and over in the period from September in the year prior to publication to July in the year of publication. The annual appears in December and the cost in that month is £8 8s ($20·50); thereafter £9 9s ($23), postage extra.

BOOKS
Book Auction Records
An annual annoted record of prices paid at book auctions in Edinurgh, Glasgow, London, Melbourne, Montreal and New York, published annually in March/April. Retail price, £10 plus inland postage 4s 6d. Orders to Book Auction Records, Dawsons of Pall Mall, Cannon House, Folkestone, Kent.

CLOCKS
Clocks and Their Value by Donald de Carle is published by N. A. C. Press Ltd at 30s. The latest edition was issued in 1969.

COINS AND MEDALS
The Standard Catalogue of the Coins of Great Britain and Ireland is published annually at 25s by H. A. Seaby.
The Standard Catalogue of British Orders, Medals and Decorations, compiled by E. C. Joslin, is published at 35s by Spink & Son Ltd, 5-7 King Street, St James's, London, S.W.1.
Coins Digest is published monthly at 4s by Morland Lee Ltd, 2 Arundel Street, London, W.C.2. Annual subscription £2 8s ($8 surface mail, $14·50 air mail).

POSTAGE STAMPS
Stanley Gibbons Priced Postage Stamp Catalogues, published annually by Stanley Gibbons Ltd, 391 Strand, London, W.C.2., in three volumes.

The British Commonwealth	£2
Europe and Colonies	£3 5s
America, Asia and Africa	£2 15s

FURNITURE

The Price Guide to Antique Furniture, by John Andrews, is published at £2 18s (post free) by Baron Publishing, Martlesham Heath, Woodbridge, Suffolk. Prices are revised twice a year by means of price revision lists, which cost £1 per annum.

SILVER

The Price Guide to Antique Silver, by Ian Harris, is published at £3 3s (post free) by Baron Publishing, Martlesham Heath, Woodbridge, Suffolk. Prices are revised three times a year by means of price revision lists which cost £2 5s per annum.

Silver Auction Records provide an A-Z annual guide giving the full description of some 4,000 pieces with assay office, silversmith, weight, price, auctioneer and date. Published at £4 4s ($15) by Hilmaston Manor Press, Dept 54, Calne, Wiltshire.

The Silver Bulletin answers investment questions and contains a regular market analysis. Published at £3 for a 12-month subscription by Morland Publications, 2 Arundel Street, London, W.C.2

POT LIDS

The Price Guide to Pot Lids and other Underglaze Colour Prints on Pottery, by A. Ball, is published at £4 4s by the Antique Collectors Club, Woodbridge, Suffolk.

3

Talking about Antiques

COLLECTORS' CLUBS AND SOCIETIES

ONE of the greatest pleasures of the collector is to meet other enthusiasts in the same field, to see their finest pieces, and to discuss matters of mutual interest. In many cases first contacts are made through collectors' clubs and societies. Details are given below of the aims and activities of some of these, together with subscription rates and other information supplied by the secretaries. One or two societies are also included which exist to promote the study of historical relics such as monumental brasses or other objects of antiquarian interest.

SPECIALIST CLUBS AND SOCIETIES IN BRITAIN

Arms and Armour Society. Hon Sec: F. Wilkinson, FRSA, 40 Great James Street, Holborn, London, W.C.1

The society was formed in 1950 and now has a world-wide membership of about 850. It exists to assist members in the study, collection and preservation of arms and armour, and is run entirely by voluntary officers.

Monthly meetings are held in London and there is a Northern Branch which holds meetings in Manchester. A quarterly journal is published, with articles based largely on original research (Hon Editor: C. Blair, MA, FSA). A quarterly news sheet is also issued. Both are free to members.

Full membership, by election, is intended for those wishing to attend the London meetings and the subscription is £2 2s. Applicants must attend two meetings as guests before being proposed and seconded by two full members.

Corresponding membership (£1 5s) is for those wishing to receive the journal only and is open to individuals, public bodies and institutions. The subscription is £2 10s or $4·00 for Canada and U.S.A. All subscriptions fall due on 1 January of each year.

Monumental Brass Society. Hon Sec: John Coates, The Elms, 90 High Street, Newport Pagnell, Bucks.

The society exists to stimulate interest in monumental brasses, indents and incised slabs and to endeavour to ensure their preservation. It promotes study by the publication of transactions and portfolios of facsimile reproductions and aims to compile a list of all extant brasses both British and foreign.

Membership is by election and the annual subscription is £2. Associate membership, for which the subscription is £1, is open to persons under the age of eighteen.

Society of Caddy Spoon Collectors. Hon Sec: Edward Kramer, 5 Verulam Buildings, Gray's Inn, London, W.C.1.

Founded in 1963, the society exists 'to promote the study of a delightful memento of a gracious era.' It provides members with a forum for discussion and is collating material for the publication of a classic textbook. It has already held an exhibition for which a catalogue was issued which was a first attempt, in print, to classify the various types of caddy spoon. The society issues regular newsletters and holds meetings, lectures and discussions. The Hon. Editor is Eric Delieb.

Membership is restricted to collectors, though dealers who are known to be collectors may be invited to become honorary members. The subscription is £2. Household membership makes it possible to include a wife or resident relative for an additional 5s. Members in the U.S.A. pay $6·00 for single or 'household' membership.

The English Ceramic Circle. Hon Sec: Mrs J. S. Frost, 23 Cliveden Place, London, S.W.1.

Membership is open to those interested in English ceramics provided they are in no way connected with the antique trade.

Meetings are held once a month in London from November to April. A summer meeting is held in June, usually outside London.

The papers read at these meetings are published annually in the *Transactions* of the Circle (Editor: Donald C Towner) which are distributed free to members. (Non-members may obtain a price list of available back numbers from W. and J. Mackay & Co Ltd, Fair Row, Chatham, Kent.)

Membership is by election. Applicants must be proposed and seconded by members of the Circle who should write to the Hon Secretary. The application will then be placed before the Committee.

The annual subscription is £5 for London members and £4 for overseas and country members. Subscriptions for additional members of the same household are £1 and 10s respectively. Subscriptions are due on November 1 each year.

The Oriental Ceramic Society. Secretary: Brigadier J. R. I. Platt, 31B Torrington Square, London, W.C.1

The object of the society, which was founded in 1921, is solely to increase knowledge and appreciation of eastern ceramics and other arts. There are about 900 members in all parts of the world.

A number of meetings are held each year, in London, usually at 20.00 hrs when papers are read or specimens discussed. Papers which add to existing knowledge are often printed, with illustrations in the *Transactions of the Society.* Exhibitions are organised from time to time to study some groups, type or period of Chinese or other eastern art.

Membership is open to candidates of any nationality who support the aims of the society and are proposed by a member. A candidate for membership is not required to own pieces or be an 'expert'. Subscriptions are payable upon election and, thereafter, on 1 October each year. They cover admission to meetings (except exhibitions held in the Arts Council Galleries) and the *Transactions,* if published during the year.

(a) Member normally living in the United Kingdom	£3 3s
(b) Husband and wife normally living in the United Kingdom	£4 4s
(c) Member normally living overseas	£2 2s
(d) Museums, libraries, institutions	£2 2s
(e) Those on the staff of group (d) members but without free copies of *Transactions*	£1 1s

The Costume Society. Chairman: Dr Roy Strong, c/o Department of Textiles, Victoria and Albert Museum, London, S.W.7.

The Costume Society was formed in 1965 to promote the study and preservation of significant examples of historic and contemporary costume. This embraces the documentation of surviving examples, the study of decorative arts allied to the history of dress, as well as literary and pictorial sources. Activities include: (a) visits to public and private collections; (b) lectures, collectors' meetings and films; (c) an annual symposium which takes place each year in a different centre: 1967 *La Belle Epoque*, London; 1968 *High Victorian*, Leicester; 1969 *Early Victorian*, Worcester; 1970 *The So-Called Age of Elegance*, Bath. Publications include *Costume* which contains articles by specialists, bibliographies, etc., and is sent free to members; proceedings of the annual symposium; and such occasional publications as *La Raffaella* (1968) and *Bernard Lens' Sketch Book* (1970).

Membership: Ordinary membership £2 0s (from January 1971); Library membership, for publications only, £1 1s.

For particulars of membership apply to Mrs Anne Thomas, 58 Padderswick Road, London, W.6.

The Doll Club of Great Britain. Hon Sec and President: Mrs Graham Greene, Grove House, Iffley Turn, Oxford.

The club was founded in 1953 and one of its objects is to ensure the preservation of old and interesting dolls, dolls' houses and accessories, though it also caters for members who make dolls and dolls' houses. Activities include lectures and expeditions, and a quarterly newsletter, *Plangon*, is issued to members who may use the 'Wants' and 'Exchange' sections free of charge.

Full membership is 17s 6d per annum with an entrance fee of 2s 6d. Associate membership is 10s per annum with an entrance fee of 2s 6d. ($2.00 in international money orders or notes only. Correspondents should enclose an International Reply Coupon.) Correspondents are asked to send a stamped addressed envelope when sending queries.

The Fire Mark Circle. Hon Sec and Treasurer: J. J. Williamson, FCII, FIAS, 21 Winston Drive, Bexhill-on-Sea, Sussex.

The Fire Mark Circle aims to encourage interest in fire marks and a bulletin of news and views is issued to members each spring and autumn.

Membership: Open to any interested candidate who is not a dealer. Home Members 10s 6d; Overseas Members £1 1s.

The Furniture History Society. Correspondence to the Assistant Secretary, c/o Dept. of Furniture and Woodwork, Victoria and Albert Museum, London, S.W.7.

The Furniture History Society was founded in 1964 to study furniture of all periods, places and kinds, to increase knowledge and appreciation of it, and as far as possible, to assist in the preservation of furniture and its records. Activities include (a) an annual conference of two to three days held at various places in the British Isles, or abroad, usually in September; (b) talks and discussions; (c) private visits to important collections of furniture; (d) an annual lecture sponsored by the society given in winter at the Victoria and Albert Museum by a person of distinction in furniture studies; (e) the annual general meeting normally held in the autumn at a place where a collection of furniture may also be visited; (f) the journal—*Furniture History*, published annually in the autumn—with important source material and articles of general interest. (g) newsletters issued from time to time with notes on recent literature, current exhibitions, and news of the society's activities.

Membership: Annual subscription £3 3s (United States $8.00). (Payable by 15 October in each year. All subscribing members receive the journal and newsletters.) Additional members of the same family can pay £1 1s each, but only one set of literature will be sent to the family.

The Glass Circle. Hon Sec: Miss Katharine Worsley, 50a Fulham Road, London, S.W.3.

The Circle of Glass Collectors arose as a result of unofficial tutorials about glass conducted by Mr John Bacon, who founded the group in 1937. From that date until 1957, Mr W. A. Thorpe was the president. The office is now held by Mr R. J. Charleston.

The Circle meets once a month between October and June and papers of interest are read and usually circulated to members.

The subscription is 35s for town members and 25s for country members. There is an entrance fee of 10s.

The Heraldry Society. Secretary: Major J. C. Riley, 59 Gordon Square, London, W.C.1.

The Heraldry Society aims to encourage and extend interest in and knowledge of heraldry, armory, chivalry, genealogy and kindred subjects. It publishes the only national heraldic magazine in Great Britain—*The Coat of Arms* (published quarterly at 5s or 65 cents in the U.S.A.). Meetings are held in London throughout the winter months and from time to time outside London and there are excursions and visits in the summer. The society awards certificates in Elementary and Intermediate Heraldry for which examinations are held annually. There is an excellent heraldic library at the society's offices where members may call between 11.00 hrs and 17.30 hrs from Monday to Friday to consult or borrow books. Membership, which entitles the holder to receive each quarter a free copy of the *Heraldry Gazette*, is £1 10s a year ($3·90c in the U.S.A.).

The Antiquarian Horological Society. Hon Sec: J. C. Stevens, 53 Woodfield Crescent, Ealing, London, W.5

The society was founded in 1953 and caters for all interested in any aspect of antiquarian horology. It has over 1,500 members and maintains premises at 35 Northampton Square, E.C.1 where there is a small library available for members to consult by arrangement with the librarian (E. F. Blunt, 8a Fulford Road, West Ewell, Surrey). In winter lectures are held at the Science Museum, South Kensington. Every other year a continental tour is arranged.

A quarterly journal, *Antiquarian Horology*, is issued free to members and the society publishes books and monographs from time to time on various aspects of the subject.

Membership is £2 2s per annum for those living within a fifty mile radius of Charing Cross and £1 11s 6d for those outside the area. Family membership is £3 3s, which entitles wives and children to join organised summer visits to collections.

Map Collectors' Circle. Editor-in-Chief: R. V. Tooley, Durrant House, Chiswell Street, London, E.C.1

The Map Collectors' Circle aims to stimulate interest in and publish material on early printed maps, atlases, cartographers, etc. It issues a 'Map Collectors'' series of pamphlets on all aspects of cartography—bibliographical, historical and aesthetic. The emphasis is on material of practical

Page 167: George II lidded tankard, the plain tapering body with reeded girdle and recurving handle, the domed cover with scrolled billet, by Robert Cox, London, 1757, 8 in high, 27 oz. Sold at Retford, Nottinghamshire, in January 1970 for £360

Page 168 : Earthenware dish, (c 1814-30) transfer-printed in blue with a view of Sidney Sussex College, Cambridge. Makers John and William Ridgway of Shelton, Hanley, Staffordshire. Sold for 9½ guineas at Goring-on-Thames, Oxfordshire, in February 1970

importance designed to help collectors, librarians and booksellers. A prospectus is available. Annual subscription is £6 10s ($17.00 U.S.A.) which entitles members to ten publications.

The British Matchbox Label and Booklet Society. Hon Sec: J. H. Luker, 283 Worplesdon Road, Guildford, Surrey. Tel: Worplesdon 2263.

Founded in 1945, the society caters for collectors of labels and bookmatch covers throughout the world, and is fully international in its membership. A newsletter is issued six times a year, there is an annual exhibition in London, and rallies are held in other parts of England. Annual subscription £1 ($3.00 U.S.A.); juniors (under 16) 10s ($1.50 U.S.A.).

The International Society of Military Collectors
The society aims to foster the study of military history and the collecting of militaria including uniforms, weapons, accoutrements, medals, model soldiers and war games. Meetings are held on the first Friday in each month in 'The Clarence' (first floor), 4 Dover Street, London, W.1. Membership is free to subscribers to the publication *Tradition*. Annual subscription rate (six issues) £5 ($12·50 in U.S.A.). Write to 'Tradition', Belmont-Maitland Publishers Ltd, 44 Dover Street, London, W.1.

The Musical Box Society of Great Britain. Hon Sec: A. R. Waylett, 'Bylands', Crockham Hill, Edenbridge, Kent. Tel. Crockham Hill 263.

The society was formed in 1962 and has now grown to include over 400 members, with collectors who are interested in musical boxes in almost every European country, the United States, Australia, Canada, New Zealand and South Africa. The Hon Editor is A. W. J. G. Ord-Hume. The annual subscription for active members is £3 and for associate members £2.

The Galpin Society for the Study of Musical Instruments. Hon Sec: Jeremy P. S. Montagu, 7 Pickwick Road, Dulwich Village, London, S.E.21.

The society was founded in 1946 for the publication of original research into the history, construction and use of musical instruments. It has a worldwide membership of about 1,000 and is open to all, of whatever nationality or country of residence; institutions may enrol as members and enjoy all rights of representation and voting. The annual Journal contains articles, reviews, notes and queries on all aspects of musical instruments. The society organizes from time to time exhibitions, symposia and other functions, including annual Winter and Summer (Annual General) Meetings. The annual subscription of £2 2s ($6), payable on or before April 1, entitles members to a copy of the Journal for that year, to a substantial reduction in the price of back numbers while still in print, and to entry to the society's meetings.

The Newspaper Collectors Club. Hon Sec: John Frost, 8 Monks Avenue, New Barnet, Herts.

The club caters for all who collect historic newspapers or study press history. It has its own amateur press publication, *Worldwide Newspaper Collecting and Press History*, which appears quarterly. Annual subscription, 30s, entitles members to receive four issues.

The British Numismatic Society. Hon Sec: W. Slayter, 63 West Way, Edgware, Middlesex

The British Numismatic Society was founded in 1903 and has over 400

L

members. It is a learned society and its activities are confined to British numismatics, interpreted in its widest sense to cover the coinage of Great Britain and Ireland and of territories that at one time or another were subject to the British Crown. Its interest also extends to token coinage, medals and badges.

Meetings are held at the Warburg Institute, Woburn Square, London, W.C.1, at 18.00 hrs normally on the fourth Tuesday in each month from September to June, (except in December, when no meeting is held). Papers are read on fresh numismatic discoveries and the results of recent research. Rare coins and medals are exhibited.

The society's journal is issued annually. Contributions, either in the form of articles or of shorter communications, should be sent to the editor at Ramsbury Hill, Ramsbury, Marlborough, Wiltshire.

Members may consult the society's extensive library at the Warburg Institute. Applications for the loan of books should be addressed to the society's librarian there.

The annual subscription is £4 4s with an entrance fee of £1 1s. The subscription is payable on election and annually on 1 January. Corporate bodies may become members. Junior members (under 21 years of age) pay a reduced subscription of 30s and the entrance fee is waived.

The London Numismatic Club. Hon Sec: Robert Seaman, 19 Darenth Road, Leigh-on-Sea, Essex, SS9 2UU.

The club was formed in 1947 and numbers nearly 200 members. Meetings are held early in each month at Friends House, Euston Road, N.W.1 at 6.30 p.m. A quarterly newsletter is circulated to members. There is a club library. Membership is by election and the entrance fee is 10s. Annual subscription 30s payable on 1 January.

The Royal Numismatic Society. Hon Sec: R. A. G. Carson, c/o Dept. of Coins and Medals, British Museum, London, W.C.1

The Royal Numismatic Society was founded in 1836 as the Numismatic Society of London. In 1904 it was granted a Royal Charter.

The society's journal, *The Numismatic Chronicle,* which is sent post free to members, is published every year. Each number averages 275 pages of articles, notes on finds, reviews and notices of selected new publications, and twenty plates (in addition to reports of proceedings and lists of members). *The Numismatic Chronicle* is £5 a volume to non-members; obtainable from Messrs Bernard Quaritch, 11 Grafton Street, London, W.1.

The society's large and increasing library is at the Warburg Institute, Woburn Square, London, W.C.1, and books can be sent to Fellows by post on request to the society's librarian, Mr N. M. Lowick, c/o The British Museum, London, W.C.1.

Meetings of the society, at which papers are read and discussed and rare coins or medals exhibited, are held monthly from October to June at the rooms of the Society of Antiquaries, Burlington House, London, W.1.

The annual subscription to the society is £4 4s. The entrance fee, except for those under 26 years of age on 1 January immediately following the date of their election, is £1 1s. Since fellowship of the society does not denote a professional qualification, the designatory letters FRNS or the name of the society, must not be used in commercial advertisement.

The Pewter Society (formerly the Society of Pewter Collectors). Hon Sec: C. A. Peal, The Wold, 12 Stratford Crescent, Cringleford, Norwich. Nor. 68F

The Pewter Society was established to promote the study of pewter and to stimulate interest in the subject and has just celebrated its fiftieth anniversary by staging the most comprehensive exhibition of British pewter ever seen, in cooperation with Reading Museum and Art Gallery. Members of the Pewter Society meet four times a year in various places. In addition to collecting, members carry out research and the society assists museums and churches with the identification, repair and restoration of old pewter. From time to time special exhibitions are staged. The society issues a journal (Editor, P. H. Starling, Beech Hill, Stoke Holy Cross, Norwich. Nor 55W) and maintains a library (Hon Librarian: R. F. Michaelis, Pelham House, Denton Road, Denton, Newhaven, Sussex).

Membership is restricted to less than forty people and is by invitation. The society is esoteric: it is confined to those who do not sell pewter to earn a living. There are, in addition, many corresponding members all over the world, mainly in Europe, Australia and the United States of America.

The Royal Philatelic Society, London. Hon Sec: George South, 41 Devonshire Place, London, W.1.

This is the oldest philatelic society in existence. It was established in 1869 as The Philatelic Society, London to promote, encourage and contribute to the advancement of the science and practice of philately. Permission to use the prefix 'Royal' was granted by His Majesty King Edward VII in 1906.

Meetings are held from October to June, as a rule on alternate Thursdays.

The first meeting of each month commences at 17.00 hrs, and is of a formal nature, at which one or more papers are read accompanied by displays by individual members. The second meeting each month consists of a display of stamps by one or more members without any accompanying paper. The latter is open from 14.30-18.00 hrs.

The library comprises a magnificent collection of several thousand philatelic works, handbooks, monographs and sets of journals and periodicals which are always available for inspection by members.

The society publishes a monthly journal, *The London Philatelist* which is sent free to members. The subscription to non-members is £3 a year.

The Expert Committee has functioned without a break for over sixty years. Any foreign stamp of catalogue status, and British Commonwealth stamps to date, may be submitted to the committee who will issue their opinion and a certificate as to its genuineness or otherwise. Members may have two free opinions a year. Prospective members need not be advanced philatelists. The essential qualification is that applicants must be amateur collectors. The council may, in its discretion, designate certain members as 'Fellows' of the society, and such Fellows shall have the right to place the letters FRPSL after their names.

On election, members are required to pay an entrance fee of £3 3s together with one of the following annual subscriptions:

£10 10s for members having a place of residence or business within a radius of 25 miles from Charing Cross.

£7 10s for members residing in Great Britain outside such area.

£5 10s for members resident overseas.

Collectors between the ages of 16 and 21 may join as associates, paying an annual subscription of £2 2s, without entrance fee. An associate of not less than two years' standing is entitled, on attaining the age of 21, to become a member without payment of the normal entrance fee.

The Pot Lid Circle, or Colour-Printed Pottery Collectors' Association. Hon Sec: J. F. Elvy, 'Vines', Hildenborough, Kent

The society aims to stimulate interest and encourage research into underglaze picture prints on Staffordshire pot lids, plates, jars, boxes, etc. Regular meetings are held for members to exchange views. Newsletters and a journal are published from time to time. A publication known as the *Pot Lid Recorder* gives the prices paid for pot lids over a period, a list which has value for the collector in indicating by price the relative rarity. Copies may be obtained from the Courier Press, P.O. Box 45, Tachbrook Road, Leamington, Warwickshire. Price £1 1s.

Membership of the Pot Lid Circle is confined to genuine collectors. The subscription for ordinary members is £2 2s payable in advance and due on 1 January each year. Corporations may pay the same subscription and nominate one individual to represent them.

Printing Historical Society. Hon Sec: David Chambers, St Bride Institute, Bride Lane, Fleet Street, London, E.C.4.

The society was founded in 1964 to encourage the study of and foster interest in the history of printing, to encourage the preservation of historical equipment and printed matter, to promote meetings and exhibitions, and to produce publications in connection with these aims. The journal (Editor: James Mosley) is issued free to members. Annual subscription for individuals and libraries, £2 2s ($5·50 for the U.S.A.); £1 1s for students ($3·00 for the U.S.A.) due on 1 July each year. Write to Membership Secretary: Pamela Robinson at St Bride Institute (address above).

The Silhouette Collectors' Club

The club was founded in 1967 and meets about four times a year to exhibit and discuss silhouettes. There is at present no membership subscription, only a postal subscription of 5s a year to cover costs. Keen collectors who wish to join in the activities of the club should write to D. Gildea, 15 Shelley Road, Bognor Regis, Sussex.

The Old Water-Colour Society's Club. Secretary: Malcolm Fry, 26 Conduit Street, London, W.1.

The club was founded in 1923 and is affiliated to the Royal Society of Painters in Water Colours. Membership is open to all interested in watercolour painting in whatever capacity. An annual volume is published with authentic articles on the old and present masters of the medium, with a large number of beautiful illustrations. This is issued to all members, who may also obtain certain back numbers at 30s each.

Members are invited to the private views of the Royal Society of Painters in Water Colours and have the privilege of free admission to all the society's exhibitions. Evening receptions, to which members may bring friends, are held periodically. Annual subscription: £3 3s.

The Wedgwood Society. Hon Sec: Mrs T. B. Jarvis, 166 Cottenham Park Road, London, S.W.20.

The society was founded in 1954 and aims to increase the knowledge and appreciation of Wedgwood ware, and to publish results of research into the history and production of the factory. Membership is around 130, including many overseas members, particularly in the U.S.A. Meetings are held about four times a year, and a weekend visit is annual. Illustrated *Proceedings* are published every other year and are obtainable from the Hon Secretary, price £1 1s each.

Application for membership should be made to the Hon Secretary. No distinction is made between dealers and collectors but the former are required to be introduced by non-dealers.

The Wine Label Circle. Hon Sec: The Rev E. W. Whitworth, Stadhampton Vicarage, Stadhampton, Oxfordshire.

This society has over 130 members in Great Britain and overseas, and exists to stimulate research, the interchange of views between members and the general study of decanter labels. A journal is published twice yearly and circulated among the members. The Hon Editors are Mr. and Mrs J. Beecroft, Rosebank, Overdale Road, Willaston, Wirral, Cheshire.

Membership is confined to collectors of decanter labels and to dealers only if genuine collectors. Annual subscription: £1 5s; Life Membership: £10 10s.

SPECIALIST CLUBS AND SOCIETIES IN THE UNITED STATES OF AMERICA

American Numismatic Society. Broadway at 155th Street, New York.

Antique Bottle Collectors' Association. P.O. Box 467, Sacramento, California. 95802.

Antique Toy Collectors' Club. 8110 Frankford Avenue, Philadelphia. Pa. 19136.

Musical Box Society International. 1765 East Sudan Circle, Greenville, Mississipi.

National Association of Watch and Clock Collectors Inc. P.O. Box 33, Columbia, Pa. 17512.

National Button Society. 7940 Montgomery Avenue, Elkins Park, Philadelphia, Pa, 19117.

Paperweight Collectors' Association. 47 Windsor Road, Scarsdale, New York.

Pewter Collectors' Club of America. 579 Grand Avenue, Lindenhurst, New York, 10533.

Print Council of America. 527 Madison Avenue, New York City, 10022.

Stevengraph Collectors' Association. Irvington-on-Hudson, New York.

United Federation of Dolls Clubs Inc. 4035 Kessler Boulevard Drive, Indianapolis, Indiana, 46220.

Wedgwood International Seminar. 55 Vandam Street, New York, N.Y. 10013.

This address is given because there are no less than eight Wedgwood clubs and societies in The United States. The seminar holds a mammoth annual meeting in a museum in a different state each year, and also publishes a periodical called *The American Wedgwoodian*. In a sense, it may be said to integrate interest in Wedgwood ceramics in the U.S.A.

GENERAL COLLECTORS' CLUBS AND SOCIETIES

There are many groups scattered throughout the country which meet to discuss antiques and often arrange visits to places where fine antiques may be seen. Some are linked together in the NATIONAL ASSOCIATION OF DECORATIVE AND FINE ART SOCIETIES, was founded in 1968 by Mrs Charles Fay and helps in the formation of new groups, issues a directory of lecturers, and generally acts as a coordinating body for societies which work for any of its objects. It encourages high standards and recommends to affiliated societies a minimum of 100 members paying at least £2 2s a year to cover a series of lectures, usually 9 or 10. The Secretary is Mrs N. Mitchell, Woodlands, Loosely Row, Princes Risborough, Bucks.

There is no individual membership. Member societies pay £10 10s on election and receive a handbook and directory of lecturers. There is a capitation fee of 1s in respect of members of member societies. The following list is of existing member societies:

BUCKINGHAMSHIRE.
The Thame Fine Art Study Group: Hon Sec: Mrs M. Gresham, Long Farthings, Haddenham, Bucks.

The Chalfont St Giles Decorative and Fine Arts Society: Chairman: Mrs P. Butterworth, Sandfords, Chalfont St Giles, Bucks.

The Gerrards Cross Antiques Group: Hon Sec: Mrs D. Bonnar, The Elms, Oak End Way, Gerrards Cross, Bucks.

The Chiltern Decorative and Fine Art Society: Hon Sec: Mrs E. Mackintosh, Hawthorn, Wycombe Road, Prestwood.

The Thames Antiques and Decorative Arts Group: Hon Sec: Mrs J. Allen, 1 Parsonage Gardens, Marlow.

HAMPSHIRE
The Hart Decorative and Fine Arts Society: Hon Sec: Mrs M. Kenning, 1 Queen Mary Close, Fleet, Hants.

HERTFORDSHIRE
The Ashridge Antiques and Fine Arts Society: Hon Sec: Mrs J. Cutts, Fullers, Cross Oak Road, Berkhamstead, Herts.

The East Hertfordshire Decorative Arts Society: Hon Sec: Mrs A. F. Stansfield, Beaumont Manor, Wormsley, Herts.

The Hertfordshire Antique and Fine Art Society: Hon Sec: Mrs J. Campbell, Annables Manor, Kinsbourne Green, Harpenden, Herts.

KENT
The Thanet Antiques and Fine Art Group: Hon Sec: Mrs J. Carte, 18 Fitzroy Avenue, Kingsgate, Broadstairs, Kent.

The North Kent Decorative and Fine Arts Society: Hon Sec: Mrs J. Brittain-Smith, Fairings, Forest Drive, Keston, Kent.

The Cinque Ports Antiques and Fine Arts Group: Chairman: Mrs H. Beacon, Undercliff House, Sandgate, Kent.

LANARKSHIRE
The Edinburgh Antiques & Fine Arts Society: Chairman: Mrs D. Thomson, 18 Belgrave Place, Edinburgh, 4.

LANCASHIRE
The Merseyside Antiques and Fine Arts Society: Chairman: Mrs R. L. Goulden, 26 Brooks Road West, Waterloo, Liverpool, 23.

LINCOLNSHIRE
The Holland and Kesteven Antiques and Fine Arts Society: Hon Sec: Mrs A. M. Baxter, 'Chestnut Lodge', Moulton, Spalding.

LONDON
The North London Decorative and Fine Arts Society: Hon Sec: Mrs D. K. Chick, 7 Martlett Lodge, Oak Hill Park, London, N.W.3.

MIDDLESEX
The Enfield Decorative and Fine Arts Society: Chairman: Mrs M. Mackintosh, 37 Essex Road, Enfield, Middlesex.
The Harrow Decorative and Fine Arts Society: Hon Sec: Mrs C. Mills, 2 Lace Road, Harrow, Middlesex.
The Moor Park Decorative and Fine Arts Society: Hon Sec: Mrs E. Price, 3 Pembroke Road, Moor Park, Northwood, Middlesex.

OXFORDSHIRE
The Banbury Fine Arts Society: Hon Sec: Mrs G. Crichton-Miller, South View, Charlton, nr. Banbury, Oxon.
The Bampton and West Oxfordshire Decorative and Fine Arts Society: Hon Sec: Mrs Spencer, Lynden Cottage, Bampton, Oxon.
The Cotswold Antiques Study Group: Hon Sec: Mrs J. Lewis, Haytor, Lavender Square, Bampton, Oxon.

SURREY
The Runnymede Decorative and Fine Arts Society: Hon Sec: Mrs M. F. Legge, Bulkeley Cottage, Englefield, Surrey.
The West Surrey Decorative and Fine Arts Society: Hon Sec: Mrs Foot, The Dower House, Wonersh, Surrey.

SUSSEX
The Adur Valley Antiques, Decorative and Fine Arts Group: Hon Sec: Mrs Bower, Bellows, Woodmancote, Henfield, Sussex.
The West Sussex Decorative and Fine Arts Society: Chairman: Mrs N. Brown, Lakers Cottage, Loxwood, Sussex.

YORKSHIRE
The Harrogate Decorative and Fine Arts Group: Hon Sec: Mrs G. Armitage, Beggar Hall, New Monkton, Yorks.
Hull and East Riding Antiques and Fine Arts Society: Hon Sec: Mrs W. E. Wilson, Boothferry Road, Hessle, E. Yorks.

There is also the Junior Museums Club organised by Mrs Frank White (8 Queens Ride, London S.W.13) which aims to show children how to enjoy visits to museums.

THE ANTIQUE COLLECTORS' CLUB, founded in 1966 by a group of private collectors, also links together a number of regional clubs. It aims to assist collectors by sending to members a monthly magazine, organising private buying and selling facilities, and issuing a year book. The annual subscription is £2 10s. Members must not be connected with the antique business. Other conditions of membership which should be read carefully are on the back of the application form which can be obtained from the proprietors—N. Steel and D. Thorpe, Clopton, Woodbridge, Suffolk. There are regional clubs (autonomous branches of the Antique Collectors' Club) in the following areas: Argyllshire—Oban; Bedfordshire—Bromham; Bristol; Buckinghamshire—High Wycombe, Marlow; Camridgeshire—Littleport; Carmarthenshire—Brechfa; Cornwall—Truro; Cheshire—Altrincham; Devonshire—Barnstaple, Exeter, Tavistock; Durham—Darlington; Essex—Black Notley, Colchester, Runwell; Glamorgan—Cowbridge; Gloucestershire—Stroud; Hampshire—Portsmouth; Hertfordshire—Welwyn; Kent—Beltinge, Bexley Heath, Farningham, Folkestone, Herne Bay; Lanarkshire—Glasgow; Lancashire—Barrow-in-Furness, Blackpool, Fence, Manchester, Southport; Lincolnshire—Lincoln; London; Middlesex—Northwood; Midlothian—Edinburgh; Norfolk—Norwich; Northants—Peterborough; Northumberland—Newcastle; Northern Ireland—Belfast; Nottinghamshire—Nottingham; North Wales; Perthshire—Dunkeld; Ross and Cromarty—Dingwall; Shropshire—Shrewsbury; Staffordshire—Wolverhampton; Suffolk—Bury St. Edmunds, Ipswich; Surrey—Cobham, Farnham, Moseley, Richmond, West Byfleet, Woking; Sussex—Brighton, Chichester, Eastbourne, St. Leonards-on-Sea; Warwickshire—Birmingham, Coventry (a Doll Club), Sutton Coldfield; Westmorland—Windermere; Wiltshire—Salisbury; Worcestershire—Malvern, Oldbury; Yorkshire—Harrogate, Hawes, Hull, Leeds, Linthorpe (Middlesbrough), Saltburn.

Other Collectors' Clubs include the following:

Airedale Antique Collectors' Society. Chairman: Mrs L. C. Asquith, Green Pastures, Toller Lane, Bradford, Yorkshire. Annual Subscription £1 10s.

Malvern and District Antique Collectors' Club. Secretary: Mrs T. Holt, The New House, Oxford Road, Malvern. Annual subscription £1 15s. Guest fee 6s. Summer membership (outings only) 5s.

Mid-Warwickshire Antique Collectors' Circle. Chairman: J. A. Park, 54 Cannon Park Road, Coventry.

Nuneaton Antique Association. Chairman: A. Ball, Garthside, 15 Arden Road, Nuneaton, Warwickshire.

South Birmingham Antiques Club. Chairman: H. C. Davies, 233 Wake Green Road, Birmingham 3. Hon Sec: Mrs I. Chapman, 67 Woodstock Road, Moseley, Birmingham. Annual subscription, £2 2s.

Tawney House Antiques Circle. Hon Sec: R. Spark, 'Sunny Bank', Matlock Road, Walton, Nr Chesterfield, Derbyshire.

West Yorkshire Antique Collectors' Society. Hon Sec: Mrs H. Lawrence, Seckar House, Seckar Lane, Woolley, Wakefield, Yorkshire. Monthly meetings are normally held at Heath Hall, near Wakefield. Summer excursions to factories, houses or private collections. Annual subscription £2 2s.

FRIENDS OF MUSEUMS

Museums and art galleries depend ultimately on the goodwill of the public. It would seem that the 1970s will show an increased all-round interest in the services provided by these establishments and a desire to help in a practical way. Many museums have had organized groups of 'Friends' for a number of years but new groups are emerging, particularly groups linked with our larger museums. *The*

British Museum Society, founded to mobilize public goodwill, stresses that its primary purpose is not to raise money but to create a body of people who will become directly aware of the Museum's needs and intentions and will share the concern of the Trustees and staff. *The Friends of the Ashmolean Museum* in Oxford, which soon attracted over 500 members, has been very active in the past year organizing exhibitions in London and planning concerts where some of the stringed instruments in the Ashmolean Collection might be heard. It is an encouraging sign of the times. The following list of such societies may be of value to those who wish to demonstrate their appreciation of the service our museums and galleries provide. Where not stated below, the addresses of museums will be found on pp 80-102.

SOCIETIES IN LONDON

The British Museum Society
Members receive free copies of a bulletin specially designed to keep them in touch with the museum's life and plans; and it is intended that these plans should include a Society Room for their use. Membership costs £2 a year (£3 for husband and wife). Correspondence to the Secretary, British Museum Society, British Museum, London, W.C.1.

Friends of the Geffrye Museum
Information may be obtained from the Curator, Geffrye Museum, Kingsland Road, London, E.2.

Friends of the Tate Gallery
Members are entitled to invitations to private views, free entry to paying exhibitions, admission on Mondays from 6.30-10 p.m., when the gallery is closed to the public, the use of the friends' private room and other privileges. Annual subscription £5 5s; Young Friends £2 2s. Full details from the Secretary, The Friends of the Tate, Tate Gallery, Millbank, London, S.W.1

SOCIETIES OUTSIDE LONDON

Barnard Castle. *Friends of the Bowes Museum* have free entry and receive a newsletter about the museum and its work, as well as being invited to private views and other functions. Minimum annual subscription £1; junior members (under 21) 5s, to be sent to the Hon Treasurer, Barclays Bank, Ltd, Barnard Castle.
Bath. *Friends of the Holburne of Menstrie Museum.*
Birmingham. *Friends of the Museum and Art Gallery* aim to increase interest and to enable people to take a more active part in the life of the museum. There is a membership of about 1,200. Minimum annual subscription 10s 6d.
Bournemouth. *Museum and Arts Society.*
Bradford. *Friends of the Art Gallery.*
Bristol. *Association of Friends of the Art Gallery.*
Cambridge. *Friends of the Fitzwilliam Museum.*
Cardiff. *Friends of the National Museum of Wales* are admitted free of charge to the museum on Sunday afternoons and receive an illustrated

report on the work of the association. Minimum subscription 10s. Those who subscribe £1 or more are admitted free to the Welsh Folk Museum. Write to The Secretary, National Museum of Wales, Cardiff.

Chelmsford. *Friends of Historic Essex.*

Colchester. *Friends of Colchester and Essex Museum.*

Doncaster. *Doncaster Arts and Music Society.*

Douglas, Isle of Man. *Friends of the Manx Museum.*

Dundee. *Tayside Museum Society.*

Eastbourne. *Friends of the Towner Art Gallery.*

Edinburgh. *Friends of the Royal Scottish Museum.*

Elgin, Morayshire. *The Elgin Society,* Elgin Museum, 1 High Street, Elgin.

Glasgow. *Museum and Art Gallery Association.*

Hull. *Hull Museums Society and Friends of the Ferens Art Gallery,* Georgian Houses, 23 and 24, High Street, Hull.

Ilkley, Yorks. *Friends of the Manor House Museum,* Castle Yard, Ilkley.

Keighley. *Friends of Cliffe Castle.*

Kendal. *Friends of Abbot Hall Art Gallery.*

King's Lynn. *Museum Society.*

Leicester. *Friends of the Museum and Leicester Museums Association.*

Manchester. *Friends of the Whitworth Art Gallery.*

Middlesbrough. *Friends of Middlesbrough Art Gallery,* Linthorpe Road, Middlesbrough.

Norwich. *Friends of the Norwich Museum.*

Oxford. *Friends of the Ashmolean Museum.* The aims of this association are to foster public interest in the museum, to encourage members of the university to enjoy the collections more fully and to use the facilities offered by the museum, and to help acquire works of art to enrich the museum's collections. Membership is by annual subscription of £2 or more, or £3 or more for a married couple. Student membership by annual subscription of 10s or more. Life membership by donation of £75 or more. Correspondence to the Secretary, Friends of the Ashmolean Museum, Ashmolean Museum, Oxford.

Plymouth. *Friends of Plymouth Art Gallery and Buckland Abbey.*

Salford. *Friends of the Salford Museums' Association.*

Salisbury. *Members of Salisbury and South Wiltshire Museum.* Application forms from the Museum Secretary.

Scunthorpe. *Scunthorpe Museum Society,* Borough Museum and Art Gallery, Oswald Road, Scunthorpe.

Sheffield. *Sheffield Museum Society.*

Southend-on-Sea. *Friends of the Beecroft Art Gallery,* Station Road, Westcliff-on-Sea.

Southport. *Friends of the Southport Art Gallery,* Lord Street, Southport.

Stowmarket, Suffolk. *Friends of Abbot's Hall Museum of Rural Life.*

Swansea. *Association of Friends of the Glyn Vivian Art Gallery.*

Tamworth, Staffs. *Friends of Tamworth Castle and Museum.*

Totnes. *Totnes Museum Society,* The Elizabethan House, 70, Fore Street, Totnes.

Tunbridge Wells. *Tunbridge Wells Museum Society.* Talks are held on the last Wednesday in each month.

Wakefield. *Friends of the Art Gallery.*

Worcester. *Friends of the Dyson Perrins Museum.* This society was formed for individuals, firms and institutions interested in Worcester porcelain who wish to associate themselves with the Dyson Perrins Museum Collection at Worcester. Life membership is £10. Ordinary membership costs a minimum of 10s a year. Junior members (under 21) pay a minimum of 5s a year. Correspondence to R. J. Collins, 14 Stanmore Road, Hanbury Park, Worcester.

York. *Friends of the York Art Gallery.*

YOUNG FRIENDS OF MUSEUMS

A number of museum societies cater particularly for children, whose interest they aim to stimulate. They are as follows:

Bedford. *Junior Friends of the Cecil Higgins Art Gallery.*
Bournemouth. *Children's Museum Club.*
Dundee. *Dundee Junior Museum Club.*
Manchester. *Young Friends of the Whitworth Art Gallery.*
Norwich. *Children's Museum Club.*

SOME USEFUL ADDRESSES

MANY of the following organisations are able to help the student of antiques with information or advice. Correspondence should normally be addressed to the secretary.

Antiquarian Booksellers' Association, 9, Stanton Road, Wimbledon, London, S.W.20.
Antiquaries, Society of, Burlington House, London, W.1.
Antiquaries of Scotland, Society of, National Museum of Antiquaries of Scotland, Queen Street, Edinburgh.
Antiques in Britain Association, 13 High Street, Wendover, Bucks. Membership (annual subscription £1) is open to all bona-fide antiques dealers.
Archaeological Association, British, Courtauld Institute of Art, 20 Portman Square, London, W.1.
Archaeological Association, Cambrian, 3 Lon Cadog, Cardiff.
Archivists, Society of, County Hall, Hertford.
Army Historical Research, Society for, c/o The Library, Old War Office Building, London, S.W.1.
Art Collections Fund, National, Hertford House, Manchester Square, London, W.1.
Auctioneer and Estate Agents' Institute, The Chartered, 29 Lincoln's Inn Fields, London, W.C.2.
Bibliographical Society, c/o British Academy, Burlington Gardens, London, W.1.
Bibliographical Society, Edinburgh, c/o National Library of Scotland, Edinburgh, 1.

British Academy, The, 6 Burlington Gardens, London, W.1.

British Antique Dealers' Association, 20 Rutland Gate, London, S.W.7. The association issues a booklet giving the names and addresses of the established dealers in antiques and works of art who are elected members. Price 10s post free ($1.50 abroad).

British Institute of Persian Studies, 85 Queen's Road, Richmond, Surrey.

Clique, The, 170 Finchley Road, London, N.W.3. The recognized medium of the antiquarian book trade. Annual subscription (trade only) £3.

Designs Registry, The Public Record Office, Chancery Lane, London, W.C.2. Records of designs registered prior to September, 1909, which include those identified by diamond-shaped design registration marks, are kept in this office. When the manufacturer's name is not given on an article but only a registration mark, fuller information can be obtained from the Designs Registry.

Dickens Fellowship, Dickens House, 48 Doughty Street, London, W.C.1.

Friends of the National Libraries, c/o the British Museum, London, W.C.1.

Gemmological Association of Great Britain, St Dunstan's House, Carey Lane, London, E.C.2.

Genealogists, Society of, 37 Harrington Gardens, London, S.W.7.

Georgian Group, 2 Chester Street, London, S.W.1.

Historical Association, 59A Kennington Park Road, London, S.E.11.

Historical Society, Royal, University College, Gower Street, London, W.C.1.

Horological Institute, British, 35 Northampton Square, London, E.C.1.

Japan Society of London, 61 Carey Street, London, W.C.2. The society organises circles covering a wide range of artistic subjects concerning Japan. Annual subscription £2 2s, or £1 1s for members under 30 years of age and corresponding members.

Library Association, Ridgmount Street, London, W.C.1.

London Appreciation Society, 8 Scarsdale Villas, Kensington, London, W.8.

London Library, The, 14 St James Square, London, S.W.1.

London Society, The, 3 Dean's Yard, London, S.W.1.

Military Historical Society, Duke of York's Headquarters, Chelsea, London, S.W.3.

Ministry of Public Buildings and Works, Lambeth Bridge House, London, S.E.1. It is possible to obtain from the Ministry (or from its Scottish Headquarters, Argyle House, 3 Lady Lawson Street, Edinburgh EH3 9SD) a season ticket which entitles the holder to visit ancient monuments and historic buildings under its control. The cost is 15s (7s 6d for old-age pensioners and children). Write to the Chief Information Officer, Dept ST.

National Art Collections Fund, Hertford House, Manchester Square, London, W.1.

Museums Association, 87 Charlotte Street, London, W.1.

National Book League, 7 Albemarle Street, London, W.1.

National Trust, 42 Queen Anne's Gate, London, S.W.1. Members of the Trust may visit National Trust properties free of charge. Annual subscription £2 or more. The address of the membership department is Bluecoat School, 23 Caxton Street, London, S.W.1.

National Trust for Scotland, 5 Charlotte Square, Edinburgh, 2.

Nautical Research, Society for, National Maritime Museum, Greenwich, London, S.E.10.

Public Record Office, Chancery Lane, London, W.C.2. Search rooms open from Mondays to Fridays 09.30 to 17.00 hrs and on Saturdays 09.30 to 13.00 hrs.

Railway and Canal Historical Society, 38 Station Road, Wylde Green, Sutton Coldfield, Warwickshire.

Royal Asiatic Society, 56 Queen Anne Street, London, W.1.

Royal School of Needlework, 25 Princes Gate, London, S.W.7., holds classes teaching the history and technique of embroidery. It also has a repair service for tapestries and embroideries.

R.V.S. Enterprises (Educational Department), Hilton House, Norwood Lane, Meopham, Kent. Runs short holidays courses or 'Teach-Ins' for the collector, investor and enthusiastic amateur at such centres as Ross-on-Wye or Banbury with expert lectures on furniture, glass, porcelain, painting, etc.

Scottish History Society, c/o Scottish Record Office, Register House, Edinburgh, 2.

Scottish Record Office, Register House, Edinburgh, 2. Search rooms open from Mondays to Fridays 09.00 hrs—16.45 hrs and on Saturdays 09.00 hrs—12.30 hrs.

Scottish Record Society, Scottish Record Office, Edinburgh, 2.

Selborne Society, 57 Corfton Road, Ealing, London, W.5.

Stationery Office, Her Majesty's, 49 High Holborn, London, W.C.1.

Theatre Research, Society for, 103 Ralph Court, Queensway, London, W.2.

Valuers and Auctioneers, Incorporated Society of, 3 Cadogan Gate, London, S.W.1.

Valuers Institution, 3 Cadogan Gate, London, S.W.1.

Victorian Society, 55 Great Ormond Street, London, W.C.1.

4

Buying Antiques

The prices given in this section were paid at public auction sales in 1968, 1969 and 1970. Variations in the price paid for similar lots may be due to the difference between the fine piece and the piece which shows signs of wear. The order of the classes follows the order of chapters in the companion volume—*Buying Antiques General Guide,* ie furniture, clocks, watches, barometers, silver, Sheffield plate, non-precious metals (brass, bronze, copper, iron and pewter), porcelain, pottery, clear glass, coloured glass and small ornamental antiques.

SALEROOMS AND AUCTIONEERS

MOST people have heard of the great London salerooms of Christie's and Sotheby's, but there are many other auction rooms in London and the provinces which hold regular or periodic sales of antiques. A few of these specialize in silver, firearms or furniture, for example. The larger salerooms publish details of their auctions in the *Daily Telegraph* (Mondays), *The Times* (Tuesdays), or *The Sunday Times*. Romeike & Curtice Ltd, of Hale House, 290-296, Green Lanes, London, W.13 (Tel: 01-882-0155) compile regular auction lists with details of forthcoming antique sales throughout the United Kingdom and these are sent by first-class mail four or five times a week to all subscribers at a cost of £18 per annum, or £5 for three months.

Members of the trade will find a useful 'Auction Calendar' in *Antique Finder* (see p 155).

The main auctioneers who hold antique sales are listed below and, when in the locality, it is often well worth while asking about current sales of antiques.

IN LONDON

Bonham, W. and F. C., & Sons, Ltd, Montpelier Galleries, Montpelier St, Knightsbridge, London, S.W.7. Tel: 01-584-9161.

Bonham's Chelsea Galleries, 75-81 Burnaby St, London, S.W.10. Tel: 01-352 0466.

Canonbury Auction Rooms, 317 Upper St, Islington, London, N.1. Tel: 01-226 6418.

Christie, Masson & Woods Ltd, 8 King St, St James's, London, S.W.1. Tel: 01-839 9060. Telegrams: Christiart London, S.W.1

Coe, W. E., & Sons, South Kensington Auction Rooms, 79-85 Old Brompton Rd, London, S.W.7. Tel: 01-589 2422.

Debenham Storr & Johnson Dymond Ltd, 26 King St, Garrick St, London, W.C.1. Tel: 01-836 1181.

Druce & Co, 54-56 Baker St, London, W.1. Tel: 01-486 4241.

Glendining & Co Ltd, Blenstock House, 7 Blenheim St, New Bond St, London, W.1. Tel: 01-499 8541.

Halletts, 280-282 Holloway Rd, London, N.7. Tel: 607-3711.

Harmer, H. R., Ltd, Specialist Stamp Auctioneers, 41 New Bond St, London, W.1. Tel: 01-629 0218.

Harrod's Auction Galleries, Arundel Terrace, Barnes, London, S.W.13. Tel: (Office) 01-748 2739; (auction room) 01-748 6615. Free parking for 200 cars.

Knight, Frank & Rutley Ltd, 20 Hanover Sq, London, WIR OAH. Tel: 01-629 8171.

Marylebone Auction Rooms, Hayes Place, Lisson Grove, London, N.W.1. Tel: 01-732 1118.

Motcomb Galleries, 19 Motcombe St, Belgrave Sq, London, S.W.1. Tel: 01-235 3636.

Phillips, Son & Neale Ltd, Blenstock House, 7 Belheim St, New Bond St, London, W.1. Tel: 01-499 8541, and at Marylebone Auction Rooms, Hayes Place, Lisson Grove, London, N.W.1. Tel: 01-732 1118.

Puttick & Simpson Ltd, Blenstock House, 7 Blenheim St, New Bond St, London, W.1. Tel: 01-499 8541.

Sotheby & Co Ltd, 34-35 New Bond St, London, WIA 2AA. Tel: 01-493 8080. Telegrams: 'Abinito', London, W.1.

OUTSIDE LONDON

Alcester, Warwickshire: John Brown & Co, Tudor House, Alcester. (Salerooms at Memorial Hall, Great Alnes). Tel: 2712/4.

Ambleside, Westmorland: Alfred Mossop & Co, Compton Rd, Ambleside. Tel: 3015/6.

Ascot, Berks: Chancellors & Co, 11 High St, Ascot. Tel: 20101.

Ashford, Kent: Burrows & Co, 39-41 Bank St, Ashford. Tel: 24321.

Banbury, Oxon: Buckell & Ballard, 3 Market Place, Banbury. Tel: 3161/2.

Bath, Somerset: Jolly & Sons, Ltd, The Auction Rooms, Old King St, Bath. Tel: 32041.

Beaconsfield, Bucks: A. C. Frost & Co, Beaconsfield. Tel: 5555.

Bedworth, Warwickshire: Butler & Grassman, 18 King St, Bedworth. Tel: 3153.

Birkenhead, Cheshire: Richard Baker & Baker, 9 Hamilton St, Birkenhead. Tel: 151-647 9104.

Birmingham, Warwickshire: Biddle & Webb, New Art Auction Galleries, Islington Row, Five Ways, Birmingham 15. Tel: 021-643 4380.

Birmingham, Warwickshire: John Chivers & Sons, 36 Cannon St, Birmingham, 2. Tel: 021-643 8681.

Birmingham, Warwickshire: Weller & Dufty, The Fine Art Salerooms, 141 Bromsgrove St, Birmingham, 5. Tel: 021-692 1414/5.

Bishop's Stortford, Herts: G. E. Sworder, Chequers, 19 North St, Bishop's Stortford. Tel: 2441.

Bishop's Stortford, Hants: Edwin Watson & Son, 26 North St, Bishop's Stortford. Tel: 2361/4.

Bournemouth, Hants: House & Son, Lansdowne House, Christchurch Rd, Bournemouth, BH1 3TW. Tel: 26232.

Bournemouth, Hants: Riddett & Adams Smith, The Auction Rooms, 24 Richmond Hill, The Square, Bournemouth. Tel: 0202-25686.

Brighton, Sussex: Graves, Son & Pilcher, 51 Old Square, Brighton, 1.

Brighton, Sussex: Philip H. Inman, 35, Temple St, Brighton, BN1 IHG. Tel: 774777.

Broadway, Worcs.: Blinkhorn & Co, 41-3, North St, Broadway. Tel: 2456.

Bristol: Lalonde Bros, & Parham, 71 Oakfield Rd, Bristol, 8. Tel: 34052.

Bristol: Taviner's, 133 Westbury Rd, Bristol, BS9 3AN. Tel: 626020.

Buckingham, Bucks: W. S. Johnson & Co, 8 Bridge St, Buckingham. Tel: 2120.

Bury St Edmunds, Suffolk: Lacy, Scott & Sons, 3 Hatter St, Bury St Edmunds. Tel: 0284 3907.

Canterbury, Kent: Worsfolds, 3 St Margaret's Sq, Canterbury. Tel: 62325.

Cheltenham, Glos: Cambray Auction Galleries, 26 Cambray Place, Cheltenham. Tel: 24679.

Chichester, Sussex: Stride & Co, Southdown House, St John's St, Chichester. Tel: 82626/7.

M

Chichester, Sussex: Wyatt & Son, 59 East St, Chichester. Tel: 86581.
Cirencester, Glos: Moore, Allen & Innocent, Corn Hall Buildings, Ciren-
    cester. Tel: 2584/5.
Crewkerne, Somerset: T. R. G. Lawrence & Son, Crewkerne. Tel: 2403/6.
Croydon, Surrey: Croydon Auction Rooms, 256 High St, Croydon. Tel:
    688-1123.
Croydon, Surrey: E. Reeves Ltd, Auction Rooms, 110-112 Church St,
    Croydon CR9 10S. Tel: 688-3137/8.
Dorchester, Dorset: Henry Duke & Son, 40 South St, Dorchester. Tel:
    1426.
Dorking, Surrey: P. F. Windibank, The Dorking Halls, 18-20 Reigate St,
    Dorking. Tel: 4556.
Driffield, Yorks: Dee & Atkinson, The Exchange, Driffield. Tel: 3151.
Dublin, Eire: James Adam & Sons, 26 St Stephen's Green N., Dublin 2.
    Tel: 63881.
Edinburgh, Midlothian: Dowell's Ltd, 65 George St, Edinburgh 2. Tel:
    225-2266.
Edinburgh, Midlothian: Lyon & Turnbull Ltd, 51 George St, Edinburgh 2.
    Tel: 225-4617/8.
Exeter, Devon: The Devon and Exeter Auction Galleries, Whitton & Laing,
    20 Queen St, Exeter. Tel: 59395/6.
Exmouth, Devon: Crews & Son, 3 Rolle St, Exmouth. Tel: 4751.
Farnham, Surrey: Weller, Egg & Co, 24 Castle St, Farnham. Tel: Farnham
    6221/4.
Fleet, Hants: Alfred Pearson & Son, 99 and 293 Fleet Rd, Fleet. Tel: 3166.
Gerrards Cross, Bucks: Buckland & Sons, Bringewood, East Common Rd,
    Gerrards Cross. Tel: 85451/2.
Glasgow, Lanarkshire: Morrison, McChlery & Co, 98 Sauchiehall St,
    Glasgow C.2. Tel: DOUglas 3386.
Glasgow, Lanarkshire: Wylie & Lockhead Ltd, 100 Kent Rd, Glasgow C.3.
    Tel: Central 9329.
Gloucester: Bruton, Knowles & Co, Albion Chambers, Gloucester. Tel:
    21267.
Godalming, Surrey: Messenger, May & Baverstock, 93 High St, Godalming.
    Tel: 7222.
Guildford, Surrey: Osentons Auction Galleries, Millmead, Guildford. Tel:
    4030.
Harrogate, Yorks: Morphet & Morphet, The Mart, 4-6 Albert St, Harro-
    gate. Tel: 2281/2.
Hexham, Northumberland: Thomas Pattinson, 4 Battle Hill, Hexham. Tel:
    3448.
Hove, Sussex: Graves, Son & Pilcher, 42 Church Rd, Hove 3. Tel: 35266.
Inverness: Fraser's (Auctioneers) Ltd, 28-30 Church St, Inverness. Tel:
    32395.
Ipswich, Suffolk: Garrod Turner & Son, 50 St Nicholas St, Ipswich. Tel:
    54664 and 53114.
Kidderminster, Worcs: Cattell & Young, 31 Worcester St, Kidderminster.
    Tel: 4754.
Kingsbridge, Devon: Charles Head, 113 Fore St, Kingsbridge. Tel: 2352.
Kirkby Lonsdale, Westmorland: James Thompson, District Bank Chambers,
    Kirkby Lonsdale, via Carnforth. Tel: Kirkby Lonsdale 555/6.
Leamington Spa, Warwickshire: Lock & England, 1-2 Euston Place, Leam-
    ington. Tel: 22341.

Leamington Spa, Warwickshire: Regent Sale Rooms, 20 Regent St, Leamington. Tel: 29679.

Leicester: Warner, Sheppard & Wade, The Auction Mart, 16-18 Halford St, Leicester, LE1 1JB.

Leominster, Salop: Russell, Baldwin & Bright, 38 South St, Leominster. Tel: 2363/6.

Lewes, Sussex: Rowland, Gorringe & Co, Gorringe's Auction Galleries, 15 North St, Lewes. Tel: 2503.

Wallis & Wallis, All Saints House, 210 High St, Lewes. (Specialists in militaria, arms and armour, coins and medals.) Tel: 3137/8.

Ludlow, Salop: Brian Cole, Royal Oak Chambers, 14 Tower St, Ludlow. Tel: 2364.

Matlock, Derbyshire: Robert E. Spark & Co, Firs Parade Auction Gallery, Matlock. Tel: 2451.

Merthyr Tydfil, Glam: E. A. M. Besley & Thomas, Central Chamber, Merthyr Tydfil. Tel: 3772.

Newbury, Berks: Dreweatt, Watson & Barton, Market Place, Newbury. Tel: 2144/6.

Newcastle-upon-Tyne: Anderson & Garland, Anderson House, Market St, Newcastle-upon-Tyne, NE1 6 XA. Tel: 26278/9.

Northampton: Northampton Auction Galleries, 33-35 Sheep St, Northampton. Tel: 0604-37263 or 0604-37282.

Norwich, Norfolk: Clowes, Nash & Thurger, 6 Tomblands, Norwich. Tel: 27261/2.

Norwich, Norfolk: Saville, Curtis & Menson, 8 and 10 Upper King St, Norwich. Tel: 29121.

Nottingham: T. Neale & Son, 34 Milton St, Nottingham. (Saleroom at 155 Mansfield Rd.) Tel: 26206.

Oswestry, Salop: C. E. Williams & Co, Salop House, Salop Rd, Oswestry. Tel: 4125/8.

Oxford: E. J. Brooks & Son, Pusey St Sale Rooms, off St Giles, Oxford. Tel: 44545.

Oxford: Franklin & Jones, Frewin Court, Oxford, OX 29LP. Tel: 48666.

Paignton, Devon: Bearne's Salerooms, 52 Hyde Rd, Paignton. Tel: 59492 and 58296.

Penzance, Cornwall: W. H. Lane & Son, Central Auction Rooms, Penzance. Tel: 2286/7.

Perth, Scotland: Love, Thomas & Sons, Ltd, St John's Place, Perth. Tel: 24111.

Peterborough, Northants: Norman, Wright & Partners, Trinity Salerooms, 26 Priestgate, Peterborough. Tel: 67361.

Plymouth, Devon: Taylor, Son & Creber, 1 Queen Anne Terrace, Tavistock Rd, Plymouth (with Auction Rooms at 3 Reservoir Rd).

Plymouth, Devon: D. Ward & Son, 11 The Crescent, Plymouth. Tel: 66251/3.

Pulborough, Sussex: King & Chasemore, Station Rd, Pulborough. Tel: 2081/6.

Reading, Berks: Nicholas, 147 Friar St, Reading, RG1 1HD. Tel: 56511/8.

Redhill, Surrey: F. G. Lawrence & Sons, 89 Brighton Rd, Redhill. Tel: 64196/7.

Retford, Notts: Henry Spencer & Sons, 15 Exchange St, Retford. Tel: 2404/3768.

Rye, Sussex: Vidler & Co, Auction Offices, Rye. Tel: 2124/5.

Saffron Walden, Essex: Cheffins, Grain & Chalk, 8 Hill St, Saffron Walden. Tel: 3656/9.

Salisbury, Wilts: Wooley & Wallis, The Castle Auction Mart, Salisbury. Tel: 27405/11.

Sheffield, Yorks: Henry Spencer & Sons, 4 Paradise St, Sheffield. Tel: 79102/5.

Shrewsbury, Salop: Hall, Wateridge & Owen, Welsh Bridge, Shrewsbury. Tel: 53151/5.

Southend-on-Sea, Essex: Elan's Fine Art Auctions, 15-17 West Rd, Southend. Tel: 48404/6.

Southsea, Hants: D. M. Nesbitt & Co, 7 Clarendon Rd, Southsea, PO 5 2ED. Tel: Portsmouth 20742.

Stafford: Hall & Lloyd, 7 Church Lane, Stafford. Tel: 4176.

Steyning, Sussex: Churchman, Burt & Son, High St, Steyning, BN 43L. Tel: 2781-4.

Swansea, Glam: John James, Uplands Saleroom, Uplands, Swansea. Tel: 56938.

Tavistock, Devon: Ward & Chowen, 1 Church Lane, Tavistock. Tel: 2458.

Tenterden, Kent: Hatch & Waterman, High St, Tenterden. Tel: 3233.

Thame, Oxon: William A. Honour, 57 North St, Thame. Tel: 2383.

Torquay, Devon: Bearne's & Waycotts, Head Office, 3 Warren Rd, Torquay. Tel: 223109.

Virginia Water, Surrey: Wentworth Auction Galleries, 22 Station Approach, Virginia Water. Tel: Wentworth 3711.

Wadebridge, Cornwall: Button, Menhenitt & Mutton Ltd, Belmont Auction Rooms, Wadebridge. Tel: 2131.

Wareham, Dorset: S. W. Cottle & Son, North St, Wareham. Tel: 2826.

Wellington, Salop: Barber & Son, 1 Church St, Wellington. Tel: 2155/9.

Welshpool, Montgomery: Harry Ray & Co, 5-6 Church St, Welshpool. Tel: 2155/9.

Winchester, Hants: Goodman & Mann, Winchester Auction Galleries, 12 Southgate St, Winchester. Tel: 2021/3.

Winchester, Hants: Alfred Pearson & Son, Walcote Chambers, Winchester. Tel: 3388.

Witney, Oxon: Habgood & Mammott, 27 Market Sq, Witney. Tel: 2633.

Wokingham, Berks: H. E. Hall & Sons, Oxford Rd Saleroom, Wokingham. Tel: 702.

Wolverhampton, Staffs: Thomas Skidmore & Son, Imperial Chambers, Lichfield St, Wolverhampton. Tel: 21491/2.

Woodbridge, Suffolk: Arnott & Calver, 14 Church St, Woodbridge. Tel: 2244/5.

Wrexham, Denbighshire: Wingett & Son, 24-5 Chester St, Wrexham. Tel: 2050-3654.

SOME AUCTION ROOM PRICES
1968-69

FURNITURE

£   s

Bookcases, Bureau-Bookcases and Bookshelves

Sheraton mahogany bureau-bookcase, swan-neck pediment, 3 ft
3 in wide — 1,650 0

George II walnut bureau-bookcase — 650 0

Georgian mahogany breakfront bookcase, 7 ft 10 in wide,
7 ft 8 in high — 450 0

Regency rosewood cylindrical swivel bookcase with shallow
pierced gilt metal gallery, 25 in diameter, 38 in high — 284 0

Large Regency mahogany bookcase with dentil cornice, the
upper part enclosed by four glazed astragal doors; the cupboards in the base enclosed by four doors with indented
panels — 160 0

Edwardian mahogany bureau-bookcase inlaid with ribbon, shell
and urn motifs in satinwood. The top with swan-neck pediment with double-glazed astragal doors. The fall flap opening
to reveal drawers and recesses. Four long drawers below on
bracket feet, 7 ft 5 in high — 132 0

Georgian mahogany secretaire-bookcase, fitted adjustable shelving enclosed by glazed barred doors and cupboard below
drawer, 2 ft 6 in wide — 120 0

Georgian figured mahogany inlaid secretaire-bookcase, the upper
part fitted with adjustable shelving, enclosed by glazed barred
doors and fitted with two short drawers enclosed by panelled
doors below, 4 ft wide — 100 0

Small oak bureau-bookcase, the top with glazed astragal doors,
the base fitted with a single drawer and double panelled
doors, 5 ft 7 in high — 95 0

A nineteenth-century mahogany bureau-bookcase with satinwood lines. Top having glazed doors. Fall flap to base, which
has four long drawers and is supported on bracket feet — 56 0

Bureaux and Writing Cabinets

Early nineteenth-century marquetry inlaid cylinder-front bureau
with pierced ormolu gallery, mounts and beading, having
interior fittings, writing slide and three drawers, on taper
legs, 3 ft 2 in wide — 475 0

George III mahogany secretaire cabinet, the upper lancet
panelled glazed doors above secretaire and panelled cupboard
doors, 8 ft 4 in high, 4 ft 2 in wide — 250 0

George II walnut bureau inlaid with boxwood lines. Interior
having central well, drawers and recesses. Two small and two
long drawers in base, on bracket feet — 210 0

	£	s
Eighteenth-century fruitwood bureau with three long graduated drawers below the fall, on bracket feet, 3 ft wide	140	0
Georgian mahogany secretaire cabinet, the top drawer opening to reveal eight drawers and recesses inlaid with shell motif and a green baize writing panel. Three long graduated drawers to the base. The upper part enclosed by panelled doors	95	0
Georgian mahogany fall-front bureau having four drawers under and on bracket feet, 3 ft 2 in high	70	0
Edwardian mahogany bureau-cabinet with pierced swan-neck pediment over glazed doors, sloping fall front over four drawers, bracket feet	66	0
George II oak bureau with fall flap and small drawers, two small and two long drawers below and supported on bracket feet, 2 ft 10 in high	60	0
Victorian mahogany bureau with sloping fall front over four long graduated drawers, on bracket feet	58	0

Cabinets

	£	s
Georgian mahogany bookcase cabinet with arched pediment surmounting astragal double doors. The base with double doors supported on bracket feet, 6 ft 6 in high	470	0
French display cabinet of Louis XVI design, mounted with ormolu female caryatids, the base with panels in the style of Vernis Martin, 3 ft 9 in wide	410	0
Regency mahogany display cabinet, the upper part enclosed by brass grilled and latticed doors, panelled cupboards to the base and supported on bold paw feet	290	0
Victorian walnut display cabinet in the Louis XVI manner, mounted with ormolu and inset with Sèvres porcelain panels, two serpentine glass doors to the side and a door to the centre, 5 ft 1 in wide	126	0
Mahogany display cabinet of Chippendale-style with two glazed astragal doors below a swan-neck pediment and supported on cabriole legs and claw and ball feet, 5 ft 3 in wide	80	0

Canterburys

	£	s
George III mahogany Canterbury with drawer in frieze on tapering legs, 1 ft 7 in wide	130	0
George III mahogany Canterbury with turned legs	115	0
Georgian mahogany four-section music Canterbury with drawer in base	85	0
George III mahogany Canterbury with slatted sides and ringed legs, 1 ft 4 in wide	60	0

Chairs—Open Arm and Elbow

	£	s
George II mahogany open arm chair in the French manner. Rectangular back and serpentine fronted seat. Arm supports and cabriole legs carved with rococo foliage and with scroll feet	150	0
George III mahogany open arm chair forming library steps, the arm supports and curved stretchers with rope twist	150	0

	£	s
Two early stick-back Windsor elbow chairs	74	0
Edwardian inlaid rosewood open arm chair with pierced splats	57	0

Chairs—Dining Sets

	£	s
Ten Sheraton-period mahogany dining chairs with cross rail backs and satinwood crestings on turned and reeded legs. Two carvers	3,100	0
Eleven Regency rosewood dining chairs with carved and reeded back rails, caned seats and on reeded sabre legs	720	0
Set of eight Regency mahogany dining chairs with padded backs, sabre legs. All are strung with brass, with brass carrying handles on the cresting rails	670	0
Set of two carving and six single Hepplewhite mahogany chairs with shield backs and pierced vase splats carved with wheat ears, on tapering legs	660	0
Set of six single and one carving Hepplewhite mahogany chairs with shield backs and pierced vase splats, supported on tapering legs	350	0
A composite set of eight eighteenth-century Dutch walnut dining chairs, inlaid with marquetry depicting floral bouquets, urns, scrolls and birds. Comprising one carving and seven single chairs	310	0
Set of six Sheraton inlaid mahogany single chairs with triple splat backs and stuff-over seats, on tapering legs	290	0
Set of nine mahogany dining chairs, one carver, in the Hepplewhite style with triple vase splats and drop-in seats	260	0
Set of two carving and six single Chippendale style mahogany ladder-back dining chairs with pierced serpentine splats and moulded legs	235	0
Set of six Regency mahogany reeded frame single chairs on sabre legs	150	0
Set of six William IV single dining chairs with leather seats and sabre legs	122	0
Set of two carving and four single Chippendale style mahogany chairs with carved and pierced splats and loose stuffed leather seats, supported on cabriole legs and claw and ball feet	120	0
Set of six Victorian walnut single chairs on slender curving legs	105	0
Set of six small Victorian walnutwood single chairs with oval backs and pierced scroll splats, on curved legs	105	0
Set of four Georgian reeded mahogany wooden seat hall chairs, crested	100	0
Set of six elm rush seat chairs with spindle backs	74	0
Set of six Victorian single chairs with slender curving legs and damask seats	68	0
Set of four Edwardian mahogany shield-back single chairs inlaid with satinwood lines and a fan	55	0
Set of six Victorian mahogany balloon-back dining chairs on turned legs	35	0

Chairs—Dining Single

Pair of George III mahogany dining chairs with moulded and rounded arched backs and pierced splats carved with foliage

	£	s
and husk pendants. Upholstered curved seats on square legs with block toes	50	0
Sheraton mahogany chair with stuff-over seat	17	0
Three early Victorian yew wood standard chairs	17	0
Pair of Victorian rosewood chairs on turned carved legs	5	0
Regency mahogany standard chair on reeded sabre legs	5	0

Chairs—Easy

George III mahogany wing armchair with an arched back, shaped sides and chamfered legs	140	0
Early Victorian mahogany frame wing easy chair	50	0
Papier mâché nursing chair with cane seat and inlaid with mother-of-pearl	30	0
Victorian button-back nursing chair	29	0

Chests of Drawers and Commodes

Chippendale mahogany serpentine chest with reeded and canted corners and with four graduated drawers, on wide bracket feet, 3 ft wide	980	0
Chippendale mahogany serpentine chest, the canted corners pendant with clusters of fruit and flowers in bold relief, 3 ft 3 in wide, 2 ft 8 in high	620	0
Georgian walnut bachelor's chest with folding top and four long drawers having brass handles and lockplates; supported on bracket feet, 29 in wide, 13 in deep, 32 in high	165	0
Eighteenth-century walnut chest of three short and three long drawers with tulip wood stringing on stand fitted with two short and one long drawer with cabriole legs and claw and ball feet, 3 ft wide	105	0
Small Georgian mahogany commode with fluted and canted corners and fitted with two small and three long drawers	66	0
George III mahogany chest of two short and three long drawers, 3 ft 2 in wide	28	0

Chiffoniers

Regency mahogany chiffonier with three stepped shelves above with gilt metal sides pierced in the Chinese style, the fronts with rope twist mouldings. The lower section enclosed by two doors panelled with radiating pink silk, 3 ft 10 in wide	150	0
Regency rosewood chiffonier, the single shelf at the top with acanthus supports. The single drawer to the front containing writing panel and fitted compartments. The whole with double brass rail and flanked by scrolled acanthus supports	110	0

Coffers and Chests

Early Charles II oak chest of four panelled drawers with panelled sides and bun feet, 3 ft 1 in wide	65	0
Late seventeenth-century carved oak coffer with a domed lid. The front carved with four arches and surrounded by stylised carving of leaves, strapwork and birds' heads, 3 ft high, 5 ft 3 in wide	60	0

	£	s
Early seventeenth-century carved oak dower chest, 3 ft 6 in wide	30	0
Seventeenth-century oak coffer with lifting top, the front panelled and carved in low relief with strapwork and foliage and the initials 'E.P,' 4 ft 2 in wide	28	0

Cupboards—Corner

	£	s
Hepplewhite free-standing, serpentine-fronted mahogany corner cupboard. Double glazed doors at the top enclose three display shelves. Base on square feet with double doors	90	0
Mahogany bow-fronted corner cupboard with glazed door enclosing shelves	60	0
Georgian standing corner cupboard with four panel doors enclosing shelves	50	0
George I blue japanned hanging corner cupboard with small open shelves above a pair of bowed doors. Decorated with chinoiseries, 3 ft 9 in high by 1 ft 11 in wide	42	0
Lacquer bow-fronted corner cupboard decorated in gilt with Chinese figures and buildings on a scarlet ground. The whole on cabriole-legged stand (not matching), 1 ft 10 in wide	40	0
Bow-fronted hanging corner cupboard with the door painted with King Solomon and the Queen of Sheba, 1 ft 11 in wide	32	0
Black lacquer bow-fronted corner cupboard with doors decorated with gilt Chinese landscapes, 1 ft 10 in wide	14	0

Davenports and Desks

	£	s
Eighteenth-century partner's desk in sabicu with tooled green leather top and fitted with eighteen drawers to the kneehole frieze, with rococo gilt metal handles; circa 1780	780	0
Queen Anne walnut kneehole desk crossbanded with fruitwood, with one long drawer and two tiers of three small drawers, 2 ft 5 in wide	400	0
George III mahogany tambour desk, the shutter enclosing fitted interior with leather-lined slope, pigeon-holes and drawers with two drawers below on square tapering legs with brass castors, 3 ft 1 in wide	260	0
Mahogany pedestal desk with leather-lined top and nine drawers around kneehole, 4 ft 8 in wide	110	0
Georgian mahogany Davenport with drawers and slide and with leather-lined fall and brass gallery, 1 ft 8 in	87	10
Victorian figured walnut Davenport with carved front supports	42	0

Dressers

	£	s
Eighteenth-century oak dresser with three small drawers with brass handles and lockplates and cabriole legs ending in pad feet, 6 ft 2 in wide	165	0
Eighteenth-century oak dresser with three small drawers with brass handles over a waved apron, with cabriole legs on pad feet, 6 ft 2 in wide	118	0
Stuart-design oak dresser, the cupboards and drawers with geometrical raised panels with gilt metal drop handles	110	0
Oak dresser, the top with a shaped frieze, two cupboard doors		

	£	s
and three shelves over three moulded drawers to the base, with cabriole legs, 5 ft 6 in wide, 6 ft 8 in high	105	0

Globes

Pair of early nineteenth-century mahogany library globes by Newton, published in 1838 and 1836. The tripod frames with out-scrolled legs ending in brass castors, 3 ft 8 in high — 780 0

Large pair of terrestrial and celestial globes by Newton; published 25 March 1875. Supported in mahogany frames on triple curving legs — 205 0

Pair of terrestrial and celestial globes in turned stands by James Wyld, Charing Cross East; published 1847 — 185 0

Knife Boxes

A pair of mahogany urn-shaped knife boxes, stamped W. Johnston, with domed lids and bodies inlaid with flowers and stripes, 2 ft 5 in high — 115 0

Sheraton inlaid mahogany serpentine-fronted knife box in original condition — 32 0

Mirrors—Mantel

Empire-style giltwood overmantel with triple mirrored panels and decorated with classical figures — 105 0

Rectangular mantel mirror in a giltwood frame carved with acanthus and shell motifs, 31 in by 25 in — 60 0

Mirrors—Toilet or Dressing

Sheraton serpentine-fronted box-frame toilet mirror fitted with two drawers, 17 in wide — 36 0

Sheraton box-frame shield-shape toilet mirror with two drawers, 18 in wide — 30 0

Mahogany box-frame toilet mirror with three drawers, 15 in wide — 15 0

Edwardian mahogany box-frame toilet mirror with three drawers to base, 22 in wide — 9 0

Mirrors—Wall

Pair of Chinese-Chippendale giltwood girandoles of rococo outline mounted with phoenix-birds and clusters of flowers from which issue two scrolled candle branches. The base enriched with acorns and oak leaves, 38 in high — 650 0

Mid-Georgian wall glass in a giltwood frame carved with scrolls and foliage and pierced, 44 in high — 200 0

Chippendale mahogany mirror with gilt gesso beading and scrolled outline — 140 0

George IV convex mirror in a gilt frame enriched with spherical ornament with two scrolled candle sconces. Crested with a gilt eagle with outspread wings — 76 0

Regency giltwood convex mirror with ball encrusted moulded frame and ebonised slip, 1 ft 11 in diameter — 15 0

Settees, Couches and Chaise Longues

Small carved mahogany sofa, the arched back carved with rococo motifs. Curved arms, carved seat rail and cabriole legs — 135 0

	£	s
Decorated satinwood cane-panelled settee with loose seat cushion, 4 ft 4 in	130	0
George III painted settee with flat rectangular back and arms, on turned legs. The arms, seat rails and legs are painted with husks and flowers on a cream ground, 6 ft wide	95	0
Early George III mahogany settee with stuffed back and arms. The seat rail and legs are carved with blind fret, 5 ft 8 in wide, (some restoration)	32	0
Victorian rosewood frame serpentine-fronted chaise longue on short cabriole legs	32	0

Settles

Eighteenth-century oak settle, 5 ft 5 in wide	60	0
Seventeenth-century panelled oak settle with box seat, 4 ft 6 in wide	52	0
Seventeenth-century carved and panelled tall-back hall settle, 5 ft 7 in wide	40	0

Sideboards

Small nineteenth-century sideboard inlaid with ebony lines. Raised back, the centre drawer flanked by a cupboard and deep drawer. Supported on six turned and tapering legs, 4 ft 8 in wide	235	0
Hepplewhite-style mahogany serpentine sideboard of rich mellow colour, cross-banded in kingwood and fitted with a napery drawer and cellaret cupboards with octagonal gilt metal handles and supported on chamfered legs, 7 ft 2 in wide	195	0
Georgian mahogany half-moon sideboard with two cupboards to the sides and two drawers with lion ring handles in the centre. Four tapering legs, 4 ft wide	175	0
Large mahogany Sheraton-style sideboard fitted with two long drawers and flanked by two deep drawers, supported on tapering legs	155	0
Regency Empire mahogany sideboard of architectural form, with a reverse breakfront with two shallow drawers to the centre flanked by deep cupboards. Supported by two curved and four simulated bamboo legs terminating in brass paw feet. The whole mounted with ormolu and brass griffins, lions' masks and sphinx and with Adams-style garlands and patera, 7 ft 6 in long	150	0
Late Georgian mahogany sideboard with shaped front, the top back rail fitted with three tambour slides. Two cupboards and a centre drawer to the base over a waved apron. Supported on six slender tapering legs, 5 ft 7 in wide	145	0
Early nineteenth-century mahogany bow-front sideboard on spiral-turned legs, 6 ft 1 in wide	95	0

Tables—Breakfast

Regency mahogany breakfast table with brass stringing on the banded top and a turned pillar ending in a reeded quadruped, 5 ft by 3 ft 5 in	265	0
Georgian mahogany oval breakfast table with reeded edge and		

	£	s
on a vase-shaped pillar ending in a plain quadruped, 5 ft by 4 ft	150	0

Tables—Card

	£	s
Chippendale mahogany card table with shaped folding top on boldly carved cabriole legs ending in claw and ball feet, 2 ft 7 in wide	370	0
Late George II mahogany card table with border of carved flowerheads and legs and frieze carved with blind fret, 3 ft wide	250	0
Regency card table in figured rosewood inlaid with brass flowers and leaves, the D-top on a ringed stem and quadruple brass capped legs, 3 ft wide	190	0
Sheraton mahogany card table inlaid with satinwood lines and on tapering legs, 3 ft 2 in wide	180	0
George II walnut card table with rectangular top on turned legs with mantled knees and club feet, 3 ft wide	95	0
Regency mahogany card table with green baize interior on curving quadruple support, ending in brass claw feet. The top is cross-banded	65	0
Victorian mahogany card table with double flap top supported on four tapering shafts, terminating in curved legs	44	0

Tables—Centre

	£	s
Regency painted centre table, the circular top simulating green marble, the border with brass mouldings hinged to a carved turned central support on a curved triangular base with lion's paw feet, 4 ft diameter	120	0
Edwards and Roberts ebonised centre table with ormolu beading on cluster column and quadruple base, 5 ft 6 in wide	38	0
Red Buhl shaped centre table with heavy ormolu mounts, two drawers and on cabriole legs. (Poor condition)	11	0

Tables—Dining

	£	s
Charles I oak dining table with a triple-plank top and the frieze carved with leaves and interlaced arcading, on column legs, 6 ft 5 in long by 2 ft 7 in wide	360	0
Large late George III mahogany dining table, the top richly carved with acanthus, ribbon motifs, satyr masks and a coat of arms. Supported on ten tapering spiral-twist legs with five loose leaves, 12 ft 4 in long	185	0
Georgian mahogany two pillar dining table with triple curving legs ending in brass-capped feet	122	0
Georgian mahogany oval drop-leaf dining table on turned legs and pad feet	75	0
Eighteenth-century mahogany oval drop-leaf cottage dining table on taper legs with pad feet, 3 ft 6 in wide	44	0
Mahogany gadrooned oval dining table with cabriole legs and claw and ball feet	40	0

Tables—Drum

	£	s
Georgian mahogany drum library table with leather top and four real and four dummy drawers. On triple curving legs with brass-capped feet, 3 ft 3 in diameter	680	0

£ s

George III mahogany library table fitted with seven drawers and
dummy drawers with gilt metal lion ring handles, the top with
gilt tooled green leather and the whole raised on a curved
quadruple support with brass-capped feet   400 0

Tables—Games and Sewing
Eighteenth-century mahogany, shaped folding top, games table
on nutcracker frame with cabriole legs and claw and ball
feet, 34 in wide   300 0
William IV games table with sliding and reversible top inlaid as
a chess board opening to reveal a backgammon board with
two drawers to the side. Central pillar supported on quadruple
curving feet   82 0
Nineteenth-century mahogany sewing table with rising top and
drawers below. The slender tapering legs ending in brass-
capped feet   76 0

Tables—Gate-leg
George I elmwood gate-leg table, the oval top with flaps on
cabriole legs carved with scrolls and leaves and ending in
pointed pad feet, 3 ft 9 in wide   150 0
Seventeenth-century oak oval gate-leg dining table with double
flaps supported on bobbin turned legs with plain cross
stretchers, 4 ft 9 in wide   70 0
Late George II mahogany gate-leg table, the oval top with two
flaps, on unusual legs fluted and ending in paw feet, 3 ft 9 in
wide   60 0
Oak oval gate-leg table on turned underframe with drawer, 4 ft
wide   58 0

Tables—Occasional
Late George II mahogany piecrust table with bird-cage support
on fluted stem with carved legs and claw and ball feet, 2 ft
2 in diameter   360 0
Large mahogany piecrust tripod table with baluster stem and
pointed pad feet, 3 ft 5 in diameter   90 0
Mahogany tripod table, the circular top with raised rim, on
cabriole feet, 1 ft 10 in diameter   40 0

Tables—Pembroke
Late Georgian mahogany oval Pembroke table with drawer, on
square tapering legs, 2 ft 7 in wide by 3 ft 6 in long   125 0
Late Georgian mahogany Pembroke table painted with a floral
border and on turned and fluted legs   110 0
Georgian mahogany Pembroke table with folding flaps and
single drawer, inlaid with satinwood lines and fan motifs, on
tapering legs, 3 ft 2 in wide   103 0

Tables—Refectory
Seventeenth-century oak refectory table of slender plain form,
the base having square ends united by a single stretcher,
7 ft 3 in long   135 0

	£	s
Oak refectory table on bulbous end supports with central stretcher, 7 ft 7 in by 3 ft wide	130	0
An exceptionally long oak refectory table with triple curving supports, 18 ft 6 in long, 3 ft 3 in wide	90	0

Tables—Side

	£	s
Queen Anne banded walnut side table with two deep and two shallow drawers on square legs, 3 ft 3 in wide	170	0
Chinese-Chippendale mahogany side table, the frieze carved with blind fret. Moulded legs, 3 ft wide	88	0
Oak side table with drawer, on turned legs, 3 ft wide	64	0
Walnutwood side table with cabriole legs carved with acanthus leaves	31	0

Tables—Sofa

	£	s
George III satinwood sofa table cross-banded with acacia, fitted with two drawers and false drawers opposite on trestle supports with splayed curved feet and brass castors, 2 ft 10 in wide	750	0
Regency banded mahogany sofa table with tulipwood stringing with two drawers on end supports and central stretcher with brass claw feet, 5 ft 10 in extended	380	0
Late George III mahogany sofa table with two drawers in frieze and raised on flat trestle supports with out-curved legs, 3 ft 2 in wide	270	0
George III mahogany sofa table banded in rosewood and with two drawers. It has trestle supports with tripod splayed legs and brass feet, 3 ft wide	250	0

Tables—Sutherland

	£	s
Mahogany Sutherland table on turned underframe, 2 ft 9 in wide	42	0
Victorian walnut-veneered Sutherland table on turned supports, 2 ft 6 in wide	36	0

Tables—Tea

	£	s
Regency mahogany tea table with folding top on a turned pillar and four curved legs, the whole inlaid with brass stringing, 3 ft wide	120	0
Late George II mahogany tea table, the top with a border of flowerheads and ribbon and the frieze and chamfered legs carved with Chinese blind fret, 3 ft wide	60	0
George III mahogany tea table with folding top, a drawer in the frieze and square tapering legs, 3 ft 8 in wide	38	0

Tables—Wine

	£	s
Hepplewhite mahogany wine table, the inlaid octagonal top supported on triple concave curving legs	105	0
Victorian mahogany wine table on pillar and tripod base, 21 in diameter	10	0

Tables—Writing

George III mahogany pedestal writing table, the gilt tooled leather top with three drawers at each side of the frieze and

	£	s
the pedestals with cupboards and drawers at either end, 4 ft wide	520	0
Early eighteenth-century banded fruitwood writing table, fitted with three drawers, a shaped apron and on cabriole legs with pad feet, 2 ft 4 in wide	130	0
Victorian lady's mahogany writing table with two short drawers on lyre end supports, 3 ft wide	30	0
Carved mahogany writing table with fitted drawer, the top lined with leather, on cabriole legs, 2 ft 5 in wide	20	0

Tallboys and Lowboys

George II walnut tallboy, the top with reeded and canted corners and three small and three long drawers. The base having three long drawers and bracket feet	480	0
Queen Anne small walnut tallboy of mellow colour, the upper chest fitted with two small and three long drawers over a brushing slide, and three long graduated drawers	270	0
William and Mary lowboy inlaid with scrolls and motifs. The top fitted with two small and two long drawers and two long drawers to the base, 4 ft 3 in high	140	0
Georgian mahogany tallboy with dentil cornice and two small and three long drawers to the top and three long drawers to the base which is supported on bracket feet	72	0
Georgian mahogany tallboy with dentil cornice, the top fitted with two small and three long drawers, the base with three long drawers and supported on bracket feet, 6 ft 1 in high	44	0

Waiters

Mid-Georgian mahogany dumb waiter with turned and carved columns supporting three trays. The whole on cabriole tripod feet, 4 ft high	190	0
George III mahogany dumb waiter with two revolving tiers and baluster centre on three curved and moulded legs and castor feet applied with roundels, 3 ft 2 in high	180	0
George II mahogany dumb waiter with three graduated revolving tiers and spiral fluting on turned central support. Plain cabriole legs, 3 ft 6 in high	120	0

Wardrobes

Mahogany breakfront wardrobe fitted with sliding trays, four drawers and panelled cupboards	92	0
Small Georgian mahogany wardrobe enclosed by two panelled doors with three drawers in the base, 3 ft 9 in wide	55	0
George III mahogany gents wardrobe with pierced swan-neck cresting, a pair of doors banded in satinwood and two short and two long drawers below, 7 ft high by 4 ft 4 in wide	48	0
Regency mahogany wardrobe the upper part with sliding trays with four drawers under on splay feet, 3 ft 11 in wide	36	0

Washstands

Late George III mahogany washstand, the top hinged and opening to form a back, the front with a pair of cupboard doors above one small drawer, on square splayed legs, 2 ft wide	60	0

	£	s
Edwardian three-tier corner washstand with basin	18	0
George III mahogany corner washstand, the slender legs joined by a stretcher with a drawer, 2 ft wide	14	0

Wine Coolers

Georgian inlaid mahogany sarcophagus wine cooler with lion mask and ring handle on paw feet	65	0
Georgian mahogany octagonal wine cooler with lifting top and short square moulded legs, 18 in wide	55	0

CLOCKS, WATCHES AND BAROMETERS

Bracket Clocks

Repeater clock by Edwardus East with signed and engraved backplate in ebonised case	600	0
A three-train musical clock by Moore of Ipswich with eight tunes in ebony case with gilt metal mounts in mid-eighteenth-century style, 2 ft 2 in high	440	0
George III fruitwood clock by Recordon, late Emery, London, with painted dial and frets at side and front of case, 1 ft 2 in high	290	0
George III walnut clock, the dial signed Joseph Smith, Chester, and of pronounced Continental character, 1 ft 6 in high	210	0
George III ebonised clock, the 7-in dial signed William Smith, with calendar and strike/silent dial. The movement is contained in an inverted bell-topped case, 1 ft 4 in high	190	0
Louis XV contra-boulle clock with enamel dial signed Darmezin, Paris, and movement signed Crepaux, Paris, in cartouche-shaped case, 3 ft 1 in high	190	0
Louis XV Boulle clock by Perrache, Paris, with an enamelled dial, the case surmounted by a youthful figure of Jove, richly mounted in ormolu, 2 ft 6 in high	170	0
George III mahogany clock by Massey, Bridge Road, Lambeth, the circular white-painted dial with a central calendar hand, 1 ft 4 in high	140	0
George III mahogany clock, the 7-in circular dial signed Lamb and Webb, London, with calendar and engraved backplate in bell-top case, 1 ft 4 in high	120	0
Mid-eighteenth-century veneered ebony clock signed John Smallwood, Lichfield, with pull quarter repeat, 1 ft 4 in high (later dial)	85	0
George III mahogany clock, the 8-in arched silvered dial signed Gravell and Tolkien, London, with engraved backplate and tic-tac escapement in broken arch-topped case, 1 ft 6 in high	60	0
Regency rosewood clock signed on dial John P. Smith, 1 ft 3 in high	20	0

Carriage Clocks

Clock in gilt case by James McCabe, London	675	0
Repeating French brass clock with white dial signed Gibson and Co Ltd, Belfast, 6¾ in high	68	0

	£	s
French brass clock with white dial signed Rowel, Oxford, 4½ in high	50	0
Repeating brass clock with white dial and glazed brass case, 5 in high	50	0
Gilt metal timepiece, the glazed case with pierced floral frets at the sides and front, 5 in high and with travelling case	48	0
Miniature silver-cased repeating clock with white dial. The case stamped J. Keller, 3½ in high	48	0

Lantern Clocks

Brass clock with engraved copper dial and an alarm disk, 1 ft 1 in high	250	0
Late seventeenth-century brass clock, the dial engraved with flowers and with pierced dolphin cresting, 1 ft 3 in high	200	0

Longcase Clocks

Late seventeenth-century marquetry clock, the 11-in dial signed Robt. Williamson, London, with calendar aperture in a walnut case inlaid with shaped panels of birds and flowers, with a bullseye in the waist door and with spirally turned columns at the corners, 6 ft 7 in high (frieze of a later date)	900	0
Tall mahogany cased clock with chimes. The elaborately foliated brass dial with a silvered chaptered ring. The case inlaid with classic urns in coloured woods, the arched hood has brass spires and the waist has a bevelled glass door	278	0
A carved mahogany cased clock with a grotesque satyr mask to the hood over a brass floral scrolled dial. Westminster, Whittington and St Michael chimes, 7 ft 7 in	230	0
Mahogany clock made by Manley of Chatham	200	0
Eighteenth-century walnut clock with domed canopy and brass face, the movement by William Stapleton, London, 7 ft 4 in high	155	0
Walnut clock, the early eighteenth-century movement signed Andr. Dunlop, London, the 12-in dial with chestnut and flower spandrels, 7 ft 4 in high	125	0
Georgian lacquer clock with brass face and striking movement. The case, with 'bullseye' door, decorated with gilt chinoiseries on a simulated tortoiseshell ground	80	0
Eighteenth-century small clock by John Lee, Cookham; with brass dial and foliated spandrels, in a black lacquer case decorated with chinoiseries in red and gilt	72	0

Mantel Clocks

An ormolu clock, the painted dial signed F. Linke, Paris, the movement in a glazed case in well chiselled ormolu with drapery, acanthus leaves and groups of fruit and ending in double cloven-hoof feet, 2 ft 11 in high	190	0
Bronze and ormolu mounted clock, the movement contained in a drum upon which is seated a Chinaman holding a parasol, the whole on the back of an elephant, 1 ft 4 in high	150	0
A French clock, inscribed Bonniere a Clermont, in a rococo porcelain case. The blue and gilt ground painted with musicians, lovers and flowers. On a similar stand	140	0

N

	£	s
Louis XVI marble and ormolu clock, the striking movement with enamel dial signed Hessen. The arched architectural case with drapery festoon, pineapple finials, an urn and fluted columns, 1 ft 5 in high	110	0
Regency rosewood clock, the movement by Dwerrihouse & Carter, Davies Street, 2 ft high	70	0
Louis Philippe clock with glass panels in gilt metal case with corinthian columns and surmounted by an urn. Decorated with coloured enamels, 18 in	68	0
An Empire marble clock mounted in ormolu, the movement with outside count-wheel, the dial surmounted by a white marble urn and suspended between fluted columns capped by ormolu pineapples, 1 ft 4 in high	55	0

Watches

	£	s
Gentleman's 18-carat gold half-hunter watch	20	0
Early nineteenth-century verge watch by D. Nevern, in a tortoiseshell case, the dial enamelled with a wharf-side scene	13	0
Gentlemen's 18-carat gold pocket watch by George Harvey, Wellington	13	0
George III verge watch by William Fowler, London, in a silver case, London 1783	9	0
Nineteenth-century verge watch by Nicoll, Great Portland Street, in a tortoiseshell case	7	10

Barometers

	£	s
Early Victorian mahogany stick barometer by E. Davis, Shrewsbury, 3 ft 3 in high	70	0
Regency rosewood inlaid with mother-o'-pearl banjo barometer and thermometer	46	0
George III mahogany banjo barometer and thermometer with engraved scales by A. M. Ortelli, Godalming, the case outlined with fruitwood lines, 3 ft 2 in high	38	0
Georgian mahogany stick barometer and thermometer by Routledge, Carlisle	38	0
Mahogany stick barometer and thermometer by Salmon, Bath	38	0
A Regency rosewood banjo barometer and thermometer by Aprile Sudbury	34	0
Early nineteenth-century mahogany banjo barometer by Lione and Tarone, London, with a thermometer and the case inlaid with Prince of Wales plumes and a whorl pattern, 3 ft 2 in high	30	0
Early nineteenth-century mahogany banjo barometer by A. Celti, Reading, the case inlaid with shells, 3 ft 2 in high	22	0

SILVER

(Troy weight: 20 pennyweights [dwt] = 1 ounce [oz])

Baskets for Bread, Cakes, Fruit, Sugar or Sweetmeats
George II oval-shaped cake basket on four cherub mask and scroll feet. The sides pierced and engraved with flowers and

	£	s
scrolls and the base engraved with a coat-of-arms, by Paul Crespin, 1753, 62 oz	3,600	0
George III oval pedestal cake basket by John Emes, London, 1804, 24 oz 10 dwt	400	0
George III boat-shaped pedestal sugar basket with engraved border, reeded edge and swivel handle by Peter, Ann and William Bateman, London, 1793, 5 oz 10 dwt	320	0
Victorian oval basket, the pierced panels embossed with beading and garlands, London, 1895, 19 oz	62	0

Candelabra and Candlesticks

Pair of George I dwarf table candlesticks, the baluster shafts upon square terraced bases by William Darkeratt, 4½ in high, London, 1726, 20 oz	1,500	0
Victorian table candelabra with two tiers of six scrolled branches issuing from a bold Corinthian column supported on a square terraced foot, with neo-classic rams' mask and husk swags by R.H. over R.H., London, 1877, 30 in high	355	0
Pair of George III table candlesticks, the tapering baluster shafts upon half-fluted circular bases by John Green & Co, Sheffield, 1800	195	0
George III chamber candlestick and snuffer, the gadrooned edge with shell motif by William Cafe, London, 1761, 12 oz	130	0

Casters

Garniture of three George II vase-shaped sugar casters of plain design by John Delmester, London, 1758, 15 oz 10 dwt	930	0
William IV Scottish baluster caster engraved with a crest above floral decoration on a granulated ground, by Elder & Co, Edinburgh, 1832, 4 oz 7 dwt	90	0
George III baluster caster with pierced cover and wrythen finial, by Thomas Satchwell, 1780, 2 oz 4 dwt	85	0
George III vase-shaped caster the otherwise plain body engraved with contemporary crest. The mark of George Giles struck over another, 1783, 2 oz 8 dwt	65	0

Coasters—Wine

Set of four partly fluted circular coasters with gadrooned rims and engraved with crests by John & Thomas Settle, Sheffield, 1818	410	0
Pair of George III coasters with pierced waved galleries, London, 1794	270	0
Pair of William IV circular-shaped wine coasters with foliate borders and crested silver bosses to the wood base, by Henry Wilkinson & Co, Sheffield, 1831	150	0
Pair of George III coasters with beaded rims, the pierced sides stamped with arcading, urns and laurel festoons, maker's mark missing, 1794	100	0

Coffee Pots

George I small plain cylindrical coffee pot with octagonal spout and low domed cover with baluster finial, by Paul De Lamerie, London, 1725, 11 oz 3 dwt	1,900	0

£ s

George II baluster coffee pot, plain with foliate decorated spout,
wood handle and hinged domed lid, probable maker Fuller
White, London, 1759, 21 oz 1,350 0

Late George III tapering cylindrical coffee pot, the plain body
engraved with contemporary armorials and a crest, by Peter,
Ann and William Bateman, London, 1802, 35 oz 2 dwt 1,200 0

George IV coffee pot, vase-shaped, with moulded bands at the
neck and waist, leaf-capped scroll handle and foliate finial
on lid, by Pearce & Burrowes, London, 1826, 22 oz 5 dwt ... 210 0

Victorian vase-shaped coffee pot engraved with key pattern
decoration, London, 1872, 24 oz 135 0

Cruets

George II five-bottle cruet frame on four shell feet with detachable baluster handle. Five cut-glass silver-mounted bottles. By
Jabez Daniel, 1750, 28 oz 7 dwt 105 0

George III cruet frame for six bottles with reeded loop end
handles, ring holders, on four feet. Five glass bottles all
chipped, one broken. By Henry Chawner, London, 1792 ...... 16 0

Cups and Goblets

Elizabeth I secular wine goblet, the bowl decorated with tulips
and strapwork motifs, on a slender baluster stem and circular
fluted foot, London, 1593, 5 oz 10 dwt 2,000 0

Pair of George III goblets of plain design, probably by William
Sumner, London, 1800, 20 oz 520 0

Pair of George III two-handled pedestal challenge cups and
covers with reeded decoration and urn knops, by Samuel
Hennell, London, 1806, 32 oz 5 dwt 400 0

George III tumbler cup engraved with armorials, gilt interior
and the base with contemporary initials. Possibly by John
Carter, London, 1766, 2 oz 1 dwt 150 0

Victorian wine cup, the beaker-shaped bowl and pedestal base
cast and chased in low relief with grape-laden vine tendrils,
by Hunt and Roskell, London, 1875, 10 oz 1 dwt 52 0

Cutlery—Canteens

George III fiddle thread pattern table silver: 24 tablespoons, 36
table forks, 12 dessert spoons, 12 dessert forks, 12 teaspoons,
6 sauce ladles, 2 soup ladles, 1 marrow scoop, majority by
Richard Crossley, 1798/1800/1804, 146 oz 9 dwt 750 0

Victorian fiddle pattern table silver: 12 tablespoons, 12 table
forks, 12 dessert spoons, 12 dessert forks, 6 teaspoons, 2 salt
spoons, by George Angell, London, 1863, 116 oz 14 dwt 260 0

Cutlery—Forks Dessert

Twelve George I three-pronged forks with crest, different
makers, 1718, 14 oz 1 dwt 1,500 0

Twelve George IV fiddle pattern forks by James Scott, Dublin,
1822, 15 oz 75 0

Six George III fiddle pattern forks by G.D., London, 1794,
8 oz 14 dwt 65 0

£   s

Cutlery—Forks Table
Twelve Queen Anne three-pronged forks engraved with a crest,
by David King, Dublin, 1708/10, 28 oz   1,000   0
Four George II three-pronged forks engraved with two crests,
1755, 7 oz 18 dwt   70   0
Eleven Victorian fiddle shell pattern forks by George Angell,
1857/61, 36 oz 16 dwt   60   0

Cutlery—Forks Toasting
George III fork with knopped shaft and scrolled handle, prob-
ably by R. Preston, London, *circa* 1767, 7 oz 10 dwt. 17¾ in
long   190   0
George III fork with knopped shaft and scrolled handle by John
Deacon, London, *circa* 1775, 8 oz. 19½ in long   180   0

Cutlery—Knives
Forty-eight Victorian table knives and twenty-four dessert
knives, kings pattern, steel blades by J.A. or T.S., 1884   270   0
Twelve eighteenth-century dessert knives, the multi-faceted
bloodstone handles with knopped urn finials and mounts
engraved, the scimitar blades of steel. *Circa* 1700, (Some
handles cracked)   115   0

Cutlery—Ladles
Four George III sauce ladles, crested Old English pattern by
Hester Bateman, 1783, 5 oz 19 dwt   150   0
Pair of George III sauce ladles with ribbed and punched beaded
bowls, by Michael Keating, Dublin, *circa* 1780, 2 oz 16 dwt   40   0

Cutlery—Spoons Dessert
Nine engraved spoons, seven by William Soame, 1741, two
1748, 12 oz   155   0
Ten Hanoverian spoons engraved with crest, 1760, 11 oz 5 dwt   120   0

Cutlery—Spoons Serving
Pair of George III Old English pattern spoons by Steven Adams,
London, 1772, 5 oz 15 dwt   40   0
Pair of Victorian spoons by George Angell, 1854, 10 oz 14 dwt   15   0

Cutlery—Spoons Table
Six George I Hanoverian pattern spoons with rat-tail bowls
by Charles Jackson, 1723, 11 oz 2 dwt   195   0
Six George III Old English pattern spoons with contemporary
initials J.G. by Hester Bateman, 1780, 11 oz 17 dwt   160   0

Cutlery—Spoons Tea and Coffee
Six William IV 'bright-cut' spoons, 1836, 3 oz 7 dwt   9   0
Eight George IV fiddle shell pattern spoons by J. McKay,
Edinburgh, 1827, 4 oz 8 dwt   8   0

Dishes
Pair of George III oval meat dishes by Frederick Kandler, Lon-
don, 1765, 73 oz 2 dwt   550   0
Pair of Victorian octagonal entree dishes and covers with

	£	s
vegetable dividers for each and ball finials, Sheffield, 1880, 120 oz 14 dwt	450	0
George III circular vegetable dish with ivory grips, pierced sides and four scroll and foliate feet, by W.S., London, 1809, 80 oz 2 dwt	360	0
William IV shaped oblong entree dish and cover with engraved armorials and foliate ring handle, by J. C. Eddington, London, 1835, 61 oz 5 dwt	260	0
George III muffin dish and cover, the domed cover with urn shaped finial, by Henry Chawner, London, 1791, 15 oz 1 dwt	210	0

Jugs—Cream and Milk

	£	s
George III helmet-shaped cream jug with 'bright-cut' engraving, loop handle and square pedestal foot, by George Smith, London, 1790, 3 oz 7 dwt	80	0
George II cream jug of conch shell type with serpent handle and three coral-like supports. *Circa* 1755, 3 oz 5 dwt	80	0
George III oblong milk jug engraved with crests and with gadroon lip and scroll handle, by R. and S. Hennell, London, 1808, 6 oz 2 dwt	70	0
Victorian baluster milk jug chased with flowers and scrolls and on three feet. Possibly by William Brawn, London, 1845, 5 oz 7 dwt	52	0

Jugs—Water

	£	s
George III pear-shaped hot-water jug, stand and lamp, the jug with rams' masks and laurel festoons, the stand on three claw feet with female bust terminals, by Andrew Fogelberg. The jug 1776, the stand 1775, 40 oz	780	0
George III vase-shaped hot-water jug, plain with wood handle and on circular foot, by William Fountain, London, 1801, 25 oz 11 dwt	460	0
George II baluster hot-water jug chased with scrolls, leaves and flowers, raffia-covered handle and rim foot, by Gurney and Cook, London, 1755, 19 oz 15 dwt	270	0

Jugs—Wine and Ale

	£	s
Queen Anne ale jug, the ground embossed with foliage and flowers and a satyr spout, by John Wisdom, London, 1712, 35 oz	280	0
Victorian wine ewer with baluster body and engraved with Grecian figures and leaves, entwined snake handle and butterfly finial, by E. and J. Barnard, London, 1862, 27 oz 11 dwt	170	0

Marrow Scoops

	£	s
Queen Anne scoop of typical form by Charles Jackson, 1713, 1 oz 10 dwt	68	0
Early George III scoop, the larger bowl engraved with initials, probably by William Tuite, London, 1767, 1 oz 12 dwt	20	0

Mustard Pots

	£	s
George III drum mustard with moulded borders, flat hinged lid and simple scroll handle, with spoon of earlier date. Pot by Emes and Barnard, London, 1813, 5 oz 10 dwt	165	0

	£	s

William IV mustard with ribbed baluster body and hinged
domed lid with floral finial, scroll handle and shell thumbpiece
and spoon of same date but different maker. Pot by C.G.,
London, 1830, 6 oz 17 dwt — 50 0

George III oblong mustard with domed cover, urn finial and
angular handle on four bun feet, London, 1813, 3 oz 11 dwt — 30 0

Salts

Four George I plain oval trencher salts with incurved sides, by
Mary Rood, 1723, 6 oz 15 dwt — 580 0

Pair of George III boat-shaped salts, reeded at the lips and
pedestal feet, gilt interiors, by Peter and Ann Bateman, 1792,
4 oz 6 dwt — 120 0

Pair of George II compressed circular salts, with plain engraved
bodies below gadroon lips each on three shell-headed hoof
supports, possibly by Isaac Cookson, Newcastle, 1747, 8 oz
1 dwt — 105 0

Salvers

George II large circular salver on four lions' mask and shell
bracket feet, the shaped border pierced and chased, by
George Wickes, 1744, 137 oz — 1,000 0

George I plain circular salver on central foot with moulded border, by W.P., 1720, 13 oz 12 dwt — 520 0

George III circular salver, engraved with initials, chased wave
border and gadroon rim, on three claw and ball feet, by
Robert Rew or Rugg, 1766, 24 oz 3 dwt — 340 0

Victorian salver engraved in the centre with an initial and also
with scrolls and foliage, moulded border, by J. and J. Angell,
London, 1845, 25 oz 14 dwt — 75 0

Sauceboats

Pair of George II plain sauceboats each on three shell and
scroll feet with gadrooned rims and double scroll handles,
by Peter Archambo and Peter Meure, 1754, 29 oz — 1,700 0

George II two-handled plain double-lipped sauceboat on collet
foot, with double scroll handles and waved rim, with a
moulded drop beneath the spout, by Peter Archambo, 1732,
17 oz 5 dwt — 1,250 0

Pair of George III sauceboats, each on fluted shaped lozenge
foot, with gadrooned borders and double scroll handles, by
William Sampel, 1766, 25 oz — 580 0

Snuff Boxes—See *Small Decorative Antiques*

Sugar Basins—See *Baskets*—*Sugar*

Tapersticks—See *Candlesticks*

Tankards

William and Mary tankard on three lion couchant feet, scroll
handle, cylindrical body and moulded base, by Robert Cooper,
1692, 31 oz — 2,100 0

£ s

George II baluster tankard with domed cover, openwork thumbpiece and double-scroll handle, on moulded spreading foot,
by William Grundy, 1755, 34 oz 5 dwt — 650 0

George III baluster tankard, with domed moulded cover and
heart-shaped lower terminal to the scrolling handle, by
William Caldecott or Cripps, 1765, 27 oz 15 dwt — 570 0

Tea Caddies

George III oval caddy, the body with two bands of bright-cut
engraving in beaded borders and the plain hinged lid with urn
finial, by Hester Bateman, 1781, 14 oz 10 dwt — 900 0

George III shaped oval caddy, the body fluted at intervals,
decorated with bright-cut engraving, hinged domed cover with
wood finial, by Robert Hennell, 1787, 14 oz 17 dwt — 480 0

Teapots and Stands

George II bullet teapot with engraved shoulder decoration of
satyr masks, leaves and flowers, straight spout, loose lid, ivory
handle and finial, by Isaac Liger, 1729, 15 oz 1 dwt — 2,100 0

George III teapot stand on four fluted panel supports, by Hester
Bateman, 1789, 4 oz 15 dwt — 280 0

George III oval teapot with moulded girdles and a matching
stand, supported on four feet, by Crespin Fuller, London,
1800, 16 oz 15 dwt — 270 0

George III oval, semi-lobed teapot, with swan-neck spout, ivory
handle and finial, by P. A. and W. Bateman, 1799, 17 oz
3 dwt — 170 0

George IV teapot, compressed circular body, ivory handle and
finial, curved spout, by Eley and Fearn, 1823, 25 oz 16 dwt — 150 0

William IV compressed circular teapot with moulded girdle,
wood finial and similar wood handle, by E. E. J. and W.
Barnard, 1830, 14 oz 2 dwt — 135 0

Early Victorian bullet-shaped teapot with engraved body, Edinburgh, 1840, 24 oz — 82 0

George III oval teapot stand, gadroon border on four panel
supports, but George Fenwick, Edinburgh, 1806, 5 oz 14 dwt — 80 0

William IV small melon-shaped teapot, with slightly domed
cover and ivory finial, scroll handle and curved spout, London, 1833, 13 oz 18 dwt — 60 0

Tea and Coffee Services

Victorian tea and coffee service of compressed circular form,
decorated with embossed flowers and foliate handles and on
scrolled feet with shell motifs, by Rawlins and Sumner, London, 1838, 72 oz — 600 0

George IV three-piece melon-shaped tea service with scroll
handles and shell decorated panel supports, by E. E. J. and
W. Barnard, London, 1829, 44 oz 7 dwt — 500 0

George III circular three-piece tea service with curved lobes,
gadroon rims and leaf decorated handles, on paw supports, the
pot with rose finial, by John Angell, 1819, 41 oz 6 dwt — 380 0

Victorian three-piece tea service of compressed circular form,

	£	s

the plain ground richly chased, by I. J. Keith, London, 1840,
48 oz — **310 0**

Vinaigrettes—See Small Decorative Antiques

Waiters
Pair of George III plain oval waiters each on four shell and
beaded bracket feet, beaded rims, by John Scofield, London,
1777, 27 oz — **560 0**

George II plain shaped square waiter on four hoof feet,
moulded border, by Thomas Farren, London, 1734, 6 oz
17 dwt — **420 0**

Early George II square waiter with raised border incurved at
the angles, 1727, 3 oz 18 dwt — **170 0**

SHEFFIELD PLATE

Candelabra and Candlesticks
Pair of candelabra, each for three lights, with reeded scrolling
arms, gadroon bordered knops, detachable nozzles and circular
bases, 17¾ in high to centres — **70 0**

Pair of three-light candelabra, the tapering vase stems, circular
bases and campana-shaped sconces decorated with chased borders, each fitted with two detachable scrolling branches, one
converting to form a five-light and bearing flame finial, 20 in
high — **60 0**

Pair of table candlesticks with V-shaped stems, gadroon shoulders, circular bases and detachable nozzles, 11¼ in high — **32 0**

Pair of table candlesticks with circular bases, vase-shaped stems
and gadroon borders, detachable nozzles, 11 in high — **22 0**

Coffee Pots
Vase-shaped coffee pot on pedestal foot with reeded borders, ball
finial and wood handle, 13 in high — **58 0**

An oval coffee pot on pedestal base, with reeded shoulder, gadroon borders and angular wood handle, 9¾ in high — **50 0**

Urn-shaped coffee pot, body semi-lobed between ribbed panels,
on pedestal base, ball finial and wood handle, 27 in high — **30 0**

Coasters—Wine
Four circular wine coasters with lobed sides below gadroon lips,
the wood bases centred by crested bosses, 5¼ in diameter — **38 0**

Pair of circular coasters with beaded and ovolo rims, wood bases,
6 in diameter — **20 0**

Caddies—Tea
Two caddies of bombé form embossed with shell motifs — **70 0**
Serpentined caddy with hinged lid and beaded borders — **10 0**

Dishes
Set of four entrée dishes and covers on heater bases, oblong
with scrolling foliate borders, 14 in wide over handles — **270 0**

	£	s
Pair of entrée dishes and covers with gadroon borders and detachable foliate handles, 11 in wide	22	0
A rectangular entrée dish and cover complete with liner, gadroon and leaf borders, wood end handles, on four supports, 14½ in wide	20	0

Teapots

An oblong teapot, body semi-lobed between gadrooned borders, short spout, ivory finial and angular wooden handles, 5½ in high	25	0
A compressed circular teapot engraved with swirling leafage, fruit finial and scroll handle, 5¼ in high	18	0

Tea and Coffee Services

Oval three-piece coffee service with vase-shaped pot, oval jug and basin decorated with bands of sprays and foliage, 10 in high the pot	160	0
Three-piece tea set with compressed circular bodies, fluted, foliate collars, scroll handles and foliate panel supports	38	0

Tea Trays

Oblong two-handled tray, engraved with armorials within a chased surround of scrolls and floral sprays, gadroon border, 30 in wide	220	0
An oblong tray, gadroon bordered and reeded end handles springing from chased foliage, 28 in wide	95	0

Tea Urns

An inverted compressed pear-shaped urn, the body engraved with a crest, foliate handles and flower finial, 16 in high	75	0
An oviform urn with an applied plain shield, the cover with vase finial, reeded loop handles, on square base with ball feet, 22½ in high	45	0

Tureens

Large shaped oval sauce tureen on four feet below heavily chased floral motifs, detachable liner, 16½ in wide	230	0
Pair of oval sauce tureens and domed covers with gadrooned rims, decorated with acorns and oak leaves at the handles, 8¼ in wide (end handles missing from one tureen)	120	0

Wine Coolers

Set of four coolers, the campana-shaped bodies engraved with contemporary armorials above lobing reeded handles and gadroon borders, on pedestal bases, 9¼ in high	520	0
Pair of coolers with campana-shaped bodies, reeded handles and on pedestal bases, 9½ in high	200	0

NON-PRECIOUS METALS

Brass

Pair of eighteenth-century andirons, with spherical finials, and masks, 29 in high	100	0

	£	s
A club fender	50	0
A Corinthian column floor standard	28	0
An embossed fire kerb	24	0
A two-handled log tub on paw feet	24	0
An alms dish with lobed centre and inscription border, the rim with punched rosettes, 15¾ in diameter	19	0
Pair of spirally-turned candlesticks on domed feet, 20½ in high	18	0
A hanging oil lamp	18	0
Pair of chambersticks, with snuffers	18	0
A heavy log tub with lion mask handles on paw feet	16	0
Brass and steel semi-circular fender	12	0
An oval fire insurance plate with a crest of a stag, dated 1774	11	0
Pair of carriage lamps	10	0
A helmet coal-scuttle	8	0
A warming-pan with turned wood handle	6	0
Pair of baluster candlesticks, 9 in high	4	0

Bronze

	£	s
Figure of a racehorse and jockey after Isadore Bonheur, 10½ in high	273	0
The Capture of Alexander by G. Halse. Two warriors hold a struggling youth. Signed and dated 1860, 24 in high	60	0
Eighteenth-century Italian figure *The Dying Gladiator* signed Canova	57	0
Figure of a dancing fawn, holding up a bunch of grapes and balanced on his left foot, 14 in high	40	0
Figure of an infant satyr playing a set of pipes, 9¾ in high	30	0
Pair of busts of Henry IV and Sully, three-quarter length, both wearing ruffs and decorations, on rouge marble socles, 20¼ in high	29	10
Pair of Art Nouveau winged figures stamped A. Moreau, 9½ in high	15	0
Pair of five-light candelabra on bulbous stems	9	0
Italian figure of Venus, 7 in high	7	0

Copper

	£	s
Early nineteenth-century tea urn on a square base	20	0
A street lamp	13	0
Three large saucepans (one with lid)	13	0
Two coal scuttles	11	0
A large kettle	9	0
Coal helmet with swing handle	8	0
Large two-handled urn and cover	8	0
A copper and brass tea urn with tap	7	0
A long turned wooden-handled warming-pan	5	0

Iron and Steel

	£	s
Steel and brass basket grate with pierced frieze and baluster uprights, 20 in wide	73	10
Seventeenth-century Sussex wrought-iron fireback, 2 ft 10 in by 1 ft 8 in and a log fork	26	0
Wrought-iron shaped fire-back	13	0
Regency iron and brass stick stand on paw feet	11	0

	£	s
Victorian cast-iron corner stick stand	5	10
Victorian cast-iron oil heater	3	10

Pewter

A charger with secondary touch of Thomas Lanyon, *circa* 1730, 20 in diameter	36	0
Five quart tankards	35	0
A four-branch candelabrum, 24 in high	22	0
Eighteenth-century circular charger, 20 in diameter	22	0
Pair of altar candlesticks, baluster-shaped stems on triangular bases, 20 in high	16	0
Pair of baluster and cup candlesticks, 18 in high	15	0
A hot-water meat dish with two handles and a grill, 22 in wide	15	0
A travelling chamber-pot, stamped Jas. Dixon	14	0
Two tankards and a mug	6	0

PORCELAIN

Bow

A sweetmeat centrepiece, formed as six scallop shells, naturally fluted, the interiors painted in colours with bouquets of flowers and with puce and gilt rims, on a pierced rockwork base encrusted with shells and coral, enriched in green, yellow, puce and ochre, surmounted by a phoenix, the birds red, green, blue and yellow plumage gilt, 8¼ in high	336	0
A figure of a girl emblematic of spring, seated on a flowering tree stump, with flowers gathered in her apron, in yellow hat, green and yellow bodice and floral skirt, on high gilt scroll base, 7 in high, anchor and dagger mark	230	0
A figure of a youth, standing before flowering bocage, his left hand on his hip, in blue lined yellow hat, yellow lined puce coat, flowered breeches and turquoise shoes, the high pierced base on scroll feet enriched in turquoise and gold, 8 in high, iron red anchor and dagger mark	168	0
A pair of figures of putti as gardeners modelled standing naked in front of a tree stump holding a basket filled with flowers in one hand and a single flower in the other, with garlands of flowers round their heads and over their shoulders, on mound bases with applied flowers, 5¼ in high, one with iron red anchor and dagger mark	84	0
A figure of a cow, modelled recumbent in front of a tree stump with head to the left and tail forward, naturally coloured in shades of brown, on a mound base with applied flowers, 3¼ in wide	50	0
A pair of vine-leaf pickle dishes painted in underglaze-blue with scattered flowers and with serrated blue-edged rims, 3½ in diameter	30	0

Bristol

A Lund's blue and white cream jug, with scroll handle, of pear shape, painted with Chinamen fishing within moulded scroll cartouches on a pleated ground, 3¾ in high	115	10

A coffee pot and cover of pear shape with a faceted spout and
crabstock handle, the sides and cover painted with sprays and
sprigs of coloured flowers and the tip of the spout and the pot
rim edged in brown, 7 in high, blue enamel cross and 10 mark   40   0
A circular bowl, the exterior painted in colours with bouquets of
flowers and flower sprays, 6¼ in diameter, blue enamel cross
mark   23   0

Caughley

A blue and white bell-shaped tankard with fluted handle, the
sides transfer-printed with a Chinese lady and child on a
terrace, the reverse with a fisherman on the banks of a river
with a man looking through a trellis, 5 in high, crescent mark   105   0
A blue and white mug of cylindrical shape, transfer printed in
underglaze-blue with 'Parrot and Fruit' by Robert Hancock,
5½ in high, crescent mark   65   0
A bowl transfer-printed in underglaze-blue on the outside with
bouquets and sprigs of flowers with butterflies hovering
around, the interior with a lily of the valley, a passion flower
and another lily, 11 in diameter, crescent mark   60   0

Chelsea

A rare pair of candlesticks of fable type, one with a hound fighting a fox and a cat climbing in a tree, the other with two
foxes beneath a tree, the animals naturally decorated in red,
brown and manganese, the trees with gilt scroll trunks and
flowering branches and bunches of grapes, supporting pierced
foliage wax pans and candle nozzles enriched with gilding on
gilt scroll bases, 13½ in high, gold anchor marks   546   0
A figure of a masquerader, standing before a tree stump in
dancing attitude his right leg raised, playing the flute, in
black tricorn hat and mask, iron red jacket with yellow
sleeves, green and yellow cloak and pink breeches, a lantern
by his side, on a florally encrusted gilt scroll base, 8 in high,
gold anchor mark at back   273   0
A rare circular fable plate, of silver shape, painted by J. H.
O'Neale, the centre with the fable of the bull and the frog,
the shell-moulded border with three naturalistic sprays of
flowers and fruit and a butterfly, the waved rim and three
moulded shell panels enriched in chocolate, 8¾ in diameter,
raised anchor period   168   0
A beaker-shaped vase, the slightly flared sides with a central
pale claret knop, on either side of which are finely painted
sprays of garden flowers, the rim and foot with gilt dentil
borders, 7¾ in high, gold anchor mark   135   0
A mazarine blue two-handled chocolate cup and cover, of bell
shape, the scroll handles and finial enriched with gilding, the
sides painted in colours with four horizontal panels of Chinese
children seated under trees, with gilt sunflower motifs below
within gilt scroll cartouches on a mazarine blue ground, 5¾ in
high, gold anchor mark   110   0
A shaped circular saucer dish painted in colours with flower

£ s

sprays including roses and tulips, with a brown rim, 9 in
diameter, brown anchor mark   71 0

Chelsea—Derby

A pair of plates, from the Duke of Northumberland service, the
bright blue borders with pink roses, 9¾ in diameter, gold
anchor and script 'N' marks   78 10

A pair of vases and covers of urn shape, the bodies decorated
with vertical gilt lines on a blue ground, reserved on either
side are two oval medallions, one with a portrait, the other
with a landscape, the whole standing on a high foot rising
from a square plinth, the double loop handles moulded with
scales and the domed top with a round knob, 9 in high
(handles repaired)   62 0

Four cups and saucers, the interlaced handles enriched with
gilding, painted *en camaieu verte* with swags of flowers
suspended from gilt dentil rims, gilt anchor and 'D' marks   44 0

A white Group of Music from a set of the Arts, modelled as a
young woman standing playing the flute, with two naked putti
by her side, one playing the viola, a column supporting a
tambourine and the rocky mound base scattered with sheets of
music and instruments, 9 in high, N217 incised   25 0

Coalport (Coalbrookdale)

A pair of vases, the shield-shaped bodies painted in colours
with pastoral scenes of lovers in rectangular panels reserved
within gilt borders on a *gros-bleu* ground, the shoulders set
with winged and crowned terms over a border of white oak
leaves on a gilt ground, the flared necks and square plinths
also richly gilt, one inscribed *Gessner's Pastorals*, the other
with a couplet by Thomson, 14¾ in high, impressed numeral
'2'   120 0

A rectangular plaque, attractively painted with a bouquet of
summer flowers, including dog roses, ranunculas and convolvulus on a white ground, 8 in by 6 in, framed   44 0

A flower-encrusted scent bottle, of slender pear shape, finely
painted with scattered insects and applied with coloured
branches of forget-me-nots, convolvulus, roses and auriculas,
the domed cover surmounted by a rose knop, 7 in long   35 0

A jug painted on either side with a bouquet of tulips, roses and
other flowers and in the centre the monogram 'JC' within a
wreath in gilding, 7 in high   24 0

Davenport

A fine turquoise-ground dessert service, each piece painted in
the centre with a cluster of fruit, including pineapples, cur-
rants, strawberries, peaches and plums, within turquoise borders edged with scrolls in apricot and gilding, and the gilt
with fruiting vine, comprising: three fruit stands in sizes,
two circular dishes on low feet and twelve plates, marks
printed in blue and pattern no. 1422   170 0

A garniture of three two-handled vases of baluster form with
scroll handles, painted in colours with garden flowers on

£   s

ledges and with picturesque landscapes, the flared necks
pierced and the royal blue grounds enriched with gilding,
9¼ in high and 8¼ in high   44   0

Derby

A tea and coffee service, each piece attractively painted in
underglaze-blue with a border of stiff leaves reserved on a
vermicular gilt band, comprising: teapot, cover and stand,
sucrier and cover, milk jug, bowl, 2 saucer dishes, 11 coffee
cups, 12 teacups and 12 saucers, crown, crossed batons and
'D' marks in red, numerals '19' and pattern no. 726   180 0

A figure of Neptune, standing on a shell with a dolphin at his
side and with billowing cloak, his hair and beard in puce
colour and his drapery in yellow with flowers and lined in
pink, 6½ in high   62   0

A landscape plaque, well-painted with fishermen unloading a
barque which lies at anchor in an estuary, with a castle on
the wooded bank and ships lying at anchor in the distance,
the light of the sinking sun reflected in the calm water, 7¼ in
by 5⅜ in, framed   60   0

A mug of cylindrical shape, with scrolled strap handle, finely
painted on one side with a traveller in a landscape with a
distant view of a mansion, the reverse with a cottage by the
side of a river in a wooded mountainous landscape, gilt
borders, 5 in high   45   0

A figure of a shepherdess, seated playing a mandolin, in pink
bodice and flowered yellow skirt, pierced scroll base with a
sheep sitting by a flowering tree, 5½ in high   44   0

A pair of figures of Turks, of small size, the boy in long yellow
coat, flowered jacket and red breeches and his companion in
long pink coat and flowered skirt, 3¾ in high   42   0

A Bloor plate with fluted and pierced latticework rim decorated
with pink-scale diaper and gilding, the centre painted with
garden flowers, 10 in diameter, printed mark in red   32   0

A candlestick group, showing the figure of Cupid, naked except
for a yellow-lined pink drapery, kneeling with his quiver of
arrows at his feet against a flowering bocage support, which
rises to support a foliate candle nozzle, the scroll base edged
in turquoise and gilding, 10 in high   26   0

Liverpool

A William Ball blue and white mug of pear shape, painted in
the oriental style with flowering plants issuing from rockwork, with a border of triangular panels above and semi-
circular panels below, 4¾ in high   63   0

A William Ball's factory blue and white saucer painted with
two vases of flowers on a terrace with mountains and birds
in the distance, the border with a herringbone design, 6 in
diameter   40   0

A part tea service painted in Chinese style in iron red, blue and
gilding with two medallions of a phoenix and stylized flowers
surrounded by scrollwork and interspersed with sprays, the

	£	s
rims with flower panels reserved on pink diaper bands, comprising: milk jug, bowl, 3 teabowls and 3 saucers	30	0
A tea pot and cover, the loop handle and spout enriched with foliage designs painted in iron red, the sides painted in colours in the oriental style with figures at various pastimes, 6½ in high	21	0

Longton Hall

	£	s
A rare sweetmeat dish moulded in the form of a leaf edged in brilliant apple-green, the centre well-painted with flower sprays, the rope-twist handle set at an unusually upright angle, 5½ in diameter	170	0
A barrel-shaped teapot and cover, with scroll handle and acorn finial, the sides transfer-printed at Liverpool in black with *The Tea Party*, and *Shepherdess and Lover*, with scattered birds, insects and flowers between, 5½ in high	44	0

Lowestoft

	£	s
A rare blue and white dated mug, of bell shape, with scroll handle, inscribed Ann Sawyer 1733 within a typical Lowestoft rococo scroll cartouche, with sprays of flowers to either side, with cell pattern border to the interior, 4½ in high, workman's mark	336	0
Two tea bowls and three saucers painted in colours with exotic birds on leafy branches, with iron red double line rims	47	0

Minton

	£	s
A dessert service painted with clusters of different flowers, including carnations, fuchias, auriculas, violas, petunias and roses, the scalloped rims edged with a border of entwined turquoise and gilt, comprising: 4 tazzas, and 14 plates, impressed marks and date cypher for 1857	100	0
A rare octagonal tray painted and signed by Samuel Bourne, the centre with a pastoral scene, the sides richly gilt with scroll-work and various diapers reserved with four vignettes, including a ducal coronet and the monogram 'H.E.G.S.', 9 in wide	100	0
An early cylindrical mug, the scroll handle and the royal blue ground enriched with gilt scrolls and foliage and reserved with flowers on a gilt shelf within a lobed gilt cartouche, 4¼ in high, interlaced L. and M mark	32	0

Nantgarw

	£	s
An ornithological plate, from the Mackintosh service, the centre with a cock pheasant standing among foxgloves in a landscape, the border gilt with scrolls enclosing bouquets of flowers in colours, 9¼ in diameter, impressed Nantgarw C.W.	504	0
A very rare oblong dish, painted by Thomas Pardoe, with a bird perched on a branch and roses and other flowers on a brown ground, the marbled gilt border with green dentil rim, 11 in wide, puce crown and Nantgarw mark	273	0
A blue and white circular plate, painted in blue enamel with bouquets of flowers enclosed by moulded 'C' and foliage scrolls, 8½ in diameter, impressed Nantgarw CW	50	0

£   s

New Hall

A part service, each piece painted with scattered flowers, within
pendant tendril and ribbon festoons and florettes at the rims,
comprising: teapot stand, 8 teabowls and 10 saucers   100   0

A punch bowl painted in 'famille-rose' style with the 'window
pattern', showing a Chinese boy gazing out of a window at
three figures on a terrace, divided by river scenes in iron red
within puce scale borders, the interior with three mandarin
figures on a terrace by a pavilion, within a border of floral
garlands, insects and diapers in bright colours, 12 in diameter,
pattern no. 425 in black   40   0

Plymouth

A very rare cylindrical mug, with fluted loop handle, painted
in lilac monochrome with the monogram 'JEM' within a
gilt rococo scroll cartouche, the border decorated in colours
with flowers entwined round a gilt chain suspending floral
swags, $4\frac{3}{4}$ in high, tin sign   367   10

A group of two putti, emblematic of spring, the two children
partly draped in yellow, puce, blue and brown, garlanded
with flowers seated on stools holding between them a long
garland, on a high scroll base enriched with puce, $5\frac{1}{2}$ in high   147   0

Rockingham

A green ground oval basket, the flared lips and elaborate scroll
handle enriched with gilding, the fluted sides and shaped
quatrefoil stand enriched with gilt designs, 6 in wide, puce
griffin mark   84   0

A set of three saucers, with petal-shaped gilt-edged rims, each
one painted with a central flower spray within a scalloped gilt
medallion reserved on a periwinkle blue ground, 6 in diameter,
marks printed in red and pattern no. 665   48   0

A pair of figures of pointers, both animals in typical alert attitude with black patches and gilt collars, on mound bases with
gilt lines, $5\frac{1}{2}$ in wide   40   0

Spode

A dessert service painted with a Japan pattern in tones of pink,
red, green, blue, yellow and gilding, with central panel of
flowers enclosed by a blue line, the rims with shaped blue and
gilt borders edged with red peonies and other flowers, comprising: centre-piece, 3 shell-shaped dishes, 2 diamond-
shaped dishes and 12 plates, marked Spode 2630   190   0

A basket of circular shape with moulded, beaded border, painted
in Imari style with oriental flowering shrubs in green, red,
underglaze-blue and gilding, $6\frac{1}{4}$ in wide, mark and pattern
no. 967 in red   60   0

A pair of pot-pourri vases of shallow campana shape, supported
on circular bases moulded and gilt with palmettes, and resting
on three gilt lion-paw feet, painted in Imari style with oriental
flowering shrubs in a fenced garden, within a border of various
diapers, $5\frac{1}{2}$ in high, marks in red and pattern no. 967   42   0

O

£   s

Swansea

A rare plate, the centre painted by Thomas Pardoe with *The
Little Brown and White Duck*, with fluted well, the border
moulded with C-scrolls and foliage enclosing bunches of
fruit and flowers, with gilt dentil rim, 8 in diameter   231   0

A pair of cushion-shaped dishes from the same service, painted
by Evan Evans, with narcissus, rose, strawberry and other
sprays, 8¼ in wide, red stencil marks   157   10

A shaped oval dish from the same service, painted by Evan
Evans, the centre with a rose and a narcissus, the border with
a strawberry and other sprays, 10½ in wide, red stencil mark   115   10

Worcester

An early leaf-moulded sauceboat, formed of overlapping cos
lettuce leaves, the crabstock handle with leaf and flower
terminals, the sides well-painted with sprigs of flowers and
insects, the interior with a flower spray, brown-edged rim,
7½ in long, First Period   115   0

A porcelain plaque of rectangular shape, painted by R. F.
Perling, signed, with a highlander leading his pony, returning from stalking, the pony laden with two stags and with
two dogs looking out over the moors, 14 in wide, framed   95   0

A pair of blue-scale teacups and saucers, each painted with
oriental flowering shrubs growing amongst banded hedge, in
tones of iron red, blue, green and gilding, within vase and
mirror-shaped panels reserved on the well-defined blue-scaled
ground, seal marks, First Period   85   0

A teapot and cover of globular shape, painted in 'famille-rose'
enamels on each side with three oriental figures in a garden,
within circular panels, divided by landscape vignettes in puce
reserved on a ground of scrolls in gilding, the domed cover
with flower knop, 5¾ in high, First Period   75   0

A pair of transfer-printed teabowls and saucers, each one printed
with *The Milkmaids* by Robert Hancock, showing two milkmaids in a farmyard with pails on their heads, a farmer help-
ing one milkmaid, and with animals in the background, the
reverse of the teabowls with a similar rural scene, and the
interior of each with a swan, First Period, each signed RH
Worcester   55   0

A pair of blue and white bowls, each one moulded on the exterior in low relief with a broad band of scrolling flowers on a
ground of scattered tear drops, the interior of each with a
naturalistic chrysanthemum head in blue, within a border of
scroll vignettes, 6 in wide, crescent marks, First Period   50   0

A blue and white basket of circular shape, the pierced sides
formed of interlacing circlets and applied on the exterior
with blue florettes, the interior with a border of trellis diaper
divided by lambrequins, and with a carnation spray in the
centre, 9¾ in, crescent mark, First Period   46   0

A coffee pot and cover transfer-printed in grey and coloured
on each side of the pear-shaped body with groups of Chinese
figures around a table, the neck and the cover with formal

	£	s

borders in underglaze-blue, the latter with flower knop,
restored, 8⅝ in high, script 'W' mark, First Period — 42 0

Worcester—Flight Barr and Barr

A circular pot-pourri vase and cover, with flared rim, the
goat's mask handles and sphinx finial gilt, the cover pierced
with alternate gilt lozenge and circle designs, the side painted
in colours with a view of Malvern Church, named on the
base within a gilt cartouche on a claret ground, on circular
stem and square gilt base, with gilt and beaded rim, 6½ in
high, script mark — 115 10

A pair of sauce tureens and covers of urn shape with double
birds heads and wing handles, decorated in Imari style with
birds and flowers, square bases, 6¾ in wide — 90 0

An interesting handle-less cup, the flared sides with two oval
portrait medallions of the King of Persia, Fath 'Ali Shah and
the Prince Royal of Persia, Abbas Mirza within burnished
gilt borders and flanked by two oval panels filled with vases
of flowers, all on an apple-green ground, gilt script marks
and titles over a sepia wash on the base — 45 0

Worcestershire—Chamberlains

A fine dessert service painted on each piece in botanical style
with an individual cut flower, within a gilt berried wreath,
the lavender blue ground moulded in white relief with sprays
of shamrock, thistle and rose, between gilt line borders, comprising : a pair of urn-shaped sauce tureens and covers, 4 shell-
shaped dishes, 3 square dishes, 2 kidney-shaped dishes, 2
lozenge-shaped dishes, and 26 dessert plates, printed red marks — 560 0

A yellow-ground beaker, of bucket shape, decorated with a
castle standing on the banks of a tree-lined river, within a
gilt-edged rectangular panel reserved on the pale yellow
ground, 4½ in high — 80 0

A flared beaker painted in the oriental style with the Bengal
Tiger pattern, with alternate mythological beasts and vases of
flowers on tables in gilt ogee panels, the border with formal
designs in iron red, green and gold, 3½ in high, base marked
Chamberlain's Worcester No. 75 — 40 0

A pair of spill vases, with flared lips, painted in colours with
flower sprays within gilt vase and mirror shaped cartouches
on a blue ground, standing on four gilt lion's paw feet on
a square base, 5 in high — 21 0

POTTERY

Creamware

A mug with loop handle, transfer-printed in black with 'The
Farmer's arms in God is our trust', 5¼ in high — 14 10

A tureen and cover, naturally modelled and coloured as a bunch
of grapes, the fixed stand formed as a leaf, 8 in wide — 12 10

£   s

Delftware

A Lambeth blue-dash portrait charger, painted in tones of blue, green, yellow and manganese with a full-length portrait of William III, the crowned king shown standing in an ermine-lined cloak, carrying the orb and sceptre, flanked on either side by trees and with the initials 'WR' above, the everted rim with dashes in blue, 13⅛ in diameter 250 0

A Lambeth plate, with flat base and everted rim, painted in tones of blue, ochre and brown with stylised half-length portraits of William and Mary, both crowned and with the initials 'WRM' above, blue line border, 8¼ in diameter 125 0

A Liverpool bowl, the flared sides painted in blue on the exterior with chinoiserie landscapes, showing pagodas amid willow trees, with mountains and flocks of birds in the distance, the interior with a similar mountainous landscape, within a cell-diaper border interspersed with scrolling flowers, 11⅞ in diameter 46 0

A Lambeth, or Bristol polychrome dish, painted in tones of iron red, green and blue with alternate vase and mirror-shaped panels containing stylised flowers and peacock feathers, reserved on an iron red trellis ground, the centre with a floral medallion, 13¼ in diameter 40 0

A set of seventeen Bristol tiles painted in blue with scenes from the Old and New Testaments, within double blue line borders, the corners with dashes and flowerheads, 5 in square 34 0

A Bristol bowl with an everted piecrust rim decorated with blue ammonite scrolls, the interior painted with a seascape centred with a willow tree behind crossed rocks on an island, flanked by fishermen and pagodas, the distance with four volcanoes and the outside decorated with flower scrolls, 10¾ in diameter 28 0

Leeds Ware

A figure of a blue roan horse, standing alert and unbridled with head raised and ears pricked a flowing mane and generous tail, the cream-coloured body well sponged in blue, and the brown hooves pegged into the flat base, marbled in green, blue and ochre, 16 in high 2,800 0

A coffee-pot and cover, pear-shaped with leaf-moulded spout having floral and leaf terminals at the base as has also the entwined handle, the neck and cover with a beaded border, 9¼ in high 90 0

A figure of Venus standing in long robes with Cupid at one side and the dolphin at the other, she clasps to her breast a pair of billing doves, 7½ in high 45 0

A creamware oval dish, the lobed rim with panels alternately pierced and painted in green enamel with sprays of flowers, the centre with another matching spray, 10⅝ in diameter 32 0

A jug, transfer-printed in black with the Coopers' Arms, the reverse with a cooper at work, 8⅜ in high 30 0

Liverpool Ware

A creamware jug of pear shape, with ribbed-strap handle,

amusingly painted on one side with a gentleman seated at a
table, holding an ale glass and a pipe, a woman carrying in
a jug closely followed by a small dog, the reverse inscribed
James; Hornniblow In the Parish of Sivern Stoke, 1783, all
in tones of green, yellow, iron red and black, 8¾ in high   100   0

A creamware jug transfer-printed in red with the American
eagle surrounded by a linked chain, each with a state name,
the reverse with a compass entitled, *Come Box the Compass,*
7 in high   26   0

Lustreware

An unusual Sunderland tureen cover and ladle, of oval silver
shape, transfer-printed on each side with a *West View of the
Cast Iron Bridge Over The River Wear, Sunderland,*
within pink lustre borders, the domed cover with a scroll knop
picked out in lustre, 12¾ in wide   65   0

A silver resist lustre jug, decorated with a crested bird perched
on a branch between flowering plants, 5½ in high   42   0

Martinware

A barn owl, naturalistically modelled with its head forming a
cover, cocked on one side with a coy expression, its fat body
with downy light brown feathers on his breast and dark brown
on the back, its claws twisted in a life-like manner, 9¼ in
marked R. W. Martin & Bros, London & Southall, 12-1892,
and on the back, wood stand   350   0

A grotesque bird and cover amusingly modelled as a crafty
starling standing on a circular base with a blue-spotted brown
breast and green, blue and brown wings, 10½ in high, signed
R. W. Martin, London & Southall, wood stand   120   0

A pair of vases decorated on the brown oviform bodies with
blue tits among apple blossom, the trumpet necks with more
blossom, all tinged in blue, green and white, 10 in high,
R. W. Martin & Bros, London & Southall, 1-1890.   32   0

Mason's Ironstone

A dessert service elaborately moulded with overlapping leaves
edged in blue and gilt and painted with sprays of pink roses
and other coloured flowers, the tureens and stand with gilt
animal's-head handles and knops, comprising : fruit stand, 2
sauce tureens, covers and stands, 3 shell dishes, 2 oval dishes,
2 shaped rectangular dishes, and 14 plates, impressed marks
lion and unicorn and Patent Ironstone China   190   0

A pair of candlesticks painted around the foot and neck with
flowers on a maroon ground and the stem with gilt bands and
grapevine, 5½ in high, impressed marks   45   0

Pratt Ware

A bull-baiting group, the bull chained to a tree-stump, being
baited by a spotted dog, both animals coloured in brown and
ochre and the mound base sponged in green, 6½ in high   260   0

A Toby jug, showing a man standing with a dog jumping up

£ s

at his side, wearing a tall brown hat, blue coat, ochre waistcoat, yellow breeches and tall brown boots, a goblet in one
hand, his other hand on his hip, 9½ in high 70 0
A group of a sheep standing with a lamb at its side, both with
sponged ochre markings and brown eyes, horns and hooves,
standing on a flat green-glazed base with shaped edge, 5 in
high 48 0
A teapot of rectangular shape with fluted corners, the sides
moulded in relief with caricatures coloured in blue, ochre,
green and brown, the ends with flower sprays and corkscrew
borders, 4¾ in high 38 0
A figure of Winter as a child wrapped in a long cloak standing
on a leaf-scroll mound with square base, sponged in blue and
ochre and covered in greenish glaze, 5 in high 25 0

Saltglaze

A bear jug and cover formed by the head, the bear clutching
with both hands a small dog and with a collar about its neck
with patterns in dark brown, the body covered with grit,
10¼ in high 70 0
A teapot and cover, the bag-shaped body moulded in relief
with pecten-shells and figures, the spout modelled in the
form of a serpent's head, with plain loop handle, on an oval
base, the ribbed cover with a high knop, 5 in high 55 0
A cup of almost bell shape, with ribbed-strap handle, crisply
moulded with upright panels of fables, animals, portrait heads,
hunting scenes and coats-of-arms, 3¼ in high 48 0

Staffordshire Figures and Groups

A figure of Tom Molyneux with fists raised in pugilistic attitude,
the American boxer with curly black hair, wearing yellow
breeches, standing on green base with brown post support,
8½ in high 380 0
A figure of a cavalry officer as a general on a red brown horse,
turned in his saddle and wearing full uniform, 10¼ in high ... 360 0
A bust of Garrick as Othello from Shakespeare's tragedy, the
actor with blackened face and red turbaned head-dress,
wearing a lilac tunic, supported on a brown marbled socle,
7½ in high 290 0
A cow creamer, modelled with a cow and calf on a high mound
base with fruiting tree support, the cow mottled in brown
and ochre, 7¼ in high 265 0
An Obadiah Sherratt group of lovers sitting under an oak tree
laden with acorns, the young man proposing to his companion
and holding a ring, the girl turned coyly away, the base
edged with coloured scrolls and applied with a label, inscribed
Perswaition, 9 in high 240 0
A group, forming a tree-trunk vase, a small boy reaching up
into the trees to a bird's nest, the base with two figures of
leopards, 8½ in high 150 0
Tithe pig group. A tree-trunk vase, showing the wife presenting
her baby with a priest at one side and her husband holding

	£	s

a pig at the other, the base with pigs, corn and a basket of eggs, 8½ in high — 100 0

Pastoral musicians. A group of a boy and a girl in front of a flowering arbour, the boy playing a pipe, in blue coat and yellow trousers, his companion playing a tambourine, wearing pink bodice and flowered skirt, pink marbled base, 9½ in high — 95 0

A figure of a fowler standing with his fowling piece at his side and a goose in his arms, wearing black hat, turquoise jacket and fawn breeches, tree-trunk support, on scroll-edged mound on a square base, 9¼ in high, numeral 48 in red — 90 0

The Cobbler and his Wife. The man working with a shoe on his knee, a hammer and pot at his side, and wearing a black-brimmed yellow hat, grey shirt with rolled-up sleeves, green jerkin, large brown apron, red breeches and blue boots, his wife holding a jug in one hand and a tumbler in the other and wearing a soft cap, green jacket, blue apron swept to one side and patched red skirt, both figures seated on stools, on flat rectangular bases, 6½ in and 6 in high — 55 0

A sheep hollow-moulded, the animal with legs spread across grassy mound base, its tightly curled body splashed in ochre, 5 in high — 40 0

Stoneware

A Nottingham mug of cylindrical form, with grooved strap handle, incised with two horizontal bands of scrolling flower sprays divided by zig-zag borders, the rim incised with the date 1727, 4½ in high — 120 0

A Nottingham loving cup of campana shape, with double-grooved strap handles, applied on each side with a rectangular panel of granular chippings, 5 in high — 50 0

A Nottingham brown-glazed tile of square shape, incised with a central stylised florette enclosed within a circular medallion, and with a quatrefoil lozenge motif at each corner, 5⅛ in square — 10 0

Wedgwood

A pair of blue jasper urns and covers decorated in white relief with Pan, dancing figures, musicians below fruiting vine borders and between stiff leaves on a pale blue jasper ground, supported on circular feet and square bases, 24½ in high, impressed marks — 900 0

A pair of campana-shaped vases and covers decorated with scenes similar to the preceding lot, the allegorical figures in white on a pale blue ground, 21 in high, impressed marks — 480 0

A Jasperware plaque of rectangular shape decorated in white relief on a black ground depicting Greek figures performing ritual sacrifices within a wreath of berried leaves, edged with a cane-coloured border, 18¼ in by 6 in, impressed Wedgwood, framed — 210 0

A pair of Wedgwood buckles, decorated in white relief on the blue jasper ground with classical figures, one with a sacrificial scene, the other with a classically draped man and woman beside a pedestal, within gold and cut steel frames by Matthew

	£	s
Boulton, and with the original clasps trimmed with blue and white ribbons sewn with sequins, overall height 2 in	130	0
A set of ten black basaltes medallions, moulded in relief with the heads of figures from Greek mythology, all treated with a smear glaze, 2¼ in wide, impressed marks	125	0
A pair of plaques in black basaltes, decorated in relief with Hercules and the Nemean lion and a boar hunter returning from the chase, 7 in wide, impressed marks, framed and glazed	100	0
A bust of Lord Nelson in full uniform, turned slightly to dexter, half length, the sash superimposed with a medal inscribed *Nile*, on a circular socle, the back impressed with his name and inscribed *Pubd July 22nd 1798 R. Shout Scp Holborn*, 11½ in high, impressed mark	100	0
A creamware teapot and cover, the ovoid body attractively enamelled by David Rhodes on one side with a young girl holding a fan in a landscape, the reverse with a tall red-roofed house in a park, the whole in bright tones of iron red, puce, green and grey, with strap handle and shell-moulded spout, the cover decorated with flower sprays and with pierced bun knop, 6 in high	75	0
A blue jasper plaque decorated in white relief with a portrait of Mrs Siddons from the model by John Flaxman in the role of the *Tragic Muse*, 5 in wide, impressed mark	50	0
A pair of creamware soup plates transfer-printed in lilac, one with two horsemen galloping past a cottage, the other with a man fishing from a river bank before a ruined tower, the rims with feather-moulded edges and printed with sprays of flowers, 9⅝ in diameter, incised leaf marks	40	0
A crocus pot, naturalistically modelled in the form of a hedge-hog, its arched brown body moulded with quills and pierced with symmetrical rows of holes, 9¼ in high	40	0
A creamware oval stand for a sauce tureen, with feather-moulded rim, attractively transfer-printed in black with exotic birds in a park, surrounded by birds in branches divided by flower sprays, 10½ in wide	12	0
A portrait medallion, bearing the white profile portrait of Sir W. J. Hooker, on a green jasper dip ground, 2⅝ in wide, impressed mark	8	0

Whieldon

A figure of a frog, crouched as if about to leap, and covered in a mottled greenish brown glaze, 3¼ in high	160	0
A teapot and cover, the round body and cover moulded as a basket of fruit and leaves which are covered in green, blue, yellow and manganese mottled glaze, with indented loop handle, leaf-moulded base to the spout, and cauliflower knop to the inset cover, 4½ in high	95	0
A teabowl and saucer, each piece covered with a mottled tortoiseshell glaze, and splashed in green and ochre	46	0

Wood—Enoch and Ralph

A Ralph Wood set of the seasons, each figure on a green and brown mound and square base, Spring with a basket and posy

£ s

of flowers, Summer with a sickle and sheaf of corn, Autumn
with a goblet and bunch of grapes, and Winter skating, the
two girls with yellow bodices and flowered skirts and the two
young men with yellow breeches and pink coats, 7½ in high   320 0
A Ralph Wood stirrup cup in the form of a hare's head, glazed
in manganese and rising above the fluted neck edged in blue,
strap handle, 6 in high   110 0
A Ralph Wood Toby jug, the grinning man shown seated on a
high-backed chair, holding a foaming jug of ale on his knees,
he wears grey tricorn hat, blue jacket, green waistcoat and
breeches and grey shoes, his coarse-featured face splashed in
brown, 9¼ in high   95 0
A Ralph Wood Fair Hebe jug, modelled by Jean Voyez, one side
of the green oak tree trunk moulded in relief with a young
man in blue jacket and yellow breeches, handing a bird's nest
to his companion, who sits wearing a blue dress at his side, a
songsheet entitled *Fair Hebe* above them, the reverse with a
toper standing with his dog, the trunk signed J. Voyez, 1788,
9¾ in high (restored)   65 0
An Enoch Wood group of the Virgin and Child, the Virgin
seated on a grassy mound and holding the infant Jesus on her
lap, she wears a white veil, a long white dress sprigged in puce
and a yellow-lined red cloak, the child with his arms out-
stretched to kiss her and wearing only a white drapery, 13 in
high   50 0
An Enoch Wood teapot and cover of Castleford type, moulded
on each side with arcaded panels of classical figures, divided
by stiff leaves, reserved on a pricked ground, below a border of
gadroons, the whole picked out in green, blue, turquoise and
iron-red, 6¼ in high, mark Wood impressed and coloured in
blue   30 0

CLEAR GLASS

Ale Glasses

A wrythen ale, the flared bowl vertically ribbed on the lower
half above a pincered knop and short stem, terminating in a
folded conical foot, 6¼ in high   210 0
Tall ale, the slightly flared bowl spirally wrythen to within two
thirds of the rim and with flammiform fringing, on a slender
dumb bell knop stem terminating in a high conical folded foot.
6½ in high   160 0
A wrythen ale, two-thirds of the tall bowl spirally ribbed and
with flammiform fringing, on a short knopped stem, terminating in a folded conical foot. 5⅜ in high   78 0
A wrythen ale, the tall round-funnel bowl spirally moulded on
the lower half, on a short stem, terminating in a folded
conical foot, 5⅛ in high   22 0

Bowls

Irish oval cut-glass bowl of canoe shape with serrated rim, band

£ s

of star cutting on sides, on square lemon squeezer foot, 13¾ in
wide   115 0
A large circular cut-glass bowl, with slightly incurving rim, the
border with formal foliage, 15 in diameter   15 10
A cut-glass bowl, the exterior cut with star pattern, with fan
cutting to the rim, on porcelain stand with four winged gilt
beasts on shaped base with gilt scroll feet, 10½ in wide   10 10

Candlesticks, Candelabrum and Tapersticks
A pair of tapersticks, the octagonal nozzles with flared rims, on
octagonal Silesian stems with lozenges to the shoulders, the
domed feet with similar lozenges, 7 in high   40 0
Hollow-blown candlestick with everted nozzle and two angular
knops between a large central ball knop, terminating in a
high domed foot, 8 in high   28 0
Ormolu mounted cut-glass two-light candelabrum, the stepped
octagonal baluster stem supporting foliage branches, from the
cut-glass wax-pans hang pear-shaped and pointed lustres, 13 in
high   26 0
Pair of cut-glass candlesticks, with oviform stems and shaped
crenellated nozzles on domed square feet, 11¾ in high   14 10

Cordial Glasses
A Jacobite cordial, the small drawn trumpet bowl engraved with
a six-petal rose and two buds, a star and an oak leaf, the
multi-spiral air-twist stem terminating in a conical foot, 6 in
high (chipped on the rim)   110 0
An unusual cordial, the small bell bowl on a collar above a swelling knop stem containing an elongated tear, terminating in a
conical foot, 6 in high   75 0
A tall cordial with small drawn trumpet bowl, the slightly tapering stem containing a double mercurial corkscrew, terminating
in a conical foot, 6¾ in high   42 0

Decanters
A Waterloo decanter and stopper of club form with fluted
lower part, engraved with a band of foliage, the neck with
three triple collars and target stopper, 10 in high. Impressed
mark   54 10
A magnum decanter and stopper, of mallet shape, with faceted
pointed stopper, 14¾ in high   42 0
Large cut-glass ship's decanter and stopper, of bell shape, the
lower part ribbed and the sides with stepped cutting, with
pointed faceted stopper, 15 in high   29 10
Pair of Victorian ship's decanters and stoppers of rounded
conical form engraved with a crest and monogram, with
faceted stoppers, 11 in high   16 10
Three cut-glass decanters and stoppers, of barrel shape, with
bands of nail's head cutting and vertical facets above and
below, with mushroom stoppers, 7½ in high   16 0

Goblets
An unusual goblet with large bucket bowl, the stem composed of

	£	s
a mushroom knop above a short baluster stem, terminating in a domed and folded foot, 7¼ in high	230	0
A rare baluster goblet, the funnel bowl with beaded lower part, the stem with a hollow true baluster and an inverted baluster divided by an annular knop on domed and folded foot, 8½ in high	140	0
Goblet with a flared bucket bowl on an inverted baluster stem containing a tear above a base knop and folded conical foot, 7 in high	45	0
An engraved goblet, the lipped ovoid bowl with loop handle and diamond engraved *John Harris/Fox and Goose, Greets Green*, supported on a hollow knop containing an 1836 three-penny piece, above a circular foot, 6½ in high	28	0
Large goblet with unusual double ogee bowl on a massive inverted baluster stem, terminating in a wooden foot, 14¼ in high	18	0

Jugs

	£	s
A cut-glass jug of helmet shape, cut with bands of lozenge ornament between vertical faceting on spreading stem and sunray base, 11 in high	21	0
Pair of jugs of pear shape, the body with nail's head cutting, the rim serrated, 5¾ in high	20	0
A Georgian cut-glass jug of helmet shape, the sides with swags and hobnail patterns, the lower part, stem and neck faceted, on lobed sunray foot, 9¾ in high	19	0

Rummers and Firing Glass

	£	s
A colour-twist firing glass with trumpet bowl above a short stem with central opaque twists of white, blue and green, terminating in a heavy foot, 4½ in high	170	0
An engraved rummer, the tall bucket bowl inscribed *Lord Nelson, Oct. R. 21, 1805*, the reverse with *Victory* at sail, 8¼ in high	85	0
Coronation rummer, the bucket bowl engraved with a portrait of the King's Champion, glove in hand, the reverse with the Royal Crown flanked by *GIVR, July 19, 1821*, 5 in high	60	0
Pair of large rummers, the rounded bowls cut with ribbons and chrysanthemum medallions, on plain stems and feet, 7½ in high	16	10

Sweetmeat Glasses

	£	s
Sweatmeat glass, the cup-shaped bowl with everted rim and heavy gadrooning on the underside, on a stout spirally ribbed stem, terminating in a folded conical foot, 4 in high	85	0
Small sweetmeat, the ogee bowl with everted rim, on a collar above an inverted baluster stem terminating in a base knop and domed and folded foot, 5 in high	48	0
Small sweetmeat, the wide cup-shaped bowl with folded everted rim, on an inverted baluster stem and base knop, terminating in a folded conical foot, 4⅜ in high	28	0

Wine Glasses—Air Twist

An unusual wine glass, the small bucket bowl on a slender air-

	£	s
twist stem with five knops of varying sizes, terminating in a conical foot, 6¾ in high	220	0
A Jacobite wine glass, the round funnel bowl engraved with a six-petal rose and single bud, on an air-twist stem, terminating in a conical foot, 5¾ in high	95	0
An air-twist wine glass, with double ogee bowl, above a double knopped stem and conical foot, 6⅛ in high	90	0
Newcastle wine glass, the round funnel bowl engraved with a band of fruiting vine, on a typical multi-knopped light baluster stem, terminating in a domed foot, 7¼ in high	85	0

Wine Glasses—Baluster

A baluster wine glass, small, the thistle bowl on a cone baluster above a base knop and domed and folded foot, 5¾ in high	95	0
A diamond-etched wine glass, the bell bowl engraved with the Arms of the Hague, above a light baluster stem, terminating in a conical foot, 7⅞ in high	55	0
A small wine glass, the round funnel bowl solid at the base and resting on an angular knop, above a baluster stem, containing an elongated tear, terminating in a domed and folded foot, 5⅝ in high	45	0
An engraved wine glass, the round funnel bowl decorated around the rim with a border of scrolls and flower-heads, on a light baluster stem terminating in a domed and folded foot, 6¼ in high	35	0
A wine glass with a bell bowl set on an annulated knop above a slender baluster stem and folded conical foot, 6½ in high	4	0

Wine Glasses—Colour and Opaque Twist

Set of six mid-eighteenth-century glasses, the bowls engraved with sun flowers, foliage and butterflies, supported on opaque twist stems and slightly domed feet, 5½ in high	260	0
A small colour-twist wine glass, with round funnel bowl on a stem composed of thick opaque white corkscrew outlined in green, within an opaque white spiral, terminating in a conical foot, 5 in high	170	0
A colour-twist wine glass, the ogee bowl supported on a stem containing a thick opaque white corkscrew entwined by blue and white spirals, terminating in a conical foot, 6 in high	140	0
A wine glass with heavy ogee bowl, on a corkscrew and spiral white opaque twist stem, terminating in a conical foot, 5½ in high	100	0
An unusual wine glass, the round funnel bowl heavily cut with honeycomb facets, on a tall opaque twist stem and terminating in an octagonal conical foot, 6¼ in high	40	0

Wine Glasses—Knop, Faceted and Plain Stems

A pair of wine glasses, engraved with butterflies and vines, on plain hollow stems and folded feet, 6¼ in high	82	0
A slender wine glass with bell bowl on a collar above a knopped stem, terminating in a folded conical foot, 6⅜ in high	35	0
An engraved wine glass of drawn trumpet shape, engraved with a martial trophy, on plain stem and folded foot, 7 in high	33	10

Wine Glass Coolers

Six cut-glass single-lipped coolers, of bucket shape with vertically
faceted lower parts and star cut bases, 4 in high   14 10

COLOURED GLASS

Blue

A pair of blue glass decanters and stoppers, of club form with
two collars to the necks, RUM and BRANDY in gilt, the flattened
drop stoppers with initials, 9½ in high   57 10

A blue glass spirit barrel, on four scroll feet, with trailed decoration to either end and pewter mount to the neck, 7 in wide   21   0

Bohemian Glass

Three Bohemian enamelled green glass overlay vases of slender
baluster form, the raised white bands with flowers on gilt
grounds, 12½ in high and 10¾ in high   78 10

Bohemian enamelled overlay scent bottle and stoppper, pear
shape with everted neck, ruby ground with white overlay cut
with facets and painted with birds on branches, 11½ in high   16 10

Cameo Glass (Webb)

An amber ground vase of pear shape with slightly flared neck,
the amber yellow ground overlaid and carved in white with
trailing blossom and with a collar of chrysanthemum medallions, 11¾ in high   367 10

A turquoise ground double scent bottle, of cylindrical form,
overlaid in white and carved with campanulas and other
flowers, hinged silver cover to one end, screw cover to the
other, 5½ in long (Silver 1884)   105   0

A small scent bottle and stopper with silver screw top, the pink
glass globular body with shells among seaweed in white relief,
2¼ in high   47   0

Daum

A beaker-shaped vase, on spreading foot, exterior overlaid in
grey and tortoiseshell and cut through with trees in Autumn
and falling leaves, interior with mottled and lilac ground,
6¼ in high (Signed Daum, Nancy)   44   0

A pair of Art Nouveau bowls, marbled in shades of purple and
red and with pale flecked interiors, 4¼ in diameter   21   0

Gallé

A globular overlay vase, the amber yellow ground overlaid and
carved in purple and blue with fuchsia, 5¼ in high   42   0

An oviform vase, the greenish ground overlaid in purple with
sprays of flowers, 5½ in high   42   0

An Art Nouveau vase, with tall cylindrical neck and short
rounded base, the purple overlay carved with trailing sweet
peas, 13¼ in high   40   0

SMALL DECORATIVE ANTIQUES

	£	s

Enamels

	£	s
Pair of Battersea blue and gilt candlesticks with panels of flowers, 9 in high	60	0
A Birmingham snuff box, the square lid, sides and base with summer flowers on a white ground, 1¾ in wide	55	0
Pair of Battersea tapersticks painted with flowers, 6½ in high	48	0
A cylindrical Staffordshire needlecase, the lid and base with landscapes and the remainder with trellis-work on a turquoise ground, 4 in long	40	0
Battersea patch box with landscape panels, 2 in wide	25	0

Miniatures

	£	s
An enamel miniature of General Thomson, by Henry Bone, signed and dated 1806, almost half-length, three-quarters sinister, gaze directed at spectator, wearing blue uniform with gold epaulettes, oval, 3 in high	250	0
A miniature of a young girl on porcelain, almost full-length, standing wearing a pink dress and holding a black and white spaniel in her arms, against a landscape background, rectangular, 4¾ in high	95	0
A miniature of a lady, in oil on copper, three-quarters dexter, gaze directed at spectator, wearing a wide white lace collar, jewels and a rope of pearls around her neck, pearls in her ears and falls of coloured feathers in her brown hair, oval, 3⅛ in high	50	0
A miniature of a child, three-quarters sinister, gaze directed at spectator, wearing a black dress tied with a blue sash, oval, 2⅝ in high	45	0
A miniature of a gentleman, by J. Bowring, signed with monogram, three-quarters sinister, gaze directed at spectator, wearing a dark brown coat and white vest and cravat, cloud and sky background, oval, 2⅜ in high	45	0
A miniature of a gentleman, three-quarters sinister, gaze directed at spectator, wearing a long curled wig, blue coat and white cravat, oval, 2⅞ in high	36	0
A miniature of a gentleman, by Patrick McMorland, signed, three-quarters sinister, gaze directed at spectator, wearing a heavy powdered wig and brown coat and vest, oval, 1½ in high	20	0
A miniature of Mrs Hebdin, well-painted, three-quarters dexter, gaze directed at spectator, wearing a white dress and red shawl, her fair hair dressed in curls, rectangular, 3⅜ in high	15	0

Paperweights—Baccarat

	£	s
A primrose weight of large size, the flower with five rich blue ogee petals outlined in white, around starhead stamens, supported on a long stalk and surrounded by numerous veined emerald-green leaves, clear glass, star cut base, 3⅛ in diameter	440	0
A dated close millefiori weight, the closely packed canes including silhouettes of animals and birds, bearing the date 1849, 2⅝ in diameter	260	0

	£	s
A mushroom weight, the upright tuft of usual type enclosed by an opaque-white muslin ring encircled by a royal-blue spiral, 2¾ in diameter	150	0
A close millefiori weight, the large canes unusually set with strands of latticinio, 2⅝ in diameter	18	0

Paperweights—Clichy

A signed scrambled weight, the variety of large brightly-coloured canes jumbled together and including part of the name of the factory CL . . CY in turquoise, 2¾ in diameter — **55 0**

A faceted weight, with a circle of pink florettes and green moss canes enclosing a central blue and white cluster, the sides cut with three rows of honeycomb facets, 2⅝ in diameter — **44 0**

A scattered millefiori weight, the clear glass with an outer ring of canes, encircling an inner cluster of coloured florettes, including pink, white, pink-and-green and green-and-white roses, 3 in diameter — **30 0**

A large scrambled weight, with a dome-shaped arrangement of brightly coloured canes of various types, 3⅜ in diameter — **28 0**

Paperweights—St Louis

A concentric millefiori weight, composed of six circles of variously coloured canes, predominantly in tones of red, pink, green, blue and white, packed closely together and centring on a central starhead cluster, 3 in diameter — **360 0**

A fruit weight of the usual type, the swirling white latticinio basket set with three pears, two orange and one green, three small red cherries and numerous serrated green leaves, 2⅞ in diameter — **300 0**

A scrambled weight, with mainly opaque-white muslin strands and coloured rods, 2¾ in diameter — **19 0**

Paperweights—Stourbridge

A pair of weights, each with a large central turquoise-and-white cane surrounded by large pastry-mould canes in turquoise, white, blue and red, set in almost concentric form, 3½ in diameter — **35 0**

A weight, composed of five concentric rows of canes in pale tones, with a brighter row in red, 3⅞ in diameter — **30 0**

Silver Snuff Boxes

A William IV rectangular box, engine turned, the lid also applied with a well chased border of matted vine leaves and bunches of grapes, interior gilt and inscribed *To Captain Canney from the Passengers of the 'Orontes' on the homeward Voyage from Calcutta to England, 1833-4*. By Reilly and Storer, 1833, 3½ in wide, 6 oz 3 dwt — **680 0**

A George III oblong box, the cover engraved with a basket-weave design enclosing a vacant oval reserve, the sides chased, gilt interior by Charles Hougham, 1813, 4 oz 13 dwt — **180 0**

A George II shaped oval box, the hinged lid chased with an exotic bird and flowers, the base later initialled, interior gilt, by G.D., 1750, 2¾ in wide — **55 0**

	£	s
William IV rectangular box, the hinged lid initialled and applied with a foliate snap, engine turned, by W.S., Birmingham, 1835, 2½ in wide	45	0
A George II shaped oval box, the lid inset with aventurine glass within a chased border of scrolls and flowers, interior gilt, by I.M. below a mullet, *circa* 1755	42	0
A Victorian shaped rectangular box, inscribed and engraved all over with scrolling leafage, Birmingham, 1851, 3 in wide	28	0
A George III oval box with dotted decoration and crested initial cover, by Phipps and Robinson, 1809, 3¾ in wide, 2 oz 13 dwt	28	0
A George IV curved oblong box engraved with flowers, swirling leafage and initials, by T. and W.S., Birmingham, 1824, 2¼ in wide	16	0

Stevengraphs (All in mint condition)

	£	s
Leda	460	0
The Last Lap (small wheel cycles only)	260	0
Spanish Bullfight	222	0
Mersey Tunnel Railway	200	0
Buffalo Bill and Chiefs	170	0
Dr W. G. Grace	145	0
The Home Stretch	145	0
Robert Burns	125	0
Declaration of Independence	125	0
The First Set	110	0
Columbus, pair	105	0
Phoebus and Aurora	105	0
Clifton Suspension Bridge	90	0
The Forth Bridge	75	0
The First Train	70	0
The Old Tyne Bridge	65	0
Queen Victoria and Premiers	62	0
The First Touch	58	0

Tea Caddies

	£	s
George II mahogany domed caddy, 10 in wide	25	0
Early nineteenth-century amboyna caddy with brass mounts and glass bowl, 14 in wide	16	0
Mahogany caddy of sarcophagus shape, 14 in wide	10	0
Georgian inlaid mahogany caddy, 9½ in wide	9	0
Late eighteenth-century tortoiseshell mounted caddy, 7 in wide (slight damage)	8	0
Georgian mahogany caddy	5	0

Vinaigrettes

	£	s
A George IV silver-gilt oblong vinaigrette with engine-turned decoration, initialled lid, applied floral borders, by Nathaniel Mills, Birmingham, 1833	43	0
A George III rectangular vinaigrette with canted corners, engraved with leaf motifs, gilt interior, by Joseph Willmore, Birmingham, 1812	24	0
A George IV oblong vinaigrette with engine-turned base and cover, reeded sides, by Joseph Willmore, 1829, 1¼ in wide	22	0

	£	s
A rectangular vinaigrette with canted corners, by Joseph Willmore, Birmingham, 1811, 1½ in wide	19	0

Wine Labels

	£	s
A set of four unusual George III labels of matted quatrefoil form, each surmounted by a polished bead and pierced on the central shaped rectangular panels for Claret, Port, Madeira and Sherry by Benjamin Smith, 1807	440	0
An unusual pair of George IV labels, each in the form of a feather-edged scroll decorated with floral sprays, one engraved for Port, the other for Sherry, and surmounted by an eagle with spreading wings by Emes and Barnard, 1824	145	0
A George III silver gilt label in the form of a well-modelled scallop shell, engraved Sherry, by Benjamin Smith, 1807	110	0
A set of four Staffordshire enamel labels, the borders painted with grape vines against a white ground, 2¼ in wide	72	0
Four George III labels for Port, Claret, Sherry and Madiera, pierced and chased, by Robert Garrard, 1814, (each with wire bottle ring)	62	0

P

SOME AUCTION ROOM PRICES
1969-70

This year's list contains rather more items in the lower price ranges. It will be noted that prices in general have dropped over the year, with the exception of those for fine and rare pieces. However, prices realized in sales in 1970 would indicate that the market has now stabilized again.

FURNITURE

	£	s
Bookcases and Bureau-Bookcases		
George III mahogany break-front bookcase, the upper part with a Greek key cornice and broken arch pediment closed by four glazed doors, and three cupboards below enclosed by panelled doors, 8 ft 4 in wide, 9 ft high	950	0
George III mahogany break-front bookcase, the upper part in three sections, with four glazed doors with interlaced lozenge bars, enclosing adjustable shelves; the richly figured and crossbanded lower part with a pair of cupboard doors at the centre and eight graduated drawers at the sides, 8ft 2 in wide, 9 ft 3 in high	620	0
George III mahogany secretaire-bookcase, the moulded cornice carved with a Greek key band, fitted with a pair of 13-panel glazed doors, the lower part with secretaire drawer, the interior being crossbanded with sycamore. Three long drawers below and on bracket feet, 3 ft 9 in wide	252	0
Late eighteenth- or early nineteenth-century mahogany secretaire-bookcase, the glazed panelled doors with arched astragals, the centre with deep drawer forming a secretaire and with cupboard below with beaded border panels. Stamped 'Thomas Mosh, 102 Wardour Street', 3 ft 8in wide, 7 ft 1 in high	189	0
Nineteenth-century oak bureau-bookcase, inlaid with motifs and birds in coloured woods, the double panel to the doors enclosing a single shelf, the fall-flap opening to reveal drawers and recesses, with two small and three long drawers below, supported on bracket feet, 6 ft 1 in high	145	0
Georgian mahogany bureau-bookcase, the fall flap opening to reveal numerous drawers and recesses over four long graduated drawers with brass handles, supported on ogee bracket feet, 3 ft 5 in wide	90	0
Georgian mahogany hanging bookcase with a tambour sliding front and one drawer below, 2 ft 2 in wide	28	0

Bureaux and Writing Cabinets
Queen Anne walnut bureau, crossbanded and inlaid with

herringbone bands, the sloping-lid enclosing drawers, pigeon-
holes and a well covered by a slide, with two short and two
long drawers below, on bracket feet, 3 ft wide   525   0

Queen Anne walnut secretaire with moulded cornice and a
convex-fronted drawer above, the fall-front of burr figure,
crossbanded and inlaid with herringbone bands, enclosing
various drawers, a cupboard, removable pigeon-holes with
secret drawers behind, the lower part with two short and two
long drawers, on bracket feet, 3 ft 7 in wide   420   0

George I walnut bureau-cabinet, the upper part with moulded
cornice and glazed doors, each with six rectangular panes,
the lower part with crossbanded sloping lid enclosing a fitted
interior and four graduated long drawers, on bracket feet,
3 ft 3 in wide   409   10

William and Mary walnut secretaire cabinet, the upper part
with a cushion drawer and a fall-front with a shaped panel
in burrwood, the lower part with two short and two long
drawers, in straight grained wood, 3 ft 6 in wide, 5 ft 5 in
high   340   0

Early eighteenth-century banded walnut fall-front bureau with
interior fittings and three graduated long drawers, 2 ft 10 in
wide   170   0

Regency mahogany cylinder bureau, with rounded tambour
shutter enclosing a slide with a rising easel, two drawers
in the frieze, on square tapering legs, 2 ft 11½ in wide   78   15

Early Georgian oak and walnut bureau in two parts, the crossbanded sloping lid enclosing a fitted interior, with two short
and three long drawers below, divided in the centre, the sides
panelled, 3 ft 3 in wide   68   5

Regency satinwood secretaire-book cabinet with a rectangular
top, shallow drawer in the frieze fitted with an adjustable
leather-lined panel, with a shelf and pilasters overlaid with
ebony guilloche, with ebonized paw feet, 3 ft 8 in wide   55   0

Edwardian inlaid mahogany roll-front bureau with numerous
drawers and writing fall, on taper legs, 2 ft 5 in wide   32   0

Early eighteenth-century oak fall-front bureau having interior
fittings, well, and three graduated long drawers, on
bracket feet, 3 ft 1 in wide   25   0

Cabinets

George III satinwood specimen cabinet with a cupboard above
three bow-fronted drawers, all crossbanded with partridge-
wood, the cupboard with oval panelled door enclosing two
drawers and pigeon-holes, the drawers all with divided interiors, with gilt brass handles and moulded legs on claw feet,
1 ft 2 in wide   441   0

Two William IV mahogany cabinets, each with brass trellis-
panelled doors to the upper part, a long drawer in the centre
and a cupboard enclosed by panelled doors below, on turned
feet, surmounted by moulded scroll pediments, 3 ft 3 in
wide, 8 ft high   294   0

Eighteenth-century walnut cabinet with moulded cornice and

	£	s
mirrored door enclosing shelving, on stand with fitted drawer and with turned legs and flat-shaped stretchers, 2 ft wide, 5 ft 2 in high	120	0
Early eighteenth-century elm and oak cabinet on stand, fitted with eleven drawers surrounding a central cupboard, cross-banded with walnut, the stand with spirally turned legs and stretchers, on turned feet, 3 ft 4 in wide	84	0
Edwardian mahogany china cabinet, inlaid with boxwood and ebony lines, the centre bow-shaped glass door enclosing two shelves, and supported on short cabriole legs, 4 ft wide	22	0
Victorian mahogany music cabinet with railed gallery and glass-panelled door enclosing three shelves, 2 ft 9 in wide	11	10

Chairs—Dining Sets

	£	s
Set of six early Charles II oak dining chairs, the spiral twist and square uprights with top-shaped finials and the splats formed of unusually slender spiral twist balusters, with solid seats and turned and square legs	1,800	0
Set of eight George III mahogany dining chairs, including a pair of armchairs, the rectangular backs with reeded uprights capped by leaves, each filled with five similar upright splats, the armchairs with reeded curved arms, the upholstered seats covered with rust velvet, on square tapering legs with block toes	1,260	0
Set of eight George III mahogany dining chairs, including two armchairs, with moulded arched backs and pierced balloon-shaped splats carved with rosettes, the drop-in seats on square moulded legs	945	0
Set of six George III mahogany dining chairs with moulded shield-shaped backs, the splats pierced with interlaced curving bars and carved in relief with husks and wheat-ears, the serpentine upholstered seats on tapering fluted square legs with block feet	630	0
Set of five Regency painted chairs, the broad curved top rails painted in colours with countrywomen and children spinning, weaving and talking in landscapes, on curved uprights with figure-of-eight horizontal bars, the caned seats on turned legs, the frames channelled with broad gilt lines and grained to simulate rosewood	577	10
Set of eight George III mahogany dining chairs, including two armchairs, with moulded shield-shaped backs and channelled upright splats headed by stiff leaves, the slightly bowed and concave seats covered with green and brown *gros-point* needlework, on moulded square legs with block feet headed by paterae (one armchair adapted from a single chair)	367	10
Set of nine Regency simulated rosewood chairs with scrolled uprights, caned seats and sabre legs, the curved backs inlaid with brass patterns	178	10
Set of six Regency mahogany rope-back dining chairs with sabre legs and drop-in seats (two having arms)	160	0
Set of six Georgian mahogany rope-back dining chairs, the stuff-over seats upholstered in green hide	155	0

	£	s
Set of four Hepplewhite mahogany dining chairs with pierced vase splats and drop-in seats	120	0
Set of six Victorian rosewood dining chairs on cabriole legs, the seats and backs upholstered in figured damask	110	0
Set of four Regency mahogany reeded frame dining chairs with sabre legs	68	0
Set of six Edwardian inlaid walnut dining chairs with stuff-over seats	50	0
Set of six Victorian mahogany-framed dining chairs with upholstered seats and backs	40	0
Set of six Edwardian mahogany shaped-back dining chairs on cabriole legs, the stuff-over seats upholstered in uncut moquette	24	0
Set of six Victorian mahogany dining chairs with upholstered seats	16	0

Chairs—Dining Single

	£	s
George III mahogany ladder-back dining chair with moulded uprights, the pierced bars centred with leaf sprays, the white damask upholstered seat on square legs and stretchers	42	0
George II mahogany dining chair with arched back and pierced splat carved with C-scrolls and wave ornament, the cut velvet seat on square legs	27	6
Nineteenth-century carved mahogany shield-back dining chair in the Hepplewhite manner, inset Wedgwood plaque	12	0
Pair of Victorian mahogany single chairs with floral seats and turned legs.	6	0

Chairs—Easy

	£	s
George III mahogany library armchair, the stuffed back with a serpentine toprail, the padded incurved arms raised on down-curved supports headed by flowerheads and trailing leaves, the stuffed seat raised on chamfered legs, upholstered in pink and blue *gros point* with a scale pattern	220	0
Victorian mahogany-frame button-back easy chair upholstered in blue velvet	24	0
Victorian walnut-frame spoon-back nursing chair on cabriole legs, upholstered in Regency stripe fabric	22	0
Victorian giltwood easy chair upholstered in damask	16	0

Chairs—Open Arm

	£	s
George II mahogany open armchair with moulded uprights and waved top carved with leaves, the pierced interlace similarly carved, with scrolled arms and drop-in needlework seat worked with mythical animals, the seat rail with nulled border, on cabriole legs with acanthus on the knees and claw-and-ball feet	504	0

Early George III mahogany open armchair, the padded arms with scrolled handles, on curved supports, on cabriole legs with carved acanthus foliage, ending in scrolled toes, with arched back and serpentine seat covered with original *petit-point* needlework, the back with flora in a landscape, the seat

	£	s

with a dog attacking a boar, in broad surrounds worked with flowers and grapes on a tobacco-brown ground — 504 0

George III mahogany open armchair with waved back and interlaced splat, the drop-in seat on cabriole legs, carved with leaves, with claw-and-ball feet — 136 10

George III pine and beechwood open armchair with moulded shield-shaped back and scrolled arms supports, carved with leaves, the bowed seat on tapering fluted legs headed by paterae — 99 15

Victorian mahogany-frame open-armchair with buttoned back upholstered in pink velvet — 18 0

Canterburys

George III mahogany Canterbury on tapering legs with a drawer in the frieze, 1 ft 6 in wide — 145 0

Late Georgian mahogany Canterbury with slatted divisions and turned uprights, a drawer in the base, on turned legs, 1 ft 7 in wide — 126 0

Edwardian mahogany Canterbury with solid rising top, for use as a piano-stool, above reeded uprights — 27 0

Chests of Drawers and Commodes

Early eighteenth-century oyster walnut chest of drawers with two short and two long drawers, the top, front and sides veneered with cross-cut oyster segments in fruitwood borders, on later bracket feet, 3 ft 2 in wide — 357 0

Pair of early nineteenth-century mahogany serpentine-fronted commodes, each fitted with four graduated long drawers, on bracket feet, 3 ft 8 in wide — 290 0

George III mahogany chest of drawers, fitted with a brushing slide and four graduated long drawers, on bracket feet, 2 ft 7 in wide — 136 10

Queen Anne banded walnut chest in two parts with four short and three long drawers, having reeded canted corners, and bracket feet, 3 ft 2 in wide — 90 0

Victorian walnut Wellington chest of thirteen drawers, 1 ft 11 in wide — 85 0

George I walnut chest of drawers, crossbanded and inlaid with herringbone bands, the top with a lobed rectangular figured panel, fitted with two short and three long drawers, 3 ft 2 in wide — 63 0

Eighteenth-century fruitwood chest of three short and three graduated long drawers, with canted corners and raised on bracket feet, 2 ft 6 in wide — 50 0

Georgian mahogany bow-front chest of three graduated long drawers, 3 ft wide — 36 0

Cupboards—Bedside and Corner

Early George II-style standing corner wig cupboard, the walnut veneer of rich patitation, with double panelled doors enclosing three shaped shelves and flanked by fluted pilasters, supported on a shaped apron with bracket feet — 85 0

	£	s
George III mahogany bedside cupboard with tray top and fitted with two doors, on square chamfered legs, 1 ft 7 in wide	52	10
Edwardian inlaid mahogany bow-front hanging corner cupboard enclosed by glazed barred door	36	0
Early eighteenth-century oak corner cupboard enclosed by panel door, on stand with taper legs and pad feet (stand of a later date)	26	0
Eighteenth-century red lacquered hanging corner cupboard	21	0
Georgian mahogany standing corner cupboard enclosed by panelled doors	20	0
Trafalgar oak corner cupboard with serpentine shelves and single arcaded panel door	13	0
Eighteenth-century oak hanging corner cupboard with shaped shelving enclosed by panelled door	9	0

Coffers and Chests

	£	s
George I leather-covered portable coffer, the leather of attractive sealing-wax red colour secured by brass-headed nails in an all-over design of scrollwork, with pierced brass corner mounts, escutcheon and royal crown, now on a frame with seventeenth-century Italian silvered wood dog masks carved in full relief, 3 ft 3 in wide	140	0
Early eighteenth-century oak dower chest raised on end supports, 2 ft 9 in wide	36	0
Early nineteenth-century oak mule chest with two small drawers to the base, and supported on bracket feet, 3 ft 10 in wide	11	0

Davenports and Desks

	£	s
Queen Anne walnut kneehole desk with rounded rectangular top, a frieze drawer and six short drawers around a kneehole cupboard, inlaid with herringbone lines, on bracket feet, 2 ft 7 in wide	840	0
Early eighteenth century yew-wood kneehole writing desk, the rectangular top lined with gilt-tooled brown leather, fitted with a long drawer and six smaller drawers surrounding recessed kneehole cupboard, a shallow drawer in the arch, on bracket feet, 2 ft 11 in wide	336	0
Early nineteenth-century kneehole desk, fitted with nine drawers, slide and recess cupboard, 3 ft 7 in wide	170	0
Regency mahogany Davenport with raised curving gallery and rising and sliding top, the base fitted with a brushing slide, four drawers and four dummy drawers, 1 ft 4 in wide	110	0
Victorian serpentine-front mahogany Davenport with writing fall, stationery compartment and secret drawers	55	0
William IV rosewood Davenport, the sloping front supported on columns, 1 ft 9 in wide	50	0

Dressers

	£	s
Eighteenth-century oak dresser of fine colour with open shelving, three short drawers with shaped apron and pot shelf under, 4 ft 10 in wide	210	0
Early eighteenth-century break-front Yorkshire dresser with open shelving, five drawers and cupboards, 6 ft 3 in wide	170	0

	£	s
Large nineteenth-century oak Welsh dresser with richly carved panels and Delft rack to the top, 6 ft 10 in wide	45	0
Seventeenth-century style oak dresser with two cupboards and three drawers over a single shelf	31	0

Globes

	£	s
Pair of terrestrial and celestial globes by W & S Jones, Holborn, the terrestrial globe showing 'The Discoveries of Captain Cook', corrected to 1802, the celestial globe adjusted to 1800, both with brass longitudinal rings, on turned supports and cabriole legs with compasses inset into platforms, 2 ft 2 in high, the globes 1 ft circumference	504	0
Terrestrial table globe by Donaldson, 1836, Niddry Street, Edinburgh, on a turned ebonized stand, 1 ft 4 in diameter	70	0

Knife Boxes

	£	s
Sheraton serpentine-front knife box converted to a stationery cabinet	22	0
Georgian mahogany knife box banded in tulipwood	14	C
Georgian mahogany knife box with three divisions and brass handle, 1 ft 5 in wide	9	10

Mirrors—Mantel

	£	s
George III design giltwood and plaster oval mirror with fluted and gadrooned frame, the resting with a lion's mask and scrolling foliage surmounted by an eagle suspending swags to the sides, 3 ft 1 in wide, 6 ft 10 in high	73	10
Regency maple overmantel with moulded borders and rectangular plate, above a coloured print of men-o'-war, 3 ft by 1 ft 11 in	26	5
Regency rosewood overmantel mirror, the frame inlaid with brass and with figures of deer in each corner, 2 ft 9 in wide	24	0

Mirrors—Toilet or Dressing

	£	s
Queen Anne red-lacquered dressing-table mirror, the base with a fall-front and one drawer below, 1 ft 6 in wide	260	0
Queen Anne walnut toilet mirror with arched bevelled plate and shaped cresting, the stepping base with five drawers and a concave cupboard, 1 ft 2½ in wide	73	10
William and Mary-style inlaid walnut dressing-table mirror, the base with seven drawers and1 a small cupboard, 1 ft 4 in wide	28	0
Old English mahogany box-frame toilet mirror, having bow-front and three drawers, 1 ft 10½ in wide	11	0
Victorian mahogany dressing-table mirror, with three drawers, 2 ft 9 in wide	4	0

Mirrors—Wall

	£	s
William and Mary silvered-wood and black-painted pier glass with a divided rectangular bevelled plate, the convex frame with continuous sprays of leaves and an outer bead and reed border, the arched pierced cresting with strapwork framed by sprays of leaves and flowers, 2 ft wide, 5 ft 11 in high	520	0

	£	s
Early Georgian mahogany and gilt landscape mirror with three rectangular bevelled plates in moulded frame with gilt border carved with wave ornament, 4 ft 6 in wide, 1 ft 4 in high	136	10
Nineteenth-century wall mirror in carved mahogany and gilt frame, surmounted by an eagle, 2 ft 11 in by 1 ft 8 in	100	0
Regency convex mirror in giltwood frame surmounted by an eagle, 1 ft 9 in diameter	60	0
Eighteenth-century carved mahogany frame wall mirror, bordered and decorated in gilt	34	0

Settees, Couches and Chaise Longues

	£	s
George III japanned settee, the quadruple chair-back pierced with a curving trellis, the arms on baluster supports, the bowed caned seat on turned legs, decorated on a black ground with gilt flowers and leaves, 5 ft 7 in wide	168	0
Early Victorian carved giltwood open-arm settee, upholstered in tapestry	45	0
Victorian mahogany button-back settee, with a serpentine front, upholstered in green velvet	38	0
Hepplewhite mahogany settee with shaped back and scrolled arms, upholstered in Regency striped fabric and fitted loose cover	32	0
Regency curved mahogany-frame settee with scrolled ends, seat cushion and bolster cushions upholstered in striped green velvet, 6 ft 8 in wide	26	0
Edwardian mahogany-frame settee upholstered in corded velvet	17	0
Victorian walnut-frame serpentine-front couch upholstered in tapestry	14	0

Sideboards

	£	s
Georgian mahogany bow-front sideboard, having three drawers and a tambour-fronted recess, on taper legs, 5 ft wide	320	0
Sheraton mahogany bow-front sideboard, crossbanded and tulipwood stringing, with three drawers and cellarete drawer, on six taper legs with spade feet, 4 ft 6 in wide	320	0
Small mahogany sideboard, with a plate drawer at the centre above a recessed cupboard flanked by two doors simulating drawers and cupboards, 3 ft 11 in wide	210	0
Regency mahogany sideboard, the narrow rectangular top with rounded break-front centre, fitted with a central drawer, a deep drawer on the left and a cupboard on the right, both with double false fronts, on turned legs, 5 ft 3 in wide	157	10
Georgian mahogany bow-front sideboard, inlaid with satinwood and ebony lines, brass rail to the back and small centre drawer flanked by a deep drawer and cupboard, supported on slender tapering legs ending in spade feet, 4 ft 5 in wide	88	0
Late George III mahogany sideboard with a rectangular top, with a long drawer in the frieze flanked by a cupboard and at one side a deep cellarete drawer with an unusual swivelling semi-circular decanter stand, 7 ft wide	50	0
Edwardian inlaid mahogany shaped-front sideboard, with centre drawer and wing cupboards, on taper supports, 4 ft wide	46	0

£   s

Tables—Breakfast

Regency mahogany pedestal breakfast table, with reeded border
to the almost rectangular top, with crossbanded border, on
turned pedestal support with four reeded, curved and
tapering legs, brass toes and castors, 4 ft 10 in wide   147   0

Georgian banded mahogany snap-top breakfast table on pillar
and splayed quadruple base, 5 ft by 3 ft 11 in   130   0

Georgian mahogany snap-top breakfast table on turned pillar
with quadruple base, 5 ft 4 in by 3 ft 6 in   105   0

George III mahogany breakfast table, with rounded rectangular
top hinged to a baluster pillar, raised on three reeded curved
square legs with lion's paw castors, 3 ft 5½ in wide   78   15

Tables—Card

George II mahogany card table with serpentine folding top, the
frieze fitted with a drawer and with gadrooned lower edge,
raised on cabriole legs carved with acanthus foliage, ending in
claw-and-ball feet, opening with double gate-leg action, the
back legs meeting at the centre when closed, 3 ft wide   441   0

Regency mahogany card table, with break-front top and a frieze
drawer, edged with contrasting lines, on square tapering legs,
2 ft 11½ in wide (the top screwed down)   157   10

George III mahogany card table, the folding top with break-
front, on square tapering legs, banded with zebra-wood, 3ft
wide   57   15

George III mahogany card table, with semi-circular baize-lined
folding crossbanded top, on square tapering legs with double
gate-leg support, 3 ft 3½ in wide   52   10

Victorian walnut card table with folding top, on end supports
with central stretcher, 3 ft wide   36   0

Early Victorian rosewood card table with folding top, on pillar
and platform base, 3 ft wide   18   0

Tables—Centre

Circular giltwood centre table with a Cretan inlaid marble slab
depicting four doves at a vase, with specimen shells to the
border, on gilt rustic column support and tripod base with
a nymph in relief, 3 ft diameter   399   0

Early Victorian small centre table, the burr-walnut top inlaid
with a band of wild roses, with ebonized border, on
gadrooned pillar and heavily moulded cabriole legs, 2 ft 8 in
diameter   47   5

Victorian walnut oval centre table with inlaid top, on cluster
column and quadruple base, 4 ft 6 in   10   0

Tables—Dining

George IV mahogany telescopic dining table with rounded
rectangular top, supported on twelve turned legs with spirally
reeded centres and castor feet, supporting two end sections
and five extra leaves, 4 ft 6 in wide by 4 ft 8 in, extending
to 12 ft 10 in   252   0

Late Georgian mahogany twin-pedestal dining table with
rounded rectangular top with reeded edge, on hinge-turned

	£	s
supports and moulded square splayed legs, with an extra leaf, 3 ft 6 in wide by 6 ft 1 in extended	210	0
George III mahogany rectangular dining table, with two narrow leaves, the moulded square legs dividing and running outwards to support extra leaves (missing) 4 ft 5½ in wide	78	15
Victorian walnut oval-end extending dining table on platform base, fully extending to 6 ft by 4 ft 6 in	28	0
Victorian inlaid walnut oval dining table on cluster column with quadruple base, 4 ft 3 in	13	0
Victorian mahogany dining table on fluted legs, 4 ft by 3 ft 9in	3	0

Tables—Drum

| George III mahogany circular drum table, the top inset with light brown leather, the frieze fitted with four drawers and alternate false drawers, on ring-turned baluster support and on square tapering legs with block feet, 5 ft 4½ in wide | 294 | 0 |
| Regency mahogany drum table, with circular leather-lined flush top, fitted with four drawers and alternate false drawers, on ring-turned pillar and four splayed square legs with brass castors, 3 ft 8½ in wide | 189 | 0 |

Tables—Games, Sewing and Work

Georgian mahogany work table on turned pillar with quadruple base	68	0
Late Georgian rosewood fitted work table with well, on central support with platform base, 1 ft 7 in wide	46	0
Victorian walnut games and work table with backgammon and chess board, 1 ft 9 in wide	35	0
Victorian mahogany octagonal games table, the top inset with chess board, on pillar and quadruple base, 2 ft 2 in	13	0

Tables—Gate-leg

George II mahogany gate-leg dining table, the oval top with two leaves, on cabriole legs with pointed and pad feet, carved behind the knees with scrolls, 4 ft wide	367	10
Stuart oval gate-leg dining table with double flaps and baluster turned legs	182	0
Early eighteenth-century cottage oak gate-leg dining table on turned supports, 4 ft 3 in wide	100	0
Early eighteenth-century country-made oak gate-leg table with drawer, 7 ft long	68	0
Eighteenth-century oval gate-leg table on turned underframe, with two drawers, 4 ft wide	48	0
Small Stuart oak gate-leg table with demi-lune flaps and barley-twist supports	44	0

Tables—Occasional

| Late Regency mahogany occasional table, inlaid with ebony lines, fitted with two small drawers and double flaps, supported on a centre pillar ending in four curving legs with brass-capped feet, 2 ft 7 in | 58 | 0 |
| Satinwood occasional table with shaped circular top, on square legs with crossed stretcher, 1 ft 6 in diameter | 33 | 10 |

£   s

Tables—Pembroke

Regency rosewood Pembroke table, the rounded rectangular top crossbanded with satinwood and with lobed projections at the corners, the frieze with a drawer and a false drawer, on turned ebonized slightly curving legs with gilded rings, 2 ft 7 in wide   367   10

Sheraton banded mahogany Pembroke table with fitted drawer, on taper legs, 2 ft 6 in wide   210   0

George III mahogany Pembroke table with serpentine-shaped leaves, fitted with a drawer, on square legs, 2 ft 8½ in wide   78   15

Tables—Refectory

Elizabeth I oak refectory table with a rectangular triple plank top, the frieze carved with a continual band of fluting and raised on six urn-shaped baluster legs with scrolled brackets and joined by moulded stretchers, 2 ft 8 in wide, 10 ft long   950   0

Eighteenth-century oak refectory table, 5 ft 1 in   280   0

Tables—Side

Eighteenth-century banded walnut side table, fitted with three short and one long drawer, on cabriole legs, 2 ft 6 in wide   110   0

Sheraton inlaid mahogany side table, having three drawers with brass loop handles, 2 ft 5 in wide   64   0

Pair of George III mahogany side tables with plain semi-circular tops, on moulded tapering square legs, 3 ft 6 in wide   44   0

George III mahogany semi-circular side table, raised on square tapering legs with block feet, 4 ft 3 in wide   25   4

Tables—Sofa

Regency rosewood sofa table with canted angles to the double-flap top, fitted with two drawers in the frieze, on turned column support with four curved and tapering legs, brass toes and castors, inlaid with brass lines, 4 ft 11 in wide, open   210   0

Regency mahogany sofa tale with satinwood banding, on end supports terminating in brass claw castors and having two drawers, 3 ft 2 in wide   150   0

Late Georgian mahogany sofa table, the deep crossbanded rectangular top with two leaves, fitted with a drawer at each side, on trestle supports and splayed square legs, 2 ft 4 in wide   60   18

Late Georgian mahogany sofa table, the rectangular top with two flaps, bleached to a golden colour, with two frieze drawers, on trestle supports and splayed square legs, 3 ft 2 in wide   57   15

Tables—Sutherland

Victorian walnut oval-ended Sutherland table on turned underframe, 3 ft   38   0

Victorian mahogany oval Sutherland table, 3 ft 8 in   26   0

Edwardian banded mahogany Sutherland table, 2 ft   22   0

Tables—Tea

George II banded walnut tea table with two frieze drawers, on carved cabriole legs, 2 ft 8 in wide   340   0

	£	s
Small Georgian mahogany tea table with folding flap and supported on pad feet, 2 ft 4 in wide	75	0
Victorian mahogany tea table, supported on turned legs, 3 ft wide	20	0

Tables—Wine

	£	s
Sheraton banded walnut wine table, on barley-twist column and with tripod base	48	0
Victorian rosewood circular wine table on barley-twist column and tripod base	24	0

Tables—Writing

	£	s
George III mahogany writing table, the rectangular top with recessed corners, a long drawer in the frieze, on trestle supports and square curved feet, 2 ft 10 in wide	157	10
Eighteenth-century oak writing table, having shaped apron and three drawers, on chamfered supports, 2 ft 10 in wide	60	0
Edwardian banded mahogany writing table with a drawer, on square tapering legs, 2 ft 6 in wide	22	0
Edwardian mahogany writing table with one pillar and four drawers, 3 ft wide	6	0

Tallboys and Lowboys

	£	s
William and Mary banded walnut lowboy with five drawers, on a stand with one long drawer, 3 ft 2 in wide	380	0
Old English mahogany tallboy in two parts, having moulded cornice and chamfered reeded corners with three short and six graduated long drawers, 3 ft 5 in wide	70	0
George III mahogany tallboy with three short and six long drawers, and a brushing slide with canted fluted corners, 3 ft 7 in wide	60	0
Old English mahogany tallboy in two parts with two short and six graduated long drawers, on bracket feet, 3 ft 6 in wide	58	0
Eighteenth-century walnut tallboy with nine drawers to the top, enclosed by two banded doors, and five drawers below, 3 ft 5 in wide	42	0

Waiters

	£	s
George II mahogany dumb waiter with three graduated circular tiers on baluster turned supports, and raised on plain cabriole legs, 3 ft 7 in high	162	15
George III mahogany three-tier dumb waiter with a turned and spirally fluted column, on a tripod support, width of largest tier, 2 ft	60	0
George II mahogany dumb waiter with three graduated revolving circular tiers, on turned supports, raised on plain cabriole legs, 3 ft 7 in high	52	10

Wardrobes

	£	s
George III hanging wardrobe with a pair of panelled doors, the lower part with two short false drawers and a long drawer, on bracket feet, 4 ft wide	55	0

	£	s

Early nineteenth-century mahogany gentleman's wardrobe, fitted
with sliding trays, enclosed by panelled doors, two small and
two long drawers to the base with ornamental gilt-metal
handles   29   0

Mid-nineteenth-century hanging wardrobe enclosed by panelled
doors, on bracket feet, 3 ft wide   10   0

Washstands

Regency mahogany washstand, having four drawers, ormolu
mounts and a white marble top, 4 ft 1 in wide   34   0

Georgian mahogany tray-top enclosed washstand, fitted with
rising top, revealing mirror with two drawers, 3 ft 6 in wide   26   0

Georgian mahogany bow-front three-tier corner washstand,
fitted with a drawer   22   0

Wine Coolers and Cellaret

George III mahogany octagonal cellaret, bound with brass, with
slightly tapering sides, on stand with square legs, 1 ft 6 in
wide   168   0

Early Victorian carved mahogany wine cooler on paw feet, 2 ft
6 in wide   50   0

Late Georgian mahogany oval wine cooler, bound with brass, on
splayed square legs, with zinc liner, 2 ft wide   31   10

CLOCKS, WATCHES AND BAROMETERS

Bracket Clocks

Regency bracket clock by Devereux Bowly, London, with
silvered chapter-ring and brass foliated spandrels, in an ebony
case with brass acorn finials   390   0

George II ebony bracket clock with striking movement signed on
face and back-plate, William Webster, Exchange Alley,
London, 1 ft 6 in high   200   0

George III mahogany bracket clock with whitened dial and
engraved back-plate, signed Perigal, London, with striking
verge movement, the plain arched case with brass lifting
handle and feet, 1 ft 1½ in high   100   10

Regency bracket clock with striking movement, the dial inscribed
James McCabe, Royal Exchange, London, No 1652, in a
rosewood case, with brass inlay, having a pineapple finial, 1 ft
9 in high   80   0

Nineteenth-century mahogany bracket clock with ornate ormolu
mounts, the silver chapter-ring by J. W. Benson, Ludgate Hill,
1 ft 5 in high   51   0

Nineteenth-century boulle bracket clock, the front inlaid with
brass scrolls on a red tortoiseshell ground, mounted with
ormolu, the sides ebonized, 1 ft 1 in high   47   0

Georgian bracket clock, the dial inscribed John Moss, London,
in a mahogany case, 1 ft 3 in high, and a bracket   35   0

Nineteenth-century mahogany bracket clock in a domed case

and supported on bracket feet, the movement by J. Smith &
Son, Nottingham, 12¾ in high 22 0

Carriage Clocks
Cloisonné enamel carriage clock with striking alarm movement,
the glazed case with column angles, inlaid with flowers and
birds, 6 in high 283 0
Gilt metal carriage clock with striking alarm movement, in plain
glazed case and leather outer case, 5½ in high 126 0
Nineteenth-century French carriage clock in a chased brass case,
with enamel dial, by A. Paul Broth, Devin & Co, Paris, 5¼ in
high 68 0
Nineteenth-century carriage clock and barometer in a brass and
glass case, the top inset with a compass, 4½ in high 39 0
Nineteenth-century French carriage clock in a brass and glass
case, 5 in high 28 0

Lantern Clocks
Brass lantern clock, signed on the dial Thomas Simonds, Fleet
Street, the bell canopy with sides pierced and engraved with a
coat-of-arms, 1 ft 3½ in high 94 10
Eighteenth-century brass lantern clock with long pendulum, by
Bent Edwards, Bungay 85 0

Longcase Clocks
Queen Anne marquetry longcase clock, the striking movement
by Jabez Stock, London, with silvered 11¼-in chapter-ring,
gilt mask and foliage spandrels, second dial and calendar
aperture, the fruitwood and walnut case with moulded cornice
and a bull's-eye window, profusely inlaid in contrasting
scorched and light woods with scrolling foliage, strapwork,
birds, angels, and a Chinaman and a monkey, 6 ft 11 in high 787 10
William and Mary longcase clock, by Joseph Foster, Exchange
Alley, in a walnutwood and marquetry case elaborately inlaid in coloured woods, a pendulum aperture to the waist, a
silvered chapter-ring with brass foliated spandrels, the square
hood with barley-twist pilasters 780 0
George II black lacquer longcase clock, the striking movement
signed William Webster, London, with pierced mask and
foliage spandrels, seconds dial and calendar aperture, and
with strike/silent regulator in the arch disguised as a second
dial, the case with arched hood, the borders decorated with
gilt chinoiseries on a distressed blue ground, the waist door
inset with bevelled mirror plate, 7 ft 4 in high 147 0
George II inlaid mahogany longcase clock with a swan's neck
pediment and a brass face inscribed, John Grundy, Whalley 130 0
George III mahogany longcase clock, the striking movement
with silvered metal chapter-ring and chased spandrels to the
arched dial, in case with fluted columns to the sides and
spirally turned columns to the hood with pierced scroll fret-
work pediment and brass finial, 8 ft 7 in high 94 10
Regency mahogany longcase clock, the striking movement with

	£	s
painted dial, the case with arched hood, fluted chamfered angles and circular glazed door to the hood, 6 ft 9 in high	29	8
Nineteenth-century oak longcase clock with swan's neck pediment, reeded columns and painted dialplate, by Burton, Kendal	14	0

Mantel Clocks

Late seventeenth-century mantel clock with 8-in silvered and brass dial engraved in the centre with tulips and draperied cartouche, with eight-day pull quarter repeating verge movement by 'Abraham Prime, Londini fecit', signed on the dial and engraved back-plate, in a walnut case with heavily moulded top and base, and spiral columns, 1 ft 4½ in, circa 1680	780	0
Nineteenth-century French mantel clock, the dial inscribed 'Julien Leroy, Paris', in an ormolu case with two female figures and surmounted by an urn, on a rectangular plinth, 2 ft 4 in wide	155	0
Nineteenth-century French mantel clock, the dial inscribed 'M. Rhode, Paris', in a white marble inlaid case, with an ormolu figure of a muse holding a book, 1 ft 4 in high	58	0
Nineteenth-century French mantel clock, the dial inscribed 'Cartier à Paris', in an ormolu case, with a bronze figure of a muse, on a white marble plinth, 1 ft 11 in wide	52	0
Nineteenth-century French mantel clock, the dial inscribed 'Miroy Brevetés', in a rustic bisque case with a woman beside a basket of fruit, 1 ft 2½ in high	32	0
French mantel clock in an ebonized and scarlet boullework case, with gilt metal mounts, 1 ft 5 in high	26	0
William IV mahogany mantel clock, inlaid with brass lines, 1 ft 5½ in high	21	0

Watches

George III 22-carat gold repeater watch by Samuel Jones of Bath, in a richly chased and pierced case with enamelled outer case and gilded and enamelled chatelaine, depicting figures in eighteenth-century dress, dated 1774	560	0
Half quarter repeating cylinder watch by Ellicott, No 8432, with white enamel dial, well pierced and engraved gold pair cases, the inner engraved with a mask, a small landscape and the number, striking on a bell, H.M. 1791, case maker V.W., with a carrying case	180	0
Georgian 18-carat gold pocket watch by Ellicott & Taylor, London, with a matt gold face and engine-turned case	60	0
Eighteenth-century verge watch by I. Donbrog, London, No 14231, with an enamel dial, in a Dutch silver outer case	23	0
Early nineteenth-century free-sprung duplex watch with compensated balance and jewelled train by Lupton & Gillam, St Martin's Lane, London, in a silver open face case, H.M., 1824. An inscription on the cuvette reads, 'The gift of H.R.H. Prince Albert to R. Cripps, 1849'	20	0
Late eighteenth-century silver pocket watch by John Cartley of Aberdeen, with duplex movement	10	0

	£	s
Half-hunter pocket watch by Barraclough, Leeds, in a silver case	10	0

Barometers

Early Victorian mahogany barometer with silvered scale and ivory urn finials, by T. & J. Mason, 3 Essex Bridge, Dublin, 3 ft 5 in high	100	0
Georgian stick barometer in a nut-brown mahogany case, by V. Cattaneo, Stockton	100	0
Georgian mahogany stick barometer, inlaid with ebony and boxwood, by Jones, London	56	0
Georgian mahogany stick barometer by F. Westley, London	45	0
Rosewood stick barometer by J. Tagliabue, London	32	0
Mahogany banjo barometer with a convex mirror at the centre by Harris, Burford, 3 ft 2 in high	28	0
Mahogany banjo barometer and thermometer by L. Pedrone	25	0

SILVER

Baskets for Bread, Cakes or Sugar

George III oval cake basket on moulded foot, pierced with arcading, the interior bright-cut and pierced with bands of foliage and arcading and the centre engraved with a coat-of-arms, with shaped reeded rim and swing handle, by Robert Hennell, 1790, *29 oz*, 1 ft 2⅜ in long	230	0
Large oval bread basket with bead edge and reeded swivel handle, by John Schofield, London, 1785, with intaglio duty mark *38 oz*	185	0
William IV oblong cake basket with swivel handle and applied acanthus foliage to the rim, by Henry Wilkinson & Co, Sheffield, 1837, *34 oz*	140	0
Large George III oval bread basket with bead edge and swivel handle, London, 1785, with intaglio duty mark	100	0
George III circular sugar basket with reeded swivel handle, London, 1799, *8 oz*	42	0

Candelabra and Candlesticks

Pair of George III table-candlesticks on circular bases engraved with bright-cut stylized foliage, the tapering octagonal stem and vase-shaped socket engraved with pendant foliage, with detachable nozzles, by Hester Bateman, 1781, 11¾ in high	2,625	0
William IV candelabrum, of elaborate rococo form, richly ornamented with clusters of roses and old English garden flowers amidst acanthus scrolls, with imperial eagles issuing from the base and supported on shell volute feet, by Paul Storr, London, 1834, *253 oz*, 2 ft 4 in high	1,920	0
Pair of George I plain octagonal table-candlesticks each on facetted base with octagonal baluster stem, with facetted vase-shaped socket and circular fixed nozzle, engraved with a crest, maker's mark Me, probably for Thomas Merry, 1714, *21 oz*, 7 in high	1,207	0
Pair of George IV three-light candelabra, the shaped circular		

Q

£ s

bases and partly fluted baluster stems chased with scrolls
and acanthus foliage, with two reeded and foliage branches
and central light each with vase-shaped socket, with detachable nozzles and flame finial to the centre engraved with a
crest, by John Watson, Sheffield, *126 oz*, 1 ft 10⅝ in high   892 0

Pair of George II table-candlesticks, each on shaped square
base and baluster stem, chased at the angles with shells,
the vase-shaped sockets with detachable nozzles, by William
Gould, 1751, nozzles unmarked, *23 oz*, 7⅝ in high   630 0

Two George III tapersticks, the domed bases chased with
rocaille ornament and flowers, the stems formed as figures
of Harlequin and Columbine supporting a fluted wax-pan,
moulded socket and nozzle, the Harlequin circa 1765, marks
indistinct, the Columbine by William Bateman, 1814, *10 oz
14 dwt*, 5⅝ in high   300 0

Two George III plain chamber-candlesticks with reeded rims,
vase-shaped sockets, detachable nozzles and extinguishers,
engraved with a crest, 1792 and 1801, *18 oz 15 dwt*   168 0

Chamber-candlestick with foliage and beaded border and floral
vase-shaped socket, with detachable nozzle and extinguisher,
engraved with a crest, by John and Thomas Settle, Sheffield,
1824, *15 oz 5 dwt*   95 0

Casters

Set of three Queen Anne plain octagonal vase-shaped casters,
each on moulded foot, the covers pierced with geometric
ornament and foliage motifs and with baluster finials,
engraved with a crest, by Charles Adam, 1713, *23 oz*, 6½ in
and 7¾ in high   1,100 0

Queen Anne pear-shaped caster on circular moulded foot, the
lower part of the body chased with vertical fluting with band
of matting and moulded rib above, the domed cover pierced
and engraved with foliage and quatrefoils and with baluster
finial, by William Denny, 1704, *6 oz 12 dwt*, 7¼ in high   399 0

George I plain pear-shaped caster on circular moulded foot,
with a rib round the body and high domed cover pierced with
slits and with acorn finial, Dublin, 1724, *4 oz 7 dwt*, 5¼ in
high   105 0

George III plain pear-shaped caster on circular moulded base,
the cover with written finial, 1769, maker's mark ID IM,
3 oz 1 dwt, 5½ in high   80 0

Coasters—Wine

Set of four George III circular wine coasters, the pierced and
trellised galleries clustered with fruiting vines, by William
Bateman, London, 1817   720 0

Pair of George III silver-gilt wine coasters, the galleries pierced
with clusters of fruiting vines, by Samuel Godbehere and
Edward Wigan, London, 1805   320 0

Pair of circular wine coasters with a band of flutes around the
sides and gadrooned foliate rims, the prints engraved with a
crest, by Waterhouse & Co, Sheffield, 1814   60 0

£   s

Coffee Pots

George I plain tapering octagonal coffee pot on moulded rim
foot with tapering polygonal spout and baluster finial to the
domed cover, engraved with a coat-of-arms in scroll and
foliage cartouche, by William Paradise, 1726, gross weight
23 oz, 9⅞ in high   2,900   0

George II plain tapering cylindrical coffee pot on circular
moulded foot with facetted curved spout and low domed
cover with baluster finial, by Gabriel Sleath, 1735, gross
weight *19 oz 14 dwt,* 8 in high   1,207 10

George III plain pear-shaped coffee pot on circular beaded
base, the curved beaded spout capped by a leaf and the
domed cover with urn-shaped finial, engraved with a crest,
by Hester Bateman, 1781, gross weight *28 oz,* 11½ in high   1,100   0

George III plain pear-shaped coffee pot on circular moulded
foot with curved spout chased with a shell and domed cover
with fluted baluster finial, (handle broken) by William Shaw,
1762, gross weight *21 oz, 9⅞ in* high   557 10

George II pear-shaped coffee pot on circular moulded foot, the
body and domed cover fluted and chased with flowers and
foliage, with shell ornament to the curved spout and flower
finial to the cover, by Thomas Whipham, 1735, with latent
silver handle, gross weight *35 oz, 9¾ in* high   440   0

Victorian coffee pot of oval form, the body crested and engraved
with bright-cut, straight fluted spout, ivory finial and handle,
by Stephen Smith, 1870, gross weight *20 oz 11 dwt,* 8¾ in
high   120   0

Cruets

George III oval cruet frame on four claw-and-ball feet with
beaded rim, the sides pierced and bright-cut with slits,
festoons and paterae, and with central loop handle, engraved
with a crest, with eight various silver-mounted cut-glass
bottles, maker's mark I.W., 1785   75   0

Victorian seven-bottle cruet frame, the sides pierced and chased
and on four panel supports, the central handle formed as
entwined foliage, with eight cut-glass bottles, three with silver
mounts, by Henry Wilkinson & Co, Sheffield, 1869, wooden
base   58   0

George III cinquefoil cruet frame on claw feet, the frame
pierced with geometric ornament and the centre with corded
handle, with five various cut-glass bottles and casters, each
with writhen finial, by E. Aldridge & Co, 1760, with additional handle and caster cover   30   0

Cups and Goblets

George III stirrup cup formed as a fox's mask, with backswept
ears and realistically chased coat, engraved with later initials,
4⅞ in long, by Henry Tudor and Thomas Leader, Sheffield,
1778, *3 oz 15 dwt*   760   0

George I plain two-handled cup on circular base with moulded
band and harp-sided handles, engraved with a coat-of-arms in

	£	s
baroque cartouche, 7½ in high, by Phillip Kinnersly, Dublin, 1717, *36 oz*	504	0
Charles II plain tumbler cup pricked with initials and dated 1677 and engraved with a later coat-of-arms, struck twice with the mark S over V in shaped cartouche and T.C. between annulets, 2½ in high, circa 1675, *5 oz 4 dwt*	367	10
George II two-handled cup and cover on circular moulded foot, the body chased with flowers, scrolls and two rococo cartouches containing a coat-of-arms and crest, with double scroll handles, the domed cover chased with vine foliage and flowers and with bud finial, 11½ in high, by Thomas Whipham, 1746, *47 oz*	252	0
Pair of George III goblets on circular stepped feet, the lower part of the campagna-shaped bodies with matted tulip and acanthus decoration, the rims engraved with bright-cut hops, 6⅜ in high, by R. Emes and E. Barnard, 1809, *22 oz*	160	0
George III goblet on rim foot chased with foliage on a matted ground, the lower part of the body applied with swirling foliage, with a band of vine foliage above, 6⅜ in high, by R. Emes and E. Barnard, 1817, *12 oz 11 dwt*	85	0
George III plain goblet on trumpet-shaped foot decorated with a band of beading, the bowl engraved at a later date with a band of scrolls, 5¾ in high, by Peter, Anne and William Bateman, 1800, *5 oz 17 dwt*	35	0

Cutlery—Canteens and Services

	£	s
Canteen of King's pattern table cutlery comprising twelve dinner forks, twelve dessert forks, twelve teaspoons, twelve dessert spoons, twelve tablespoons, soup ladle, by William Smiley, London, 1857, 160 oz. Matching serving spoon, London, 1898. Matching set of twelve dinner knives and twelve dessert knives with stainless steel blades, by Messrs Viners, Sheffield	520	0
Victorian table service with shell and thread decoration, comprising twenty-four table forks, twelve table knives, twelve dessert forks, twelve dessert knives, twelve tablespoons, twelve dessert spoons, twelve steak knives, twelve tea knives, twelve soup spoons, two soup ladles, two serving spoons, twelve pastry forks, twelve teaspoons, twelve fruit spoons, two sauce ladles, pair of salad servers, set of six fish knives and forks, an asparagus set, London, 1898, *296 oz*	400	0

Cutlery—Forks Dessert

	£	s
Six George III three-pronged dessert forks bearing two maker's marks, I.C. and M.G., one presumably on resale, Dublin, 1774, *5 oz 18 dwt*	105	0
Five George II three-pronged dessert forks, each engraved 'Spread Eagle, Gracechurch Street', probably by James Whitthorne, Dublin, circa 1745, *4 oz 10 dwt*	95	0
Twelve Victorian fiddle-pattern dessert forks, London, 1844 and 1845, *20 oz 10 dwt*	44	0
Set of six early Victorian dessert forks, Exeter, 1853	19	0

	£	s

Cutlery—Forks Table

Twelve Queen Anne three-pronged table forks engraved with a crest and motto, by William Ged, Edinburgh, 1710, Assay-master Edward Penman, (marks on three worn), *23 oz* — 360 0

Twelve George II three-pronged table forks engraved with a crest by Philip Roker, 1748, (marks on most indistinct) *25 oz* — 252 0

Twelve three-pronged old English pattern table forks, each engraved with a crest, seven by Richard Crossley, 1782, five 1780, 1781, etc, *25 oz* — 145 0

Set of six Victorian table forks with acanthus handles and shell decoration to the reverse, London, 1898, *20 oz* — 20 0

Three George III table forks by Richard Crossley, London, 1804, *6 oz 10 dwt* — 10 0

Cutlery—Knives

Twelve George I table knives and twelve cheese knives, the tapering cylindrical handles with ball finials, with steel blades, circa 1725, (maker's mark only T.S. legible on six of each category) — 270 0

Eighteen table knives with Victorian silver handles — 57 0

Forty-three Victorian table knives with silver reeded handles engraved with a crest — 25 0

Cutlery—Ladles

George III old English pattern soup ladle engraved with initials, by Hester Bateman, 1788, *4 oz 7 dwt* — 48 0

King's husk pattern soup ladle by William Eley and William Fearn, 1822, *10 oz 4 dwt* — 20 0

George II plain punch ladle engraved with a monogram, with baluster wood handle, possibly 1723 — 12 0

Cutlery—Spoons Dessert

Set of six George III silver-gilt dessert spoons of plain design by William Sheen, London, 1785, intaglio mark, *8 oz* — 72 0

Six George III old English pattern dessert spoons by Peter, Anne and William Bateman, 1804, *5 oz 17 dwt* — 40 0

George IV fiddle pattern dessert spoon by William Eley, London, 1825 — 2 0

Victorian dessert spoon, London, 1845 — 1 10

Cutlery—Spoons Serving

George IV long-handled serving spoon, London, 1825 — 13 0

Victorian long-handled serving spoon, London, 1852, *6 oz 10 dwt* — 10 0

Cutlery—Spoons Table

Twelve various rat-tailed tablespoons, mainly engraved with initials or monogram, 1718, 1721, 1726, etc, *18 oz 16 dwt* — 75 0

Pair of Queen Anne rat-tailed tablespoons with dog-nose tops, each engraved with the initials T.R.M. and a later monogram, by Isaac Dalton, 1709 — 37 16

Pair of George III silver-gilt tablespoons by William Eley and William Fearn, London, 1817, *7 oz* — 18 0

George III tablespoon, London, circa 1820 — 4 0

£   s

Cutlery—Spoons Tea and Coffee
Set of seven William IV teaspoons of plain design by Mary
    Chawner, London, 1835, *5 oz*   20   0
Set of six Victorian teaspoons with reeded handles and
    engraved crests, London, 1838, *5 oz*   9   0

Dishes and Plates
Twelve George III dinner plates with shaped gadrooned
    borders, engraved with two crests and a motto, maker's
    mark W.S., perhaps for William Stroud, 1805, *227 oz*, 9½ in
    diameter   1,680   0
Set of four George III plain octagonal entrée dishes and covers
    with moulded gadrooned borders, each engraved with a coat-
    of-arms and three crests, the raised covers with a bud finial
    (two missing), by J. Wakelin and R. Garrard, 1798, *168 oz*,
    12¼ in long   735   0
Pair of William IV plain oblong partly fluted entrée dishes and
    covers, the dishes with foliage scroll borders and the covers
    with similar loop handles, engraved with a coat-of-arms,
    maker's mark HH, Birmingham, 1834, *115 oz*, 1 ft 1 in long   390   0
Large oval vegetable dish and cover, the dish with shaped shell
    and scroll border the domed cover with pomegranate finial,
    with tripartite division, engraved with a coat-of-arms and
    motto, by Robert Garrard, 1828, *102 oz*, 1 ft 2½ in wide   273   0
Victorian oval entrée dish with moulded rim and semi-
    gadrooned cover, Sheffield, 1897, *49 oz*   100   0

Jugs—Cream and Milk
George II plain pear-shaped cream jug on three hoof feet with
    scalloped rim and double scroll handle engraved with a crest,
    Bristol, circa 1740, *3 oz 6 dwt*   440   0
George III plain helmet-shaped cream jug on square base with
    beaded border and loop handle, engraved with initials, by
    Hester Bateman, 1790, *2 oz 8 dwt*   105   0
George III helmet-shaped cream jug on three lion's mask and
    paw feet, the body chased with festoons of fruit and flowers,
    scrolls and wave ornament, with shaped rim and double scroll
    handle, engraved later with two crests and a coronet, maker's
    mark WW, probably for William Ward, Dublin, circa 1800,
    4 oz 14 dwt   52   10
George III oval cream jug of shaped outline with reeded rim
    and loop handle, engraved with bands of bright-cut ornament
    and an escutcheon, maker's mark IM, 1802, *3 oz 1 dwt*   42   0

Jugs—Water
Plain vase-shaped hot-water jug on circular foot with gadrooned
    shoulder and foliate lip, the body and curved cover engraved
    with the cypher of William IV, crown and garter motto and
    royal ducal coronet and monogram AS, for Princess Augusta
    Sophia, by Robert Garrard, 1834, gross weight *18 oz 19 dwt*,
    7 in high   190   0
Victorian Scottish hot-water jug of tapering form, the chased
    body with satyr mask spout and leaf-capped handle, crested,

	£	s
maker's mark M.C. & Co, Edinburgh, 1874, *27 oz 14 dwt*, 10½ in high	90	0
Victorian cone-shaped hot-water jug with spherical knop, London, 1870, gross weight *12 oz*	28	0

Jugs—Wine and Ale

George II plain pear-shaped covered wine jug on circular moulded foot, with double scroll handle capped by a leaf and domed cover with corkscrew thumbpiece, with moulded drop beneath the spout, by Jacob Marsh, 1743, 9 in high — 520 0

Victorian circular wine jug with matted finish and gilt interior, short neck, everted lip, flat hinged cover and baluster finial, by Stephen Smith, 1878, *15 oz 10 dwt*, 6 in high — 35 0

Marrow Scoops

George III marrow scoop by J. and J. Perkins, London, 1796 — 24 0

George III plain marrow scoop, engraved with a crest, probably by Christopher Haines, Dublin, circa 1785 — 22 0

Mugs

George II large plain cylindrical mug on circular moulded foot and with boldly modelled scroll handle, engraved with a monogram, by Edward Lothian, Edinburgh, 1742, *25 oz*, 6⅜ in high — 300 0

Two plain George III mugs, each of shaped outline on circular moulded base with double scroll handles and slightly flaring lips, engraved with a monogram, by Patrick Robertson, Edinburgh, 1775, *18 oz 5 dwt*, 3½ in and 4⅞ in high — 200 0

Mustard Pots

George III mustard pot, London, 1802, *4 oz* — 41 0

Oval mustard pot engraved with drapery festoons and a monogram, and pierced above with slits and circles, with domed cover and reeded scroll handle, with glass liner, by Robert Hennell, 1788, *3 oz 5 dwt* — 38 0

Early Victorian cylindrical mustard pot with pierced body and initialled cover with flower finial, leafy handle, by Elizabeth Eaton, 1847, *5 oz 6 dwt*, 3¼ in high — 37 0

Large early George III vase-shaped mustard pot with pedestal foot, London, circa 1762, *7 oz 10 dwt* — 16 0

Salvers

James II plain circular salver on central spreading foot, the salver with moulded reeded border, engraved with a later monogram, maker's mark WE mulled above and below, 1688, *16 oz 8 dwt*, 10¼ in diameter — 651 0

George II circular salver on four foliage scroll feet, the shaped moulded border decorated at intervals with shells and foliage, the centre chased with a band of scrolls, trelliswork and flowers and engraved with a coat-of-arms in rococo cartouche, by John Robinson, 1745, *64 oz*, 1 ft 4 in diameter — 388 10

George I small plain salver on bracket feet with incurved corners and moulded border, the centre engraved with a

	£	s

coat-of-arms, maker's mark missing, 1724, *16 oz 18 dwt*, 8¼ in square — 273 0

George III plain circular salver on three bracket feet, the border stamped with a band of laurel between two beaded bands and the centre engraved with a monogram within flower sprays, by Robert Jones, 1779, *27 oz*, 1 ft diameter — 252 0

George III circular small salver on three hoof feet with shaped shell and scroll border, the centre chased with a broad band of birds, pagodas and scrolls, engraved with a crest, by Richard Rugg, 1767, *12 oz 9 dwt*, 8 in diameter — 60 18

Salts

Set of six George III silver-gilt circular salt cellars, each on three lion's mask and paw feet with applied shields, with partly fluted bodies and chevron patterned borders, on circular plinths with bracket feet and similar borders, engraved with a coat-of-arms and motto, by D. Scott and B. Smith, 1803, *97 oz* — 1,202 0

Six circular silver-gilt salt cellars with gadrooned borders and open wirework sides, each with circular cut-glass bowl, maker's mark C.C., 1806, in fitted wood case, *16 oz 8 dwt* — 420 0

Four circular salt cellars each on three mask feet, the bombé sides chased with flowers and foliage on a matted ground, engraved with a crest and motto, maker's mark C.P., perhaps for Charles Plumley, 1819 and 1821, *22 oz* — 94 10

Pair of plain boat-shaped salt cellars on collet bases and with reeded rims, engraved with a crest, by Samuel Hennell, 1800, *4 oz 17 dwt* — 55 0

Pair of George III two-handled boat-shaped salt cellars, each on oval moulded foot with reeded borders and loop handles, one salt cellar with partition, by Robert Sharp, 1788, with a pair of old English salt shovels, 1793, *9 oz 18 dwt* — 39 18

Sauceboats

Pair of George II plain oval sauceboats, each on three paw feet with moulded scrolls above, the shaped rim chased with a narrow band of wave ornament, flowers and scrolls, with double scroll handle capped by a leaf, engraved with a monogram, by Robert Lowe, Edinburgh, 1748, *14 oz 4 dwt* — 800 0

Pair of George II plain sauceboats, each on three hoof feet with shaped rims and double scrolled handles, engraved with initials, by Bennett Bradshaw & Co, 1740, *15 oz 5 dwt* — 441 0

George II plain sauceboat on three hoof feet with gadrooned rim and rising scroll handle capped with a leaf, maker's mark illegible, 1754, *13 oz 1 dwt* — 120 15

Plain large sauceboat on three shell feet with scalloped rim and rising double scroll handle, engraved with a crest, probably 1758, *12 oz 4 dwt* — 65 0

Snuff Boxes—See Small Decorative Antiques

Sugar Basins—See Baskets—Sugar

£   s

Tapersticks—See *Candlesticks*

Tankards
Queen Anne cylindrical tankard and cover on fluted low domed
  base with a moulded rib round the body and scroll handle,
  the stepped domed cover chased with bands of flutes and
  punched motifs, with openwork scroll thumbpiece, the front
  engraved with a strapwork and scrolling cartouche enclosing
  a later applied medallion, by Isaac Dighton, 1703, *31 oz,*
  7⅛ in high   756   0
Charles II cylindrical tankard and cover on reeded foot, the
  raised cover with corkscrew thumbpiece, chased in the
  Chinese taste with figures, exotic birds and plants and
  engraved with a coat-of-arms in plume mantling, maker's mark
  R in script, pellet below, 1677, *19 oz 12 dwt,* 6 in high   720   0
George II plain tankard of shaped outline on circular moulded
  foot with a rib round the body, double scroll handle and
  openwork scroll thumbpiece to the domed cover, engraved
  with a monogram in a scroll and foliage cartouche, by
  Wililam Grundy, 1756, *30 oz,* 8 in high   483   0
George III plain cylindrical tankard and cover on spreading
  base with a moulded band around the body, the domed cover
  with pierced scrollwork thumbpiece, by S. Godbehere and E.
  Wigan, 1786, *24 oz,* 7⅜ in high   350   0

Tea Caddies
Set of two George II silver-gilt tea caddies and an oval sugar
  box each of inverted pear shape, the foot chased with panels
  of scalework and flowers, the body chased with foliage and
  flutes, and repoussé with sunflowers, roses and other flowers,
  the domed cover similarly chased with bud finial, engraved
  twice with a coat-of-arms within chased rococo surrounds
  and with two crests, by William Grundy, 1744, *44 oz,* 7½ in
  high   950   0
George III oval tea caddy with shaped domed cover, urn finial
  and beaded borders, engraved with two bands of wrigglework
  enclosing quatrefoils and two oval cartouches enclosing a
  coat-of-arms and monogram, by Hester Bateman, 1790,
  10 oz 1 dwt   651   0
George III shaped oval tea caddy, the body bright-cut with
  formal floral borders, engraved twice with an initial, the
  domed cover with similar border and urn finial, with original
  key, by Joseph Scammell, 1791, gross weight *12 oz 10 dwt*   220   0
Plain oval tea caddy, the raised hinged cover with urn finial,
  engraved with a crest, maker's mark JS in script, perhaps for
  John Sanders, 1794, *10 oz 15 dwt,* 5⅞ in high   162   10

Tea and Coffee Services
George III tea and coffee service comprising compressed
  spherical teapot, sugar basin and cream jug, oval tea-kettle,
  stand and lamp and vase-shaped coffee pot, stand and lamp,
  each piece on rim foot and with high collar, the stands on

	£	s

four reeded scroll feet, engraved with a crest and coronet, by
William Burwash, 1812, gross weight *143 oz* — **900 0**

George III parcel-gilt tea service comprising teapot, sugar
basin, and cream jug, each on circular ovolo foot and with
ovolo rim applied with silver-gilt satyr's masks entwined with
snakes, the teapot with gilt foliage spout and ivory handle
terminating in a satyr's mask and a winged monster, the
slightly domed cover with baluster finial engraved with a
rosette, the basin and cream jug with gilt double serpent
loop handles, engraved with a coronet, motto and initial, by
Paul Storr, the teapot and cream jug, 1812, the sugar basin,
1813, *69 oz* — **787 10**

George III tea and coffee service comprising circular teapot,
pear-shaped coffee pot, two-handled sugar basin and cream
jug, each on circular foot chased with flowers, scrolls and
shellwork on a matted ground and engraved with a crest and
monogram, the tea and coffee pots with curved spouts and
twig finial to the domed cover, the sugar basin and cream jug
with scroll caryatid figure handles, by Thomas Wallis and
Jonathan Hayne, 1817, gross weight *89 oz* — **588 0**

Victorian tea and coffee service richly decorated with flowers,
fruit and foliage, scrolls and cartouche panels, by J. Muir-
head & Son, Glasgow, 1861, *70 oz* — **400 0**

Teapots and Stands

George I plain octagonal pear-shaped teapot on rim foot with
curved spout and baluster finial to the domed cover, by Joseph
Ward, 1717, gross weight *13 oz 9 dwt* — **2,600 0**

George II bullet-shaped teapot on circular moulded foot, the
curved spout with stylized foliage base, the shoulder and flat
cover chased with strapwork, shells and scrolls, engraved with
a vacant baroque cartouche, the scroll wood handle capped
with silver leaf, by Sampson Bennett, Exeter, 1759, gross
weight *14 oz 1 dwt* — **682 10**

George I plain circular teapot stand on four bracket feet with
moulded border, the reverse engraved with initials, maker's
mark indistinct, 1718, *6 oz 15 dwt*, 6 in diameter — **315 0**

George III oval teapot on moulded foot with straight spout,
centrally domed cover and beaded borders, engraved with
a crest and motto and later monogram, maker's mark, perhaps
S.W. for Samuel Wood, 1785, gross weight *14 oz 16 dwt* — **126 0**

George III circular teapot of plain design, London, 1808, *21 oz* — **108 0**

Early Victorian teapot, plain compressed melon-shaped body,
fluted curved spout, melon finial and loop handle, on four
anthemion feet, by Joseph and Albert Savory, 1843, gross
weight *26 oz 1 dwt*, 6½ in high — **95 0**

George III teapot of compressed circular form, the matt ground
chased with upright acanthus leaves and a girdle of lozenge
and foliated motifs, a melon knop to the cover, by Peter and
William Bateman, London, 1805, *19 oz* — **60 0**

Trays

George III two-handled oval tray on four gadrooned feet, the

fluted out-curved border with gadrooned rim and with gadrooned and foliage handles, engraved with a coat-of-arms
within plume mantling, by Thomas Hannam and John
Crouch, 1801, *89 oz*, 1 ft 9¼ in wide   850   0

Early Victorian two-handled oval tea tray engraved with
armorials, leafage and flowers, applied scroll border with
flowers and beads, similar handles and four pierced panel
feet, by E. E. J. and W. Barnard, 1840, *136 oz 17 dwt*, 2 ft
4 in wide   460   0

George II snuffer tray of hourglass shape on four shell and hoof
feet, with scalloped edge and double scroll handle, engraved
with a monogram in scrolling foliage cartouche, by William
Cafe, 1757, *7 oz 12 dwt*, 7¼ in wide   110   0

Vinaigrettes—See Small Decorative Antiques

Waiters

George II shaped circular waiter on three bracket and scroll
feet, the outcurved fluted border with shaped rim, engraved
with a narrow band of beads with foliage at intervals, the
centre with a crest in a foliage cartouche, by S. Herbert & Co,
1757, *6 oz 18 dwt*, 6½ in diameter   126   0

George III small circular waiter on hoof feet with shell and
scroll border, the centre chased with a band of flowers, by
Ebenezer Coker, 1760, *8 oz 17 dwt*, 7¼ in diameter   81   18

Circular waiter on claw-and-ball feet, chased later with flowers,
scrolls and wave ornament and engraved with the royal
crown and cypher of William IV and a monogram, by R.
Jones and J. Schofield, 1776, *7 oz 17 dwt*, 7 in diameter   38   0

Wine Coolers

Pair of George III campagna-shaped wine coolers on circular
feet chased with a band of quatrefoils and acanthus foliage,
the bodies fluted below and with entwined vine tendril
handles, extending below the lip with everted ovolo border,
engraved twice with an initial, by Paul Storr, 1817, *137 oz*,
10⅛ in high   950   0

Pair of Victorian wine coolers and liners with plain fluted
campagna-shaped bodies, shaped gadroon-knopped stems and
shaped circular bases, by John S. Hunt, 1855, *178 oz 18 dwt*,
12¾ in high   950   0

SHEFFIELD PLATE

Candelabra and Candlesticks

Pair of seven-light candelabra on shaped square bases, chased
with a band of floral foliage, the tapering stems with vase-
shaped sockets, with six scrolling reeded branches and central
light, 1 ft 7¼ in high   73   10

Pair of table candelabra, the double scrolled and reeded
branches with acanthus decoration   42   0

	£	s

Pair of table candlesticks on circular bases and baluster stems
with circular nozzles and foliage borders, 10⅝ in high — **14 0**

Pair of table candelabra, each with three reeded and scrolled
candle branches issuing from beaded and tapering shafts,
supported on pedestal feet, 1 ft 2½ in high — **10 0**

Coasters

Set of twelve wine coasters, lobed and fluted and with turnover
rims, 6¼ in diameter — **200 0**

Pair of wine coasters with fluted sides below ovolo rims, wood
bases and zinc liners, 6 in diameter — **26 0**

Pair of wine coasters, the sides pierced with scrollwork, with
applied scrollwork borders — **9 0**

Coffee Pots

Fluted compressed baluster coffee pot with applied leaf and
flower borders, loop handle and curved spout, 8¾ in high — **28 0**

Oval coffee pot on pedestal foot engraved with an initial above
an applied gadroon girdle, curved spout and wood handle,
detachable cover, 10 in high — **10 0**

Dishes

Pair of shaped oblong entrée dishes and covers with gadrooned
and flower rims, the domed covers with stylized foliage
borders, with foliage finials on a leaf ground, 11 in wide — **89 5**

Oblong toasted-cheese dish, the detachable domed cover with
spherical finial, with detachable wood handle and silver liner
engraved with a crest, the liner Sheffield, 1802, weight of
liner 9 oz 9 dwt, 8 in long — **42 0**

Pair of oblong entrée dishes with gadrooned handles, and the
covers and handles — **22 0**

Oval turn-over breakfast dish with reeded and claw supports,
with liner and drainer — **17 0**

Tea Caddies

Large tea caddy of baluster rectangular form, lightly chased
with leafy scrolls and flowers, the hinged cover with flower
finial, on four curved supports, key, 8 in high — **38 0**

Globular tea caddy and cover with wrythen-fluted ground — **21 0**

Teapots

Small oval teapot, the straight sides plain between reeded
borders, with wood handle and finial, 5 in high — **42 0**

Compressed circular teapot, plain with moulded girdle and loop
handle, 4¾ in high — **14 0**

Circular teapot with reeded girdles — **2 10**

Tea and Coffee Services

Four-piece tea and coffee service, on bun feet with shell and
leaf decoration on gadroon rims and moulded bodies, the
milk jug and sugar basin with gilt interiors, the tea and coffee
pots with wood handles — **125 0**

	£	s
Three-piece tea set of melon form, the sugar basin and milk jug with gilt interiors, on anthemion decorated feet	55	0
Victorian engraved tea and coffee service, surmounted by acorn finials, comprising teapot, coffee pot, hot-water jug, sucrier and cream jug	22	0

Tea Trays

Oblong two-handled tea tray, engraved with cartouche panels and applied floral decoration	240	0
Victorian oblong two-handled tea tray, chased below the applied grape and vine leaf border, on four feet, 2 ft 4 in wide	38	0

Tea Urns

Tea urn of plain hemispherical form on four scroll and paw feet, and shaped square plinth, with two lion's mask drop-ring handles to the body, gadrooned border to the shoulder and domed cover with ball finial, engraved with a monogram within foliage wreath, with central vase-shaped burner, circa 1810, 1 ft 4¼ in high	70	0
Olong tea urn complete with burner, crested below a lattice-work band, gadroon borders, lion's mask ring handle, on four slender supports, 1 ft 1½ in high	60	0
Circular tea urn supported on four bold paw feet, with lion's mask ring handles and spirit burner	15	0

Tureens

Oval soup tureen and cover, semi-lobed, with loop handles, urn finial, on matching pedestal foot, 1 ft 4½ in wide	210	0
Pair of plain two-handled boat-shaped sauce tureens and covers in the Adam taste, each on square plinth and with foliage loop handles to the domed covers	150	0

Wine Coolers

Pair of campagna-shaped wine coolers on spreading feet, with reeded handles, gadroon borders, detachable rims and liners, the bodies engraved with arms, 8¼ in high	240	0
Pair of wine coolers with gadrooned bands and lion masks, the upper parts detachable, 11 in high	90	0
Wine cooler, richly embossed with foliage and flower-heads and vacant cartouche panels, with double satyr handles	50	0

NON-PRECIOUS METALS

Brass

Seventeenth-century brass chandelier with baluster centre and large pendant sphere and twelve scrolling branches, 3 ft high	200	0
Brass chandelier of six S-scroll branches rising from a gadrooned bowl and short baluster shaft, hung from a chain and coroner, 2 ft high	60	0

Pair of brass candlesticks of Régence style, with elaborately

	£	s
chased shafts with shells, strapwork and sprays of leaves and flowers, the bases chased with marks, C-scrolls and sprays of leaves, 10 in high	45	0
Brass sundial, signed A. Abraham, Liverpool, 1 ft diameter	41	0
Regency brass inkstand, of boat shape with scrolling serpent handles and three lidded containers, 9 in wide	33	10
Georgian brass kettle stand, formed as a tripod table with circular top, turned support and cabriole legs, 9½ in diameter	14	0
Seven horse brasses on two straps	6	10
Pair of baluster brass candlesticks, 9¼ in high	3	5

Bronze

	£	s
Pair of French nineteenth-century figures of Amorini holding ormolu floral garlands, 1 ft 2 in high	155	0
Set of four French nineteenth-century figures of putti, as the Seasons, 7½ in high	82	0
Pair of bronze figures of cupids on marble bases, signed 'Aug. Moreau', 9 in high	60	0
Pair of classical bronzes, Hermes and Iris, Heralds of the Gods, on black marble mounts, 2 ft 10 in high	40	0
Bronze figure of Napoleon, signed 'V. Riviere', on marble base, 9 in high	31	0
Bronze plaque of the Duke of Wellington, signed 'C. C. Adams', in ebonized frame	10	10

Copper

	£	s
Nineteenth-century ship's copper lantern with fluted cover, marked 'Anchor'	21	0
Early nineteenth-century two-handled tea urn with lid and brass top	19	0
Set of four early eighteenth-century copper saucepans with covers	13	0
Copper long-handled warming pan	9	10
Copper two-handled preserving-pan, 16 in diameter	7	10
Copper kettle with raised brass decoration	6	0
Copper coal-helmet with swing handle	4	0

Iron and Steel

	£	s
Pair of iron andirons of sixteenth-century style, with turned and knopped bodies and splayed bases with female busts, 2 ft 5 in high	38	0
Adam serpentine brass and cast-iron fire-basket and fire-back	36	0
Empire brass and steel fire-kerb	21	0
George III iron basket grate, the back with Christ and the Woman of Samaria and with a pierced serpentine brass apron and brass urn-shaped finials, 2 ft 5 in wide	10	0
Pair of wrought-iron fire dogs	6	0

Pewter

	£	s
Three eighteenth-century measures of standard form with acorn thumbpieces to the flat covers, the handles variously engraved with initials, 10½ in high	79	0

	£	s
Pair of early nineteenth-century circular basins with everted rims and hammer surface, by Samuel Cocks, London, 10½ in diameter	63	0
Georgian flagon of bulbous form on circular moulded foot, with scroll handle and raised cover, 8¼ in high	47	0
Eighteenth-century plain pear-shaped jug with curved spout, domed cover and shell thumbpiece, 7½ in high	42	0
Pair of Queen Anne circular dinner plates with moulded rim, the border of each stamped 'Burrough of Newbury', enclosing a castle, by H. Perchard, 1709, 9¾ in diameter	26	0
Large pair of table candlesticks, each on domed circular base, with baluster stems and vase-shaped sockets, fitted with ejectors, X crowned, maker's mark B and P, 11½ in high	19	0
Pair of early eighteenth-century plates, London touch mark	16	0

PORCELAIN

Bow

	£	s
Pair of finely modelled figures of musicians seated between flowering branches, the man playing a flute, and with side drum, in pink hat and pink and yellow cloak, his jacket with green and pink spots and his blue breeches reserved with iron-red flowers, the woman playing the harp, in pink hat, blue bodice and pink skirt reserved with flowers, the mound bases encrusted with flowers and moulded with pink and gold scrolls, on three green and gold scroll feet, 8½ in high, red anchor and dagger and rare blue dagger marks	399	0
Pair of octagonal plates in the *famille rose* style, painted with a child on a buffalo, with a dog, two storks and a bird in flight on islands in a river landscape, the borders with iron-red and yellow scrolling foliage, 8¾ in wide	294	0
Pair of figures of a gardener and companion standing before wide flowering bocages, the man holding a spade, his coat with iron-red flowers, with blue apron and pink breeches, the woman with a sheep beside her, her dress with iron-red flowers and her apron encrusted with flowers, the bases moulded with green and pink pierced scrolls, 9½ in high	252	0
Figure of a seated nun reading a bible, in pink-lined black cowl and black and white habit, the base with two books and a rosary, 4¾ in high	115	10
Pair of figures of putti standing before flowering tree stumps, holding baskets of fruit, with floral garlands, draped in cloaks decorated in blue and gold, the green and gold scroll bases applied with flowers, 5¼ in high, iron-red anchor and dagger marks	78	10
Rare pipe, modelled as the head of a gipsy woman, with puce-spotted scarf round her head and neck, with brown hair and yellow earrings, the bowl and stem with metal mounts, 3½ in wide	57	10
Figure emblematic of smelling from a set of the four senses, standing beside a pillar, holding flowers to her nose and resting her arm on a vase, in yellow and blue striped cloak,		

	£	s
her dress painted with flower sprays, the base and pillar with manganese splashes and encrusted with foliage, 10 in high	52	10
White shell-shaped sweetmeat dish, formed as a fluted scallop shell resting on naturally modelled rockwork, shells and coral, 4¾ in wide	42	0
Three white coffee cups with loop handles, the sides applied with a large spray of prunus and two smaller	26	0

Bristol

Pair of candle cups, covers and stands, decorated with a simple neo-classical pattern of a two-toned iron-red coil, wreathed in gold, ground with floral sprays in gilding, cross marks in brown and numeral 3 in gilding, the stand 6⅜ in diameter	175	0
Chinoiserie bowl with gadrooned sides, painted in colours with Oriental figures, insects and flower sprays, the interior with central flower spray and brown wave and dot rim, 4¼ in diameter, mock Meissen mark and blue enamel cross	84	0
Tea bowl and saucer, the sides painted in green monochrome with floral swags suspended from gilt rings, the rims gilt, blue B and cross marks	44	0
Circular bowl, the exterior painted in colours with bouquets of flowers and flower sprays, 6¼ in diameter, blue enamel cross mark	21	0
Saucer, decorated in blue enamel with flower sprays, the border with scrolls and foliage and the rim gilt	6	0

Caughley

Basket of circular shape, with scalloped rim, moulded on the exterior with interwoven basketwork hoops and printed in underglaze-blue with insects and sprays and sprigs of flowers, the interior with nuts and pine cones, and with carrots, radishes, lettuce and other vegetables round the rim, 9¼ in diameter, crescent mark	72	0
Blue and white bridge pattern bowl, painted in the Oriental manner with a stylized bridge joining two islands with buildings and trees on them, the border with cross-hatched designs, 6 in diameter	36	10
Blue and white circular bowl, transfer printed with Orientals on terraces, amongst flowers in vases, with trees and buildings in the distance, the interior with a vase of foliage and with blue rim, 5½ in diameter, crescent mark	21	0

Chelsea

Lobed and fluted botanical plate, painted in colours with two beetroots and leaves, five sliced lemons, four shadowed insects and a bluebell spray, with lobed chocolate rim, 9¾ in diameter, red anchor mark	735	0
Botanical plate, the centre painted with a flower spray, two butterflies, an insect and another flower, with chocolate rim, 8¼ in diameter, red anchor mark	367	10
Pair of Mazarine blue plates of Mecklenburg-Strelitz type, the centres painted in colours with exotic birds and insects, the borders alternately gilt with insects on mazarine blue		

grounds in moulded gilt scroll cartouches and painted in colours with floral swags, the lobed rims gilt, 8¾ in diameter, gold anchor marks · 210 0

Pair of fable candlestick groups, one with a fox and bird, and the other with a dog goring a fox, before flowering trees, the mounds applied with flowers, on pierced gilt scroll bases, 6¼ in high, gold anchor marks · 126 0

Pair of figures of a harvester and companion, the man standing before a flowering tree stump with a scythe over his shoulder, in a pink-lined sea-green coat, his breeches enriched with gold, pink and blue designs, with a knotted scarf and barrel beside, his companion in pink coat and iron-red bodice, her dress with blue and gold designs, on mound bases encrusted with flowers and moulded with scrolls, 7¼ in high, gold anchor marks at back · 100 0

Custard cup and trembleuse saucer, painted with a loose bouquet and scattered flowers, with chocolate rim; and a trembleuse saucer *en suite*, red anchor marks · 99 10

Claret ground circular bowl decorated in the atelier of James Giles, the lower part with pine cone moulding and painted in colours with loose bouquets and scattered flowers, the claret border enriched with gilt *cailloute* and edged with gilt cornucopia-shaped scrolls, 6¾ in diameter, gold anchor mark · 73 10

Green ground vase of baluster form, the elaborate scroll handles enriched with gilding and the neck with pierced arches, the sides painted in colours with a putto on cloud spray and a flower spray, in gilt scroll cartouches on the green ground, the rims gilt, 5½ in high, gold anchor mark · 52 10

Chelsea Derby

Botanical shaped oval dish, painted in colours with two pink lilies and leaves and a small red-flowered plant, with gilt dentil rim, 9 in diameter, gold anchor mark · 94 10

Part tea service painted with flower sprays, the blue borders enriched with gilt dots and arrow heads, consisting of : slop bowl, four large tea bowls and saucers, four coffee cups; gilt marks · 89 0

Quatrefoil teapot and cover painted *en grisaille* with laurel swags supporting classical medallions, the handle and spout with blue enclosed by gilt *feuille-de-choux*, the waist with gilt foliage and the shoulder with entwined foliage swags, 8¾ in wide, gilt mark · 29 10

Two-handled cup, the sides with floral swags suspended from gilt scrolls, the shaped claret scale border enriched with gilding and with gilt rims · 20 0

Coalport (Coalbrookdale)

Six odd Coalport plates, the centres similarly painted with Chinese figures and birds, named on the backs, the iron-red borders with different designs and with gilt rims, and two oval meat dishes, the borders painted in red monochrome with chinoiseries in gilt cartouches on iron-red grounds · 126 0

Pair of Coalport ice pails and covers with gilt scroll handles, the

R

£ s

sides reserved with Chinese horsemen and figures on iron-red
grounds enriched with horizontal gilt scale, the borders with
iron-red sphinxes and scrolls and with gilt rims, 11½ in high | 78 10

Coalbrookdale perfume bottle and stopper, of cushion shape
painted with scattered sprays and moulded with elaborate
gilt scrolls, with claret lower part, 5 in high, blue C-Dale
mark | 29 10

Coalbrookdale rectangular basket with loop handle, painted with
a bouquet of flowers, the angles with flower sprays in relief
and the rim gilt, 7 in high | 14 10

Coalbrookdale shaped inkwell, painted with flower sprays and
encrusted with flowers and foliage, enriched in colours, the
borders moulded with green and gold scrolls, 7 in wide | 12 10

Davenport

Pair of wall jardinieres, of wedge shape, with concave crests
moulded with foliage, the sides painted with flower sprays and
birds on branches, the borders enriched with gilt bands and
foliage and with gilt serrated rims, 7½ in wide, plush velvet
mounts | 126 0

Pot-pourri bowl with gilt animal mask handles, the sides painted
with chinoiserie scenes, the gilt rims with beading, 3¼ in
high, red mark | 12 10

Pastille burner and stand, of conical form, painted in pink and
gold with roses, the square stand on gilt paw feet, 4 in high | 10 10

Derby

Pink ground cylindrical cup and saucer, painted by Jockey Hill
with a view near Ashburn, Derbyshire, in circular gilt band
and foliage cartouches on the 'Bloom' pink ground, the border
to the saucer with gilt foliage, and with gilt rim, blue mark | 399 0

Group of lovers walking arm in arm, the man in pink tricorn
hat, green coat and iron-red breeches gilt with flowers, the girl
in yellow hat, pink bodice and green and yellow striped
dress, with fruit and foliage in her apron, the mound base
applied with grapes, 6 in high | 294 0

Oval vine-leaf dish, the borders moulded with yellow-green
vine leaves and brown stalks, the centre painted in colours
with a loose bouquet and scattered flowers, with brown rim,
11 in wide | 100 0

Pair of biscuit figures of putti reclining beside tree stumps, one
with a dog beside, the rockwork bases applied with foliage,
4 in high, incised No 213 | 84 0

Bloor figure of Shakespeare, after the original by Scheemakers
intended for Westminster Abbey, the poet in pink cloak, his
clothes enriched with gilding, leaning on a pedestal, supporting three books and a manuscript, on an oblong octagonal
base enriched with gilding, 10 in high, iron-red mark,
incised No 305 | 52 10

Figure of Britannia in plumed helmet, gilt cuirass and florally
decorated cloak, the lion and martial trophies beside, the
base moulded with pink and gold scrolls, 1 ft 1½ in high | 31 10

Blue and white lobed oval sauce boat with scroll handle, the

	£	s

interior painted with Oriental river landscapes, the exterior with foliage trellis and cell patterns to the order, 8 in wide   **30   0**

Nightlight stand of castellated form painted with a view near Chester in a gilt oblong octagonal cartouche on a lime-green ground, the rims gilt, the border with alternate white and gold foliage, $5\frac{3}{4}$ in high, iron-red mark   **29   0**

Liverpool

Botanical bowl of attractive shape and fine quality painted in colours with rose, tulip and dahlia specimens, $4\frac{3}{4}$ in diameter   **220   0**

Unusual (William Ball) blue and white bowl painted with an upside-down design of a Chinaman fishing by a bridge, and with a pagoda and trees on a rockwork formation, with a long fence and fishermen behind, the reverse with an island vignette and arrowhead formation of birds, the interior with island and trellis border, 9 in diameter   **78   10**

Baluster vase painted with bouquets and scattered flowers in gilt scroll and circular cartouches on an unevenly applied wet blue ground, $6\frac{3}{4}$ in high   **57   10**

Globular teapot and cover with loop handle and knop finial, the sides painted in colours with scattered flowers, the borders with waved blue and gold designs, $8\frac{1}{4}$ in wide   **42   0**

Blue and white bowl, the exterior transfer-printed with three loose bouquets, the interior with central bouquet, the border with a band of half-moons, 8 in diameter   **25   0**

Longton Hall

Two rare figures of pug dogs, inspired by J. J. Kändler at Meissen, seated on their haunches facing left, their tails curled with blue collars, their bodies with manganese splashes, on mound bases, $3\frac{3}{4}$ in high   **603   0**

Pair of figures of a gardener and companion standing beside scrolling pillars, the man in black hat, pink coat, puce-striped breeches and white apron, with a spade and flowerpot beside, his companion in black hat, yellow skirt and white apron, on puce green and gold scroll bases, $4\frac{1}{4}$ in high   **294   0**

Bullet-shaped teapot and cover with loop handle, the fluted sides painted in colours with loose bouquets and scattered flowers, the pink borders of lobed outline, the cover with strawberry finial, $6\frac{3}{4}$ in high   **57   10**

Blue and white cylindrical coffee cup with angular scroll handle, painted with a continuous Oriental landscape, $2\frac{1}{2}$ in high   **50   10**

Lowestoft

Sugar bowl and cover, with floral finial, the sides painted in a soft palette with a loose bouquet in a gilt floral cartouche and with scattered flowers, the puce trellis orders enclosed by gilt scrolls, $5\frac{1}{4}$ in high   **168   0**

Pear-shaped cream jug with loop handle, *en suite* to the preceding lot, $4\frac{1}{4}$ in high   **84   0**

Blue and white shaped oval cream jug of fluted form, the sides painted with Oriental figures in boats in a river landscape,

<table>
<tr><td></td><td align="right">£</td><td>s</td></tr>
</table>

in moulded foliage cartouches, the borders with stylized foliage and the interior with a flower spray, 5¾ in wide   49   0

Minton

Two-handled pot-pourri bowl, cover and stand, with globular body, the handles formed as entwined crab-stocks with flower-spray terminals, painted with a view of Chillingham Castle, the reverse with a bouquet of garden flowers, the cover encrusted with flowers and with fruit finial, the stand on three scroll feet, 11 in high, blue crossed swords mark   115   10

Pair of tea cups and saucers with loop handles, painted *en camaieu rose* with landscape vignettes, the rims gilt, mock Sèvres mark, pattern No 294   35   10

Bowl, with loop handles, painted *en camaieu rose* with landscape vignettes, the rim gilt, 7 in diameter, mock Sèvres mark, pattern No 294   12   10

Nantgarw

Fine plate from the MacIntosh service, the centre brilliantly painted with an exotic bird in a landscape, the border with flower sprays in gilt sea scroll cartouches and with elaborate gilt scrolls and foliage, the gilt mantle rim with alternate large and small lobes, 9½ in diameter, impressed Nantgarw CW mark   420   0

Cushion-shaped dish painted in green, blue and red, with scattered wild cornflowers, the lobed rim gilt, 9½ in wide, impressed Nantgarw CW   44   0

Plate, painted in colours with pink roses and buds, the lobed rim with traces of gilt dentil pattern, 9¼ in diameter, impressed Nantgarw CW   29   10

New Hall

Spirally-fluted tea and coffee service decorated in blue and gold with floral swags to the orders, consisting of: teapot, cover and stand, sugar bowl and cover, slop bowl, cream jug, two saucer dishes, twelve tea bowls, twelve coffee cups, twelve saucers, pattern No 165   199   10

Punch pot and cover of globular shape, the curved spout and scroll handle, boldly painted in bright colours on each side with a bouquet of garden flowers among sprigs, 9½ in high   180   0

Plymouth

Set of figures of the Seasons comprising a figure of Spring, another of Autumn and two of Summer, each as an almost naked putto on a rococo scroll base and with relevant seasonal attributes, 5¾ in high   280   0

Bell-shaped mug with ribbed strap handle, painted in colours with bouquets and sprigs of roses and other flowers, below a border of rococo scrolls in puce, 6¾ in high   40   0

Vase of tall slender baluster shape with waisted neck, painted in *famille-rose* enamels with a red-headed bird perching on a bamboo, with insects in flight, 12¾ in high   26   0

£   s

Rockingham

Pair of shaped oval dishes with entwined branch loop handles,
the centres painted with bouquets of flowers in gilt foliage
cartouches, and the borders moulded with white leaves and
encrusted with foliage, 9¼ in wide, puce griffin marks   367 10

Pair of figures of poodles, modelled leaning on their front paws,
their necks, tails and ears encrusted, one wearing a top hat,
on maroon and green bases with yellow and gold tassels, 4½ in
wide   105 0

Pair of leaf-moulded cups and saucers, moulded with alternate
green and yellow leaves with gilt veins, the rims gilt and with
gilt entwined handles, puce griffin marks and red 873 nos   73 10

Cylindrical spill vase, with spreading lip, painted with a flower
spray within a gilt rectangular cartouche on a claret ground,
the waist moulded with two bands enriched with gilding and
the rim with gilt bands, 4¼ in high, puce griffin mark   58 0

Plate, the centre painted with a bouquet of flowers, and the
border with green all-over leaf design, the rim moulded with
foliage and enriched with gilding, 9 in diameter, puce griffin
mark   40 0

Two small pastille burners, modelled as castles with two turrets,
the brown walls pierced and encrusted with foliage, on green
mound bases with yellow walls, 3¾ in high   36 10

Spode

Dessert service, the centres transfer-printed and decorated in
colours with landscape scenes, the blue borders with flower
sprays in white relief and with gilt rims, consisting of : oval
centre dish, two sauce tureens with fixed stands and one
cover, four oval dishes, four heart-shaped dishes, twelve plates   220 10

Garniture of three campana vases of pattern No 1166, the gilt
loop handles with rams' mask finials and the sides painted
with flower sprays on blue grounds enriched with an all-over
gilt scale pattern, the rims gilt, on fixed circular plinths, 6 in
to 6¾ in high   99 10

Pair of vases, painted in blue, red, green and gold with stylized
Oriental flowers and fences, the rims gilt, 5¼ in high, red
Spode 967 mark   31 10

Jug, with scroll handle, the sides painted in colours and moulded
with floral bouquets, 11¾ in high   19 0

Lobed deep plate, the centre painted with a view of a cottage
near Chester, the border moulded with foliage and with lobed
dentil gilt rim, 8½ in diameter   6 10

Swansea

Fruit stand of rectangular shape with double foliate handles in
gilding, painted in the centre, probably by William Pollard,
with a spray of flowers including stocks, roses, convolvulus
and periwinkle, the elaborate gilt borders with pendant swags
in green and gilding, high foot, 12¾ in high   100 0

Spill vase, of flared form painted in colours in the style of
William Billingsley with pink roses and green foliage, the rims
gilt, 5½ in high   84 0

£   s

Oval teapot and cover, the spout enriched with gilt foliage, the
sides painted in colours with bouquets of flowers with gilt
foliage in between, the borders with gilt foliage and dentil
rim, 11 in wide, and a cream jug and slop bowl *en suite*   37   0
Plate, the centre painted in colours with two roses on a
stalk and the border with green, puce and gold stylized
foliage, with gilt rim, 8½ in diameter   23   0

Worcester
Fine Dr Wall pierced oval chestnut basket, cover and stand, the
brown and yellow branch handles with floral terminals, the
moulded sides and pierced cover and border to the stand
with green-centred pink rosettes, the rims with yellow bands
and the centre to the stand with a bouquet of flowers, the
rims gilt, the stand 10¼ in wide   273   0
Dr Wall blue scale teapot, cover and lobed hexagonal stand, the
sides painted in iron-red, green, blue and gold with flowering
chrysanthemums and bamboos in gilt scroll vase and mirror-
shaped cartouches on the blue scale grounds, the rims gilt,
the cover with floral finial, 7 in wide, blue square seal marks   189   0
Dr Wall spirally-fluted cream jug, with snake handle, the lower
parts moulded with foliage enriched with green, the sides
painted with flower sprays, 4¼ in wide   157   10
Dr Wall blue scale circular dish of Blind Earl type, the branch
handle with two rose buds, the sides lightly moulded with
leaves, and similarly decorated to the preceding on the blue
scale grounds, the lobed rims gilt, 6 in wide, blue square sea
mark   136   10
Blue and white pierced oval basket, the branch handle with
floral terminals, transfer-printed with pine cones and foliage,
the border with trellis and foliage, and the exterior to the
pierced basketwork sides applied with rosettes, 7¼ in wide,
crescent mark   84   0
Dr Wall apple-green coffee cup and saucer, of 'Marchioness of
Huntly' type, the apple-green borders enclosed by shaped gilt
scrolls suspending floral swags, the rims gilt, blue crossed
swords and six marks   68   0
Blue and white junket dish, the centre transfer-printed with
cones, flowers and foliage, the border with scrolling trellis and
foliage designs, 10¼ in diameter, crescent mark   40   0
Blue and white shaped hexagonal teapot stand, transfer-printed
with the 'Pleasure Boat' and 'Fisherman' design, 6 in wide,
disguised numeral mark   26   0
Blue and white lobed oval tureen stand, 9¼ in wide, crescent
mark   23   0

Worcester—Flight Barr & Barr, and Barr Flight & Barr
Flight, Barr and Barr claret ground dessert service with central
gilt motifs, the claret borders with gilt beaded rims, consisting
of : two sauce tureens and covers, circular centre dish, four
oval dishes, four cushion-shaped dishes, four circular dishes,
twenty-two plates : impressed marks   189   0
Small pair of Barr, Flight & Barr vases, the handles formed as

£   s

gilt entwined snakes and the sides finely painted in colours by Thomas Baxter with country scenes illustrating the poems of Cowper, in gilt wedge-shaped cartouches on buff yellow grounds, the borders with gilt foliage and with gilt and beaded rims, 5¼ in high, script marks and Coventry Street address and with the relevant lines of poetry   168 0

Flight, Barr & Barr pot-pourri bowl and pierced cover with flared floral finial, the sides with alternate green and pink panels, divided by gilt bands, the borders encrusted with shells and seaweed enriched in colours, the rims with gilt beading, 6¼ in diameter, the cover with script mark   57 10

Barr, Flight & Barr white spill vase with fixed ring handles from eagles' heads, painted in colours with 'The Woodman', after Gainsborough, and with a band of pink roses and foliage on a square base, 5¼ in high, script mark and Coventry Street address   57 10

Worcester—Chamberlains

Chamberlains dessert service painted in iron-red, blue, green and gold with an all-over pattern of stylized foliage in the Oriental style, the rims gilt, consisting of : oval centre dish, oval dish, two kidney-shaped dishes, four heart-shaped dishes, twelve plates, some dishes with script or printed marks, one plate with the mark of the supplier, P. Smith, No 22 The Strand   399 0

Pair of Chamberlains armorial plates, the centres painted with the achievements of Lt-Gen Sir Charles William Doyle, Ar. three stags head erased gu. with a palm branch in bend and under it the word 'Egypt', the first crest an equestrian marmeluke charging, the second a stag's head gu. from an eastern crown, to right and left a soldier of the 87th and 12th Regiments, with the motto *Fortitudine Vincent,* all in a laurel wreath, the border with gilt classical fret, 9½ in diameter, script marks   78 10

Chamberlains miniature basket, the centre painted with a river running through a town, with gilt seaweed borders, the rims with shells and coral enriched in colours, with gilt branch handle, 4 in wide, script mark   70 10

Pair of Chamberlains armorial breakfast cups and saucers   31 10

Chamberlains cushion-shaped dish, 8¼ in wide   11 10

POTTERY

Creamware

Neale variegated small two-handled vase, the gilt loop handles with rams' masks below, the body marbled in brown, grey and red brown, and moulded with beaded and key pattern borders on spreading foot and black basalt base, 5¾ in high   63 0

Creamware mug, the side transfer-printed and enriched in colours with a gaff-rigged yawl and another in the distance, and inscribed 'AMJ Brazen 1792', 6¼ in high   33 10

Pair of creamware pierced oval baskets and moulded basket-

work stands, the sides with alternate green and white pierced
strapwork, the stands 7¾ in wide   29 10

Pair of creamware armorial plates, the centres transfer-printed
in black, with a coat-of-arms, formed as a nymph emblematic
of wisdom with putti beneath and the motto 'Let Wisdom
Unite Us' with dead game suspended at the sides, the borders
moulded with swags and with black rims, 9¾ in diameter   25   0

Delftware

Lambeth charger, the sides painted with an all-over design of
green vine leaves and blue and yellow grapes, 13 in diameter   168   0

Liverpool polychrome plate, painted in the 'Fazackerly' style
with a long-tailed bird sitting perched on a flowering branch
with a fence below and a flying insect above, 13¼ in diameter   147   0

Bristol polychrome bowl, the exterior painted with stylized
flowers, the wide blue border reserved with similar flowers,
the interior with central blue flower spray and with circle and
dot designs, 11¾ in diameter   126   0

Bristol blue and white rectangular flower brick painted with a
figure crossing a bridge joining two houses, the top with
circular perforations, 6¼ in wide   73 10

Six Bristol manganese square tiles, the centres painted in blue
with buildings in landscapes in octagonal reserves on
powdered manganese grounds, the angles with blue foliage,
5¼ in square   21   0

Pair of Bristol blue and white plates, the centres painted with
houses on wooded islands in a river landscape, the borders
with alternate trellis and flower sprays, 9¼ in diameter   16 10

Leeds Ware

Leeds creamware variegated coffee pot and cover of pear shape,
decorated in the Wedgwood style, the spout with stiff foliage,
the variegated sides applied with white floral swags, 10 in high   57 10

Leeds creamware Dutch perforated teapot and cover, the
entwined and reeded strap handles with foliage terminals
and with turquoise floral finial, the sides painted with a single
flower in dark brown cartouches on a mottled iron-red
ground, 6¾ in wide   52 10

Leeds creamware perforated sauce tureen, cover and stand,
of fluted form, the cover with flower finial and the stand
with a border of moulded swags, 8¾ in diameter   40   0

Leeds creamware quintal, the five necks moulded with foliage
and with serrated rims, 8¼ in high, impressed Leeds Pottery
mark   26   0

Liverpool Ware

Printed teapot and cover of globular shape, leaf-moulded
handle and spout, transfer-printed in black on one side with
John Wesley with hand raised, signed 'Green, Liverpool',
6 in high   150   0

Coffee pot and cover painted with birds swooping in flight, one
with a lizard in its beak, landscape below with snails, the
domed cover with pierced ball knop, 9⅜ in high   24   0

£   s

Lustreware

Sunderland Crimean War bowl, transfer-printed in black and
enriched in colours with views of the Iron Bridge over the
river Wear and patriotic slogans, 11¾ in diameter   50   10

American Market Sunderland pink lustre bowl, transfer-printed
with the arms of the United States, Republican inscriptions,
and portrait medallions of Washington, Lafayette and
Franklin, the interior with the Shipwright's Arms, 8¼ in
diameter   31   10

Staffordshire pottery copper-lustre jug, the sides decorated in
copper lustre with two scenes of figures and buildings in a
landscape, the border with key pattern, 5½ in high   27   0

Staffordshire pottery silver-lustre jug, the sides transfer-printed
in black with two scenes of a house in parkland, with splashes
of silver lustre between and with silver lustre neck, 5½ in high   19   0

Martinware

Fantastic toad, with leering expression, its knobbly back and
scaled body covered in blue, green and ochre glazes, 7 in wide,
incised 'Martin Southwark', dated 12.78   157   10

Grotesque fish spoon-warmer of massive size, the bulbous body
and twisting tail in tones of brown saltglaze, its head with
wide-set staring eyes and gaping mouth, 11 in wide, incised
'R.W. Martin, Sc. London 1883' and 'Martin, London and
Southall, 30.5.83'   135   0

Prattware

Fair Hebe jug, after the 'Voyez' model, the jug formed as a tree
stump with branch handle and moulded in high relief with
three figures and a dog, their clothes enriched in green, yellow
and blue glazes, the grey stump with green foliage and the
notices 'Fair Hebe' and 'A Bumper', 8¼ in high   222   10

Martha Gunn Toby jug, the woman holding a mug, her dress
with brown and ochre scrolls, 9½ in high   105   0

Lord Vernon jug, the admiral standing holding a pipe and a
frothing jug, his suit striped in blue and ochre, 9¾ in high   68   0

Sauceboat formed as a monstrous fish, its tail as the handle
and its mouth as the spout, the scale-moulded body enriched
with green and brown glazes, 8¼ in wide   40   0

Oval medallion moulded in relief with Hercules and the Nemean
lion, enriched in green and manganese, the gadrooned border
spotted in green and blue, 5½ in high   26   0

Saltglaze

Blue ground King of Prussia teapot and cover, with green
crabstock handle, spout and pierced ball finial, the side
painted in colours with a bust of Frederick of Prussia inscribed on a pink hand above *Fre Prufsiae Rex*, the reverse
with a crowned eagle above martial trophies inscribed on a
pink band *Semper Sublimis*, in green cartouches on the
mottled grey blue ground, 7 in wide   199   10

Teapot and cover, with crabstock handle and spout, one side
painted in colours with lovers in a landscape and the reverse

	£	s
with a wanderer beside a river, the border with black scrolls on a green-washed ground, the design echoed on the cover, 7½ in wide	84	0
Staffordshire dish, the sides moulded with scrolls, basketwork, trellis and herringbone, the shaped borders with pierced lozenge designs, 12¼ in diameter	29	10

Staffordshire Figures and Groups

	£	s
Pottery bust of Clive of India, in iron-red tunic with purple sash and yellow insignia, the green socle with brown rims, 9¼ in high	157	10
Group of the Death of Nelson, the dying admiral resting his shoulders on an officer seated on a chair with another kneeling beside, their clothes enriched in blue, pink and ochre, named in gilt script on the base, 7¼ in wide	100	0
Cow creamer and cover, naïvely modelled, its body with ochre splashes and with brown horns and feet, on a rectangular base, 6¾ in wide	99	10
Equestrian figures of the Prince and Princess of Wales, their clothes enriched with gilding, named in gilt capitals on the bases, 10½ in high	63	0
Pair of figures of Napoleon and Nelson, their clothes decorated in colours, the mound bases with gilt rims, 8 in high	57	10
Figure of Washington, his features enriched in colours, his clothes with gilding, named on the base in gilt script, 14¼ in high	52	10
Group of Queen Victoria holding hands with Napoleon III and the Sultan of Turkey, their clothes enriched with blue and gold, named in gilt capitals on the base 'Turkey, England, France', 11 in high	44	0
Tithe Pig group, the husband, wife and rector standing before a tree, their clothes enriched in colours, the mound base with pigs, eggs and sheaves of corn, 6¾ in high	40	0
Figure of Uncle Tom, seated on rockwork with Eva beside, their clothes enriched in colours, the base with script, 7½ in high	26	0
Group of the Vicar and Moses, the vicar asleep in the brown pulpit while Moses preaches below, 9½ in high	23	0
Figure of Elijah, seated before a flowering tree with a raven on his shoulder and another by his side, in iron-red robes and pink and green cloak, the mound base applied with flowers, 9¾ in high	12	10

Stoneware

	£	s
Large Fulham saltglaze tankard, the lower part applied with hounds chasing a hare and above two Beefeaters standing holding staves to either side of the bust of King George II, with the date 1729 incised beneath, the upper part with mottled brown glaze; the border incised 'On Bansty downes a hare we found which led us all smoking Round', with silver rim, 8¼ in high	68	0
Large Doulton and Watts flagon formed as a bust of Admiral Lord Nelson, covered in a brown glaze, in full-dress uniform		

£   s

with insignia, orders and medals, the base inscribed 'Trafalgar, 1805, England Expects Every Man to do his Duty', 12½ in high, impressed mark   58   0

Large flask formed as the head and shoulders of a man wearing a beret, which forms the mouthpiece, 10¾ in high   17   0

Wedgwood

Rectangular plaque, incised and painted in colours by Emile Lessore after Boucher, with Venus at her toilet surrounded by putti and a nymph, 16 in by 11¾ in, signed, reverse with Wedgwood Etruria mark   651   0

Pair of blue and white jasper oval portrait medallions, decorated in white relief with profiles of King George III and Queen Charlotte, impressed 'Geo. III' and 'Q. Charlotte', 2¼ in wide, impressed lower case Wedgwood and Bentley marks, the contemporary ormolu frames with pierced ribbon finials   472 10

Black basalt library bust of Mercury, the god in winged helmet, on a waisted socle, 18½ in high, impressed marks   100   0

Dessert service painted in colours with landscape vignettes, with wide blue borders and gilt rims, consisting of : shaped rectangular centre dish, four shaped dishes, two shaped circular dishes, twelve plates, impressed Wedgwood Etruria mark   78 10

Blue and white jasper vase of inverted pear shape with goat's head handles, the sides with white stiff foliage on a blue jasper ground, on a cylindrical plinth with floral swags suspended from rams' heads, 5½ in high, impressed mark   78 10

Blue and white jasper rectangular plaque, moulded in white relief on the blue ground with putti bringing a goat to be sacrificed on an altar, 9 in by 6 in, impressed mark   58   0

Garniture of three sage-green and white jasper vases of urn shape, the sides decorated in white relief with classical scenes and floral swags on sage-green grounds, the borders with the signs of the Zodiac, the covers with stylized foliage and with stiff leaves to the lower part, 10 in high, impressed and three letter marks   50 10

Pair of Rosso Antico and black basalt bucket-shaped jardinieres and stands, the borders with black basalt fret suspending stylized foliage and triangles, 5¾ in high, impressed marks   44   0

Blue and white jasper cream jug of helmet shape, the white handle with foliage in relief, the dipped blue ground with fluted lower part and with scenes of domestic employment in white relief, the spreading foot with stiff leaves, 5 in high, impressed mark   26   0

Black basalt lobed oval teapot and cover, with Widow finial, the sides moulded with cupids and nymphs and with stiff foliage to the lower parts, 8½ in wide   14 10

Blue and white jasper portrait medallion of a lady in profile to the left, on a dipped blue ground, 1¾ in high, impressed mark, gilt metal frame   12 10

Whieldon

Tortoiseshell hot-milk jug and cover of pear shape, with scroll

£   s

handle and floral finial, the side applied with flowers on a scrolling branch and covered in variegated tortoiseshell glazes, 6¼ in high   294   0

Tortoiseshell oviform teapot and cover, with crabstock handle and spout and floral knop finial, splashed with blue, green and manganese glazes, 8 in wide   147   0

Tortoiseshell plate, the border alternately moulded with basketwork and trellis and splashed with yellow, green and blue patches on the mottled brown tortoiseshell ground, 9¼ in diameter   29   10

Wood—Enoch and Ralph

Ralph Wood Lord Howe Toby jug seated on a barrel with a pipe at the side and his foot on a dog, holding a frothing jug, in black tricorn hat, ochre coat and pale yellow breeches, the square base with chamfered corners, 9¾ in high   199   10

Ralph Wood Planter Toby jug, the seated man holding a frothing jug, his clothes splashed in mottled brown and greygreen glazes, the rectangular base with canted corners, 9¼ in high   115   10

Ralph Wood group of a sheep and two lambs, their fleeces with blue splashes and with brown noses and eyes, on a green bombé base, 5½ in wide   105   0

Two Enoch Wood figures of a Turk and companion, their clothes decorated in red, yellow, blue and brown, on grassy mounds and square bases, 5¾ in high   42   0

Enoch Wood figure of Elijah, seated on rockwork with a yellow bird beside, in red and blue cloak and dark blue robes, on rocky mound, named on square base, 9¾ in high   23   0

CLEAR GLASS

Ale Glasses

Ale glass with tall slender bell bowl, solid at the base, and supported by a straight stem with an angular knop containing a tear, terminating in a conical foot, 7⅞ in high   85   0

Engraved ale glass, the funnel bowl decorated with hops and barley, above an opaque-twist stem and conical foot, 6¾ in high   34   0

Ale glass, the round-funnel bowl supported on a double-series opaque-twist stem and conical foot, 6⅛ in high   22   0

Bowls

Circular bowl, the rounded sides engraved with a rose spray, perhaps intended as a Jacobite emblem, supported on a circular foot, 8¼ in diameter   85   0

Pair of oval cut-glass bowls and stands, of slightly flared form, the sides with lozenge and foliage cutting, 8½ in wide   23   0

Cut-glass bowl on circular stem and square base, the bowl cut with hobnail and ray ornament with waved rim, 9¼ in high   14   10

£   s

Candlesticks

Pair of cut-glass candlesticks, with faceted vase-shaped stems, six pointed canopies suspending six small topaz and six pear-shaped large drops in clear glass, with thistle-shaped nozzles, on hexagonal stems and square bases, 11 in high — 50 10

Pair of Georgian candlesticks, the hollow vase-shaped stems with notch cutting, supported on stepped square bases, the nozzles with separate drip-pans hung with icicle drops, 9½ in high — 30 0

Cordial Glasses

Cordial glass, the small straight-sided bowl vertically moulded and supported on a tall stem with a central opaque-white gauze encircled by two spiral tapes, terminating in a domed foot, 6½ in high — 90 0

Deceptive cordial, the deceptive funnel bowl supported on a heavy inverted baluster stem containing a tear, terminating in a wide folded conical foot, 4¾ in high — 80 0

Deceptive cordial, the funnel bowl solid at the base, containing a tear, supported on a hollow inverted baluster stem, above a folded conical foot, 4¾ in high — 65 0

Decanters

Pair of large engraved ale decanters with globular bodies, tall necks, and slight kick-in bases, engraved on one side with a pendant bunch of hops and on the reverse with four crossed ears of barley, 11¾ in high — 105 0

Pair of decanters, the mallet-shaped bodies petal-cut near the base, with vesicar stoppers, 7½ in high — 65 0

Decanter of cruciform type, the quadrangular body with vertical fluted corners, surmounted by a tapering neck with lipped rim and triple collar, high kick-in base, 9½ in high — 26 0

Set of three cut-glass spirit decanters of square section with canted corners, the shoulders with lozenge borders, mushroom stoppers, 8½ in high — 16 10

Cut-glass decanter and stopper of cylindrical form with a band of diamond cutting, the shoulder faceted, 9¼ in high — 11 10

Goblets

Pair of baluster goblets, the round-funnel bowls supported on baluster stems, composed of a large cushion knop above a short straight section and base knop, terminating in a domed and folded foot, circa 1705, 10¼ in high — 490 0

Attractive goblet, the cup-shaped bowl supported on a multi-spiral air-twist stem and conical foot, 6¼ in high — 70 0

Attractive goblet, the ogee bowl resting on a double-series opaque-twist stem, terminating in a conical foot, 7⅛ in high — 24 0

Goblet, the drawn-trumpet bowl supported on a columnar stem containing a small tear, terminating in a wide folded foot, 10⅜ in high — 20 0

Engraved goblet having a large ogee bowl decorated with a continuous band of floral sprays, supported on an opaque-twist stem and conical foot, chipped on the rim, 7⅜ in high — 18 0

£   s

Jugs

Cut-glass jug, the globular body with two snakes and the initial
K, each within circular medallions and diamond-cut borders,
supported on a star-cut circular foot, the rim with fan and
geometric cutting, the high loop handle with scale cutting,
8½ in high   72   0

Cut-glass claret jug and stopper, decorated with medallions
and swags with faceted neck and flattened drop stopper,
11¾ in high   12 10

Rummers and Firing Glasses

Engraved Newcastle rummer, one side with a coat-of-arms above
a monogram, the reverse with a sailing ship passing under
Sunderland Bridge, 8¼ in high   47   0

Pair of engraved rummers, the ovoid bowls inscribed with the
monogram JMW, supported on small square bases, 6 in high   25   0

Pair of Masonic firing glasses, engraved 'Hirams Lodge No 458'
and with dividers and emblems, thick feet, 3¾ in high   19   0

Sweetmeat Glasses

Sweetmeat glass, the shallow flared bowl with folded rim,
supported on an inverted baluster stem with base knop and
folded foot, 4 in high   48   0

Sweetmeat glass, the shallow double-ogee bowl supported on a
star-studded Silesian stem, terminating in a domed foot, 5⅞ in
high   35   0

Massive sweetmeat glass, the ogee bowl on a collar and octagonal
Silesian stem, with a three-ringed collar on domed and folded
foot, 8¼ in high   21   0

Wine Glasses—Air Twist

Jacobite wine glass, the round-funnel bowl engraved with a six-
petal rose and single bud, with a moth on the reverse,
supported on a central-swelling and shoulder-knopped air-
twist stem, terminating in a conical foot, 6⅛ in high   140   0

Engraved wine glass, the double-ogee bowl engraved around
the rim with fruiting vine, supported on a multi-spiral air-
twist stem, terminating in a heavy conical foot, 6¼ in high   80   0

Air-twist wine glass, the bell bowl resting on a beaded knop,
above a multi-spiral shoulder-knopped stem, terminating in
a conical foot, 6⅛ in high   70   0

Wine glass, the double-ogee bowl resting on a shoulder-
knopped air-twist stem, swelling at the base and terminating
in a conical foot, 6 in high   60   0

Wine glass, the double-ogee bowl resting on a central-swelling
air-twist stem, terminating in a conical foot, 6¼ in high   38   0

Engraved wine glass, the bell bowl decorated around the rim
with fruiting vine, above an air-twist stem and domed foot,
6⅝ in high   30   0

Engraved wine glass, the round-funnel bowl finely engraved
around the rim with a border of fruiting vine, resting on an
air-twist stem and terminating in a conical foot, 6 in high   26   0

	£	s

Wine Glasses—Baluster
Attractive wine glass with a straight-sided bowl supported on an acorn baluster stem containing a tear, above a base knop, terminating in a folded conical foot, 7 in high — 260 0

Baluster wine glass with a bell bowl supported on a swelling-knop stem, above a base knop and larger beaded knop, terminating in a domed foot, 7⅛ in high — 85 0

Wine glass, the tall bell bowl supported on a triple collar, above a true baluster stem, terminating in a conical foot, 7⅛ in high — 80 0

Small baluster wine glass with bell bowl, on two collars, baluster section and base knob, on folded foot, 4¾ in high — 6 0

Wine Glasses—Colour and Opaque Twist
Colour-twist wine glass, the bell bowl supported on a stem containing an opaque-white corkscrew, encircled by alternate translucent-blue and red spirals, terminating in a conical foot, 6⅛ in high — 150 0

Set of four wine glasses, the ogee bowls with petal-moulding on the lower halves, resting on opaque-twist stems and conical feet, 6 in high — 60 0

Pair of engraved wine glasses, the ogee bowls decorated around the rims with fruiting vine, supported on double-series opaque-twist stems, terminating in conical feet, 5½ in high — 40 0

Wine glass with an ogee bowl resting on an opaque-twist stem, terminating in a conical foot, 5⅞ in high — 22 0

Pair of wine glasses, the round-funnel bowls supported on opaque-twist stems and conical feet, 6 in high — 20 0

Wine Glasses—Knop, Faceted and Plain Stems
Rare wine glass, the straight-sided bowl solid at the base, supported on a hollow four-sided Silesian stem, star studded on the sides, the shoulders impressed with crowns at the corners, terminating in a folded conical foot, 6 in high, circa 1715 — 460 0

Newcastle wine glass, the large bell bowl engraved with the arms of Overyssel, supported on a slender multi-knopped stem, terminating in a good conical foot, 7½ in high — 90 0

Wine glass of Newcastle type, the tall round-funnel bowl supported on a slender multi-knopped stem, including a teared knop, terminating in a domed foot, chipped on the rim, 8 in high — 75 0

COLOURED GLASS

Blue Glass
Three Bristol blue glass spirit decanters and stoppers of barrel shape, gilt with the names 'Brandy', 'Rum' and 'Hollands' in script in oblong octagonal cartouches suspended from chains and with polygonal stoppers, 7½ in high — 63 0

Ten finger bowls of plain rounded form, 4¾ in diameter — 33 10

A coiled snake enriched with gilt spots — 21 0

£   s

Bohemian Glass

Engraved armorial goblet of ruby glass, the bell bowl with a coat-of-arms with scroll mantling and the date 1770 on incised twist stem and domed foot, 8¾ in high   61   0

Encased overlay scent bottle and stopper, the clear glass body overlaid in white and blue and cut with lozenge, star and spiral patterns, enriched with gilding and white enamel with painted stopper and hexagonal foot, 12 in high   31   10

Cameo Glass (Webb)

Cameo scent bottle of elongated ovoid form, the turquoise glass overlaid in white and cut with two large floral sprigs surmounted by a silver screw top, 6½ in high   95   0

Encased overlay scent bottle of globular form, the yellow ground gilt in the Japanese style with a flying bird and a trailing branch among iron red stars, 4½ in high, the silver-gilt screw cover, London 1885   73   10

Red and white cameo vase of compressed form carved with butterflies and trailing sprays of chickweed, 5¼ in wide   52   10

Gallé

Art Nouveau elephant vase, overlaid and carved with six elephants walking nose to tail among palm trees, the shoulder with green cloud scrolls, the lower part incised with a Chinese-style signature, 14½ in high   840   0

Art Nouveau vase of tapering cylindrical form, the greenish ground overlaid in purple and carved with aquatic plants, 9¾ in high   58   0

Art Nouveau flared vase, the cloudy ground overlaid in purple and carved with flowering lotus, the foot flecked in orange, 17½ in high   40   0

Wine Bottles

Early bottle of dark green tint, the squat body applied with a seal bearing a coat-of-arms, below a short tapering neck with string rim, kick-in base, 6½ in high   55   0

Sealed bottle, dark-green in colour, the squat form surmounted by a tapering neck with string rim, the seal impressed with a coat-of-arms, a chevron between three birds, kick-in base, 7 in high   42   0

Set of three bottles, of transitional shape and dark green tint, each bearing a large seal inscribed 'W. Daubeny, 1776', 8¾ in high   40   0

SMALL DECORATIVE ANTIQUES

Enamels

Pair of Staffordshire enamel candlesticks with vari-baluster stems and fluted bases, alternately painted in colours with flowers and gilt with foliage on a purple diaper ground, the stems similarly decorated and embellished with raised gilt flowers and scrolls, with lobed wax pans, 10½ in high   84   0

	£	s

Staffordshire enamel drop-shaped scent bottle, raised and painted in colours with fruits and flowers within blue panels on an orange diaper ground, embellished with black and white pellets and scrolls, the metal-gilt stopper pierced with scrolls, 3¼ in high ... **63 0**

Limoges enamel bowl of circular form with shaped sides painted with flowers and birds on a white ground, centred by a grisaille portrait medallion of Julius Caesar, the exterior with two handles and raised gilt and white scrolls on a black ground, seventeenth century, 5¾ in diameter ... **32 0**

Miniatures

A gentleman, by John Smart, signed with initials and dated 17—, three-quarter face to the right, wearing a pale blue coat, gold-embroidered waistcoat and white cravat, his hair powdered, 1½ in high, in gold bracelet clasp frame ... **609 0**

A gentleman, by Thomas Hazlehurst, signed with initials, nearly full face, wearing a blue coat with black collar, white waistcoat and cravat, oval, 3⅜ in high, in gold frame, the reverse with a lock of hair and initial 'R' in gold ... **163 0**

A gentleman, by George Place, signed, three-quarter face to the right, wearing a blue coat, blue and yellow striped waistcoat, red undervest and white cravat, oval, 3½ in high ... **73 10**

A lady, by Richard Cosway, three-quarter face to the left, wearing a frilled fichu and bonnet with ribbons, pencil and some colour on card, rectangular, 4½ in high ... **58 0**

A nobleman, by Charles Boit, three-quarter face to the left, wearing armour and a crimson sash with powdered wig, oval, enamel, 1¾ in high ... **47 0**

Miss Trower, by Thomas Hull, signed, three-quarter face to the right, wearing white dress and bandeau, with narrow yellow sash, oval, 2½ in high ... **10 10**

Paperweights—Baccarat

A rare pansy weight, the concave base painted in coloured enamels with a pansy supported on a stalk with small buds and green leaves, enclosed by a garland of blue forget-me-nots, the top and sides of the weight cut with circular windows, 3⅛ in diameter ... **450 0**

A dated close millefiori weight, the colourful canes closely packed, including animal silhouettes, inscribed 'B. 1848', 2¾ in diameter ... **200 0**

A patterned millefiori weight with a ring of yellow and green canes and five circles of red and green canes, the whole enclosing a ring of white star-dust canes and a central florette, 2⅞ in diameter ... **30 0**

Paperweights—Clichy

A miniature swirl weight with a central pink and green rose, from which issue alternate blue and white swirling ribbons, 1¾ in diameter ... **135 0**

A patterned millefiori weight with a compact cluster of pink roses and dark blue florettes, set above latticinio strands

s

£ s

within a ring of green pastry-mould and smaller pink florettes,
reduced, 2⅝ in diameter   95   0
A colour-ground sulphide weight, the brilliant opaque-blue
ground set with a portrait of Queen Victoria and Prince
Albert, in profile to the right, 3⅛ in diameter   45   0

Paperweights—St. Louis
A rare encased white-overlay weight with an upright bouquet,
composed of a central orange flower with a mauve centre,
flanked by a white, a red, and a blue flower, together with
three canes, set amidst several green leaves, the whole set in
clear glass and enclosed by an opaque-white overlay cut
with seven circular windows, and further encased with clear
glass, star-cut base, 3 in diameter   1,050   0
A rare and attractive wood strawberry weight with two large
pink fruits supported on a pale green stalk, surmounted by a
five-petalled white flower with yellow centre and with four
green leaves, the whole set above an unusual ground of single
swirling white strands, 3⅛ in diameter   450   0
A patterned millefiori weight, the clear glass set with a ring of
alternate blue and lime-green canes surrounding five pink
and white florettes and another in the centre, 2⅛ in diameter   20   0

Paperweights—Stourbridge
An attractive pair of door-handles with an outer row of white
corrugated canes, enclosing four rows of florettes in tones of
pink, white and blue, set concentrically around a pastry-
mould cane, 3 in diameter   60   0
Pair of concentric millefiori weights, each composed of four rows
of canes in pale pink, blue and green, centred on a large
corrugated cane, 3¾ in diameter   40   0
A concentric millefiori weight with four rows of corrugated canes
in pink, blue and white, 3⅞ in diameter   20   0

Pot Lids
A pot lid, inscribed 'Shakespeare's House, Henley Street,
Stratford-on-Avon', a view of the exterior of Shakespeare's
birthplace at Stratford-on-Avon, Warwickshire, in the street
a pageant in progress   15 10
A pot lid, inscribed 'The Room in which Shakespeare was
born, 1564, Stratford-on-Avon', with three figures and a dog
in a Tudor and Jacobean furnished room, the border of pearl-
like dots   11   5
A pot lid, inscribed 'Pegwell Bay, Established 1760', with a view
from the cliffs, a fisherman with a net, the border line and
dotted   8   0
A pot lid, inscribed 'Walmer Castle', favourite residence of the
Duke of Wellington, built by Henry VIII, with two horsemen
on the road   7   0
A pot lid, inscribed 'Uncle Toby', with Uncle Toby and the
Widow Wadman in the sentry-box, a scene from Laurence
Sterne's classic *Tristram Shandy*, the border line and dotted   7   0

	£	s

Snuff Boxes

Rectangular silver 'pedlar' snuff box, the cover embossed in high relief with the bust of a jester holding a knife, torch and jug on a matted ground, with reeded borders to the plain sides and base, maker's mark JL, probably that of John Lacy or John Law, London, 1824, 3¼ in wide — 441 0

Rectangular gold snuff box, the cover engraved with flowers and scrolling foliage on a hatched ground, with waisted engine-turned sides and base and with shell and scroll thumbpiece, the interior of the cover with presentation inscription, by Henry Frost and William Charman, London, 1834, 18-carat gold, 3¼ in wide — 273 0

George III snuff box in the form of a book, the covers engine-turned and the spine engraved with reeded bands, marked on base and lid, by Thomas Eley, 1819, *3 oz 14 dwt*, 3 in wide — 195 0

Rectangular silver-gilt singing bird box, engraved with scrolls, and panniers of flowers on an engine-turned ground, the turret engraved with scrolling foliage and opening to disclose the brilliantly plumed bird, the reverse with hinged compartment for the key, 3¾ in wide — 157 10

George II rectangular pinchbeck snuff box, the centre of the cover inset with jasper plaque within a *rocaille* cartouche, chased with scrolls and wave ornament, the waisted bombé sides chased with scrolls and flower pendants, circa 1760, 3 in wide — 94 10

William IV rectangular snuff box, engine-turned all over within applied plain moulded borders, the interior gilt, by Nathaniel Mills, Birmingham, 1833, 2¾ in wide — 52 0

George IV snuff box of curved oblong form, engraved with foliage and scrolling sprays, marked on base and lid, by John Bettridge, Birmingham, 1825, *1 oz 2 dwt*, 2½ in wide — 38 0

Stevengraphs

The First Innings	100	0
William, Prince of Orange, Crossing the Boyne	100	0
The Last Lap (small wheels)	80	0
Leda	70	0
The Mersey Tunnel Railway	52	0
The First Set	50	0
Ecce Homo	40	0
Baden-Powell	22	0
Houses of Parliament	20	0
Field-Marshal Sir John French (remount)	16	0

Tea Caddies

George III oval satinwood caddy, the lid inlaid with conch shell, the front with bird on branch, 8 in wide — 35 0

Tortoiseshell caddy on ivory bun feet with cut-glass bowl, 12½ in high — 34 0

William IV rosewood casket-shaped caddy — 26 0

Papier-mâché caddy by Jennens and Bettridge, with painted and gilded decoration, impressed mark — 15 10

£   s

Vinaigrettes

Victorian rectangular vinaigrette, the initialled lid inset with jasper and bloodstone, the sides and base engine-turned, the interior gilt, maker's mark B and C, Birmingham, 1860, 1¾ in wide — 60 0

George III vinaigrette, gilt, engine-turned, oblong with chased floral edges, 1⅜ in wide — 43 0

George III vinaigrette, gilt, with reeded sides, 1½ in wide — 38 0

Wine Labels

Two George III escutcheon-shaped wine labels with thread borders, engraved for Madeira and Sherry and surmounted by a pierced and engraved crest, a demi-lion rampant holding a banner and rising from a castellated tower, by Thomas Watson, Newcastle, 1819 — 180 0

Six early Victorian wine labels in the form of matted vine leaves, for Montilla, Benicarlo, Malaga, Manzanilla and Valdepenas, by Reily and Storer, 1837 and one 1835 — 88 0

Three large George IV shaped oval wine labels, pierced for Sherry, Port and Madeira, by Matthew Boulton, Birmingham, 1827 — 75 0

William IV silver-gilt wine label in the form of a circular medallion engraved with a crest and for Brandy, within a chased wreath of oak leaves and acorns, by Rawlings and Summers, 1835 — 75 0

George IV silver-gilt wine label pierced for Madeira, within a chased surround of flowers, leafage and bunches of grapes, surmounted by a shell, probably by Charles Rawlings, 1823 — 65 0

REGULATIONS GOVERNING THE EXPORT
AND IMPORT OF ANTIQUES

IMPORT REGULATIONS

These are simple. Antiques that can be shewn to be over 100 years old may be imported into Britain free of tax, or import charges. A declaration signed by the vendor (which may be in the form of a receipt) is normally required by the inspecting customs officer.

EXPORT REGULATIONS

These are complicated, since the regulations governing the import of antiques varies from country to country. Both vendor and purchaser must be familiar with the relevant requirements. As far as the British vendor is concerned, two points should be borne in mind :

(1) An export licence must be obtained from the Export Licensing Branch of the Board of Trade in respect of any article over 100 years old which is of a value of £2,000 or more. This value limit does not apply to diamonds or articles mounted or set with diamonds, documents, manuscripts or archives, or archaeological material of U.K. origin for which export licences are required irrespective of value. Applications for licences (Form C) are obtainable from the Export Licensing Branch. Exports of all items to Southern Rhodesia are subject to licensing control.

(2) To export antiques over £2,000 in value an exchange control declaration (Form C.D.6) is also needed. This form may be obtained from the Customs and Excise or from any bank.

When antiques are shipped abroad, any packer or shipper who is familiar with procedures will normally advise on the regulations in force in the importing country. A list of packers and shippers is given in *The British Antiques Year Book*.

INDEX OF PLACES

INDEX OF SUBJECTS

(Figures in italics refer to pages on which saleroom prices are quoted.)

292